Social Problems
A Critical Approach

Social Problems
A Critical Approach

Kenneth J. Neubeck
Department of Sociology, University of Connecticut

Scott, Foresman and Company   Glenview, Illinois
Dallas, Tex.   Oakland, N.J.   Palo Alto, Cal.
Tucker, Ga.   London, England

Library of Congress Cataloging in Publication Data

Neubeck, Kenneth John, 1943–
  Social problems.

  Includes bibliographical references and indexes.
    1. Social problems.   2. United States—Social
conditions—1960-   3. Social history—20th
century.   I. Title.
HN18.N47   362'.042'0973   78-15294
ISBN 0-673-15201-4

ACKNOWLEDGMENTS

Introduction: From "The Politics of Analyzing Social Problems," *Social Problems,*
Vol. 20:1 (Summer 1972). Reprinted by permission of the authors and The Society for
the Study of Social Problems.

Chapter 1:   From *Working: People Talk About What They Do and How They Feel
About What They Do,* by Studs Terkel. Copyright © 1972, 1974 by Studs Terkel.
Reprinted by permission of Pantheon Books, a Division of Random House, Inc. and
Wildwood House, Ltd.
Table 1.1. © 1976 by The New York Times Company. Reprinted by permission.

Chapter 2:   William H. Form and Joan Rytina, "Ideological Beliefs on the Distribution
of Power in the United States," *American Sociological Review,* Vol. 34, Feb. 1969.
Reprinted by permission of the authors and the American Sociological Association.
From *Political Alienation in Contemporary America* by Robert S. Gilmour and Robert B.
Lamb. Copyright © 1975 by St. Martin's Press, Inc. Reprinted by permission.
Table 2.1. The first two items © 1976 by The New York Times Company. Reprinted
by permission; poll conducted by the Times and CBS News. The last four items are
from a press release by Peoples Business Commission, Washington, D.C., September
1, 1975; poll conducted by Hart Research Associates.
Table 2.2. Reprinted from *U.S. News & World Report.* Copyright 1977 U.S. News &
World Report, Inc.

Chapter 3:   From *Barred from School,* copyright © 1976 by Thomas J. Cottle.
Reprinted by permission of New Republic Books, Washington, D.C.
Table 3.1. American Council on Education, Copyright 1974.

Chapter 4:   Copyright © 1971 by Frank L. Keegan. From *Blacktown: U.S.A.* by
Frank L. Keegan, by permission of Little, Brown and Co.

Chapter 5:   From "How can a little girl like you teach a great big class of men? the
Chairman Said, and Other Adventures of a Woman in Science" by Naomi Weisstein,

For Gig and the children

Preface

Social Problems: A Critical Approach was written to help students critically analyze the implications of many of the serious social problems confronting us today. It is intended to provoke thought, discussion, and debate, rather than to simply present a series of facts.

As the table of contents indicates, *Social Problems: A Critical Approach* opens with an introductory chapter that presents different approaches to the study of social problems and describes the critical approach that is taken in this book. The critical approach involves examining two different types of social problems—problems of societal organization and problems of individuals—and analyzing their causes, effects, and—in many cases—possible solutions or steps toward mitigating the problems.

In the first part of the book, students are introduced to eight macro problems—key organizational features of American society that are harmful to millions of people. In the second part, students are presented with five micro problems—individual behaviors that have an adverse impact on other people and/or may be self-harmful. The book is organized to make it possible for instructors to assign the chapters they wish to use in the sequence they prefer.

As a teaching tool, a textbook must be comprehensible to students and must engage their interest. This book presents information in a straightforward and highly readable manner, even when rather complex and abstract ideas are being addressed. Tables, charts, and photographs are directly linked to the text in order to underscore important ideas. Specialized terms and concepts are defined and illustrated in the text, and a comprehensive glossary is provided at the end of the book as an extra aid to students.

Each of the chapters on macro and micro problems contains a reading that poignantly illustrates the impact of the social problem on individuals. These readings, entitled "Public Problem, Private Pain," are carefully chosen excerpts from published interviews, autobiographies, and modern novels. This special feature will not only increase student interest but will also give students an opportunity to see how real people experience and react to the problems under consideration. For example, in the reading in Chapter 8, an assembly-line worker discusses his reactions to the boredom, danger, and lack of freedom in his job. Some of the other Public Problem, Private Pain readings present the views and feelings of a woman who needs welfare assistance in order to raise her children, a disabled Vietnam veteran, and a woman who has helped her cancer-stricken sister commit suicide.

Another feature that will promote student involvement is the series of provocative discussion questions at the end of the chapters. These questions can form the basis of classroom discussion or may be used in conjunction with outside assignments. Many of the questions are designed to encourage debate in which different positions on problem-related issues are formulated. Other questions promote investigation by students of particular problem areas.

Thanks to the efforts of John Hearn of the University of Connecticut, a comprehensive Instructor's Manual is available to accompany this book. The manual contains suggestions for class activities and assignments, multiple-choice and essay test questions, and suggested readings and films.

Many people have selflessly contributed to the completion of this project. My appreciation is owed to the staff of Scott, Foresman, especially to Walter Dinteman and Sybil Sosin. I am grateful to colleagues at the University of Connecticut and at other schools who made many useful suggestions for improving the manuscript. In addition, I wish to thank my students. Their reactions—both in and out of the classroom—to many of the materials incorporated into this book helped guide its direction and development.

Finally, I am deeply indebted to my wife and children. They know best the role they played in helping me get this book done.

Kenneth J. Neubeck

Overview

Contents

Part 2 Micro Problems 283

Social Problems
A Critical Approach

Introduction

I n 1976 the United States celebrated its two-hundredth birthday by holding ceremonies and festivities in cities and towns across the country. There were speeches and parades, picnics and fireworks displays; new plaques and monuments sprang up everywhere. The year-long Bicentennial celebration was especially marked by recollections of the historical milestones and achievements that are said to have made this country great.

But beneath the optimism and cheer of the Bicentennial there was— and is today—plenty of reason for dissatisfaction and unease. Serious social problems plague the United States in this last part of the twentieth century—problems that are far from being resolved. Many Americans are poor, and most feel politically powerless. People are worried about jobs, pollution, and street crime. This society's ability to celebrate its three-hundredth birthday may well depend upon how we deal with such problems.

Social Problems: A Critical Approach analyzes several of the most serious of today's social problems, ranging from economic inequality and poverty to drug abuse. The book looks at the causes and effects of these problems and considers solutions to many of them. None of the social problems analyzed in this text has a simple solution, and all pose challenges to our collective wisdom and ingenuity.

We begin this introduction with a review of the various approaches sociologists have traditionally taken toward the study of social problems. Next, the approach taken in this book—a *critical approach* to social problems—is set forth. Finally, we will discuss some reasons why the level of societal concern with particular problems often shifts with time.

TRADITIONAL APPROACHES TO THE STUDY OF SOCIAL PROBLEMS

Sociologists have long been interested in the problematic aspects of social life. In fact, the nineteenth-century scholars who pioneered in the development of sociology did so out of deep concern over social conditions, particularly the problems in the nation's rapidly expanding cities. During the 1800s this society experienced the almost simultaneous impact of industrialization, urbanization, and the arrival of millions of immigrants from abroad. Crime, violence, alcoholism, and mental troubles seemed to be on the increase. The early sociologists hoped that a better understanding of America's problems might provide clues on how to improve conditions. The new discipline of sociology was not simply an academic exercise; rather, its proponents saw sociology as a means to an end—the reduction of suffering, strife, and destructive behavior.

Historically, there have been two major approaches to the study of

Sociologists of the eighteenth and early nineteenth centuries hoped that their new discipline could be used to help eliminate socially undesirable behavior. Many of them thought that the behavior of industrial workers, who at that time included young children, was often deviant and in need of change.

social problems.[1] The first, the *social pathology approach,* was popular primarily during the nineteenth and early twentieth centuries. Social pathologists were largely concerned with individuals whose behavior they thought deviant. They assumed that this deviant behavior was to a large degree due to biological or psychological deficiencies. After World War I, the social pathology approach gave way to a second orientation toward the study of social problems—the *social disorganization approach.* This approach also focused on the deviant behavior of individuals. But much more attention was given to the influence of the social environment in explaining deviance.

The Social Pathology Approach

The approach to the identification of social problems taken by the scholar-reformers of the nineteenth and early twentieth centuries has earned them the title of *social pathologists.* Borrowing ideas from the biological sciences, these sociologists preferred to conceive of American society as an organism. Like living organisms, said the social pathologists, society is subject to the dangers of disease and illness—in this case, such undesirable behavior as criminality and mental disorders. Social pathologists

[1]Our treatment of these approaches is based on Earl Rubington and Martin S. Weinberg, eds., *The Study of Social Problems,* 2nd ed. (New York: Oxford University Press, Inc., 1977); and Ritchie P. Lowry, *Social Problems* (Lexington, Mass.: D. C. Heath & Company, 1974).

defined as social problems those behaviors which, in their judgment, ran contrary to the maintenance of a healthy society—a society that harbored little or no deviance.

The social pathologists typically cast the blame for such behaviors onto the individuals involved. They explained phenomena like criminality largely in terms of such presumed personal weaknesses as character deficiency and psychological inadequacy. Many suggested or implied that criminals and other "undesirable" individuals were genetically or biologically inferior to "normal" people. While social pathologists were aware of the unsettling changes underway in America, they were less concerned with the effect of these changes on individuals than they were with the effect of "defective" people on society. As social pathologist Samuel Smith suggested, "defective" people created more "defective" people:

> In social pathology the interrelation of the abnormal classes is one of the most impressive facts. Paupers often beget criminals; the offspring of criminals become insane; and to such an extent is the kinship of the defective, dependent, and delinquent classes exhibited, that some have gone so far as to hold that under all the various forms of social pathology there is a common ground in the nervous morbid condition of individuals.[2]

Although Smith and other social pathologists were concerned with what they called "bad environment," they believed that social problems primarily involved "weakness of the individual mind or will, the lack of development and the lack of self-control" among certain groups of people in society.[3]

Carefully selected family histories were often used by social pathologists to support their views. One such history, which was to become widely cited, concerned the Jukes family.[4] Max Jukes, a backwoodsman born in 1720, was described as an extremely ignorant man who married an equally ignorant woman. Allegedly, most of their descendants between 1730 and 1874 turned out to be criminals, paupers, and mentally troubled individuals.

Another family history concerned the Kallikaks.[5] Martin Kallikak, a soldier in the revolutionary war married a young girl who was said to be feeble-minded. Of their 480 descendants, all but 46 were criminals, prostitutes, illegitimate children, or other types of "deviates." In his second marriage, Kallikak took a wife who was said to come from "good stock." This marriage produced 496 descendants, almost all of whom were doctors, lawyers, and other well-regarded members of their communities. Such family histories were regarded as proof that "defective" people

---

[2]Samuel Smith, *Social Pathology* (New York: The Macmillan Company, 1911), pp. 8–9; reprinted in part as "The Organic Analogy," in Rubington and Weinberg, eds., *The Study of Social Problems*, pp. 24–25.

[3]Ibid., p. 25.

[4]Richard L. Dugdale, *The Jukes* (New York: Putnam and Company, 1877).

[5]Henry H. Goddard, *The Kallikak Family* (New York: The Macmillan Company, 1914).

produced offspring whose behavior constituted the social problems of the day.

Modern-day scholars have harshly criticized such family studies as scientifically worthless.[6] For example, the studies are said to have reflected bias in the choice of families investigated and in the categorization of various family members as "defective." The most common criticism is that the social pathologists failed to address the impact of social and cultural influences on those whose behavior was singled out for scrutiny.

Nonetheless, social pathologists used their findings as the basis of their proposals for solutions to social problems. According to these scholars, individuals whose behavior interfered with societal health had to be dealt with. Depending on the illness, the cure might entail education, counseling and moral guidance, disciplinary punishment and forced labor, or even involuntary confinement. Since the social pathologists blamed many social problems on the growing immigrant population, they frequently suggested denying various "defective" ethnic groups entry into the country. In fact, this idea influenced federal legislation; the Immigration Act of 1924 drastically reduced the legal quotas of Jews, Italians, Russians, Poles, Hungarians, Spaniards, Greeks, and other Eastern and Southern Europeans, who, along with nonwhites, were considered "racial defectives."[7]

These early analysts of American society clearly were making moral and political judgments about who and what were to be considered social problems. These judgments seem to have been based on social class biases and rigid personal moral codes that viewed anything other than white, Protestant, middle-class attitudes and behavior as "bad." What we would today call *racism,* prejudice against Southern and Eastern Europeans and nonwhites, also appeared to guide their judgments. The social pathology approach was consistent with widespread public beliefs in *Social Darwinism.*[8] This body of ideas was based on the belief that people's social-class position was linked to their biological quality. Those living at the bottom levels of the socioeconomic scale were thought to be less "fit" for survival than the more affluent.

The approach taken by the social pathologists also implicitly embodied a belief that the United States—a rapidly growing, industrial, capitalist society—was basically benign and wholesome, as social orders go. Certainly, no major overhaul or transformation of American society was thought to be needed. Instead, certain defective individuals were seen as the real social problems of the day. Though there were "bad environments," these were localized conditions of an exceptional nature, and they could easily be eradicated. The major reform efforts, then, were to

---

[6]See Allan Chase, *The Legacy of Malthus* (New York: Alfred A. Knopf, Inc., 1977), pp. 138–75.

[7]Ibid., pp. 289–91.

[8]Richard Hofstadter, *Social Darwinism in American Thought,* rev. ed. (Boston: Beacon Press, 1965).

focus on the troublesome populations. Thus, social pathologists defined social problems in such a way as to make them solvable within the boundaries of the prevailing social order.

The social pathology approach still lingers on in sociology, although only among a minority of social thinkers. Edward Banfield's work on the urban poor is perhaps the best example. In *The Unheavenly City*, Banfield—a former White House adviser on urban affairs—explained the plight of America's slum-dwellers in terms of their alleged personal deficiencies:

> The lower class individual lives in the slum and sees little reason to complain. He does not care how dirty and dilapidated his housing is, either inside or out, nor does he mind the inadequacy of such public facilities as schools, parks and libraries; indeed, where such things exist he destroys them by acts of vandalism. Features that make the slum repellant to others actually please him.[9]

Banfield's proposed solutions to urban poverty are consistent with the social pathology approach. He suggested the involuntary sterilization of poor people and the removal of newly born infants from their parents for placement in more "normal" middle-class surroundings. Such solutions are virtually identical to those proposed to handle "defective" European immigrant groups in the not-so-distant past. Unlike his predecessors, though, Banfield did not expect his ideas to be carried out, since they would not be seen as politically feasible in today's society.

The Social Disorganization Approach

After World War I, a number of sociologists had grown dissatisfied with the biological analogy that social pathologists used to discuss the workings of American society. They also began to feel that the behaviors identified as social problems by the social pathologists were not totally the fault of those involved. Seeking an alternative way to explain such behaviors, sociologists moved toward a new approach involving the concept of *social disorganization*. As we shall see, this concept enabled scholars to pay more attention to the immediate environments within which problematic behaviors were found. As they focused on such environments, they discovered that "deviant" behavior was likely to be expressed only under certain kinds of societal conditions.

This shift in scholarly focus was not only an advance toward a better understanding of deviance; it was also a step forward in the intellectual sophistication of the new discipline of sociology. During the post–World War I period, sociologists were increasingly concerned with establishing credibility as *scientists*. In order to obtain greater scholarly recognition

[9]Edward C. Banfield, *The Unheavenly City* (Boston: Little, Brown & Company, 1970), p. 62.

and respect within the academic world, they were required to separate the study of social problems from reformist moralizing. A more objective approach was deemed desirable—one in which sociologists might consciously stand back and examine problems within the context of basic social laws and processes, just as other scientists objectively study physical phenomena. The concept of social disorganization was thought to provide a scientifically neutral and value-free approach to social phenomena. In focusing on the workings of society, rather than on presumed psychological or biological traits of individuals, the new approach was also more distinctly *sociological*. This fit well with the desire of sociological practitioners to clarify the boundaries of their new academic field.

Normlessness and social disorganization.　Those who emphasized the social disorganization approach rejected the social pathologists' biological conception of society. Rather, they saw society as a complex organizational unit—a *social system*—whose parts were all interrelated and interdependent. The organization of society was made possible by sets of *norms,* or rules for appropriate behavior. Norms were dictated by and flowed from American culture. If all members of society accepted and adjusted their behavior to these norms, that is, if they fulfilled their appropriate *social roles,* the social system would function smoothly. In this case, the social system would be in a state of equilibrium and would grow and progress by means of natural evolutionary tendencies.

Against this theoretical background, sociologists still had to explain why all was not well in America. Why did such phenomena as violence, crime, and alcoholism exist, and why did America's growing urban centers particularly seem to be the scenes of these problems? Their answer was that certain sectors of the population were overwhelmed by the very difficult demands associated with change. Deviant behaviors were due to the existence of social disorganization within parts of the social system.

For example, the progressive movement of people from rural areas to crowded cities that accompanied industrialization meant that many migrants had to make great life adjustments. The norms that regulated interpersonal relationships and life-styles in a small town were often inapplicable to fast-paced city living, much to the surprise of new migrants. Urban life often meant daily contact with strangers, new and stressful living conditions, and subservience to the impersonal demands of officialdom at work and in the realm of law. Past experiences provided little support and few guidelines for a quick adjustment to the city, it was suggested. In the absence of clearly defined norms, or with the failure of migrants to readily internalize existing norms, deviant behavior was likely to occur. Deviance was thus viewed as an indication of *normlessness,* a response to the confusion and disorientation associated with being caught up in change.

As a result of such ideas, sociologists began to examine America's urban scene and tried to relate its features to nonconforming behavior. A famous series of studies was carried out in Chicago.[10] Urban sociologists noted that Chicago consisted of several ecological zones, each of which differed in terms of economic status, neighborhood stability, and the degree to which relations among residents were closely knit. They found that such phenomena as mental disorders and juvenile delinquency appeared most frequently in unstable areas of the city—neighborhoods that were in a constant state of flux because most of the inhabitants were new arrivals and transients. They concluded that neighborhood instability caused social disorganization—the absence of norms to guide people's behavior—and that, as a result, deviant behavior abounded.

Similar difficulties were said to confront new immigrants from abroad. Many foreigners entering the United States came from rural backgrounds and followed others of their national origins into ethnic enclaves in the nation's cities. Also, sociologists suggested, the native cultures of many of these people were at variance with the dominant culture of white Anglo-Saxon Protestant America. The demands of "Americanization" meant that many immigrants had to shed their traditional and taken-for-granted ways of living. Often they were caught between wanting to learn and adapt to the American way and wanting to cling to the ethnic identities and ancestral life-styles with which they felt most comfortable. Furthermore, the norms of behavior of the old country seemed out of place in America. Hence, sociologists saw the *culture conflict* arising out of immigration as yet another source of deviant behavior. Culture conflict was also thought to be a result of change processes taking place within this society.

Perhaps the most influential study in this area was *The Polish Peasant in Europe and America,* by William I. Thomas and Florian Znaniecki.[11] Basing their findings primarily on an analysis of letters to and from Polish immigrants, these researchers documented the personal troubles caused by dealing with American culture. This society's emphasis on individualism, competition, and material gain, for example, ran counter to traditional Polish communal values. The stresses associated with adapting to a new culture and its norms frequently led to marital problems and family instability. Conflict between the generations was common, as chil-

[10]See, for example, Robert E. L. Faris and H. Warren Dunham, *Mental Disorders in Urban Areas* (Chicago: University of Chicago Press, 1939); and Clifford Shaw and Henry McKay, *Juvenile Delinquency and Urban Areas* (Chicago: University of Chicago Press, 1942).

[11]William I. Thomas and Florian Znaniecki, *The Polish Peasant in Europe and America* (New York: Alfred A. Knopf, Inc., 1927), 2 vols.

In the nineteenth century, the United States became the new home of millions of immigrants from abroad, many of whom settled in ethnic enclaves in the nation's cities. As this photograph of New York City's Hester Street indicates, the new immigrants were often faced with overcrowded conditions and poverty in the decaying areas of the cities to which they were relegated. Many social disorganization theorists explained the deviant behavior that sprang up as resulting from culture conflict between traditional ways of life and the demands of Americanization.

dren came in contact with American cultural values at school. The Polish immigrant was finding it hard to become integrated into American society, and deviant behavior was often the result.

Merton's anomie theory.   The concept of social disorganization also led some sociologists to look at America's opportunity structure and its role in nurturing deviant behavior. The best example is Robert K. Merton's influential *anomie theory*.[12] American culture, Merton observed, places a great deal of emphasis on getting ahead and attaining material success. Yet the means for pursuing these cultural goals are not equally distributed within the population. People do not have the same family resources, access to educational opportunities, and important connections. Some people are discriminated against because of their racial or ethnic backgrounds. Moreover, aside from race and class membership, not everyone has equally internalized the approved norms governing the pursuit of material success.

If an individual has the means to pursue cultural goals and has internalized the socially approved norms for doing so, deviance is unlikely. In Merton's terms, such a person will be a *conformist*. Otherwise, an individual may experience *anomie* (normlessness) and act in accordance with other norms of behavior.

Anomic individuals may respond to their situations in any one of four ways, according to Merton. (1) In *innovation*, a person pursues cultural success goals by socially disapproved means. This category encompasses, among others, those who commit crimes against property—from purse-snatching to white-collar offenses by corporate executives. (2) *Ritualism* takes place when an individual slackens the pursuit of material success by lowering aspirations and rejecting the pressures to compete and get ahead, but still accepts the societal means. The low-level bureaucrat who has little hope for upward mobility and simply plods along year after year, enforcing the bureaucratic rules, exemplifies the ritualist. (3) In *retreatism*, a person rejects and abandons both the goals and the means of pursuing them, simply withdrawing from the "game." The seriously mentally troubled, the chronic alcoholic, the drug addict, and the Skid Row vagrant are examples. (4) Finally, *rebellion* involves the attempt to change both the cultural goals and the means by which they are pursued. This category includes individuals who have committed themselves to radical revolutionary change in the values and structure of social life.[13]

In sum, Merton and other social disorganization theorists blamed social problems on the uneven workings of the societal opportunity structure, industrialization, urbanization, and immigration, which, they said, carried

[12]Robert K. Merton, "Social Structure and Anomie," *American Sociological Review*, 3 (October 1938): 672–82.
[13]From Robert K. Merton, *Social Theory and Social Structure*, rev. ed. (New York: The Free Press, 1964), pp. 140–57.

disruptive consequences for some segments of the American population. Changes taking place in society often rendered norms unclear, difficult to learn and adjust to, and even of questionable utility. Persons caught up in situations of social disorganization were problems. But the explanation for deviant behavior went beyond questions of individual character and personality deficiency. Instead, the major problem was social disorganization itself, which meant that parts of the social system were out of kilter and in need of some minor adjustment.

Social disorganization and the ideal society. Like the social pathologists, those sociologists who turned to the social disorganization approach made certain moral and political judgments about the nature of social problems in American society. Their approach was not totally scientific and objective. Rather, it reflected a set of assumptions about the ideal state of society. These sociologists believed that society *should* be a well-organized social system characterized by relative homogeneity in cultural beliefs, individual conformity to the norms of the dominant culture, and the absence of behavior that deviated from accepted norms.

As we have seen, the way in which a social problem is defined has a great deal to do with possible solutions. For theorists of social disorganization, the solutions seemed to require a two-fold strategy. First, the norms of the dominant culture had to be clarified, and efforts had to be made to bring deviants in line with these norms. Second, means had to be found to slow down change or, at least, to reduce the harmful effects of change and to take some of the kinks out of the opportunity structure. In practical terms, the first strategy was probably easier. It was also consistent with the solutions to social problems that had already been advanced by the social pathologists.

Thus, the focus of those employing the social disorganization approach was largely on deviant individuals, although there was sympathetic consideration of the difficulties imposed by their immediate environments. Consequently, solutions to social problems were essentially viewed as matters of administration. Deviant behaviors could be taken care of by proper intervention, without reorganizing or transforming the entire social system. Some minor adjustments to some parts of the system were perhaps necessary, but for all practical purposes it would be much easier if the deviants were to do most of the adjusting.

The social disorganization approach continues to have a following among sociologists. During the 1960s, for example, Daniel Moynihan wrote a federal report that attempted to explain why black Americans continue to be overrepresented among the poor.[14] Moynihan argued that the era of slavery created a tradition of family instability and disorganization among blacks. The black family, he alleged, was still in a state of

[14]See Lee Rainwater and William L. Yancey, *The Moynihan Report and the Politics of Controversy* (Cambridge, Mass.: The M.I.T. Press, 1967).

breakdown; and illegitimacy, crime, delinquency, unemployment, and welfare dependency were among the results of this breakdown. Only if the black family were strengthened and stabilized would equality with whites be achieved.

Critics have pointed out that Moynihan was talking about only a small proportion of black families and that he was ignoring the continuing existence of white racism as a hindrance to black advancement. Instead, Moynihan was subtly blaming blacks for their historical and current position of social, economic, and political subordination. Consistent with the social disorganization approach, Moynihan's solution was for blacks to become better adjusted to society and model their families after an ideal that many whites have failed to achieve.

Both the social pathologists and the social disorganization theorists have tended to view various forms of deviant behavior as the principal focus for the study of social problems. Proponents of both approaches have, to one degree or another, failed to see the organization and operation of American society as problematic. In reaction to this, an increasing number of sociologists have begun to move away from the more traditional approaches.[15] These sociologists contend that scholars should not simply accept the prevailing order as a given, but that they should instead treat it as worthy of examination and critical review. Few would deny that the troublesome and troubled behavior of individuals continues to merit serious attention. But certain key features of American society are at least as problematic as individual deviance.

In the next section we shall set forth the critical approach to social problems that will be followed in the remaining chapters of this book. This approach focuses not only on problems associated with the behavior of individuals, but also on aspects of the larger society that are harming millions of people.

A CRITICAL APPROACH
TO SOCIAL PROBLEMS

In identifying America's social problems, a sociologist's own values are inevitably brought into play. In particular, it is impossible to state that a specific phenomenon is a social problem without making implicit reference to an assumed ideal societal state. The social pathologists valued a

[15]See, for example, Judith Carnoy and Marc Weiss, eds., *A House Divided* (Boston: Little, Brown & Company, 1973); William Chambliss, ed., *Problems of Industrial Society* (Reading, Mass.: Addison-Wesley Publishing Co., Inc., 1973); James M. Henslin and Larry T. Reynolds, eds., *Social Problems in American Society,* 2nd ed. (Boston: Holbrook Press, Inc., 1976); Milton Mankoff, ed., *Poverty of Progress* (New York: Holt, Rinehart & Winston, 1972); Robert Perrucci and Marc Pilisuk, eds., *The Triple Revolution Emerging* (Boston: Little, Brown & Company, 1971); and Jerome Skolnick and Elliott Currie, eds., *Crisis in American Institutions,* 3rd ed. (Boston: Little, Brown & Company, 1976).

"healthy" society, one in which the illness of socially undesirable behavior was absent. Proponents of social disorganization theory valued a smooth-working, culturally homogeneous social system in which people adapted their behavior to accepted norms.[16] All these theorists possessed a vision of the ways in which society should work. And it was against this vision that they determined who and what were to be identified as social problems.

The *critical approach* taken in this book is likewise based on a vision or ideal against which the societal status quo is judged. This vision has informed and guided the identification of social problems that are addressed in the chapters that follow. By placing this vision in full view, we are making it possible for readers to determine whether the critical approach furthers understanding of the realities of life in American society.

The vision or ideal against which this text measures the status quo possesses the following characteristics:

1. Differences in personal wealth and income should be minimal, so that the life chances of all Americans are relatively equal and so that all share more equitably in the goods and services being produced.
2. Members of American society should be able to actively participate in or directly influence those political and economic decisions that affect them.
3. Each individual should have ready and continuing access to the education and training needed to develop his or her interests and capabilities to the fullest extent.
4. There must be no personal and institutionalized discrimination against individuals on the basis of group membership (e.g., race, ethnicity, and sex).
5. None of America's resources should be devoted to military aggression and violence against other peoples of the world. Instead, our nation and others must move toward disarmament and the peaceful settlement of differences.
6. Resources must be devoted to the preservation and conservation of the natural environment, and technological decisions must take into account the well-being of future generations.
7. Work must be freely available to all. It should be organized cooperatively, with special attention to providing meaning, dignity, and satisfaction.
8. Members of American society should be at peace with themselves and with one another. The vicarious rewards associated with such activities as crime, violence, and drug abuse should have no attraction, and the anxieties that provoke mental troubles and suicide should be absent.

[16]C. Wright Mills, "The Professional Ideology of Social Pathologists," *American Journal of Sociology,* 49 (September 1943): 165–80.

Having said this much, it should be obvious that this approach to social problems is necessarily "critical." Given the gap between our vision and the stark realities, we are forced to find fault with and judge severely the very structure and operation of American society as a whole. We do not take our society as a given; we instead see it as problematic in and of itself. At the same time, we find ourselves looking with understanding—though not always with approval—at the variety of troubled and troublesome behaviors of individuals who find themselves cast as deviants within the prevailing order.

Our vision of the ideal society is, obviously, rather utopian. No society in the world today comes close to matching its features, though we expect that some society will someday manage to do so. Our vision of the ideal society is simply a tool, a measuring rod that provides a set of criteria by which to assess the real-life status quo.

In line with the critical approach, we shall examine two major types of problems in this book. The first, *macro problems,* are key features of American society that are problematic. The second, *micro problems,* are forms of individual behavior that may be harmful to others and/or to the person.

Macro Problems

Certain very fundamental organizational features of American society stand in the way of our individual and collective development as human beings. That is, certain economic, political, social, and technological arrangements that have come to prevail in America are problematic because these arrangements harm millions of people. In Part I we focus on these problematic organizational or structural features of American society. We shall be looking at ongoing processes and patterned group relationships that are empirically observable over time.

For example, Chapter 1 examines economic inequality—the unequal distribution of wealth and income—as an integral feature of American society that has a vast impact on the life chances of millions. This and other structural features—the concentration of power, unequal educational opportunity, the subordination of people on the basis of race and sex, militarism, environmental abuse, and work—are matters with which Americans are confronted daily. We shall be referring to such large-scale, systemic features as *macro problems* in order to underscore their scope and pervasiveness.

Because macro problems are rooted in societal organization, their reduction or elimination may well require an eventual transformation of the prevailing order. Macro problems will not yield to minor technical or administrative reforms. They can be dealt with only if the majority of men and women in this society work consciously and collectively to bring about change. To do so, Americans must analyze, plan, and seek to

Micro problems—or problems of individuals—are not limited to urban areas. For example, problems of crime, alcoholism, and drug abuse are common even in the suburban communities to which many middle-class people have gravitated in their pursuit of the American Dream. In ways we still do not fully understand, micro problems may be caused by the organization of society.

reorganize society with a vision in mind. The kind of transformation our own vision suggests cannot come about by wishful thinking. Nor is it likely to happen if we simply back away and trustingly leave our future in the hands of societal elites and their appointed "experts." We must all be involved in the solution of macro problems.

Micro Problems

While our critical approach emphasizes the harmful effects of key features of American society, we cannot ignore the troublesome and troubled behavior of individual societal members. Millions of Americans are engaging in behavior that adversely affects other people and/or is at times self-destructive. Though theories on the causation of such behavior abound, we really understand very little about criminality, mental illness, suicide, alcoholism, and drug abuse.

We shall refer to such forms of behavior, which are analyzed in Part II, as *micro problems*. The term *micro* is not used in order to belittle the significance of this behavior. Rather, it simply underscores the difference between problems largely involving the macro order—the structure of American society—and those arising from the actions of individuals, or the micro order.

In the traditional approaches to social problems, the behaviors we consider micro problems were seen as forms of *deviant behavior*. We wish to avoid this term, for it carries unnecessarily negative connotations. Those whose behavior is troubled or troublesome can in many instances be considered to be acting normally, given the life situations with which they may be faced.

Moreover, the concept of deviance implies that people are being judged unacceptable and that they should be made to adjust to society and its norms. Yet, the behavior in question could be viewed in quite a different manner. In ways we still do not fully understand, some forms of deviance may be caused by the organization of American society. It is senseless to ask people to adjust or conform to societal conditions that may be harming them. The more logical solution is to alter these conditions.

THE LIFE CYCLE
OF SOCIAL PROBLEMS

For decades sociologists have claimed that social problems have a natural history or *life cycle*. As early as the 1940s, attempts were made to specify the general stages through which problems were believed to go. One such early attempt, which still influences contemporary thinking on the matter, was developed by Richard Fuller and Richard Myers.[17] According to this approach, the cycle begins when people become aware of some objective situation which, in their estimation, is problematic. They are not quite sure what to do about it, and they begin to communicate their concern to others. What often follows is public debate over the problem, with conflicting ideas put forth as to why the situation exists and what is to be done. In the course of public debate, the various groups whose interests are affected by the problem and/or its solution make their positions known. Finally, we come to the stage of reforms. Official policies for dealing with the problem, which were hammered out through debate and influenced by the jockeying of various interest groups, are finally implemented.

Not long ago, two sociologists attempted to update and extend earlier efforts to specify problem life cycles. Many of their ideas are supportive of our critical approach. According to these sociologists, Robert Ross and Graham Staines, the following process takes place during the career of a social problem:

---

[17]Richard C. Fuller and Richard R. Myers, "The Natural History of a Social Problem," *American Sociological Review,* 6 (June 1941): 320–28.

Private or interest group recognition of the social problem; political recognition of the problem as an appropriate issue for public discussion; public debate and social conflict about the causes of the problem; a set of political outcomes of this sequence.[18]

Defining a Social Problem

Ross and Staines note that an individual or group defines a given phenomenon as problematic in terms of their *ideology* or sense of what the ideal state of affairs should be. (This is much like what we have been calling a vision against which objective reality can be compared.) They suggest that social problems are defined largely in terms of an individual's or group's perceived self-interest. Thus, the initial definition of a social problem can be a highly political event, particularly when opposing interests get involved.

Take, for example, the denial of voting rights that until quite recently confronted many black citizens in the southern and border states. Unrealistic qualifications were often set up to prevent blacks from voting, and persons who pushed too hard to exercise the franchise were frequently threatened or harmed. The civil rights movement of the 1950s and 1960s denounced the discrepancy between black voter participation and the rights granted to all citizens under the Constitution. As the civil rights movement saw it, blacks should be voting and electing political representatives who would respond to their interests. Many whites, on the other hand, viewed black involvement in politics as an erosion of their monopoly over political affairs. Opposing interests were thus involved in the definition of racism in politics as a social problem.

Transformation into a Public Issue

The next stage in the sequence involves the transformation of a problem into what Ross and Staines call a *public issue*. In their opinion, this transformation will take place only if the privately recognized problem is seen as publicly important and legitimate for public consideration. A number of different "social actors" are typically involved as a problem becomes an issue. Coverage by the mass media is critical in terms of making a problem visible and in determining its importance and legitimacy.

The changes demanded by the civil rights movement required that racism in politics be seen as a public issue. Hence, large-scale demonstrations were organized in the early 1960s—demonstrations that drew

---

[18]This section is based on Robert Ross and Graham L. Staines, "The Politics of Analyzing Social Problems," *Social Problems,* 20 (Summer 1972): 18–40; quotation from p. 18.

In order to become a public issue, a problem must be seen as important to the public and a matter of legitimate consideration. In recent years, for example, numerous groups and individuals, including civil rights organizations and some big-city mayors, have expressed concern over deteriorating conditions in our nation's inner cities. If other Americans—especially high-ranking public officials and important opinion-leaders in the news media—agree that this problem is serious and legitimate, then it may be given the status of a public issue for which solutions must be sought.

thousands of blacks and sympathetic whites. The demonstrations were covered in the national news media, and they were considered even more newsworthy because of the violent responses they frequently met. Television viewers saw peaceful marchers with placards being beaten with police batons, shocked by cattle prods, battered by the spray from high-pressure hoses, and trampled by horses. Other violent events during the early 1960s, including the murders of civil rights workers and the bombing of black churches, simply underscored the issue of racism in politics.

Ross and Staines see the reaction (or even nonreaction) of public officials as an element in the equation. Sometimes there is conflict between media representatives and public officials over whether a given problem deserves the status of public issue. Again, this may be a matter of perceived self-interest, as officials can attempt to downplay the importance of problems and provide their own interpretation of events. For example, many southern politicians, who had been elected with white votes, saw civil rights as nothing to get excited about. In their view, a handful of "outside agitators," racemongers, and riffraff who did not understand or appreciate the "southern way" were stirring up trouble. While the media brought racism in politics and white resistance to change into the limelight, many southern officials tried to deny there was any issue deserving such concern.

Debating Causes and Solutions

Once a privately recognized social problem becomes a public issue, according to Ross and Staines, debate about its causes begins. This stage is extremely important, for perceived causes have a definite relationship to the types of solutions that are considered. Ross and Staines distinguish between two different causal interpretations commonly brought to bear on social problems. On the one hand, a problem may be given a *systemic attribution:* the system itself is problematic and/or generates difficulties for individuals. Our critical approach falls into this category. On the other hand, a problem may simply be blamed on the people involved; it is their deficiency, their faults, that "causes" the social problem. This second causal interpretation is termed *personal attribution.* Earlier we saw how the social pathology approach and, to a lesser extent, the social disorganization approach tend to lead in such a direction.

For participants in and supporters of the civil rights movement, the lack of black participation in elections was a result of a well-organized system of racist exclusion and denial of voting opportunities. The outcome was black political powerlessness and the election of white candidates who served only white interests. Engaging in systemic attribution, the civil rights movement demanded that this system be changed and that black efforts to exercise the franchise be protected. Many southern officials, on the other hand, claimed that blacks could vote if they were "qualified," but that most were not really interested in doing so. If the "outside agitators" and "liberal media" had not come in to stir up trouble, there would be no problem. Here, the causal interpretation of personal attribution was being employed; those demonstrating and demanding change were the *real* problem, not the "southern way."

Different groups find either systemic or personal attribution in line with their perceived self-interest. Ross and Staines observe that public officials often prefer to blame the people facing problems for their troubles, rather than to encourage a belief that the prevailing order is itself somehow problematic and deserving of transformation. It seems likely that all dominant groups will tend to favor personal attribution, for they manage, control, and profit from the system that could be called into question.

After the opposing groups make public their interpretation of the causes, serious debate begins. As Ross and Staines put it: "since causal diagnoses of social problems are reached by different people in different political situations, conflict between alternative patterns of attribution becomes inevitable."[19] The result is a complex bargaining process between authorities and the "partisans" of the social problem that eventually results in a compromise between the groups. The political outcome is often in the form of legislation or administrative changes through which the problem, as it has come to be defined, is addressed.

In the case of the demands of the civil rights movement, the compromise was debated and reached at the national level. The Voting Rights Act of 1965 outlawed the formal procedures used by many southern states to block black voter participation, and the federal government provided observers at polling places to check on overt efforts to intimidate black voters. Though the law could not address the more informal means by which whites attempted to discourage blacks from voting, it did put the force of national policy behind those who wanted to enter the polling booth. Whites still dominate the political scene in the southern and border states, except in communities in which blacks predominate. And Congress found sufficient reason to extend the protections provided by the Voting Rights Act in 1975. Nonetheless, the civil rights movement had won something—even if it was only a slow acquiescence to the presence of blacks in the voting booth. Southern political leaders are now beginning to take black votes into account and to curry black support by avoiding the racial issues that were long a major theme in southern politics.

The Role of Power

The message implicit in Ross and Staines' discussion is that *power* and its exercise determines how problems are ultimately defined and, thus, what solutions are likely to be considered and implemented. By power, sociologists usually mean the probability that individuals or groups can implement their desires even though they may be resisted. Groups have different self-interests to advance or protect, and those that cannot mobilize power (even if only to disrupt the status quo) are likely to lose out to those whose dominance is well established.

[19]Ibid., p. 32.

"THE SUGAR SHACK"

One of the outcomes of the attempt by the civil rights movement to solve the problem of racism in politics was the passage by Congress of the Voting Rights Act of 1965. This photograph shows black voters in Wilcox County, Alabama, waiting to enter the polling place in the spring of 1966. Prior to the passage of the Voting Rights Act, no blacks had been registered to vote in this county.

People or groups who possess power are in the best position to:

1. Determine whether a privately recognized problem will be permitted to become a public issue;
2. Advance their self-interested version of the sources or causes of a problem;
3. Control the ways in which a given problem will come to be defined; and
4. Determine what, if anything, will be done to solve the problem.

The power of the civil rights movement lay in its ability to mobilize public opinion against racism in politics, thus pressuring government officials to take steps against denial of blacks' constitutional rights.

The life cycle of social problems and, especially, the role of power have direct implications for the critical approach. The macro problems discussed in this book can be reduced or eliminated. But attempts to do so are a threat to the perceived self-interests of those who benefit from the ways in which American society is now organized. Thus, those who derive power and special privilege from maintaining the status quo will prefer to keep macro problems from becoming public issues. If the problems do become issues, dominant groups will actively push for solutions that are consistent with their self-interests. To the degree to which they are successful, either nothing will change, or those changes that are made will be easily incorporated into the prevailing order.

Take, for example, economic inequality. Millions of Americans are poor or near-poor, while a small minority lives in almost unimaginable affluence. The sharp reduction of economic inequality would require a drastic shift in the ways in which income and wealth are distributed, with the affluent few giving up much of their wealth. Certainly the affluent are not about to bring the fact of economic inequality before the public. Nor are they likely to champion a movement for redistribution. Such a position would not be in their self-interest. But, when the poor and their support--ers do cry out, when economic inequality does come to public awareness, affluent groups will take an active interest. They will sanction solutions that do not make serious inroads on their economic privilege.

This occurred during the 1960s, when poverty became a public issue. At that time, the solutions came from Congress and the president (offices of the affluent) and focused almost entirely on changing the poor. These solutions included family planning, support for self-help organizations, extensions of free legal aid, and some minimal training for the hard-core unemployed. Such solutions to the macro problem of poverty were easily incorporated into the prevailing order, satisfying dominant economic groups. Yet, neither poverty nor affluence were measurably reduced by these programs, and the "war on poverty" was ended by the Nixon Administration (1968–74). Since then, public awareness and concern over poverty have been permitted to dissipate.

On the other hand, it *is* in the interests of dominant groups to permit micro problems to enter public awareness and to be seen as the *real* problems of the day. Micro problems are easily blamed on the traits of individuals rather than on the character of the American system—in other words, they lend themselves to personal attribution. Each year more resources are earmarked for handling micro problems as economic, political, and social elites throw their support behind enlarged police and penal systems, campaigns against drug and alcohol abuse, and expanded mental health services, among other programs. The point is that these social problems are widely considered amenable to administrative and technical adjustments—more research, more tax money, more experimental programs, and more surveillance and control of people. Since none of these strategies threatens the existing order from which dominant groups draw benefits, such groups obviously see it as better for the public to focus on "deviance" when they reflect on problems of this society. In this way public attention is diverted from the societal arrangements that are harmful and that may even contribute to the generation of the "deviant" behavior.

SUMMARY

In this chapter we have looked at various approaches to the study of social problems and have set forth the approach that will be followed in this text. The chapter began with an overview of the two approaches that have dominated the field. The *social pathology approach* saw deviant behavior as the major social problem and blamed this behavior on biological and psychological deficiencies of the people involved. The *social disorganization approach*, on the other hand, focused on disruptions in social life as the cause of social problems. Like the social pathology approach, this approach tends to focus on deviant behavior of individuals.

The *critical approach* to social problems looks mainly at problems in the structure and organization of society. Like the two older approaches, the critical approach identifies social problems on the basis of moral and political judgments. The judgments behind our critical approach are set forth within the context of our vision of or hope for American society.

Macro problems are organizational features of American society that do harm to millions of people, while *micro problems* involve individuals whose behavior is self-harmful or has an adverse impact on others. The reduction or elimination of macro problems may well require an eventual transformation of the ways in which American society is organized.

The *life cycle* or career of a social problem is a political process in which power plays a decisive role. As problems enter public awareness, those who benefit from the maintenance of the status quo have a stake in ensuring that the accepted causes and solutions do not infringe upon their perceived self-interest. In practical terms, this means that macro problems—even when they somehow are brought into public awareness—may fail to be "solved." Since preferred solutions tend to be those that do not disrupt the prevailing order, macro problems tend to remain with us.

The degree to which a solution to a macro problem can be incorporated into the prevailing order will affect what is done about it. At the same time, dominant groups have no real reason to discourage public awareness and concern with micro problems, since attacks on these can more easily be accommodated without appreciably altering the status quo.

DISCUSSION QUESTIONS

1. What is the most serious social problem facing us today? Discuss the criteria you used to choose this problem.
2. Are people who are poor, or mentally troubled, or involved in heavy drug use "normal"? What assumptions or set of values does your answer to this question reflect?
3. Edward Banfield blames the plight of America's urban slum-dwellers on their attitudes and behavior—a case of personal attribution. What factors would one look to if trying to explain the slum-dwellers' plight in terms of systemic attribution?
4. Look at the front page of today's newspaper. What "social problems" are reported? Take one problem and discuss alternative solutions to it, considering the individual or group self-interests the various solutions would affect.
5. The mass media, according to Ross and Staines, play a major role in rendering problems into public issues. What does this suggest about the significance of the attitudes and values of those who own or work for the mass media?
6. It is not expected that you necessarily share the same vision of the ideal society that the author set forth. Where do you disagree? What elements or characteristics of the ideal society would you eliminate or add? Why?

Macro Problems

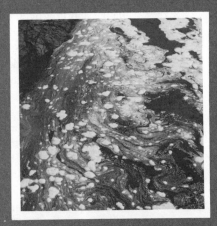

T he study of social problems is not a cheerful pursuit. No one enjoys closely examining the things that are wrong with society. But because societal conditions are demonstrably harming millions of people, it is important to undertake the study. As we saw in the Introduction, only when harmful conditions become public issues is there hope of change and improvement.

In the first part of this book we address eight *macro problems*—organizational features of American society that stand in the way of our individual and collective development. Macro problems are not "out there," harming someone else. Rather, they are directly or indirectly impinging on each of us from the day we are born to the day we die.

Income and wealth are unequally distributed among Americans (Chapter 1). While a small number of people live in almost unimaginable luxury, millions of others suffer in poverty. In the absence of mechanisms to reduce the vast gap between rich and poor, we are paying for social welfare programs that are widely acknowledged to be inadequate.

The expression "money talks" reflects the fact that the concentration of income and wealth in the hands of a few has implications for the workings of the American political system (Chapter 2). At the national level, government is conducted largely by affluent people and their appointees. Wealthy people outside of government use funds and lobbyists to influence national policy. Bureaucratic elites often ignore or manipulate the majority of Americans, and decisions tend to be made *for* rather than by the people.

Economic inequality is also reflected in the amount and quality of education we have opportunity to receive (Chapter 3). Bright children from poor families are far less likely to go beyond high school and complete college than are less intelligent children from rich families. Since educational credentials dictate where one will enter the occupational structure, unequal educational opportunities produce a waste of talent that ultimately affects the quality of life for all.

In terms of income, wealth, and occupational position, members of minority groups are grossly disadvantaged in comparison to the white population (Chapter 4). While formal practices of discrimination and exploitation have been outlawed, subtle practices of racism remain. The result is continued interracial distrust, periodic conflict, and the suppression of talent that could be used in the interests of all.

Subtle practices of sexism work to subordinate women (Chapter 5). Men hold a monopoly over America's opportunity structure, thwarting the potential contributions of women. The expression "You've come a long way, Baby," ignores the inequalities that women have yet to overcome.

America's economic system, which allows a few to be rich while others must compete for scarce financial resources, increasingly relies on production for death. Our economy is highly oriented toward defense spending, and our federal tax dollars feed the process of militarism

(Chapter 6). Investment in military-related activity uses funds that could be used to improve the quality of life that the military was set up to protect. The proliferation of weaponry for American use and sales abroad increases the probability of war—war that would most likely involve nuclear weapons.

America's economic success has been bought at the price of environmental sanity (Chapter 7). By gobbling up limited natural resources, manufacturing ecologically questionable products, and spewing harmful wastes into the air, water, and earth, our economic institutions have been destroying the natural environment. The long-range effects of environmental abuse are likely to threaten future generations.

America's economic system, which is buoyed by militarism and intrudes upon nature, figures in everyone's life through the medium of work (Chapter 8). The economy is not organized to provide work for all who want and need it. And the structure and content of many jobs create stress and dissatisfaction. We pay for the problems of the unemployed, and we must endure the poor quality of goods and services produced by people whose work is a source of dissatisfaction.

1 Economic Inequality and Poverty

Differences in personal wealth and income should be minimal, so that the life chances of all Americans are relatively equal and so that all share more equitably in the goods and services being produced.

THE REALITY OF ECONOMIC INEQUALITY
Concentration of Wealth and Ownership
Unequal Distribution of Income
Minorities and Economic Inequality

PERPETUATION OF ECONOMIC INEQUALITY
Wealth Begets Wealth
The Unequal Burden of Taxation
Ideological Supports for Inequality

POVERTY AMIDST AFFLUENCE
What Is Poverty?
Who Are the Poor?
Why Are They Poor?

THE EFFECTS OF ECONOMIC INEQUALITY
Inequality and Life Chances
The Need for Government Intervention

SUMMARY

A s we go about our everyday lives, most of us are too busy to reflect deeply and critically about inequality in society. Our "personal orbits" revolve around school, work, and home, with some time left over for leisure and personal enjoyments.[1] While glancing through newspapers or watching television, we may be reminded that serious inequities exist in American society. But many of us feel that such inequities do not affect us, and we may find it hard to identify with the people they do affect.

At least part of our complacence stems from the knowledge that we are members of one of the most affluent societies in the world. America's material abundance stands in stark contrast to the scarcity experienced by most of the world's peoples. And our sense of national well-being is reinforced and supported in many ways. Political leaders periodically conjure up visions of our society's historical progress and international economic leadership. Economic problems are usually portrayed as temporary situations that can be righted. Our Gross National Product, one measure of our nation's economic vitality and growth, has boomed well over the two trillion dollar mark—a figure unmatched by any society in history.[2] Stores and shops are filled with an amazing array of items awaiting consumption. Detroit continues to pump out huge numbers of new vehicles each year. Time- and labor-saving devices for the home and workshop abound. Indeed, we cannot flip through a magazine or newspaper without being reminded of the wide diversity of goods and services available for our use and enjoyment.

The sense of material well-being many of us possess, or to which we aspire, can easily be assumed to permeate all corners of America. Of course, we will readily admit that, unfortunately, some people in the United States lead poverty-stricken and economically insecure lives. But are that many people really poor or near-poor? Hasn't poverty pretty much disappeared from our affluent society?

To the extent we think along such lines, it seems proper to think of the American population as economically middle class. Since the vast majority of Americans appear to be well-fed, well-housed, and well-clothed, it must be true that they share equitably in the nation's total wealth and income. In fact, the very suggestion that there is significant economic inequality in the United States seems rather absurd. If extreme cases are momentarily shunted aside, could we not safely conclude that, economically at least, our society is almost classless?

This chapter will not question the fact that the United States is extremely affluent, particularly when compared to the majority of countries around the world. But it does question the belief that our population is

---

[1]For a classic discussion of the desirability of looking beyond our "personal orbits" toward an understanding of the workings of society, see C. Wright Mills, *The Sociological Imagination* (New York: Oxford University Press, Inc., 1959), Chapter 1.

[2]The Gross National Product (GNP) is the total value of goods and services produced in a given year.

economically middle class and that our society is classless.[3] We will look at evidence of the greatly unequal distribution of wealth and income and the prevalence of poverty and near-poverty in our society. As we shall see, gross economic inequality is an integral feature of American life. Such inequality is not in the process of disappearing, and its continuance poses consequences that each of us, despite our everyday preoccupations, should be willing to confront.

THE REALITY
OF ECONOMIC INEQUALITY

The economic status of an individual or family is based on the possession of wealth and income. In this section we will examine data indicating that both wealth and income are disproportionately concentrated in the hands of a few. Moreover, we will see that minority group members are particularly disadvantaged in terms of sharing the wealth and income that is available.

Concentration of Wealth and Ownership

Any consideration of economic inequality in the United States must recognize that ours is basically a capitalist economy. The key institutions that comprise the economy—business and industry—are privately owned. Ownership of the largest, most economically significant businesses takes the form of shares of corporate stock. These shares increase or decrease in dollar value in rough accordance with the economic success and profitability of the corporation.

Corporate stock is, and has long been, one of the principal forms of wealth available to members of this society. Income is derived from stock ownership in two ways. First, the directors of the corporation pay shareholders an annual dividend for each share held—a significant form of income for those who hold many shares. Second, owners of shares may buy and sell holdings in such a way as to realize substantial monetary gains. The distribution of stock ownership can tell us a lot about economic inequality in the United States.

Stock ownership is concentrated in the hands of an extremely small percentage of the population. As of mid-1975, there were only 25.2 million individual stockholders in America. In other words, our largest and most significant economic institutions are owned by about 10 percent

[3]See Richard Parker, *The Myth of the Middle Class* (New York: Liveright, 1972); and Robert L. Heilbroner, "Middle-Class Myths, Middle-Class Realities," *Atlantic* (October 1976): 37–42.

of the American people. Moreover, the *ownership class*—roughly, the richest 1 percent of the population (about 2.1 million people)—controls 56.5 percent of available corporate stock. As shown in Table 1.1, this stock has a dollar value of almost $500 billion. The remaining stock is distributed among the shareholder population, while the vast majority of Americans lack the surplus cash to lay out for the purchase of stock and thus own no shares at all. The ownership of a share of stock gives an individual a vote on corporate policy. This franchise is monopolized by a highly privileged few.

The concentration of heavy stock ownership within what amounts to a few hundred thousand households is not a new and unique phenomenon. Ownership has been concentrated for many decades, and there is no reason to believe that this situation will change. Stock is often passed along from one generation to the next through gifts and inherited estates. Intermarriage among members of the miniscule ownership class has also contributed to continued concentration of stock holdings by individuals and family groupings.

Among the most significant members of the ownership class are the top managers and directors of business and industry, and their heirs. High-level executives not only receive large salaries, annual bonuses, expense accounts, and other benefits of rank, but they are also typically granted options to purchase stock in their own companies at attractive rates. The rationale behind granting stock options is that they provide an added incentive for executives to push for increased profitability, since this enhances the value of their own holdings.

Wealth other than corporate stock is also generally concentrated in the hands of a few—not surprisingly, the same richest 1 percent of the population that controls more than half the stock. Table 1.1 indicates that

Table 1.1. Personal Wealth Distribution in the United States, 1972, in Billions of Dollars

Asset	Value Held by All Persons	Value Held by Richest 1 Percent	Percentage Held by Richest 1 Percent
Real estate	$1,492.6	$225.0	15.1%
Corporate stock	870.9	491.7	56.5
Bonds	158.0	94.8	60.0
Cash	748.8	101.2	13.5
Debt instruments	77.5	40.8	52.7
Life insurance	143.0	10.0	7.0
Trusts	99.4	89.4	89.9
Miscellaneous	853.6	83.3	9.8
Total assets	**4,344.4**	**1,046.9**	**24.1**
Liabilities	808.5	131.0	16.2
Net worth	**3,535.9**	**915.9**	**25.9**

Source: *New York Times*, July 30, 1976, p. D11. Data are attributed to James D. Smith and Stephen D. Franklin, "The Distribution of Wealth Among Individuals and Families," 1975.

The benefits of rank for the top business executive who is a member of the ownership class include more than a large office with a view and a key to the executive washroom. High-level managers take home large salaries and bonuses and stock in the company, which they can purchase at a price lower than the going rate. Their economic situation contrasts sharply with the financial insecurity experienced by the majority of Americans.

a disproportionate amount of all tax-exempt state and local bonds, cash, mortgages, life insurance reserves, real estate, and other property of major economic value is owned by 1 percent of the population. One consequence is that a small number of wealthy people—among whom are the directors and managers of our largest economic institutions—possess an inordinate degree of economic power. This economic power includes more than the ability to spend and consume; it also includes the ability to influence decisions that bear on the direction in which our overall economy will go.

Thus far we have concentrated on the holdings of a small ownership class. What about the distribution of wealth within the American population as a whole? Data here is limited. In *The Rich and the Super-Rich*, Ferdinand Lundberg summarized findings from a 1962 survey of American households, in which wealth simply referred to the value of a household's assets after subtracting debts. This survey, which was based on data from the U.S. Bureau of the Census, revealed that some 10 percent of American households either had no wealth at all or were in debt. Another 50 percent of all households (about 34 million units) possessed wealth of under $10,000.[4] Such data suggests that the average American household falls short of any real affluence. One way of comprehending the meaning of this concentration of wealth is to imagine how long the majority of family units could survive on their "wealth" if they had to live on the sale of what they owned, and to contrast this with the ownership class, where survival would not be much of a problem.

In order for the nation's total wealth to be more equitably distributed among the American population, property holdings worth hundreds of billions of dollars would have to be removed from the ownership class and reallocated among tens of millions of households. This is an unlikely event. For, as we shall see in Chapter 2, "Concentration of Power," there is a definite relationship between the ability to command great economic power and the ability to exercise influence over political questions of national significance.

Unequal Distribution of Income

The members of the ownership class derive much (if not most) of their annual incomes from returns on their property holdings. Most Americans are not so fortunate. Instead, they are forced to base their economic well-being on the sale of their labor to others (less than 10 percent are independently self-employed). In return for the sale of their labor, members of the work force receive annual salaries or hourly wages, and their earned income rests on their *marketability*—the demand for their labor on the part of public and private employers. The many people who cannot work—because of age, disabilities, or the lack of a buyer for their labor—must depend on alternative sources of income, such as retirement benefits, pensions, social security payments, veterans' benefits, welfare payments, and unemployment compensation.

Like wealth, income is not distributed equally among members of the American population. And, as with wealth, the unequal distribution of income does not seem to be undergoing any change. Though median family income has gone up through the decades, the relative distribution of income has remained almost exactly the same since World War II.[5]

Figure 1.1 shows how imbalanced the distribution of income is in the United States. In this figure, the total number of American families is divided into five equally sized groups, ranked from high to low in order of annual family income. The top fifth, consisting of the 20 percent of

[4]Ferdinand Lundberg, *The Rich and the Super-Rich* (New York: Bantam Books, Inc., 1969), p. 18; and Dorothy S. Projector and Gertrude S. Weiss, *Survey of Financial Characteristics of Consumers* (Washington, D.C.: Board of Governors of the Federal Reserve System, 1966).

[5]Daniel S. Rossides, *The American Class System* (Boston: Houghton Mifflin Company, 1976), pp. 114–17.

Figure 1.1. Distribution of Income Among American Families, 1976

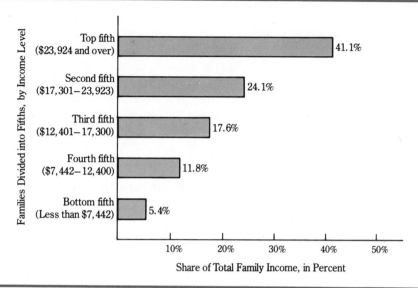

Source: U.S. **Department** of Commerce, Bureau of the Census, *Money Income and Poverty Status of Families and Persons in the United States: 1976* (Washington, D.C.: U.S. Government Printing Office, September 1977), p. 11.

families having the highest annual incomes, received 41.1 percent of the total family income in 1976. The bottom fifth, the 20 percent of families having the lowest annual incomes, received 5.4 percent of the total. If income were equally distributed among families, each group would receive 20 percent of the total—no more and no less.

To carry this a bit further, the top two fifths, or most affluent 40 percent, received 65.2 percent of total family income, while the bottom three fifths—the majority of American families—had to make do with 34.8 percent. It seems clear that a minority of family units appropriates the majority of income and consequently possesses unequal access to the goods and services of the affluent society. After the ownership class and other high-income earners take out their share, the remaining economic resources are divided among the many.

The economic well-being of the majority of Americans would be even more tenuous were it not possible for them to charge consumer purchases on credit cards and take out loans for major expenditures. By buying on the promise of future income—in effect, by going into planned debt—many members of the work force are able to gain an additional share of the goods and services they help produce. It is on this rather shaky basis that the supposed "middle classness" of the American people rests.

With inflation eating away at the purchasing power of the dollar, and with constant increases in the prices of essential goods and services, the income stability of the average American household has been threatened in recent years. Lacking funds to invest as a hedge against inflation—a luxury taken for granted by members of the ownership class and others with surplus income—many members of the labor force find themselves running in place. Income gains are quickly eaten up by the rising costs of living. Old debts must be paid off, and new ones seem to constantly emerge. Increasingly, families can remain in the middle class only by accumulating new debts and/or increasing the number of family members who work outside the home. Yet even with the steady increase in the percentage of married women entering the labor force since World War II, overall income inequality has remained largely unchanged.

Minorities and Economic Inequality

Economic well-being depends to a large extent on whether or not one belongs to a minority group. In 1976 the median family income for white families was $15,537 (see Table 1.2). In that same year, the median family income for black families was $9242. Or, using the government

For the majority of Americans, pursuit of a middle-class life-style means taking out loans and using revolving credit plans to obtain goods and services—a home, a car, home furnishings, and equipment for leisure pursuits. As inflation continues to increase, many families are finding that they cannot maintain the standard of living considered typical of and suitable for the American middle class.

Table 1.2. Family Income by Race, 1976

Total Money Income	Whites	Blacks	Blacks and Other Nonwhites	All Races
Median income, in dollars	$15,537	$9242	$9821	$14,958
Percent				
Under $3000	3.1%	10.1%	9.6%	3.9%
$3000–4999	5.3	16.0	14.9	6.5
$5000–6999	7.3	12.5	11.8	7.8
$7000–9999	11.5	14.9	14.4	11.8
$10,000–14,999	20.4	18.9	19.1	20.2
$15,000–24,999	33.4	20.8	21.8	32.0
$25,000 and over	19.1	6.8	8.3	17.8

Source: U.S. Department of Commerce, Bureau of the Census, *Money Income and Poverty Status of Families and Persons in the United States: 1976* (Washington, D.C.: U.S. Government Printing Office, September 1977), p. 9.

poverty-level figure of $5815 for an urban family of four, we find that in 1976 9.1 percent of the white population was poor, while 31.1 percent of blacks fell into this category. Other minorities have not been faring much better. For example, 24.7 percent of Spanish-surnamed Americans were living in poverty in 1976.[6]

We do not need elaborate tables to realize that minority group members are dramatically underrepresented in the upper-income ranges and grossly overrepresented in the lower ranges. And we may be sure that America's ownership class is virtually "lily-white." It is also clear that only a massive reallocation of economic resources can change the distribution of wealth and income between whites and racial or ethnic minorities. These economic resources have to come from somewhere. Thus it becomes easier to understand the uneasiness displayed by many running-in-place white Americans as minorities press for an increased share of the economic pie. In the absence of any reallocation of income and wealth, most whites are forced to compete with minority group members for the relatively small amount left over after the affluent have taken their bite. Intergroup hostilities may be increased under the prevailing competition for scarce resources—in this case job slots at higher income levels.

Despite periodic governmental announcements, the white-minority differential is not in a state of decline. It is true that the median family income of blacks, for example, has risen substantially since World War II. But so has the median income of whites, and black income has not risen appreciably *relative* to that of the racial majority. Blacks must make even greater annual percentage gains than whites just to keep the already wide income gap from widening further. For example, if each group's median

[6]U.S. Department of Commerce, Bureau of the Census, *Money Income and Poverty Status of Families and Persons in the United States, 1976* (Washington, D.C.: U.S. Government Printing Office, September 1977), p. 20.

family income for 1976 increases by 10 percent, each white family picks up $155, while each black family receives only $92. So if both groups improve their median annual family incomes at the same percentage rate, the white-black differential actually increases over time. In recent years, black income has increased by a slightly higher percentage than white income, but the gap between the two groups remains.

PERPETUATION
OF ECONOMIC INEQUALITY

As we have seen, income and wealth are far from equally distributed among individuals and families in the United States. The net worth of most households is minimal, a reflection of what little property people have been able to collect on the basis of the sale of their own labor to employers. Real wealth, on the other hand, is monopolized by a small ownership class. In this section we will look at the reasons why inequality remains such a permanent part of our economic life.

The financial resources of members of the ownership class enable them to purchase and consume luxurious goods and services without imperiling their financial standing. The very rich can afford the most expensive leisure-time pursuits —vacations in exclusive resorts, opening nights at the opera or ballet, elaborate dinner parties and balls —and still have plenty of money left over for investment. This photograph shows a fox hunt, an expensive sport enjoyed almost exclusively by the wealthy.

Wealth Begets Wealth

What does the ownership class *do* with all its money? Enormous wealth makes possible a great deal of luxurious consumption. Wealth can be used to obtain the best available goods and services. Yet, while members of the ownership class are capable of material acquisition far beyond the level of most Americans, such spending can be managed without making much of a dent in their overall holdings.

More important, wealth is used to accumulate more wealth. With professional financial and legal assistance, members of the ownership class are able to keep their wealth active. Their money managers advise them on buying and selling holdings and guide them to investments in profitable income-producing properties that will further enhance or protect their net worth. Through such activities, wealth recreates itself, and the increased wealth recreates itself. The problem facing the very rich is one of deciding how best to increase their affluence in the face of a host of opportunities, not how to hold on to it. As wealth begets wealth, the economic gap between the ownership class and the majority of Americans is maintained over time.

On the other hand, even if the majority of Americans could afford to pay for financial and legal assistance, they would have little money to invest. They certainly would not have assets on the magnitude required to get involved in the most profitable large-scale investments open to the ownership class. Thus, one might also say that nonaffluence begets nonaffluence. The economic condition of most Americans is one of relative stagnation and almost total dependence on the sale of their labor and/or various government benefits for continued economic maintenance. If you have wealth, it is easy to parlay it into more; if you have little or none, then that is likely to remain the case.

The Unequal Burden of Taxation

Many people view the various taxes levied at different governmental levels as means of decreasing economic inequality, particularly income inequality. But is the existing tax structure really a progressive force, a mechanism of income leveling and income redistribution? Or does it simply support economic inequality? When we examine the tax structure and the ways in which the burden of taxation is distributed, we must conclude that the outcome (if not the intent) is to perpetuate economic inequality.[7]

Many Americans believe that more affluent people bear a heavier tax burden than those who are less well off. But periodically we read about very wealthy people who, for example, pay little or no federal income tax in a given year. The affluent, with the financial and legal talent only they

---

[7]See Philip M. Stern, *The Rape of the Taxpayer* (New York: Vintage Books, 1974).

can afford to employ, are able to seek out and take advantage of various tax loopholes that effectively reduce their tax burden to a minimum.

For example, the profit derived from buying and selling corporate stock is not taxed at the same rate as income derived from employment. Those who gain substantial annual incomes from playing the stock market are taxed at a lower rate than if their only source of income came from working for a living. Ideally, this situation exists in order to encourage everyone to invest in the American economy, but in reality it works out as a form of welfare for the rich. Similarly, another way the affluent invest surplus cash is by purchasing tax-exempt state or local bonds. Such bonds are sold to help finance many worthwhile public projects. The interest received from these bonds is tax-free. This is quite unlike the interest the average person receives on a savings account, on which taxes must be paid. In effect, it is another form of welfare, a reward or subsidy for being wealthy enough to buy such bonds.

Certain common taxes affect the average worker more than they do the affluent. We are all familiar with the sales tax, levied by states and localities around the country. Most families must spend a substantial percentage of their annual incomes on essentials; what is left over may go toward some luxury items. This means that a large amount of their income is spent on items subject to the sales tax. The more affluent do not spend most or all of their income in this manner. Instead, they save or invest surplus income, and the returns on these investments offset much of the burden stemming from sales tax on their consumer expenditures. Hence, the burden of sales tax weighs most heavily on the average family, who can neither avoid nor offset the tax. Low-income families, who must spend literally all of their income, feel the burden of this type of tax more than anyone else. Thus the sales tax, rather than being a progressive form of taxation that decreases economic inequality, is actually a regressive tax that penalizes the nonaffluent.

A similar situation prevails with regard to social security taxation. As this tax is set up, workers pay a certain percentage of their annual wages or salaries to the government up to a specified dollar cutoff point. In 1978, for example, workers earning up to $17,700 were taxed at a rate of 6.05 percent. Since the majority of workers earn no more than this, the average worker's entire income tends to be subject to this form of taxation. In the case of the affluent, however, only a small percentage of annual income may be subject to this tax, since this group makes so much money above the official cutoff point. Again, this tax hits hardest at the nonaffluent majority, while the economically privileged pretty much escape its impact.

As these examples indicate, the majority of American working people bear the brunt of taxation out of all proportion to their ability to pay. The tax structure, rather than reducing economic inequality, permits such inequality to continue unabated. In Chapter 2 we will look at the relationship between economic power and political influence in order to understand why this is the case.

Ideological Supports for Inequality

Thus far we have considered two primary reasons why extreme economic inequality is such an integral feature of American society. Wealth begets wealth in a cumulative process that favors the propertied few. And the overall tax structure is organized so that economic inequalities go virtually unaffected. A third reason economic inequalities persist is that our own culture favors these inequalities. That is, American values and beliefs support the economic status quo and hinder criticism of it.[8]

An important component of the American value system is a belief in what might be called *competitive individualism.* From the time we are children, we are taught that nobody gets or deserves a free ride in this society and that hard work, a willingness to strive, and winning out in competition against others will result in success. Appropriate attitudes toward work and economic rewards are typically instilled in the home as a part of childhood socialization. And, as we shall see in Chapter 3, the schools also drill children in competitive individualism. In both school and the labor market, individuals are encouraged to believe that they are fully responsible for their own economic fates.

In any truly competitive situation, there will be both winners and losers. Not all can win out in the competition for economic success—for high incomes and accumulation of wealth. Some will do much better than others. So we are encouraged to believe that economic success, or the lack of it, is almost totally an outcome of individual effort and competitive capabilities. The value system does not take into account the fact that the race may be rigged—that some start out just in front of the finish line, while others run the race wearing concrete boots.

When we internalize the belief in competitive individualism, we are simultaneously adopting an explanation of why economic rewards are unequally distributed. The affluent, we logically conclude, must deserve their privileged economic status or else they would not have it. And the nonaffluent must equally deserve their plight.

Obviously, this explanation of economic inequality leaves much to be desired. It simplistically ignores some factors that result in generations of affluence for a few, hard-earned subsistence for most, and economic

---

[8]See Joan Huber and William M. Form, *Income and Ideology* (New York: The Free Press, 1973).

Soon, a new home built on a wooded lake site will give John and Cheryl Muirhead lots of room for their growing family. (Photo: Frank Cowan)

Americans are encouraged to believe that wealth means personal worth—that we are "somebody" only if we have money. This message forms the basis not only of lessons we learn at home and in school but also of the advertisements that appear in magazines and newspapers and on television.

deprivation for all too many. We have already seen how, for example, inheritance and the tax structure help perpetuate the concentration of wealth and disparities in income over time. In the next section, additional inadequacies of our taken-for-granted beliefs will be suggested.

If we really believe that achieving economic well-being is like running a race, that the race is open and equally fair to all, and that people then get what they deserve, then we have no reason to be critical of the economic inequality that prevails in American society. Those at the very top, in the middle, and at the very bottom deserve their economic status. Possession of wealth and income becomes a measure of personal worth. If we believe all this, then we will not question inequality. But who benefits the most from our failure to engage in such questioning? Obviously it is the ownership class, the most affluent—for so long as most members of

American society accept economic inequality as natural and proper, the economic position of the most privileged is in no danger of being threatened.

POVERTY AMIDST AFFLUENCE

According to the American system of values and beliefs, the poor are the losers in fair competition for economic rewards. So it is not surprising that most Americans believe that poverty is a result of supposed faults of the poor themselves.[9] Among these supposed faults are individual character deficiencies, lack of motivation to achieve, and unwillingness to strive to better their position. Some claim that the poor possess a unique set of cultural values that places little or no emphasis on hard work and economic success. A less common explanation for poverty (but not as uncommon as one might expect) suggests that one's genes determine one's economic status. The poor, presumably, are those persons who are genetically inferior to everyone else.

Beyond all this, the word *poverty* is often a synonym or code name for a racial or ethnic minority group. When someone says "the poor," many persons immediately think of blacks, Puerto Ricans, American Indians, or Chicanos. The typical poor person is often envisioned as a young, able-bodied nonwhite, living willingly (even happily) at the lowest income levels. Some people suggest that the poor are really rather affluent in their poverty, living quite well on the welfare rolls. Many think that the typical poor person chooses not to work, preferring public welfare benefits to employment.

This view of poverty, while fitting well with our system of values and beliefs about economic inequality, is more myth than reality. Poverty is a matter of economic deprivation, not of character deficiency. Whatever the deficiencies of the poor, they do not include mindless acquiescence in being poor. Most of the people who are poor in the United States are white. Rather than being able-bodied and available for employment, most members of the poverty population cannot find employment because they are too old, too young, disabled, or are mothers who cannot readily leave their children. Eligibility for welfare is quite restricted, and many poor persons do not receive welfare benefits. Those who are on welfare find that it provides a bare basis for survival as opposed to a life of comfort, and recipients tend to feel humiliated and degraded by their dependence on it.

In this section, we shall examine poverty and the plight of the poor. We shall see that, just as there are mechanisms at work to ensure affluence

---

[9]Joe R. Feagin, "Poverty: We Still Believe That God Helps Those Who Help Themselves," *Psychology Today* (November 1972): 101 ff. See also Joe R. Feagin, *Subordinating the Poor* (Englewood Cliffs, N.J.: Prentice-Hall, Inc., 1975).

and continued economic well-being for a privileged few, there are also mechanisms to provoke and perpetuate poverty for many millions. The tendency is for poverty to beget poverty, creating a cycle from which few can completely break away on their own.

What Is Poverty?

Poverty is first and foremost an economic state. Being poor means, essentially, lacking a means of subsistence capable of providing what—in this society and at this time—could be considered a secure and adequate standard of living. On the one hand, poverty is an absolute state—by any objective measure the poor are materially deprived to the point where survival often becomes an issue. And, on the other hand, poverty is a relative state—the poor are materially deprived in comparison with the majority of the population.

Many of the people living in or near poverty hold full-time jobs, for which wages are so low that they cannot count on attaining a secure and adequate standard of living. For those food-service workers, domestic helpers, textile workers, and others who work long hours for small wages, economic success is an unattainable goal that cannot be achieved through hard work.

Persons living in poverty typically have *some* means of subsistence. For many poor families it is public welfare, while most others who are poor or near-poor receive either a primary or partial source of subsistence from employment. For the employed poor, the income derived from working is too low to provide a secure and adequate standard of living. Thus, even though an individual may be eager to work, no one may want to employ him or her or the wages offered may be below the level necessary to move out of poverty. Being poor does not necessarily mean that the person is unwilling to embrace the notion of competitive individualism, but rather that the person is not marketable.

Likewise, a person who is too old or too young to sell his or her labor, too disabled to go to work, or who must place the responsibilities of child care ahead of full-time employment may effectively be cut off from a secure and adequate standard of living. Apparently, unless one can contribute to the American economy as a worker, one is useless to it, no matter what the underlying reasons. Uselessness is underscored by according nonworkers the most negligible share of the nation's economic resources. Consequently, many persons are also rendered useless as consumers.

The poor, in essence, are the millions of people who are economically obsolete—those men, women, and children whose contribution to production and consumption is considered peripheral to the ongoing operation of the American economic system. Unable to produce or unable to demand rewards for their contributions to production, and thus unable to consume, millions live out their lives in a state of economic deprivation. The promises of the consumer society remain well beyond their reach.

Who Are the Poor?

While the poor comprise a numerical minority within the United States, this minority is by no means an insignificant one. Census data for 1976, in which only the most destitute were considered poor, revealed that almost 25 million persons were living in a state of poverty—nearly one out of eight Americans.[10] These 25 million poor people included approximately 5.3 million families and an additional 5.3 million unattached individuals (see Table 1.3). The official definition of poverty used in this census varied for different categories of people; for example, a nonfarm family of four was considered poor if its annual income was under $5815. But in all cases the dollar definition of poverty encompassed those who were worse off both in absolute and relative terms. According to the census, another 10 million persons had incomes that placed them in the category of *near-poor*—that is, their incomes were so low that any slight

[10]U.S. Department of Commerce, *Money Income and Poverty Status*, p. 21.

Table 1.3. Number of Individuals Under the Poverty Line, in Thousands, 1976

Family Status	All Races	White	Black	Spanish Origin
Total	**24,975**	**16,713**	**7,595**	**2,783**
65 years and older	3,313	2,633	644	128
In families	19,632	12,500	6,576	2,516
Heads of families	5,311	3,560	1,617	598
Related children under 18	10,081	6,034	3,758	1,424
Other family members	4,240	2,906	1,201	494
Unattached individuals	5,344	4,213	1,019	266

Source: U.S. Department of Commerce, Bureau of the Census, *Money Income and Poverty Status of Families and Persons in the United States: 1976* (Washington, D.C.: U.S. Government Printing Office, September 1977), pp. 21 and 24.

drop (as a consequence of job loss, layoffs, serious illness, or disability) would place them below the official poverty line.[11]

If we break down the poverty figures further, we get a better idea of which groups comprise the poverty population. The census data showed that 40 percent of the poor were under eighteen years of age and that 17 percent were sixty and older. Thus, the majority of the poor (57 percent) are very young, school-age children and youth, and the elderly. To this we can add another 24 percent of the poor—females who are heads of families and unattached females.[12] In other words, about 80 percent of the poor fall outside of the category of persons we usually think of as breadwinners.

Though approximately seven out of ten poor persons in the United States are white, nonwhites are poor out of all proportion to their representation in the total population. Blacks comprise less than 12 percent of the population but are 30 percent of the poor. The prevalence of poverty among minority families contributes substantially to the white-minority income differential discussed earlier.

Why Are They Poor?

As we saw earlier, poverty is very often considered the fault of the poor themselves. Our system of values and beliefs suggests that we must blame the victim for lack of economic success.[13] But poverty is an economic state. People are poor because they lack money. And they lack money because they are unable to sell their labor or because they are able to earn only very small incomes. In other words, the cause of poverty is not the victim but is instead the nature of the American economic system and the ways it deals with people.[14]

[11]Ibid., p. 28.
[12]Ibid., pp. 3 and 20.
[13]See William L. Ryan, *Blaming the Victim* (New York: Vintage Books, 1971).
[14]This section is based on Gabriel Kolko, *Wealth and Power in America* (New York: Praeger Publishers, Inc., 1962).

Business practices contributing to poverty. Among the forces contributing to poverty has been *technological change*. Decisions by executives in business and industry to automate or increase mechanization of their operations—in order to increase efficiency and profits—have resulted in the displacement of many workers and have closed opportunities for new entrants into the labor force. Those most affected by technological change are unskilled and semiskilled workers. Thrown out of jobs or denied them in the first place, such persons find it difficult to find any work, not to mention work that pays enough to provide a secure and adequate standard of living.

Worker displacement is not limited to large industrial centers. Over the decades, the nation's farms have become large mechanized corporations, requiring fewer and fewer people to produce food for the population. Today some 4 percent of the work force feeds us all. As mechanization of agriculture has spread and intensified, millions of farm workers who lack the training and skills required to compete successfully in the urban labor market have found themselves economically obsolete. Displaced farm workers have contributed substantially to the size of the poverty population as a consequence of decisions over which they had no control.

Employers contribute to the creation and perpetuation of poverty in other ways as well. For example, many of our largest corporations have become international operations with plants around the world. In order to increase profits and thus reward stockholders, corporate executives have been channeling resources into other nations. Such investments are often undertaken because the costs of materials and labor are lower in these nations than in the United States. Many products that were once made by American workers are now being made elsewhere. In effect this has meant the export of jobs, increasing the competition for employment in this country and contributing to the high rates of unemployment that constantly prevail.

The pay scales of business and industry also contribute to poverty. Many blue-collar workers have a certain amount of job security, somewhat higher wages, retirement pensions, and other worker benefits as a result of union membership. But for those millions of workers who do not belong to unions, wages are often so low as to place them near (if not in) a poverty situation. While federal and state governments have established minimum wages for a variety of occupational areas, the minimum wage is generally set so low that it does not provide families with a secure and adequate standard of living. And periodic upward revisions in the minimum wage have not been sufficient to offset annual inflation and increases in the cost of living.

Government benefits. Many members of the work force—particularly those in unskilled and semiskilled positions—are subject to periodic unemployment. Layoffs and seasonal unemployment most affect those with marginal skills. Contrary to popular belief, the *unemployment compensation* provided by government agencies for these and other workers does not necessarily prevent poverty. Unemployment compensation does not protect all members of the labor force, pays only a percentage of the wage formerly earned by the unemployed, and is cut off after a given period of time. Unless a worker can find a new job or get the old one back, welfare may be the next resort.

The rules concerning eligibility for *welfare* differ from state to state, as do the type and amount of benefits available.[15] In no state does welfare provide more than a basis for subsistence at a poverty level. Potential recipients are subjected to a degrading screening process in which the state probes into virtually every area of their personal lives. Benefits are given grudgingly, and recipients are continually rechecked for eligibility and to make sure they do not have other sources of income. While welfare cheats have been found, only a tiny percentage of recipients cheat the system (despite the publicity accorded them).[16] Yet far more Americans have negative feelings about welfare recipients than about the "welfare benefits" the affluent routinely collect under the law.

Other economic and social factors.   As we have seen, *age* is closely linked to poverty. Many adults reach retirement age only to find that their savings and other economic resources are inadequate and that poverty is their future state. Senior citizens on fixed incomes (e.g., income from many insurance programs and pension plans, which does not increase with inflation) find that they cannot keep up with annual increases in the costs of living. Food costs, medical costs, rent, and utilities escalate—but incomes do not keep pace. For many, welfare is the only answer—and not much of an answer at that. Roughly one person in six who is over sixty-five is poor, and many more are near-poor. Age, of course, works against finding or holding employment.

Like the aged, the young are confronted with the societal rule that people will be permitted to consume in accordance with their output (marketability), not in accordance with their requirements. Of the 40 percent of the poor under eighteen years of age, most are too young to work at all (even if jobs were available) and must depend on others to provide for them. A large proportion of those old enough to work are of school age, and sacrificing schooling for work typically means employment in the most low-paying, dead-end occupations. In general, the young are powerless to overcome poverty completely on their own volition; their situation is quite similar to that of the elderly poor.

[15]For a historical analysis of public welfare and some of its functions, see Frances Fox Piven and Richard A. Cloward, *Regulating the Poor* (New York: Vintage Books, 1971); see also Betty Reid Mandell, ed., *Welfare in America* (Englewood Cliffs, N.J.: Prentice-Hall, Inc., 1975).

[16]Al Sheahen, "The Real Welfare Chiselers," *Commonweal,* February 13, 1976, 105–7.

Sex and *marital status* are also linked to the probability that one will be poor and will find it difficult to extricate oneself from poverty. Over time there has been an increase in the percentage of American families headed by women, and in 1976, 48 percent of all poor families fell into this category. As we shall discuss in Chapter 5, "Institutional Sexism," employed women earn less than do men, on the average. This is partly a result of sex discrimination in hiring, which limits the types of jobs available to women. But even when women perform the same jobs as men, the women are often paid less. The woman who heads a household faces many problems, not the least of which is finding a job that will keep her family out of poverty. The general absence of reliable and inexpensive child-care facilities for women desiring employment makes it even more difficult for female heads of households to avoid poverty.

To this add *racism*. We have seen, for example, that blacks are disproportionately represented among the low-income and poverty populations. For blacks a vicious cycle seems to be operating, involving educational discrimination and the failure of public schools to equip blacks to compete on an equal basis with whites for decent jobs; discrimination by employers, who hire whites over blacks, and/or pay black workers less than whites for the same jobs; exclusion of black workers from union membership, particularly in the skilled trades; and frequent unemployment, a reflection of the fact that the black worker is most likely to be in a job that is insecure and subject to either periodic layoffs or disappearance through mechanization. The black unemployment rate is normally at least twice that of whites. Finding that they cannot keep a job or earn enough while working to support a family, black men, like similarly situated white men, often define themselves as failures. Their sense of economic obsolescence, felt as personal worthlessness, often creates tensions in the home that contribute to family breakup. We then have a female-headed household which, as we have seen, is quite likely to be poor or near-poor.

As was implied above, another factor that contributes to the creation and perpetuation of poverty is *education*. It is clear that without the kind and degree of education or training that will make one marketable, a decent-paying job is beyond one's reach. While it is questionable whether many jobs today really require the amount of schooling employers demand, a high-school or college diploma is a necessity for marketability. But the dropout rates in schools serving poor children are enormous, and many children of the poor emerge from years of schooling as functional illiterates. Insofar as public schools fail to provide an adequate education or salable skills for children of the poor, the probability is increased that such children will replicate their parents' low-income position. The failure of educational institutions to equip low-income children for participation in the economy is an important factor begetting and sustaining a permanent poverty population.

Parenthetically, we should stress that increasing the educational achievements of the poor and near-poor will not alone guarantee an end to poverty. The American economy must be capable of providing work for all—and work at levels of remuneration above the poverty level—in order for increased education to be put to use. Without such changes in the employment picture, the reduction of poverty through education is bound to be thwarted.

The structural basis of poverty.   To answer the question "Why are they poor?" we must look well beyond the alleged personality characteristics, values, and genetic makeup of the poor. The organization of the economy and its machinations; the profit-oriented decisions made by top executives in business and industry; governmental policy; discrimination on the basis of age, sex, race, and ethnicity—all bear on the poor and tend to be outside their immediate control. The propensity to blame the victims for the economic deprivation under which they labor, while consistent with our values and beliefs regarding inequality, ignores all too many realities. Under the existing structure of our society, any of us could be poor if deprived of adequate means of subsistence by virtue of forces and decisions originating outside our "personal orbits."

Just as our economic system perpetuates the privilege of the ownership class, so does it perpetuate the life situation of the poor. Many members of the ownership class earn more in one year than poor persons can reasonably expect to accumulate in a lifetime—a stark reflection of the extremes of economic inequality in the United States.

THE EFFECTS OF ECONOMIC INEQUALITY

Economic inequality is not simply an abstract, intellectual concept. And the previous brief assessment of some of its dimensions and underlying causes barely begins to cover the topic. But at this point we shall turn away to suggest some of the consequences of economic inequality for American society. We will then consider potential solutions.

Inequality and Life Chances

We live in a society in which wealth and income have an undeniable bearing on a citizen's life chances. To some extent, at least, we must "buy" life just as we purchase any other commodity. Our economic situation will determine whether we eat and whether we can afford nutritious foods. It will determine whether we are safely and comfortably housed

The structural basis of poverty is evident when one considers the plight of the elderly. After a lifetime of hard work, many Americans have been forced to retire at age sixty-five and live on whatever savings they have plus, perhaps, small social security and pension benefits. According to census data, persons who are sixty years of age and older make up 17 percent of the poverty population.

and whether we can afford to buy quality health and medical care. Our economic situation will determine the area in which we can afford to live and the quality of educational opportunities available to our children. It will determine whether we have leisure time, how much we have, and how we can use it. It will determine whether our children live through birth, as well as the future life expectancy for us and them. Our economic situation will be inextricably linked to our sense of security, personal well-being, and self-worth. To the degree to which economic resources—wealth and income—are unequally distributed, life chances are also unequally distributed. By accident of birth and little more, a child born into the ownership class will be able to "buy" a life that is both longer and qualitatively different from that of a child born into poverty. While we all may have unalienable rights to "life, liberty, and the pursuit of happiness," economic inequality—with its impact on life chances—obviously stands in the way of the exercise of these rights.

Economic inequality also means that American society is incapable of harnessing and utilizing the potential talents and abilities of all its members. For example, educational opportunities closely correspond to economic position. It is the children of the affluent minority who most frequently go to private schools and academies, receive special tutoring, are "broadened" by travel, and are sent to elite colleges and universities. These advantages are conferred not because the children of the affluent deserve them more than anyone else, but because their parents can easily afford them. The children of the poor and of the average working family, on the other hand, must be happy with what little educational opportunity they receive in return for their parents' tax payments. Education, like color television, is a commodity; basically, you get what you pay for.

The denial of educational advantages means that much human talent remains hidden and repressed. Talent that goes unrecognized and insufficiently cultivated is not going to be utilized. The shortage of imaginative teachers, inventive medical practitioners, participants in the creative arts, and sensitive administrators and politicians is an arbitrary shortage. We have no real way of knowing how much potential talent goes to waste annually because millions of families lack the economic resources to ensure their children an opportunity to cultivate and demonstrate it. As a consequence, the whole society is poorer both culturally and materially.

Furthermore, economic inequality is becoming increasingly costly. How much does the United States devote to welfare relief, to unemployment compensation, and to paying the salaries of the armies of bureaucrats and workers who administer relief funds? How much do we devote to cleaning up the physical and mental damage done to those persons whose economic situation exerts a negative influence on their bodies and minds? How much do we devote to processing through the legal, judicial, and penal systems those who steal in order to secure temporary increases in their disposable incomes? The expenditures are enormous, and they are a result of the pervasiveness of economic inequality and poverty. In the absence of a shift in the distribution of wealth, income, and opportunity, the costs of maintaining the status quo can only be expected to continue to grow.

Some mention must also be made of the psychic costs of economic inequality. The competition for scarce economic resources, and thus life chances, leaves no one untouched. The thought of being a loser, of being or becoming economically obsolete, is a permanent nightmare for members of American society.[17] Competition separates people from one another and contributes to intergroup jealousies and hatreds, periodic

[17]Jules Henry, *Culture Against Man* (New York: Vintage Books, 1965).

Public Problem, Private Pain
A WELFARE MOTHER

Jesusita Novarro, who went on welfare when her husband deserted her, holds a part-time job at a neighborhood settlement house. At the time of this interview, she had just recovered from a serious illness for which she had been hospitalized.

I start my day here at five o'clock. I get up and prepare all the children's clothes. If there's shoes to shine, I do it in the morning. About seven o'clock I bathe the children. I leave my baby with the baby sitter and I go to work at the settlement house. I work until twelve o'clock. Sometimes I'll work longer if I have to go to welfare and get a check for somebody. When I get back, I try to make hot food for the kids to eat. In the afternoon it's pretty well on my own. I scrub and clean and cook and do whatever I have to do.

Welfare makes you feel like you're nothing. Like you're laying back and not doing anything and it's falling in your lap. But you must understand, mothers, too, work. My house is clean. I've been scrubbing since this morning. You could check my clothes, all washed and ironed. I'm home and I'm working. I am a working mother.

A job that a woman in a house is doing is a tedious job—especially if you want to do it right. If you do it slipshod, then it's not so bad. I'm pretty much of a perfectionist. I tell my kids, hang a towel. I don't want it thrown away. That is very hard. It's a constant game of picking up this, picking up that. And putting this away, so the house'll be clean.

Some men work eight hours a day. There are mothers that work eleven, twelve hours a day. We get up at night, a baby vomits, you have to be calling the doctor, you have to be changing the baby. When do you get a break, really? You don't. This is an all-around job, day and night. Why do they say it's charity? We're working for our money. I am working for this check. It is not charity. We are giving some kind of home to these children.

I'm so busy all day I don't have time to daydream. I pray a lot. I pray to God to give me strength. If He should take a child away from me, to have the strength to accept it. It's His kid. He just borrowed him to me.

I used to get in and close the door. Now I speak up for my right. I walk with my head up. If I want to wear big earrings, I do. If I'm overweight, that's too bad. I've gotten completely over feeling where I'm little. I'm working now, I'm pulling my weight. I'm gonna get off welfare in time, that's my goal—get off.

It's living off welfare and feeling that you're taking something for nothing the way people have said. You get to think maybe you are. You get to think, Why am I so stupid? Why can't I work? Why do I have to live this way? It's not enough to live on anyway. You feel degraded.

The other day I was at the hospital and I went to pay my bill. This nurse came and gave me the green card. Green card is for welfare. She went right in front of me and gave it to the cashier. She said, "I wish I could stay home and let the money fall in my lap." I felt rotten. I was just burning inside. You hear this all the way around you. The doctor doesn't even look at you. People are ashamed to show that green card. Why can't a woman just get a check in the mail: Here, this check is for you. Forget welfare. You're a mother who works.

This nurse, to her way of thinking, she represents the working people. The ones with the green card, we represent the lazy no-goods. This is what she was saying. They're the good ones and we're the bad guys.

Studs Terkel, *Working: People Talk About What They Do All Day and How They Feel About What They Do* (New York: Pantheon Books, 1974), pp. 303–304.

conflicts, and tragic episodes of personal and collective strife. It means that the only people who are honored or revered are the winners—the affluent minority. And the anxieties, tensions, and frustrations economic inequality and competition generate may well be a contributing factor to many expressions of individual "deviance"—ranging from criminal behavior to mental illness. All these costs, though difficult to measure, are felt in real ways.

The Need for Government Intervention

Economic inequality is a deeply rooted but by no means inevitable feature of American society. It is possible to minimize differences in personal wealth and income in order to make the life chances of all relatively equal and so that all can share more equitably in the goods and services being produced.

One of the first steps involves a change in attitudes toward economic inequality and poverty. Americans must become much more familiar with the facts about inequality and the harm stemming from it. Members of this society must also begin to reject the notion that extensive economic inequality is part of the natural order of things, and that therefore nothing meaningful can be done about it. Inequality can be attacked, but only if people are willing to collectively press this issue in the national political arena.

The next major step is to work out precise mechanisms to redistribute wealth and income. The goal should be to provide a decent standard of living for all persons, while placing restrictions on the senseless accumulation of wealth by a few. In recent years, various ideas on how to achieve equality have been put forth by individual scholars and a few legislators. It is time that such proposals become a matter of public debate, so that members of this society can decide which show the most promise.

For example, one proposal involves providing a guaranteed minimum income through the *Negative Income Tax* (NIT). Essentially, the NIT would be based on a periodic report on income, which each person or family would file with the federal government. If the income reported was above a set minimum amount, taxes would be paid on the excess above the minimum, with tax rates set low on earnings just above the minimum. If, on the other hand, the income reported was below the minimum, the federal government would issue a direct cash payment to make up the difference. The minimum must obviously be set high enough to move people out of poverty.

The NIT would provide an income floor for all needy individuals and families. Its primary beneficiaries would be members of low-income groups, who would no longer have to struggle along on poverty-level wages or plead for welfare assistance. The present welfare system could be reduced in scope, at a substantial savings to taxpayers, and reoriented toward providing human services to anyone in need.

Mechanisms to eliminate poverty and enhance the standard of living of low-income groups must be accompanied by major changes in America's tax structure. In particular, income taxes must be made progressive in reality as well as in theory, so that those who have higher incomes are made to pay their fair share. Profits from stocks and other forms of wealth, including state and local bonds, could be taxed at the same rate as income derived from working. In general, all the loopholes that provide a form of welfare for the rich must be closed, and the tax structure should restrict the maximum levels of income and wealth that can legally be accumulated by an individual or family.

Ways must also be investigated to redistribute wealth and increase the net worths of the millions of Americans who own little or nothing. The federal government could, for example, place a *net worth tax* on millionaire families, of whom there are currently about two hundred thousand. This tax would provide the federal government with sufficient revenue to permit special tax reductions for less affluent families who have put a certain amount of money into savings accounts (thus accumulating an estate). The net result would be a gradual reduction in the concentration of wealth among the rich and greater economic independence for large numbers of Americans.

No matter which mechanisms are adopted to reduce inequality, any surplus tax funds that are generated must be used to expand the supply of *free or low-cost services* available to members of this society. Such services include education and job-training, child-care facilities, efficient networks of public transportation, and health care. The purpose of attacking economic inequality is not simply to redistribute money, but also to improve the quality of living for all. Basic services should be readily available to all Americans.

The reduction of economic inequality will involve costs—but primarily for the most affluent, who will be most adversely affected by tax reforms aimed at the redistribution of income and wealth.[18] To the degree to which redistribution fosters increased equality in material terms, the economically derived status differences between the affluent and everyone else will be diminished. Such costs seem minor in comparison with the costs accompanying maintenance of the status quo, in which many millions are being forced to suffer.

As we have seen, the problem of economic inequality cannot be solved unless it is pressed in the national political arena. In Chapter 2 we shall analyze the national political system and some of the political obstacles that must be overcome in dealing with inequality.

[18]See Herbert Gans, "The Positive Functions of Poverty," *American Journal of Sociology*, 78 (September 1972): 275–89.

SUMMARY

In this chapter we have seen that the United States is a class-divided society. Wealth is heavily concentrated in a small ownership class, and a minority of family units receives the majority of the total annual family income. Gross economic inequality is perpetuated as wealth begets wealth, the taxation structure leaves inequalities untouched, and American cultural values provide a rationale for viewing such inequalities as natural and proper.

Those worst off within this class-divided society are the millions of poor and near-poor. While most are white, the poverty among racial and ethnic minority group members is far out of proportion to their numbers in the population. Contrary to myth, most poor people are very young, very old, disabled, and females who are heads of families. They are poor not because of individual deficiencies; rather, they are victims of decisions and circumstances outside of their immediate control. Just as social mechanisms help the rich maintain their affluence, there are economic, political, and social factors that render it difficult for people to escape poverty.

In a society in which one's opportunities and life-style are closely linked to having money, economic inequality translates into unequal life chances. As millions suffer in poverty, the potential talents and abilities of such persons go untapped—the entire society is poorer culturally and materially. The costs of poverty are also felt in the increasingly costly welfare, health care, and penal systems. More generally, the competition for scarce resources leaves no one untouched and is a source of individual anxiety and intergroup conflicts.

Gross economic inequality is not inevitable. It can be altered through government intervention. Mechanisms to change the distribution of wealth and income exist, for example, the Negative Income Tax and net worth tax. But such measures will only be implemented when people press the issue of economic inequality in the national political arena.

DISCUSSION QUESTIONS

1. What is the probability that you or your children will ever become part of the ownership class (roughly the richest 1 percent of all Americans)? What factors stand in the way?
2. Is it true that *anyone* can be economically successful if he or she really tries? Why?
3. What are your feelings about economic inequality? Should poverty be eliminated? If so, how should the costs of this be shared?
4. It is commonly held that any serious move toward the equalization of wealth and income will reduce people's incentive to work. What are the arguments for and against this view?

5. If you were a member of the ownership class, what arguments would you make against tax reforms that would take away much of your money to help eliminate poverty? If you were a member of the poverty population, what arguments would you make in favor of such tax reforms?

6. If America's economic growth falters in the coming decades (e.g., due to energy shortages and costs), job opportunities—even for college graduates—may undergo a marked decline. Moreover, opportunities for upward mobility may be restricted so that workers are locked in place. Under such circumstances, what arguments might be made for the redistribution of wealth and income?

2 Concentration of Power

Members of American society should be able to actively participate in or directly influence those political and economic decisions that affect them.

I t is common to refer to the United States as a democracy. From kindergarten on, children are taught about the democratic character of the American political system. Ours, it is often said, is a government "of, by, and for the people." Students are encouraged to study the U.S. Constitution and to learn about the various branches of government. Frequently, the American political system is favorably contrasted with others that are called totalitarian or dictatorial. In short, the schools act as agencies of political socialization; they function to provide future adult citizens with a belief in the noble origins and operation of the American political system and to urge faith in its democratic workings.[1]

Unfortunately, the schools too often fail to distinguish between democratic ideals and political realities. Everyday observations and practical experiences have led many Americans to harbor doubts about the democratic character of the American political system. Many contend that political power has become concentrated in the hands of a select few and that, to the degree such concentration exists, we do not have a government of, by, and for the people. Instead, decisions affecting all Americans are made by persons primarily concerned with the pursuit of their own self-defined interests.

This chapter begins by examining the conventional pluralist perspective on the distribution of political power. This perspective holds that power is equitably distributed and that America is a democratic society in which no one group is politically dominant. While this conventional view is widely held, we shall point to indications of doubt and disagreement that have emerged in recent years among the public. Next we shall set forth two alternative perspectives on the distribution of power.[2] The power elite perspective sees power as having become concentrated among those holding top positions in America's bureaucratic organizations. The governing class perspective emphasizes the power-wielding capabilities of the wealthy and their representatives. Finally, we shall consider some of the broad consequences of the concentration of power and suggest some steps that might move America's political system closer to the democratic ideal.

POWER IN AMERICA: WHO RULES?

Is the United States a democratic society? Those holding the *pluralist perspective* would say that it is. In this section we shall present the views

[1]See, for example, David Easton and Jack Dennis, *Children in the Political System* (New York: McGraw-Hill, Inc., 1969).

[2]Contending perspectives on the true nature of the American political system might be considered a struggle amongst conflicting intellectual "paradigms." See Thomas S. Kuhn, *The Structure of Scientific Revolutions* (Chicago: University of Chicago Press, 1962).

The pluralist belief that farm organizations and other veto groups have a direct impact on national policy-making has not been substantiated by recent events. Though farm groups have protested against economic policies that limit their income in a time of high expenses—presenting their case to the federal government and staging demonstrations like this one in Chicago's financial district in 1978—their demands have essentially gone unmet.

of David Riesman, whose book, *The Lonely Crowd,* cogently expresses the pluralist position.[3] We shall then look at survey results that indicate that many Americans entertain doubts about the validity of this perspective.

The Pluralist Perspective

In *The Lonely Crowd,* sociologist David Riesman commented on American politics while making a large-scale assessment of our nation's culture and personality. Riesman argued that great changes have taken place in the American political system during the twentieth century. At various times during the nineteenth century, Riesman noted, wealthy businessmen and industrialists exercised an inordinate amount of power over the federal government and its policies. It almost appeared that an economic upper class, much like the ownership class described in Chapter 1, "ruled" America. Riesman contended that upper-class domination over government has disintegrated in the present century and that our society has become pluralistic in its national politics. That is, there are now many other groups capable of countering the great political powers

[3]David Riesman, *The Lonely Crowd,* abridged ed. (New Haven, Conn.: Yale University Press, 1961), Chapter X. A more recent variant of Riesman's ideas can be found in Arnold M. Rose, *The Power Structure* (New York: Oxford University Press, Inc., 1967).

historically held by men of wealth and economic power. Riesman used the term *veto groups* in referring to those organized bodies strong enough to make a direct impact on key national policy decisions. In his view, farm groups, labor and professional organizations, and ethnic and regional groups, among others, have all developed the political strength to veto policies that might adversely affect their interests. And, to a somewhat lesser extent, such groups can also initiate actions and mobilize pressures to gain the adoption of policies they want.

The pluralist perspective, as espoused by Riesman, essentially contends that political power is dispersed and distributed among a multitude of competing and contending interest groups. No group is capable of dominating at all times, nor is any group even interested in all questions of national policy. The distribution of power in America is a constantly shifting and rather amorphous phenomenon. Occasionally, political alliances form among different interest groups, only to be dissolved when new issues revive conflicting interests. The federal government is assumed to be a neutral body—an arbitrator, a compromiser—which soothes conflict and works out matters in the best interests of all. It is responsive to all groups and dominated by none.

Thus, from the pluralist perspective, the United States is a democratic society. All persons are free to join or otherwise support organized groups that promise to represent their interests in the national political arena. And the leaders of such groups, in order to gain strength and make themselves felt at the national level, must appeal to the citizenry for support. Organizations representing great business interests, according to the pluralist perspective, are just like any other group in this respect.

Not coincidently, *The Lonely Crowd* dismissed the idea that there are continuing, large-scale economic inequalities in American society. In fact, according to Riesman, "America is a middle-class country." He asked rhetorically "whether one would not find, over a long period of time, that decisions in America favored one group or class . . . over others." He answered that this was not the case. "Does not wealth exert its pull in the long run? In the past this has been so; for the future, I doubt it."[4] The rise of a multitude of veto groups has neutralized the historical power of wealth, according to Riesman. The ownership class is just like any other group: it must compete and struggle to be heard.

We are thus presented with an orthodox picture of the national political scene, one that coincides with the content of many American social studies textbooks. Riesman in his own way expressed the dominant belief about the distribution of power in the United States. But is political power really so completely dispersed throughout American society? Is the federal government just a neutral body that responds to the best interests of the American people? Is political decision-making at the national level

[4]Riesman, *The Lonely Crowd*, p. 222.

divorced from the interests of wealth and ownership? Is the ownership class just another group scrambling for power? Does one group or class really run things in this society? Let us look at recent public beliefs about these issues.

American Beliefs About Political Power

In recent years, there have been several major surveys of American beliefs about political and economic power. These surveys, which have been conducted on both the local and national levels, have found that a significant proportion of Americans do not believe in the pluralist position. Instead, the results indicate that many Americans feel that they are powerless and that the United States is run by a small group of powerful people.

The Muskegon study. During the 1960s William Form and Joan Rytina conducted a survey on beliefs about the way power is distributed in the United States. They carried out a series of interviews with a sample of persons residing in the city of Muskegon, Michigan. The researchers selected participants from three economic groups—the rich, the middle class, and the poor.[5]

During the course of interviews, participants were asked to decide which of the following three statements best described the national distribution of power:

A. No one group really runs the government in this country. Instead, important decisions about national policy are made by a lot of different groups such as labor, business, religious, and educational groups, and so on. These groups influence both political parties, but no single group can dictate to the others, and each group is strong enough to protect its own interests.

B. A small group of men at the top really run the government in this country. These are the heads of the biggest business corporations, the highest officers in the Army, Navy and Air Force, and a few important senators, congressmen and federal officials in Washington. These men dominate both the Republican and Democratic Parties.

C. Big businessmen really run the government in this country. The heads of the large corporations dominate both the Republican and Democratic Parties. This means that things in Washington go pretty much the way big businessmen want them to.[6]

Three fifths of those interviewed selected statement A, which is a summary of the pluralist perspective. But there was not an overwhelming consensus. Roughly one fifth selected statement B and the remaining fifth

[5]William H. Form and Joan Rytina, "Ideological Beliefs on the Distribution of Power in the United States," *American Sociological Review,* 34 (February 1969): 19–31.

[6]Ibid., p. 22.

chose statement C. An intriguing finding emerged when the researchers matched the economic level of the participants with the statements they chose. The higher their family income, the more likely persons were to state that pluralism best described our national system of power. Lower income persons and members of minority groups in the poor and middle classes were far more likely to select the alternative statements.

Form and Rytina concluded that persons in different economic positions see the structure of power from different vantage points and in terms of their own perceived interests. Those at higher income levels, finding that the political system generally works for them and in their class interests, are apt to voice the conventional view that this is a democratic society. On the other hand, the poor and members of minority groups have not found the political system so responsive to their needs and perceived interests; they have experienced domination and thus feel the absence of a pluralist democracy. Statements B and C, which imply dominance, fit quite well with the everyday reality of their lives. More recent surveys, conducted nationally, underscore the feelings of powerlessness many Americans have come to hold. These national surveys reveal that such feelings extend well beyond the poor and members of minority groups.

The Senate survey.   In 1973 the U.S. Senate commissioned a major survey of public attitudes toward government and other major American institutions.[7] The results revealed an extraordinary degree of dissatisfaction with the workings of the national government. Americans decried secrecy and corruption in government and claimed that their interests were being sacrificed in favor of powerful special interest groups. Fifty-five percent described themselves as alienated and disenchanted, feeling "profoundly impotent to influence the actions of their leaders." A similar percentage agreed with the statement that "people running the country don't really care what happens to you." Such expressions of alienation were not only due to the events of 1973 (e.g., the Watergate scandal, which led to the resignation of President Richard Nixon in 1974), for the survey report showed that such feelings had been on a steady increase at least since 1966.

Along with political alienation, the survey found a marked loss of respect for the institutions of national government during the 1966–73 period. By 1973 only 19 percent of Americans were able to state that they had "a great deal of confidence" in the executive branch of the federal government. Other branches fared only slightly better: roughly a third of the American people had great confidence in Congress and the Supreme Court. By contrast, over half had a great deal of confidence in "local trash collection."

[7]Data and direct quotations from U.S. Senate, Committee on Government Operations, Subcommittee on Intergovernmental Relations, *Confidence and Concern: Citizens View American Government, Part 1* (Washington, D.C.: U.S. Government Printing Office, December 3, 1973).

But the survey also indicated that the American people strongly believed that their government *could* be made to work effectively and meet their needs. They were not ready to toss the political system out the window in favor of something new. People saw a need for "an increased diffusion of power—both inside the structure of government and through greater scrutiny of its workings and leadership. The mandate is for participation, not direction . . . . And the message is . . . that people want to be included and informed, not managed and ignored." The survey report went on to note that "the people are opting strongly for a restoration of open, democratic government, where the people are trusted and consulted." This seems to indicate that, while the American people may feel managed and dominated from above and are dissatisfied over their plight, they are not willing to continue with such a situation. On an ominous note, the survey report concluded that "if the preconditions for open government are not met, then frustration, alienation, and polarization are likely to proceed apace. And the distrust of the governed for those who govern is a dangerous development indeed."

A society in which over half the people feel that they cannot influence their governmental leaders, one in which people trust garbage collection more than Supreme Court justices, does not seem to be a *democratic* society. Instead, it appears to be a society marked by the erosion of political democracy and the concentration of power in the hands of a few.

Polls on attitudes toward business.   One of the other key participants in the exercise of power over the American people—the corporate world—has also undergone a crisis of faith in recent years.[8] Most Americans continue to believe in the basic principles of the capitalist economic system—for example, that business and industry belong under private control and ownership. Survey reports indicate that Americans oppose the notion of nationalization, or federal takeover, of industries (by a government they distrust). But 77 percent believe that the national government should be "tougher" on big business, according to a 1973 public opinion survey. The fact that only 23 percent believed that corporate power would actually be curbed demonstrates the public's sense of impotence both in the face of their national government and the power wielded by the corporate world.

Between 1966 and 1973 the percentage of the American people expressing a "great deal of confidence" in business dropped from 55 to 27 percent. During this same eight-year period, public confidence in the quality of goods and services being sold also dropped markedly, and people expressed an ever stronger belief that they were paying out more and receiving less for their money. There were more complaints about the failure of the corporate world to provide enough steady jobs for people. Fewer Americans thought business offered young people a

[8]Data in this section are from Louis Harris, *The Anguish of Change* (New York: W. W. Norton & Co., Inc., 1973), Chapter X.

Public Problem, Private Pain
FEELING POWERLESS

In the course of conducting a large-scale study of political disillusionment and alienation in the United States, political analysts Robert S. Gilmour and Robert B. Lamb interviewed numerous Americans from all walks of life. The excerpts from their interviews reprinted below provide an indication of the depth of distrust of government and feelings of political meaninglessness and powerlessness experienced by these and other Americans. As these interviews indicate, political alienation and frustration are not confined to one class but are instead felt by people from most social classes and occupational groups.

One cannot help but wonder where such attitudes are likely to lead. Will political alienation remain at this level—will their distrust and cynicism encourage Americans to remain in a position of spectators chafing under the governance of other people? Or will this alienation become transformed into grass-roots activism around issues that are being ignored or mishandled by America's elites? Presumably, it is up to those whose voices are heard in this selection—and to others like them—to make the decisions that will answer these questions.

Despite vague and contradictory meanings of "political alienation," there is broad agreement that alienation does indeed exist. Informed but less optimistic observers, such as Louis Harris, claim that the proportion of Americans who are alienated from their national government is 50 percent and higher. The evidence for such a judgment is all but overwhelming from the news-paper, magazine, TV reports; opinion polls; and surveys we reviewed and analyzed. But it was the extended personal interviews we held with a variety of people that brought the point most forcefully and convincingly home.

The characteristic comment was made by a retired fireman: "Watergate has convinced me that what I thought happened sometimes happens *all* the time." A similar view was stated by a Denver druggist: "Perhaps I felt this way even without Watergate. My taxes go up after every election, while politicians take their junkets to Europe, get contracts for their friends and kickbacks on roads and other projects. They always seem to have their hands in the till. It sure beats working for a living."

The widespread sense of *distrust* resulting from the Watergate scandals, the numerous indictments and convictions, and the investigation and subsequent resignations of Vice President Spiro Agnew and President Richard Nixon should not be allowed to obscure the view of other, almost equally widespread aspects of disillusionment and political alienation that have now become well rooted in the public mind. A sense of the *meaninglessness* of choice between poor candidates and outmoded parties was echoed wherever we went. "It doesn't matter which way you vote; they're all the same, talk the same, promise the same. But all out for themselves, that's all," was a Boston doorman's way of summing up this meaninglessness of choice.

A sense of *powerlessness* to make any political impact or to make needed changes of direction was another repeated theme. "I am powerless to influence any political vote, any political decision, or any politician," a New Jersey housewife explained. "There's no relation between my vote and what any politician does," a New York City cabdriver said. "It's like worshipping a pagan god, 'cause once you vote for them they never again have any contact with you." A heavy-equipment operator in Iowa summed up all these feelings. When asked about representative government, he shot back, "What representation of the people? They don't even know who the people are. The Democrats and Republicans are just the same. They only represent one thing: Number One, and maybe a crony or two." While he rolled silently across a crowded golf course in his electric cart, a Chicago investor remarked, "We used to joke about politics in '1984' but now it's hitting you in the face, and it's frightening."

In spite of the keen sense of distance, disdain, and even fear felt by the governed for their governors, many of our informants agreed with the widow of a TV repairman in Memphis: "We don't need to change the Constitution. Not one bit. The problem is what they're doing with it. They're twisting it all out of shape." The people we interviewed consistently saw a basic difference between "the constitution" or "the government" and elected officials: "Kick them out and start over again!" a summer stock stagehand demanded. "Why?" we asked. "I can't trust any of them. It's just a feeling I have. I don't care if it's a judge or the President or the parking meter guy. Everybody knows they're crooks." "Vote out everybody in office, is what I say," an upstate New York mason said. Others saw the distinction between government structure and the politicians clearly enough, but they were less optimistic about the effectiveness of an electoral clean sweep. "I guess they all gits crooked when they gits that high up," the wife of an elderly New England potato farmer said. "Guess they has to be." An estranged student put an ideological cast on the same theme: "They're all just in there tight with the big capitalists and the big bucks. The whole system's set up that way now. What's my vote gonna mean to that? Nothing!"

Robert S. Gilmour and Robert B. Lamb, *Political Alienation in Contemporary America* (New York: St. Martin's Press, 1975), pp. 3–5.

chance to get ahead or that it allowed people to utilize their full creative talents. In 1973 only 22 percent of the American people agreed that business really cared about the individual. There was a feeling that the corporate world was not making an adequate contribution in such areas as pollution control and the support of educational, cultural, health, and charitable activities.

At the same time, the majority of the American people believed that business could and should be doing more to improve the public welfare. Americans expected business to use its money and power to eliminate racial discrimination, wipe out poverty, rebuild the cities, control crime, and raise moral standards. While public expectations of business rose steadily as confidence in governmental effectiveness declined, the corporate world failed to respond.

As a result, public respect for the corporate world has markedly declined. While the public looked to business and industry to fill the vacuum created by government ineffectiveness, the corporate world chose to concentrate on the pursuit of narrow economic goals. From the perspective of the American people, the corporate world was unresponsive to their needs and outside the realm of popular control through governmental restraint.

Americans continue to hold negative attitudes toward government and business, with more than half feeling themselves powerless in the face of corporate and governmental interests (see Table 2.1). It seems clear that the pluralist perspective does not coincide with the views and experiences of millions of Americans. In the view of a significant proportion of citizens and of many scholars, the United States is not working as a democracy of, by, and for the people. Power, like wealth, is not distributed equally.

Table 2.1. Public Opinions on Business and the Federal Government

Statement	Percent Agreeing
The federal government is unresponsive to the needs of the citizenry.	58%
The government can be trusted only some of the time.	56
America's major corporations tend to dominate and determine the actions of public officials in Washington.	58
Democratic and Republican parties are in favor of big business rather than the average worker.	57
Big business is the source of most of what's wrong in this country today.	49
It would do more good than harm to develop a political movement to challenge the influence of big business.	49

Sources: The first two items are from the *New York Times,* February 24, 1976; poll conducted by the *Times* and CBS News. The last four items are from a press release by Peoples Bicentennial Commission, Washington, D.C., September 1, 1975; poll conducted by Hart Research Associates.

THE POWER ELITE PERSPECTIVE

Shortly after the publication of *The Lonely Crowd,* another sociologist, C. Wright Mills, directly challenged the pluralist perspective, offering a different version of the way power is distributed in American society.[9] His work, *The Power Elite,* set off a debate that has not yet ceased. Mills' study has caused many sociologists to take a new and more critical look at the national political system.

The Attack on Pluralism

In *The Power Elite,* C. Wright Mills attacked the pluralist perspective as a form of romanticism. The position taken by scholars like Riesman, Mills felt, reflected what we might *like* American society to be rather than what it is. The United States is not a democratic society, despite whatever vestiges of pluralism might be said to exist. Rather, in Mills' eyes, it is a society dominated by a set of *elites*—the men who hold the very highest offices in the large-scale bureaucratic hierarchies that have come to prevail in the United States.

Mills did not deny the existence of farm groups, labor and professional organizations, and other interest groups. Such groups clearly exist, but Mills felt they exist at a secondary level of power. The power to make decisions of national and international significance is on another level altogether, a level above and beyond the reach of the multitude of veto or interest groups deemed so significant by Riesman. It is the *power elite* alone that makes the decisions that shape the nature and course of the society in which we live. And, to Mills, Congress is not part of this power elite. It too exists on the secondary level of power. The decisions made by Congress—often under the buffeting pressures of one or another set of interest groups—are made within an overarching political and economic framework determined and promoted by the power elite.

Identifying the Power Elite

Who are the members of the power elite? Mills answered this question by tracing the historical ascendancy of three major components of American society. The first component is *big business and the corporate rich.* Unlike Riesman, Mills denied that the political significance of economic elites has undergone a decline in the twentieth century. To Mills, the men who sit

[9]C. Wright Mills, *The Power Elite* (New York: Oxford University Press, Inc., 1956). Mills' influence is readily detectable in other works; see, for example, Ralph Miliband, *The State in Capitalist Society* (New York: Basic Books, Inc., 1969). Critiques of Mills' work can be found in G. William Domhoff and Hoyt B. Ballard, eds., *C. Wright Mills and the Power Elite* (Boston: Beacon Press, 1968).

at the very highest levels in America's giant corporations and other financial institutions still retain enormous political strength. Whether through direct participation in national government, campaign contributions to political candidates, or other forms of political activity, economic elites work to ensure that their particular interests are met.

Second, Mills identified the *military* as a bureaucratic entity whose top officials possess membership in the power elite. Mills traced the historical ascendancy of the American military from a marginal arm of civilian government, important only in times of war, to a vast hierarchical institution that has become an integral part of the American scene. Reaching preeminence during World War II, it has since grown in size and in political and economic importance. As do members of the nation's economic elite, the highest officers in the military establishment have particular interests to pursue and protect. Their positions at the very top provide them with the means to do so.

Third, Mills focused on the *executive branch* of the federal government. Top officials of this branch, including the president, have come to reign over an immense bureaucratic network. The office of the president and the cabinet agencies under this office have progressively expanded in size and importance. In Mills' view, the executive branch overwhelms Congress in terms of power, and Congress largely responds to initiatives and decisions that flow from the executive branch. The two governmental bodies are not coequal, in Mills' estimation, and those persons in the top positions of the executive branch are prominent members of the power elite.

Thus Mills presented a complex of elites in which there is a three-way sharing of power, a triumvirate that sits in judgment over major national and international decisions of the day. No segment of the elite—economic, political, or military—dominates, though a close reading of Mills' book can easily lead one to conclude that he saw economic elites as first among equals. Nevertheless, each segment of the power elite has definite interests it wishes to pursue. These interests can be met only by close cooperation with the others:

> The power to make decisions of national and international importance
> is . . . seated in the political, military, and economic institutions. As each
> has assumed its modern shape, its effects on the other two have become
> greater and the traffic between the three has increased. As each of these
> domains has coincided with the others, as decisions have become broader,
> the leading men of each . . . have tended to come together to form the
> power elite of America.[10]

The men who participate in this powerful triumvirate, in Mills' judgment, form a self-contained, cohesive social group. In his study, Mills attempted to show the bases of their group cohesion. The members of

---

[10]Mills, *The Power Elite*, p. 9.

Among the ways in which the wealthy influence political policies is by contributing to political campaigns. When wealthy donors give candidates direct contributions, attend political fund-raising dinners (photograph), or provide other forms of aid, they earn the gratitude of the candidates and may thus feel somewhat assured that those candidates who are elected will not work against their interests.

the power elite, he argued, come from rather similar social origins. Close personal and family ties exist among those whose bureaucratic positions provide elite status. And there is a frequent interchange of personnel between the hierarchies commanded by the elite. Top corporate executives are tapped for key appointments in the executive branch, and men of wealth are routinely invited to take on ambassadorial posts around the world. Such persons move in and out of government with ease. High-ranking executive branch officials and retiring military officers frequently enter key offices in business and industry. The ease of movement, to Mills, is a visible indication of the close ties among those at the top, as well as an indication that such men tend to think alike. To Mills, members of the power elite are of a similar social type, thereby contributing to the unity of the power elite as a group.

The Erosion of Public Involvement

As we have seen, Riesman argued that Americans exert political influence through the medium of organized veto or interest groups. Mills did not have so optimistic a view of the role of the public. According to Mills, dominance by the power elite produced the *massification* of the American people. By this he meant that the public, in succumbing to manipulation by the powerful, had become increasingly unable to define and act on its own political interests. In Mills' terms, the American majority had turned into a *mass society* and existed on the third or lowest level of power.

The power elite manipulates the American public through careful orchestration of the mass media, the major means by which people find out what is going on. By selective censorship of information, by limiting the realm of national debate, by emphasizing entertainment over messages that inform, the mass media minimize serious political discussion and controversy. This is to be expected, since the national media are owned, controlled, and financed (by advertising) by the economic component of the power elite. The American public is not properly informed and thus cannot participate in deciding the issues that affect all people. Thus, Mills argued, members of the mass society are progressively incapable of understanding issues and comprehending decisions that are allegedly made in their interest by those at the top.

As a result of manipulation from above and their powerlessness over important national decisions, citizens of the mass society have become less and less interested in politics. Political democracy becomes less possible, and the majority of Americans find themselves at the mercy of forces they can neither understand nor control. Slowly but perceptibly, the members of the power elite have become more inaccessible and less accountable to those affected by their high-level decisions.

The Case of Defense Spending

As we have seen, the power elite perspective divides the American political system into three levels of power. At the top is the power elite, composed of those men who hold top positions in big business, the military, and the executive branch of the federal government. The second level of power is filled by interest groups and members of Congress, while the general public can be found at the third, or lowest, level. Mills pointed out that the general public is manipulated by the power elite, and that this manipulation has resulted in the massification of the public.

The power elite perspective can be applied to an annual event in American politics, the consideration of the federal budget by Congress. This budget is drawn up by the office of the president and sent to Congress in January of each year. Each year, the budget calls for expenditures of hundreds of billions of dollars, and each year a large percentage of it is devoted to defense purposes. In January 1978, for example, $115.2 billion of President Jimmy Carter's $500.2 billion budget was earmarked for defense.[11]

Obviously, decisions regarding how much money the government will

---

[11]*New York Times,* January 24, 1978, p. 15C.

spend on defense are of major importance to all Americans. Whose power holds sway over these decisions? The pluralist perspective would have it that the American people hold the power. A brief examination of the budgeting process, however, demonstrates that defense-spending decisions largely involve the corporate world, the military, and the president.

The federal budget is prepared by an agency of the executive branch, the Office of Management and Budget (OMB), whose top officials are appointed by and report directly to the president. The process begins when all agencies of the executive branch, including the military (through the Department of Defense), send their budgetary requests to OMB. Officials of OMB essentially decide which budgetary requests to approve and which might be reduced or eliminated. Agency heads can appeal such decisions to the president, who makes the final decision. Each year, as we have seen, OMB and the president grant the military the largest slice of the budgetary pie—roughly a quarter of it in 1978—leaving the remainder to be divided by all the other federal agencies.

Once the White House and the military have, for all intents and purposes, decided on defense expenditures, another power elite component—big business—enters the picture. Buried in the overall defense budget are tens of billions of dollars to be spent on weapons systems and equipment. Thus the aerospace/defense industry, like the military, has a vested interest in large-scale defense spending. When the time comes, industry lobbyists join with White House and military officials in efforts to ensure that Congress approves the proposed defense budget with minimal cuts. Not only profits but also stockholders' dividends depend on keeping military spending up.

Congress is ordinarily quite cooperative. Members of Congress rely on defense spending for their home states and districts. Any dramatic decreases in defense expenditures could mean the closing of military facilities or cutbacks in production by aerospace/defense firms. The specter of economic decline, rising unemployment, and resultant voter dissatisfaction provides an incentive for Congress to approve expenditures whether they are necessary or not.

And what of the public? Americans receive very little objective information about the necessity of defense spending; most information comes directly from the power elite. This information is channeled to the mass media and Congress. And, of course, the power elite does not solicit public opinion about budgetary decisions.

The decision to allocate $115.2 billion to defense, rather than to use some of this money to subsidize health care or higher education, is essentially made *for* the American public. In introducing his budget proposals, President Carter stated: "The nation's armed forces must always stand sufficiently strong to deter aggression and to assure our security."[12] Few would disagree with this premise. But one is struck by the absence of any words inviting public debate over how American security

[12]Ibid.

might best be protected and at what cost to the taxpayers. C. Wright Mills' perspective on the distribution of political power indicates that no such invitation is likely to be extended.

THE GOVERNING CLASS PERSPECTIVE

A second alternative perspective, which differs slightly from Mills' emphasis on bureaucratic elites, is the *governing class perspective*. This view emphasizes the power-wielding capabilities of the wealthy and their representatives. The governing class perspective has been set forth by G. William Domhoff in *Who Rules America?*—a study that appeared in the late 1960s.[13]

America's Social and Economic Upper Class

Domhoff began by trying to establish the existence of a social upper class of national dimensions—that is, an exclusive social grouping that reigns supreme in terms of status and prestige. As evidence of the existence of such a class, Domhoff pointed to the social registers that have long been maintained in a score of major American cities. The individuals and families listed in these registers are there by virtue of family pedigree and economic circumstance. They are members of "high society."

Domhoff also identified a set of institutions and events that cater to the exclusive tastes and interests of upper-class individuals. These include private schools, elite universities and colleges, clubs and resorts, and parties and balls. Domhoff argued that they provide a basis for cohesiveness among members of the upper class, for it is at such institutions and events that these people mingle with one another. The outcomes are the formulation of friendships, the establishment of business and social contracts, and the exposure of youth to potential marriage partners of the "right kind." Adults and children of this social upper class readily sense their high status and are easily able to differentiate themselves from others who do not "belong."

Having established to his satisfaction that such an upper class exists, Domhoff turned to another question. Is this *social* upper class also an *economic* upper class? He found a great overlap between those with the greatest wealth and highest incomes (the ownership class of Chapter 1) and those who are considered at the top in social terms. Members of the social upper class are, for the most part, wealthy businessmen and their families or descendants of such men. They compromise that component of society Mills called the economic elite.

[13]G. William Domhoff, *Who Rules America?* (Englewood Cliffs, N.J.: Prentice-Hall, Inc., 1967). Domhoff answers critiques of his work in *The Higher Circles* (New York: Vintage Books, 1971).

America's Governing Class

Domhoff was particularly interested in discovering whether this national social and economic upper class is also a ruling or *governing class* (he preferred the latter term) in a political sense. Domhoff defined a governing class as "a social upper class which owns a disproportionate amount of a country's wealth, receives a disproportionate amount of a country's yearly income, and contributes a disproportionate number of its members to the controlling institutions and key decision-making groups of the country."[14] Thus Domhoff looked at the ways in which members of the social and economic upper class participate in the nation's major institutions.

One place major decisions are made is in the dominant economic institutions that, by virtue of their overall size, sales, and assets, are the foundation of the American economy. Decisions made at the top levels of these institutions often have an impact on the economic well-being of the entire nation. The largest corporations and financial institutions, according to Domhoff, are under the control of the upper class. Upper-class individuals either themselves play the roles of directors and managers of such institutions or handpick persons from non-upper-class backgrounds for such key decision-making roles.

Obviously, high-ranking officials in the federal government also hold a great deal of power. In Domhoff's words, "Members of the American upper class and their employees control the Executive Branch."[15] To support this assertion, he examined the ways in which presidential nominees are controlled. The key here is money. Financing a national political campaign has become an increasingly expensive proposition. Candidates are generally unable to support much of the costs themselves, and contributions by the public are generally insufficient. Thus, private benefactors must be sought out. Upper-class individuals are most likely to support candidates who best articulate upper-class goals and values and who are unlikely to threaten upper-class economic interests. Donations or loans implicitly mean favors in return, and the debts of successful presidential candidates to wealthy benefactors are reflected, in Domhoff's view, in key policy decisions.

Furthermore, the president appoints individuals to key posts in the federal bureaucracy and the judiciary. Appointees to such positions of importance, according to Domhoff, tend to come from the social and economic upper class in far greater frequency than one would expect, given its size. Those individuals who lack upper-class backgrounds, Domhoff suggests, are appointed on the basis of their past demonstrated performance in understanding and serving upper-class interests. Through this and through data on financial contributions, Domhoff was able to support his argument that the upper class is, in reality, a governing or ruling class.

[14]Domhoff, *Who Rules America?* p. 9.
[15]Ibid., p. 84.

Pluralism Below

Congress is influenced but not controlled by the upper class, in Domhoff's view. Members of Congress are often dependent on upper-class contributions for their election campaigns. They are also directly subject to influence by the powerful, well-financed lobbies that represent upper-class economic interests. While many legislators are themselves from upper-class backgrounds, most are not. Moreover, Congress is subject to pressures from many groups that do not represent upper-class interests. Thus senators and representatives are subject to influence but not total upper-class control.

It is with regard to Congress and on the local and state levels of government that Domhoff feels the pluralists may have a point. While decisions and policies made in the executive branch of the federal government and in the corporate world may be under the control of upper-class individuals or their representatives, political diversity exists below. Domhoff saw no incompatibility between top-level control by the upper class and pluralism at another level. Here he seems to be siding with Mills, who also conceptualized a secondary level of power operating within a framework of domination imposed from above.

But Domhoff departed from Mills by insisting that, despite the existence of a governing class, the United States is still democratic. He

According to the governing class perspective, it is at the state and local levels that the people are most likely to have a voice in political policies and decisions. For example, neighborhood organizations that have formed across the country in order to make city governments more responsive to such issues as tenants' rights and improved city services have often succeeded in having their concerns adopted.

argued that the governing class is not monolithic, and that there are splits and divisions within it. Not all members of the upper class agree on just what policies and decisions will best coincide with their short-term and long-term interests. Domhoff suggested that competing factions within the upper class may find themselves forced to indirectly seek support from non-upper-class groups in order to meet their self-defined needs. Thus members of the upper class may be divided over whether to throw their weight behind Democratic or Republican candidates for national office. It is a question of which party and candidate promises to protect—or at least not to verbally threaten—those aspects of the societal status quo the upper class wishes to preserve. Domhoff suggests that American democracy is based primarily on cleavages within the governing class itself, at the same time that this class effectively shapes the nature and course of American life.

The Case of Social Security

The governing class perspective portrays upper-class control over the corporate world and the executive branch of the federal government. Moreover, it is said that Congress is influenced by the upper class. The 1977 decision on how to save the faltering social security system may serve to illustrate the presence of such class interests in politics.

During the 1970s it became increasingly evident that the funds out of which social security benefits were paid would soon be depleted. Benefit levels were being increased; more people were receiving benefits; and new benefit programs were being added, while funds coming into the federal government were inadequate to offset costs. The White House and Congress were faced with a choice. The social security system could be bailed out using general tax funds obtained through increased individual and corporate income taxes. Or the social security tax, identified in the preceding chapter as a regressive tax that disproportionately affects the average worker, could be substantially increased. This increase would affect both workers and employers, as the latter must match workers' payments to the social security system.

Of these two alternatives, increasing individual and corporate income taxes is clearly against the interests of members of the governing class. There is too great a possibility of general tax reform that would penalize the affluent. Well-paid federal officials—both in the executive branch and in Congress—do not pay the social security tax. They instead pay into (and receive generous benefits from) a federal pension plan. Raising their income taxes to bail out a social security system in which they do not participate is not in their interests.

In late 1977 Congress considered and passed increases in the social security tax payments of individuals and employers. The president strongly approved, and he signed the bill into law. As Table 2.2 indicates, the tax would progressively increase so that only the affluent would

Table 2.2. Social Security Tax Payments

	Employees and Employer Each				Self-Employed		
	Worker's maximum annual pay taxed	Tax rate	Maximum tax per worker	Increase from old law	Tax rate	Maximum tax	Increase from old law
1977	$16,500	5.85%	$ 965.25	—	7.90%	$1,303.50	—
1978	$17,700	6.05%	$1,070.85	—	8.10%	$1,433.70	—
1979	$22,900	6.13%	$1,403.77	$ 260.32	8.10%	$1,854.90	$ 324.00
1980	$25,900	6.13%	$1,587.67	$ 353.47	8.10%	$2,097.90	$ 445.50
1981	$29,700	6.65%	$1,975.05	$ 595.35	9.30%	$2,762.10	$ 933.45
1982	$31,800	6.70%	$2,130.60	$ 656.40	9.35%	$2,973.30	$1,019.40
1983	$33,900	6.70%	$2,271.30	$ 702.60	9.35%	$3,169.65	$1,090.50
1984	$36,000	6.70%	$2,412.00	$ 748.80	9.35%	$3,366.00	$1,161.60
1985	$38,100	7.05%	$2,686.05	$ 928.35	9.90%	$3,771.90	$1,442.25
1986	$40,200	7.15%	$2,874.30	$ 978.00	10.0%	$4,020.00	$1,521.00
1987	$42,600	7.15%	$3,045.90	$1,033.50	10.0%	$4,260.00	$1,608.00

Source: *U.S. News and World Report,* December 26, 1977, p. 89.

continue to earn income above the official cutoff point. Meanwhile, the average worker would be paying out even more money to the federal government. In order to offset social security tax increases, employers in the corporate world could simply raise the prices of their goods and services. Workers may thus be hit again by the social security tax changes, as their dollars would go to buy less.

These changes in the social security system were made by officials in the governing class-controlled White House and the governing class-influenced Congress, by people who do not pay the social security tax and whose incomes are well above those of the average worker. Thus, ironically, those who made these tax decisions would largely be unaffected by them. Domhoff would no doubt argue that, since the affluent are unlikely to endorse taxation policies that would adversely affect themselves, the solution to save the social security system was predictable.

By early 1978 there were signs of a taxpayer revolt as workers—already bothered by inflation and rising costs of living—began to bridle at the prospects of increases in social security taxes. Should Congress and the White House be pressured to once again alter the basis of social security funding, one can only hope it will be in a less openly class-biased direction.

THE CONSEQUENCES OF POWER CONCENTRATION

It seems clear that political power in the United States is monopolized by a small number of individuals—whether these individuals comprise a power elite or a governing class. The concentration of power invites abuse. There can be no better contemporary example of extreme abuse of power than the so-called Watergate affair. Discovery of abuse of power can only increase the level of political alienation that exists in the United States. In this section we shall consider the larger meaning of Watergate as well as additional indications of political alienation.

Watergate and the Abuse of Power

Few people have forgotten the revelations during 1973 and 1974 as news reporters and government investigators uncovered the illegal acts we call the Watergate affair.[16] From the discovery by an alert security guard of the burglary of Democratic headquarters prior to the 1972 presidential election to the forced resignation of President Richard M. Nixon in 1974, the Watergate affair demonstrates the logical and almost predictable outcome of the concentration of power.

The term *Watergate* has come to stand for all the illegal, amoral, and unethical practices that the Nixon administration allegedly engaged in beginning in 1968. Among these practices were political espionage and "dirty tricks" against campaign opposition; interference with the judicial process and obstruction of investigations; maintenance of an "enemies list" of persons to be harassed by federal agencies; use of campaign funds to pay off the men caught burglarizing Democratic headquarters to keep them from implicating higher-ups; evasion of tax payments; use of public funds to beautify and enhance the value of personally owned properties; approval of a "secret plan" that would have abrogated guaranteed civil liberties in order to combat change-oriented groups; and favoritism in decision-making in response to large campaign contributions from the ownership class.

Many people believe that the Watergate affair occurred only because men with criminal propensities happened to attain high office. This is only partly the case. Watergate was made possible by a bureaucratic system of government that places power in the hands of a few. Abuses of power similar to those revealed in 1973 and 1974 had been engaged in by prior presidents and in the corporate world for years. Nixon and his aides extended the abuses, and they got caught.

Watergate was possible because the president and other top officials of the executive branch are formally unaccountable to those below them and use the power of their positions to keep their activities secret. Because of their power, they are able to convince lower level government employees to follow their orders. They are able to "sell" government favors to campaign contributors, and they are able to institute many

[16]See Leon Jaworski, *The Right and the Power* (New York: Reader's Digest Press, 1976); and J. Anthony Lukas, *Nightmare: The Underside of the Nixon Years* (New York: The Viking Press, 1976).

measures under the guise of "national security." Watergate-type abuses can only be avoided by capturing popular control over government, so that important decisions are made by more than one or a few top officials and so that illegal activities are too difficult and costly to execute. If persons who command both economic and governmental institutions remain inaccessible and unaccountable to any but their cohorts, if they make decisions *for* the people rather than carry out decisions made *by* the people, and if they are freely able to define the national interest in terms of dominant class and institutional interests, more Watergates (in one form or another) should be anticipated. This is particularly true insofar as the penalties for such white-collar crimes remain relatively light in contrast to the rewards possible through the successful exercise of concentrated power.

Watergate and similar usurpations of the public trust—both within and outside of government—are *systemic* phenomena that cannot be fully explained by reference to the character traits of the individuals involved. The system is set up so as to allow power that can be abused. While we may gain some sense of relief when a few "rotten apples" are uncovered, the continued concentration of political and economic power is a problem larger than those few who are caught abusing it.

Political Alienation

As we have seen, many Americans are asking whether our political system is truly democratic and whose interests political representatives are serving. Feeling that their voices are not being heard, a significant proportion of citizens have become alienated and have withdrawn from participation in national politics.

Unofficially, the United States maintains a two-party system. The Democratic and Republican parties dominate elections for national office.

Table 2.3.   Participation in Elections for President and U.S. Representatives, 1960–76

Year	Estimated Resident Population of Voting Age	Vote Cast			
		For president	Percent of voting age population	For U.S. Representatives	Percent of voting age population
1960	109,674	68,838	62.8%	64,133	58.5%
1962	112,958	x	x	51,261	46.3
1964	114,085	70,645	61.8	65,886	58.1
1966	116,638	x	x	52,900	45.4
1968	120,285	73,212	60.9	66,109	55.2
1970	124,498	x	x	54,173	43.5
1972	140,068	77,719	55.4	71,188	50.9
1974	144,928	x	x	52,397	36.2
1976	150,000	80,000	53.3	NA	NA

Source: *Statistical Abstract of the United States, 1975* (Washington, D.C.: U.S. Bureau of the Census, 1975), p. 450. Data for 1976 reported in *New York Times,* November 4, 1976. x: not applicable; NA: not available.

The political dissatisfaction and alienation of Americans is dramatically illustrated by the declining participation of eligible voters in elections. Anywhere from half to two thirds of voters have stayed away from the polls on election days in recent years. Many political observers feel that low voter turnout is caused by feelings of powerlessness on the part of citizens.

In the past three or four decades, an ever increasing percentage of the voting population has been unwilling to identify with either major party. According to Gallup poll data, a substantial bloc of people are choosing to call themselves "independents."[17] The growth of this bloc reflects numerous factors, among which is the substantial dissatisfaction that has developed over the conduct of national politics.

Even more serious a reflection of political alienation is the apathy of eligible voters. Many people do not register to vote. And, as Table 2.3 indicates, participation of eligible voters in elections has been declining for a long time. In 1976 barely more than half of all eligible voters participated in the choice of the new president. An even greater level of indifference is discernible with regard to the election of persons to the U.S. Congress. Low voter turnout could simply be due to satisfaction (or dissatisfaction) with all competing candidates. But given the other indices of political alienation we have mentioned, it seems more likely that declining turnouts represent cynicism and disgust over the workings of the political system in general.

The term *democracy* refers to a political system through which it is

[17]Data on political party identification appear periodically in *Gallup Opinion Index.*

possible—and in which members of society want—to have a say in those decisions that affect them. In such a system, the people themselves play an informed and active role in determining the nature and course of their society. Power rests in the hands of the people, and government expresses their will. It seems clear that the American political system is not meeting these criteria.

The concentration of power in the hands of a few—be it a power elite or a governing class—means that many of the crucial issues of our times are decided for us, if they are even raised at all. Shall we have an equitable system of taxation, one that minimizes economic inequalities? Shall we set up mechanisms to redistribute wealth and income in the interests of eliminating poverty? Shall we reorganize this society's productive apparatus so as to eliminate unemployment and fully utilize our productive capabilities? Are there particular elements of business and industry that should be taken out of private hands and placed under public ownership and control? Shall we limit defense expenditures in favor of improving the quality of life? Would the resources devoted to space exploration be better used for more earthly needs? Shall we require corporations to bear the full costs of ending their pollution and environmental destruction, instead of passing the costs on to the consumer and taxpayer?

In a democratic society these issues would be debated and decided by the people. In the United States, they are decided by a minority of men, many of whom have more than a passing interest in protecting the status quo. With power concentrated in the hands of a few, the majority of society's members cannot help but feel powerless and alienated from their "rulers."

TOWARD THE DEMOCRATIC IDEAL

If the concentration of political and economic power is to be arrested and reversed, those persons who are presently disenchanted must inject themselves into the political arena and make their concerns felt. Staying silent is equivalent to sanctioning the status quo. For some reason, Americans do not seem to be taking advantage of the lessons of the 1960s, when the collective political activities of people committed to change had a significant impact on national policies.

In the early 1960s, centuries of American tradition were overturned by the efforts of an active and aggressive grass-roots civil rights movement. Segments of the black and white populations entered into the political arena, stirring up a major shift in race relations in this country. Governmental elites, as indifferent to racism as their predecessors, were pressured into providing federal legislation to protect and enhance opportunities for racial minorities. If those who dared to launch and join that civil rights movement had written off change as hopeless, governmental indifference would have continued.

By the late 1960s, a series of presidential decisions, made secretly and without reference to the public, had embroiled the United States in a war in Southeast Asia. As American involvement escalated and as the costs of the war became clear, tens of millions of people voiced their outrage in the national political arena. Governmental elites were forced to alter their stance on the war and withdraw from involvement in it, in response to the popular pressures placed upon them. If those who attacked America's presence in Southeast Asia had not done so, the wartime carnage might still be going on.

Today, too many of us assume that our participation in political activity will make no difference. In fact, as the above examples indicate, the fabric of national politics is much more delicate and vulnerable to change from below than we often choose to recognize. The disenchanted must cease being spectators to decisions of national consequence and must instead help shape them.

College students are in an excellent position to analyze and reflect on major political issues. Indeed, students played key roles in the initiation and conduct of the civil rights and antiwar movements of the 1960s. By joining or creating organizations that are outspokenly dedicated to progressive societal change, students can help generate the public discussion necessary for such change to be realized. Such discussion and the pressures for change to which it is likely to give rise are unlikely to be generated from other than grass-roots directions. Certainly those whose political and economic power depends on maintaining the status quo are unlikely to stimulate discussion of change.

Along with grass-roots movements for change must come major alterations in the procedures of government. In the aftermath of Watergate, Congress passed campaign financing laws to limit direct private contributions to presidential candidates and to collect public funds for use in campaigns. These laws should be progressively strengthened, and loopholes eliminated. (For example, wealthy candidates can still use their own personal funds to outspend less affluent ones in political campaigns; and Congressional campaigns are not subject to the new financing laws.) All candidates for national political office and all elected and appointed officials and their staffs should be required by law to make regular full disclosure of their economic interests. Members of Congress, for example, should not be permitted to sit on committees or vote for bills that are directly connected to their economic holdings. The tie between self-interest and political behavior must be completely broken if the concerns of the American public are to be addressed effectively.

It is also important to facilitate greater public involvement in national politics. The federal government should be working to encourage all citizens to register to vote. It should be subsidizing regular television coverage of significant congressional debates and committee hearings.

During the late 1960s and early 1970s, increasing numbers of Americans participated in demonstrations and voiced their outrage over the war in Vietnam. Their sustained pressure on the government ultimately led to the withdrawal of American troops from South Vietnam in 1975. With similar organization and commitment, Americans could overcome their powerlessness and help shape national policy on the issues that concern us today.

Election procedures should be simplified so that anyone can run for public office without going through a great deal of red tape. Presidential primaries and elections should be conducted on a national basis, rather than state by state. All such changes would bring more people into politics and increase the probability that democracy will become more than a symbolic ideal in this society.

SUMMARY

There are three major perspectives on the workings of America's political system. The conventional view is that America is democratic and pluralistic and that no one group or class dominates politics at the national level. Yet many Americans feel dominated and see themselves as powerless to affect decisions that affect them.

Two alternative perspectives suggest that political power has become concentrated in the hands of a few. The power elite perspective emphasizes the important role played by those in top positions in the corporate world, the military, and the executive branch of government. The governing class perspective emphasizes the power-wielding capabilities of the rich as they participate in or otherwise influence government decisions. While differing in their emphases, these two perspectives seem closer to the reality experienced by many Americans than does the pluralist view.

To the degree to which political power is concentrated in the hands of a few, abuses of power can be expected. With such concentration and abuses comes political alienation. Americans must overcome this sense of alienation and challenge concentrated power, seeking changes and reforms that will bring the political system closer to the democratic ideal.

DISCUSSION QUESTIONS

1. How were you taught to view the workings of the American political system in elementary school? In high school? How much of what you were taught seems to fit with reality?
2. How important is it for people to vote in elections? Do you feel that voting or not voting makes a difference? In what way?
3. How do your family and friends view politics and politicians at the national level? To what degree and in what ways do you share their views?
4. While the 1960s and early 1970s were years of widespread protest, especially by college students, very little of this kind of activity is going on now. Why do you think this is the case?
5. Are you optimistic or pessimistic about whether America's political system can be moved closer to the democratic ideal? On what do you base your optimism or pessimism?

3 Schooling and Unequal Educational Opportunity

Each individual should have ready and continuing access to the education and training needed to develop his or her interests and capabilities to the fullest extent.

I n the previous two chapters, we examined two macro problems that harm millions of Americans—economic inequality and the concentration of power in the United States. As we suggested, part of the reason these problems continue to plague our nation may be found in our educational system.

In this chapter, we will examine American ideals and beliefs about the educational system and evaluate their accuracy. We will consider the impact of schools on the socialization of children and on inequality in America. The chapter concludes with proposals for altering the educational system.

THE "GREAT SCHOOL LEGEND"

Historians of American education generally provide a positive view of the contributions of the educational system. They claim that education has strengthened the American political system, that it has helped energize our economy, and that it has contributed to lessening class inequalities. [1] In this section, we examine these claims and look at contrary views that suggest that the contributions of the American educational system have not been totally positive.

Beliefs About American Education

When America's system of mass public education was established in the 1800s, the men and women who founded the various local school systems presumably wanted, among other things, to improve the readiness of people to participate in the political system. They felt—as do many today—that only with an educated citizenry could the United States function as a democracy. Since that time, the schools have sought to instill common political values in millions of members of our otherwise diverse population. Among these values has been respect for existing political institutions and procedures. American education, in the view of many historians, has contributed to political stability and has helped foster democratic ideals.

Historians have also pointed to the contribution made by our system of education to the economic development of the United States. Mass public education was introduced into America during a period of rapid industrialization. At this time, literacy and the creation and transmittal of new knowledge became more and more important to continued economic growth. Business and industry had to have people who could fill positions

[1]See, for example, Bernard Bailyn, *Education and the Forming of American Society* (New York: Vintage Books, 1960); and Lawrence A. Cremin, *The Genius of American Education* (New York: Vintage Books, 1965).

in the increasingly complex world of work. The schools responded by providing literacy and skills training, thus increasing our technological know-how and aiding the efficiency and productivity of America's economic system.

Finally, historians have suggested that mass public education has enhanced the ability of citizens to protect or better their socioeconomic positions. In the public schools, all children compete on the basis of individual merit, rather than on family position. This has made it possible for the poor to change their circumstances. We have, historians point out, moved a long way from the time when education—particularly higher education—was readily accessible only to the children of the affluent. Today, almost all youngsters attend school (see Figure 3.1).

There is certainly some truth to such historical generalizations. Our system of education has been handed vast responsibilities and has carried many of them out—often with very meager resources. But education has not only acted as a force for change and improvement. It has functioned as a conservative force as well. The positive picture of the contributions of education has recently been challenged by so-called revisionist historians.

Figure 3.1.   Participation in Public Schools

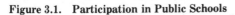

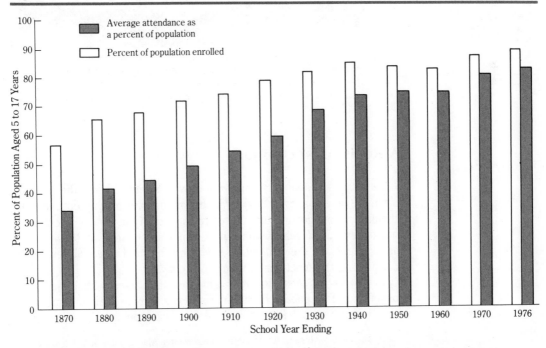

Source: U.S. Office of Education, National Center for Educational Statistics, *The Condition of Education, 1977* (Washington, D.C.: U.S. Government Printing Office, 1977), p. 27.

One of the major goals of mass public education in the nineteenth century was to Americanize immigrants—to teach them to fit into the existing political and social order. This goal was met not only by developing curricula for the children of immigrants but also through a system of adult education in which citizenship was taught along with lessons on the English language.

A Revisionist Critique

In recent years, some scholars have grown dissatisfied with the historical claims reviewed above. Revisionist historians have attempted to balance the picture, suggesting that there are aspects of the history of education not deserving of celebration.[2] It is important to look at these critical assessments of the history of education in the United States before considering the functions of education today.

In *The Great School Legend,* Colin Greer has taken a fresh look at the belief that mass public education was developed in order to democratize the United States.[3] According to Greer, mass public education was an

[2]The need for historical revisionism is stressed in Marvin Lazerson, "Revisionism and American Educational History," *Harvard Educational Review,* 43 (May 1973): 269–83.

[3]Colin Greer, *The Great School Legend* (New York: Basic Books, Inc., 1972).

important part of the Americanization movement of the nineteenth century. This movement was aimed at indoctrinating the millions of people who immigrated to the United States, so that they would "fit into" the American political order. Wealthy and politically influential people encouraged the development of local school systems and adult education programs during the nineteenth century in the hope that schooling would head off political dissension and conflict. They felt that if poor and working-class immigrants could be brought to accept the elite-dominated political system and to work within it, class and ethnic grievances could be channeled into manageable directions. Citing historical documents and statements by nineteenth-century elites, Greer suggests that the mission of education "was to maintain and transmit the values considered necessary to prevent political, social, or economic upheaval."[4] In other words, instead of enhancing the democratic process, education was expected to function as a mechanism of social control.

Revisionist historians have also found documentary evidence suggesting that the role of education in industrialization was not exactly what earlier historians claimed. Nineteenth-century industrialization caused changes in the nature of work. In particular, more and more workers were becoming employees of enterprises owned by others. A way had to be found to smooth the transition into this new world of work. According to Samuel Bowles: "An ideal preparation for factory work was found in the social relations of the school, specifically in its emphasis on discipline, punctuality, acceptance of authority outside the family and individual accountability for one's work."[5] By organizing mass public education to resemble the bureaucratic economic organizations of nineteenth-century America, schooling was intended to foster a disciplined labor force—one that would not question managerial privileges and authority.

The claim that American education has made a substantial impact on class inequalities has also been questioned. In a reexamination of the development of mass public education in the nineteenth century, historian Michael Katz has shown that American public education has always been class-biased.[6] Though it was introduced with the intention of opening up opportunities for all, education has both reflected and helped perpetuate class inequalities over time:

> It is the children of the well-to-do, not the children of the poor, who have benefited most from public education. That is especially true of the higher levels of schooling, one important function of which has been to secure differential advantage to the children of the affluent.[7]

[4]Ibid., p. 74.

[5]Samuel Bowles, "Getting Nowhere: Programmed Class Stagnation," *Society,* 9 (June 1972): 43. See also Samuel Bowles and Herbert Gintis, *Schooling in Capitalist America* (New York: Basic Books, Inc., 1976).

[6]Michael Katz, *Class, Bureaucracy, and Schools* (New York: Praeger Publishers, Inc., 1971). See also Michael Katz, *The Irony of Early School Reform* (Cambridge, Mass.: Harvard University Press, 1968).

[7]Katz, *Class, Bureaucracy, and Schools,* pp. 109-10.

Furthermore, Katz observed that public schooling has historically functioned to secure such advantage primarily for children from affluent *white* families. Generations of black Americans, for example, were subjected to substandard education in racially segregated schools—a situation that has only been addressed in the last two decades.

Thus, the efforts to balance educational historians' celebration of American schooling have led to some critical findings. If the American system of mass public education performed in the way the revisionist historians claim, what about education today? As we will see, there is evidence to suggest that not too much has really changed. Education still seems organized to foster political stability, to nurture a literate and compliant labor force, and to conserve existing economic inequality.

SCHOOLING AS AN AGENT OF SOCIALIZATION

Though laws pertaining to school attendance vary from state to state, most children are required by law to attend until the age of fifteen or sixteen. State governments dictate the number of hours and days per year that children must spend in school; indeed, state financial aid to local schools is often based on average levels of attendance. A local school system may lose money if absenteeism and truancy are high. Truancy is a crime, and parents may not withhold children from school attendance without providing a state-approved substitute.

Because of compulsory attendance, the majority of American children are exposed to schooling for many hours every year, whether they prefer to attend school or not. What are children expected to learn during these many hours? Sociologists of education generally agree that two distinct kinds of lessons are presented in the classroom.[8] First, there are the formal lessons—reading, arithmetic, history, and so forth. Second, certain standardized ways of thinking and behaving are also being encouraged. The second kind of lesson is often called the *hidden curriculum,* due to its subtle nature.

School systems differ from locale to locale, and community control over public schools ensures diversity across the nation.[9] Still, most school systems are organized bureaucratically. Authority over children is vested in the hands of administrators and teachers, who are in turn responsible to an elected board of education. Students are urged to accommodate themselves to a system of administrative rules and regula-

[8]See Christopher J. Hurn, *The Limits and Possibilities of Schooling* (Boston: Allyn & Bacon, Inc., 1978), Chapter 7.

[9]Efforts by the federal government to shape this diversity toward a national curriculum are described in Joel Spring, *The Sorting Machine* (New York: David McKay Co., Inc., 1976).

tions, and school authorities judge and reward students on the basis of how they respond to directions and commands. Such bureaucratic arrangements are said to be necessary in order to process large numbers of children each school day in a relatively impersonal, orderly, and efficient manner. The same rationale for bureaucratic organization is often applied to prisons and mental hospitals.

Several years ago, the Carnegie Corporation of New York sponsored an inquiry into the state of public education across the country. Charles E. Silberman, a well-known journalist and scholar, spent three years crisscrossing the country before presenting his findings in *Crisis in the Classroom*. His observations of school systems in action led Silberman to the conclusion that *docility* is being emphasized. Outbursts of spontaneity, originality, and nonconformity are commonly discouraged, while passivity and adherence to routine are stressed.[10]

Silberman and others have argued that compulsory participation in bureaucratic school settings fosters the formation of certain personality traits. Mass public education, it is said, promotes attitudes and habits of behavior that fit well with highly structured settings, those calling for rationality and predictability. While there has not been definitive research supporting such broad generalizations, several in-depth case studies of schooling do provide some evidence that this is the case.

The "Organization Child"

Sociologist Rosabeth Moss Kanter spent seven months studying a typical suburban nursery school located in the Midwest.[11] According to Kanter, the teachers in this school believed that children who followed orders and exerted self-control were mentally healthy children. As a result, the teachers constantly urged the children to adapt to the planned classroom routine, and they set up a round of activities each day conducive to promoting, in Kanter's terms, the *organization child*—the child who is most comfortable when those in authority provide supervision, guidance, and roles to be fulfilled. In requiring children to adapt to such experiences, Kanter concludes, the schools both reflect and support the trend toward bureaucratization of life in American society.

Similar conclusions have also been reached by Harry L. Gracey, a sociologist who studied classrooms in an eastern elementary school.[12]

[10]Charles E. Silberman, *Crisis in the Classroom* (New York: Vintage Books, 1970), pp. 113–57.

[11]Rosabeth Moss Kanter, "The Organization Child: Experience Management in a Nursery School," *Sociology of Education*, 45 (Spring 1972): 186–211.

[12]Harry L. Gracey, "Learning the Student Role: Kindergarten as Academic Boot Camp," in *Readings on Introductory Sociology*, 2nd ed., Dennis H. Wrong and Harry L. Gracey, eds. (New York: Macmillan, Inc., 1972), pp. 243–54. Gracey examines elementary education in *Curriculum and Craftsmanship* (Chicago: University of Chicago Press, 1972).

One part of Gracey's research focused on kindergarten, which he came to call *academic boot camp*. Kindergarten works to teach the student role to children not previously conditioned to organized schooling. The content of the student role is "the repertoire of behavior and attitudes regarded by educators as appropriate to children in school."[13] Such behaviors include willingness to conform to teacher demands and to perform the "work" at hand without resistance. Educators believe that children who have successfully learned the student role in kindergarten will function smoothly in the later grades.

Gracey found that school administrators best liked the teachers who most quickly and effectively produced order and routine. Such teachers elicited desired responses from the children with no more than a look, a few words, or a simple command signal. Gracey believed that these teachers were grooming the children to respond without question to officialdom and to follow orders without dissent. Even though many of the requests did not seem to make much sense to them, most of the children obeyed. Those who broke away from routines or resisted classroom authority were likely to be treated as "bad children" and to be sent to the school psychologist for guidance on how to adapt.

Both Gracey and Kanter concluded that the experience of organized schooling fosters certain personality traits. Since, if Silberman is correct, children are urged to conform for hours, days, and years on end, the outcome may be the *organization adult*—the team-oriented person who fits well into nonschool bureaucracies, such as corporations, the military, and the government. As Silberman puts it, "the teacher, although he may disclaim the title, is the students' first 'Boss.'"[14]

Of course, organized schooling is only one of the factors influencing personality traits and habits of behavior. Students—especially as they move into the advanced grades—often find enough strength in peer support to resist and sabotage the routines set up for them. In his classic study, *The Adolescent Society,* James Coleman found that the peer values of many young adults ran counter to those promoted by high-school teachers and administrators.[15] In his view, the high schools often failed to motivate students into conformity with academic routine because educators did not understand how to counter peer influence.

In recent years, the matter of school discipline—enforcing school routine—has become a major issue in many city and suburban school systems. Violence and vandalism have plagued schools across the country. For example, a recent government report estimates that fifty-two hundred high-school teachers will be physically attacked in any given month of 1978, while some six thousand will be robbed. In more general

[13]Gracey, "Learning the Student Role," p. 245.
[14]Silberman, *Crisis in the Classroom,* p. 141.
[15]James Coleman, *The Adolescent Society* (New York: The Free Press, 1961). See also Arthur Stinchcombe, *Rebellion in a High School* (Chicago: Quadrangle Books, 1964).

The failure of many urban and suburban school systems to enforce school routine is exemplified by increasing violence and vandalism. It has been estimated that moderate to severe problems of vandalism, theft, and violence currently occur in a quarter of all American schools. Vandalism alone costs school systems nearly $600 million a year. Such figures indicate that many American schools are not attaining their goal of producing "good children."

terms, educators talk about a loss of respect for authority.[16] Parents and educators seem to feel that renewed efforts at discipline are needed in the schools.[17]

Hence, the degree to which bureaucratically organized mass public education actually succeeds in producing adult prototypes of the organization child is open to question. Nonetheless, it seems that organized schooling today, as in the nineteenth century, is oriented toward doing so. "Good children" are presumably the sought-after result.

Learning to Participate in the Economy

Besides attempting to expose students to bureaucratic values, schools are said to promote attitudes and habits of behavior that are unique to a

[16]"The ABCs of School Violence," *Time*, January 23, 1978, pp. 73–4. See U.S. Office of Education, National Institute of Education, *Violent Schools—Safe Schools* (Washington, D.C.: U.S. Government Printing Office, 1977).

[17]Discipline is seen as the main school problem in public opinion polls. See U.S. Office of Education, National Center for Educational Statistics, *The Condition of Education, 1977* (Washington, D.C.: U.S. Government Printing Office, 1977), p. 20.

capitalist society. Jules Henry, a social anthropologist, conducted extensive field research on this topic over a period of years.[18] He compiled data for a case study by careful observation of a midwestern elementary school. On the basis of his research, Henry concluded that "school is an institution for drilling children in cultural orientations."[19]

Henry pointed out that public schools are faced with two incompatible tasks. On the one hand, they are expected to transmit dominant cultural values and beliefs; while on the other hand, they are charged with liberating the minds of young people. Typically, according to Henry, they resolve this dilemma in favor of the first of the two tasks, keeping creativity—which may involve questioning and rejecting accepted ways of thinking about and doing things—under strict control. Henry's research indicated that the schools direct creative talent into certain channels, such as science and mathematics. Creative children generally are not encouraged to expend their energies on social studies, since this might require analysis and criticism of prevailing social and economic arrangements and conventional political and religious beliefs. Henry suggested that talent is pushed toward areas that serve the American technological economy and its ability to conduct sophisticated warfare.

In his research in the elementary grades, Henry was interested in what he came to call *noise*—that is, what children absorb in school aside from the formal subject matter. As part of his research, Henry recorded children's reactions to the games teachers introduced to make learning pleasurable. Whether involved in singing contests or spelling bees, children were constantly being pushed to compete against one another. On occasion, competition revolved around gaining the teacher's attention and winning the rewards only she or he could provide. Children quickly learned that their loss in a competitive arena meant someone else's gain. The winner's elation and excitement were, by definition, at the expense of the loser's depression and unhappiness.

Henry concluded that schooling teaches children (as noise) to be afraid of failure, to dislike themselves when they do fail, and to resent those who succeed at their expense. Children learn to compete at an early age and learn to see competition as natural. This, according to Henry, prepares them to compete with others throughout the course of their school careers and beyond. People learn to be motivated by the fear of failure and to be driven by the specter of personal obsolescence. They find themselves working hard to become a success—even if it means pushing others aside.

Children who fail to play competitive games, for whatever reason, are likely to be viewed as out of step with the expectations of school authorities. In the words of Edgar Friedenberg, a sociologist who has conducted research on the values of high-school students:

[18]Jules Henry, *Culture Against Man* (New York: Vintage Books, 1965), pp. 283–321.
   [19]Ibid., p. 283.

Competition is an extremely important part of the school curriculum from kindergarten through college. High-school students are encouraged, for example, to compete for a place on the basketball team or cheerleading squad—where they can compete against students from other schools for the coveted position of "championship team."

[The school] helps to see to it that the kinds of people who get ahead are those who will support the social system it represents; while those who might, through intent or merely by their being, subvert it are left behind as a salutory moral lesson.[20]

Again, one may question such broad generalizations, based as they are on very limited empirical evidence. But schools are arenas of competition—whether it be for grades, for dates, or for glory on the playing field. The noise is, in each such instance, "do not be a loser." It seems logical that such attitudes and values continue to guide people's behavior in adult life.

[20]Edgar Z. Friedenberg, *Coming of Age in America* (New York: Vintage Books, 1965), p. 49.

The Political Impact of Schooling

In the words of Joel Spring, contemporary mass public education is an "instrument of power." It prepares the young "for the acceptance of control by dominant elites."[21] To experience schooling is to be exposed to political indoctrination, for schools, whether consciously or unconsciously, make a contribution to the political outlook and behavior of the young.

Studies by political scientists have led them to conclude that public education functions to legitimate existing power relationships in America.[22] We should not be surprised that this is the case. Education in every known society—be it formal schooling or learning from one's parents—involves the transmission of the society's culture. That typically means transmission of the dominant cultural values, including the support of prevailing political arrangements. Or, as Ralph Miliband has put it: "Educational institutions at all levels generally fulfill an important conservative role and act, with greater or lesser effectiveness, as legitimating agencies in and for their societies."[23]

Research shows that children develop political consciousness in stages.[24] At a very early age they are encouraged to have positive ideas about their society and government. In the first years of schooling, a simple form of patriotism is fostered. Children are taught to respect the symbols of government and political authority—from the American flag to the uniform of the police officer and the soldier.

As children slowly become capable of grasping more abstract political ideas, they are introduced to such concepts as democracy, voting, and civil liberties in their classes. They are taught about local, state, and national government. The political order is depicted largely in terms of political authority that should be respected and accepted in much the same way as children are expected to treat authority in the schools. Not surprisingly, the political status quo is presented as a given, not as an entity against which people might have valid reasons to struggle.

According to political scientist Jerry Tucker, students are encouraged to celebrate the political status quo as a rather idealized state of affairs. Tucker calls this kind of political education the *tooth fairy approach*.[25] His experience with college students leads him to believe that, by and large,

[21]Joel H. Spring, *Education and the Rise of the Corporate State* (Boston: Beacon Press, 1972), p. 152.

[22]See Harmon Ziegler and Wayne Peak, "The Political Functions of the Educational System," *Sociology of Education*, 43 (Spring 1970): 129–42; and Edgar Litt, "Civic Education, Community Norms, and Political Indoctrination," *American Sociological Review*, 28 (February 1963): 69–75.

[23]Ralph Miliband, *The State in Capitalist Society* (New York: Basic Books, Inc., 1969), p. 239.

[24]Michael Rush and Phillip Althoff, *An Introduction to Political Sociology* (Indianapolis: The Bobbs-Merrill Co., Inc., 1972), pp. 30–37.

[25]Jerry Tucker, *The Experience of Politics* (San Francisco: Canfield Press, 1974), p. 133.

public schools teach slogans and rhetoric instead of encouraging substantive inquiry. Children in classrooms are too often sheltered from controversial issues and from the often seamy underside of modern political life.

The tooth fairy approach to political education has also been noted in analyses of commonly used classroom materials:

> Textbooks generally present an unrealistic picture of American society and government. . . . In statements about democracy and the good life, textbooks often do not separate prescriptions from descriptions.[26]

Because they are led to confuse the political system as it should be with the political system as it is, according to Tucker, young people are likely to be bewildered and disillusioned when they run into political facts at variance with what they were taught.

The daily experience of organized schooling also fails to encourage active political participation. We have noted that mass public education is both compulsory and bureaucratically organized. Students are drafted into school; they cannot choose to stay away. Once there, they are subject to rule from above and are likely to be punished if they resist the demands of authority. Much like inmates in a prison or mental institution, people in school are permitted little or no input into policies and decisions that directly affect them. Thus, though children are taught the rhetoric and slogans of democracy, they are simultaneously denied democracy in practice.

Consider, for example, the widespread phenomena of class elections and student governments. These activities are said to have educational merit. Yet, in reality, they are only an artificial exercise in political education, taking place in a vacuum. Elected student officers or representatives are rarely permitted a role in school decision-making. At best, they may be invited to advise administrators and teachers. Student governments, ironically, exist only at the discretion and under the supervision of higher authorities. "Democracy" of this kind is an empty activity that does not prepare people to struggle in their own interests.

A similar situation exists with regard to the typical school newspaper. Freedom of the press, one of the principles underlying any truly democratic order, is usually sharply restricted. Censorship rights over student publications are reserved by school authorities. The right of censorship typically extends even to "creative" student publications, such as literary magazines, in which one might reasonably expect to find expressions of political discontent and heretical views. In the larger society, newspaper publishers and other media groups fight to maintain the concept of freedom of the press, but students are discouraged from doing so.

The Constitution of the United States guarantees freedom of assembly and speech. Public schools are tax-supported institutions—which means

---

[26]Thomas R. Dye and L. Harmon Ziegler, *The Irony of Democracy,* 2nd ed. (Belmont, Calif.: Duxbury Press, 1972), p. 143.

that they are paid for by citizens, including the parents of the students. But the use of school property is subject to approval and control by educational authorities, who alone determine what groups of students may gather and for what purposes. The assembly of large numbers of students, no matter what the official reason, is always carefully monitored (allegedly for safety reasons).

Politics is very much a part of schooling. For one thing, the tooth fairy approach to political education is itself a form of politics. Moreover, politics often directly intrudes into the conduct of public schooling through the actions of elected school boards. The members of such boards hold authority over administrators and teachers and may use this authority to impose their own views about proper educational experiences for children and young people.

In an environment so dominated by authority, it is highly unlikely that citizens' rights and responsibilities and political expertise could be taught. Rather, "Our schools teach passivity instead of responsible activism."[27] To the degree that the schools are successful in teaching this lesson, they are turning children into candidates for political manipulation. Never having been exposed to real-life political struggle, and armed largely with an unrealistic view of the political order, too many people are rendered impotent in the face of concentrated power. This is in large part the cause of the high levels of apathy, cynicism, and alienation from the prevailing political structure we saw in Chapter 2.

Once again, we do not wish to overstate the degree to which schools are successful in their intended or unintended socialization practices. Many factors—from peer influence to nonschool environmental forces—may function to undermine the effectiveness of such practices. Our knowledge of the ultimate impact of schooling on attitudes and behavior remains rather limited. We suggest, however, that the momentum of schooling lies in one direction: the encouragement of social conformity, fear of personal failure, and political passivity.

SCHOOLING AND INEQUALITY

Aside from and related to its role in socializing youngsters, the American educational system also functions as a *gatekeeper*. That is, it operates to guide people from and into one or another level of the class system—or to keep them at the same level. Where one stands in the class structure bears a direct relationship to the type, quality, and amount of formal education one is likely to receive. A person's class position is likely to be reaffirmed by the treatment received in school.

Children from poverty-level areas face a real problem. They are most

[27]Tucker, *The Experience of Politics*, p. 136.

Figure 3.2. Occupations of Young Males, by Educational Attainment

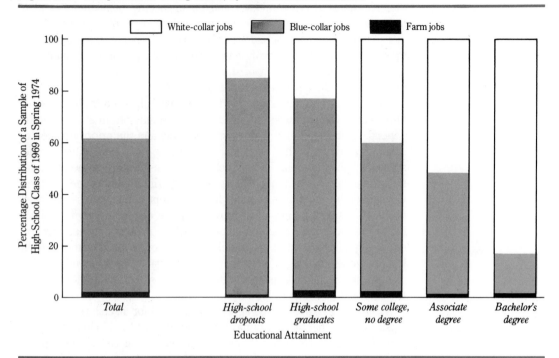

Source: U.S. Office of Education, National Center for Educational Statistics, *The Condition of Education, 1976* (Washington, D.C.: U.S. Government Printing Office, 1976), p. 114.

likely to attend public schools with a limited range of educational resources. Failure and dropout rates tend to be high in schools serving low-income populations. Many poor children, dissatisfied with their school experiences and/or drawn by the need to find employment to help their families, quit when they are old enough. As Figure 3.2 indicates, dropouts are most likely to wind up with low-paying blue-collar jobs. Lacking the credentials that would help their marketability in the world of work (see Chapter 1), children from low-income families are likely to find themselves in the same position in the class structure as their parents. Mass public education, rather than helping low-income children change their class position, often functions to reaffirm their poverty.

By contrast, children who come from more affluent communities tend to have a more positive experience. They are likely to enter public schools with a built-in head start, since their parents are best able to provide the time, energy, and money to prepare their children for school. It is in affluent homes that expensive educational toys, games, and books are likely to be found. Children may gain experience from travel and preschool enrollment in enriched settings. They then enter schools whose structure and climate are in line with their childhood experiences.

Of equal importance is the fact that the public schools are ready for them. Schools serving middle- and upper-income populations tend to have the best teaching resources, the widest array of educational services, and high expectations for performance. Dropout rates are low, and movement into higher education is common. Thus, with the assistance of quality treatment, children of the affluent are channeled into positions that replicate their parents' class standing.

There are a number of outside factors that help keep the gatekeeper functioning. Expenditures on public education differ from state to state, depending on the state's economic well-being and the priority placed on school spending. Within each state, local per pupil expenditures differ among school systems. Though school systems receive some state and federal funds, local school financing is based primarily on property taxes. Consequently, inequities abound. More affluent communities—in which property values are high—can provide a great deal of money for schooling at low tax rates. In communities in which property values are low, even very high tax rates will generate little money for education. In the last few years challenges have been brought against such inequities in the courts, but a child's education often continues to reflect the worth of the land and buildings in his or her community.

Even where expenditures appear to be equal for all children, this may mask the fact that special outlays may be needed to aid children whose families were unable to get them ready for school success. Equal spending does not necessarily mean equal educational outcomes, given the damage that poverty-level living can do to the development of a small child. And children from low-income families are often faced with discriminatory treatment when attending school with more affluent children. Teacher expectations, the channeling of children into special groups for instruction, and the use of questionable testing devices are all part of the gatekeeping process.

In this section we shall go into more detail about the relationship between education and inequality. We shall be examining the mechanisms and processes through which organized schooling ensures that the class position of less affluent children is not appreciably altered.

Tracking and Testing—An Overview

When mass public education was introduced into the United States in the nineteenth century, increasing numbers of children enrolled in tax-supported school systems. Soon the population of the public schools began to be dominated by members of the poor and working classes.[28] This was

---

[28]This section draws heavily on the ideas of Samuel Bowles, "Unequal Education and the Reproduction of the Social Division of Labor," in *The Education Establishment*, Elizabeth L. Useem and Michael Useem, eds. (Englewood Cliffs, N.J.: Prentice-Hall, Inc., 1974), pp. 17–43; and David K. Cohen and Marvin Lazerson, "Education and the Corporate Order," *Socialist Revolution* (March–April 1972): 47–72.

particularly the case when school attendance became compulsory under the law. In general, however, the low-income children left school early to go to work. The higher grades primarily served those from affluent backgrounds.

But by the beginning of the twentieth century, a shift began to take place in the composition of the higher grades. Laws passed to keep children in school longer (and thus reduce the number of children in the labor pool) began to be effective. The occupational structure itself was changing, and new employment opportunities existed for people with literacy skills. More people could afford to let their children remain in school, instead of sending them out to find work at the first legal opportunity. Finally, there was a growing belief in education as a route to self-improvement and movement upward in the class system.

The result was that public high schools were faced with an influx of students from poorer families. Educators tried to find a solution to the problem of accommodating these students. They came up with the idea—deemed innovative at the time—of organizing high-school curricula around a system of *tracks,* each geared to a different occupational or educational end. The tracks were set up to prepare students for what they would most likely be doing upon graduation. Educators assumed that children from economically disadvantaged backgrounds were destined for similar futures. Thus a *vocational track* was created for this group. The affluent were steered into an *academic track* on the assumption that they were likely to go on to college or to enter occupations in which academic skills would be useful.

Placement into one of these tracks was not only based on the socioeconomic standing of students' parents. Earlier performance in school was also taken into account. But since performance in academic subjects tended to reflect the environmental advantages associated with class background, the end result was the same. Placement in a vocational or academic track generally reflected class differences.

At the same time, educators were able to argue that all children were receiving an equal opportunity to be educated—that the schools had simply been organized more efficiently in order to take different abilities into account. In the early twentieth century, the notion of efficiency was of particular relevance, for public school systems were under political pressures to demonstrate that they were using tax funds in a businesslike manner.[29] The track system was offered as proof that this was being done.

But despite the track system, the quest for efficiency, and other innovations, the dropout and failure rates in public schools were extremely high. By any real standard, mass public education was failing. In a recent examination of school surveys from a number of big-city school systems, Colin Greer found that, during the early part of this century, educators

[29]See Raymond Callahan, *Education and the Cult of Efficiency* (Chicago: University of Chicago Press, 1962).

Since the start of this century, students from poor and minority backgrounds have been channeled into vocational education, while their more affluent peers have been placed in college-preparatory courses. This tracking system has helped perpetuate patterns of poverty and discrimination.

were more concerned with how many students were being enrolled than with what happened to them once they were in school. Greer argues that, ironically, the failures of American education were (and still are) signs that it has been succeeding in maintaining the status quo. High dropout rates, for example, have guaranteed a continuous source of labor for low-paying, low-status jobs.[30]

Shortly after World War I, another innovation began to spread through public school systems. Under the impetus of the newly developing science of psychology, special tests were developed that were said to be useful in measuring intelligence and native ability. Educators quickly grasped onto these tests. Here, presumably, were tools with which individual differences could be discovered among students. With testing, children could be guided to those educational programs for which they were most suited—another step toward making schools efficient.

Needless to say, psychological testing fit well with the already accepted concept of tracking. And performance on the tests largely reflected the advantages associated with class background. Students from low-income backgrounds tended to perform poorly on the new tests, enabling school authorities to justify their placement in tracks demanding little in the way of academic work. The reverse tended to hold true for students coming from economically privileged backgrounds. The combined effects of testing and tracking were to further rigidify differential treatment of children on the basis of their class origins.

[30]Greer, *The Great School Legend*, pp. 105–51.

The logical accompaniment to the testing movement, and one that followed closely on its heels, was the growth of the guidance counselor profession. New experts were required to administer and interpret the results of the tests. Counselors trained in educational psychology and statistics were hired to work with students and parents. Not only did students from different class backgrounds continue to be channeled into different tracks; now the guidance counselor could show that they "deserved" the placement.

Today, testing remains a common method of ascertaining the so-called intelligence and ability of students. Children from low-income families, including minority children, by and large perform poorly on IQ tests, for the forms of knowledge and the thought processes required by these tests are most likely to be acquired in white middle-class homes and schools. But the use of IQ tests to measure intelligence is still widespread despite the generally acknowledged biases of the testing instruments.

In most public school systems, too, a track system still exists. Guidance counselors continue to play the role of test administrators and help guide students into the appropriate curriculum. In sum, it is hard not to conclude, along with Colin Greer, that:

> The fact of the matter is that American public schools in general, and urban public schools in particular, are a highly successful enterprise. Basic to that success is the high degree of academic failure among students. . . . The schools do the job today they have always done. They select out individuals for opportunities according to a hierarchical schema which runs parallel to existing social class patterns.[31]

If the public schools attempted to ensure academic success for every child, the supply of school- and self-defined losers would rapidly dwindle. In Greer's view, this would mean trouble, since there would be too many academically successful people from low-income backgrounds who would probably be very restive if forced to perform America's least desirable jobs.

An Elementary-School Case Study

A case study that focused on a group of children in an urban elementary school dramatically illustrates the impact of tracking and testing.[32] The study was conducted by Ray C. Rist, a student of the late Jules Henry, whose work on noise we discussed earlier. Rist followed the progress of

[31]Ibid., p. 152.
[32]Ray C. Rist, "Student Social Class and Teacher Expectations," *Harvard Educational Review*, 40 (August 1970): 411–51. See also Rist, *The Urban School: A Factory for Failure* (Cambridge, Mass.: The M.I.T. Press, 1973), and "On Understanding the Processes of Schooling," in *Power and Ideology in Education*, Jerome Karabel and A. H. Halsey, eds. (New York: Oxford University Press, Inc., 1977), pp. 292–305.

a group of black children who were attending public school in St. Louis, Missouri.

In the school Rist studied, teachers typically knew something about each child before the child began kindergarten. For example, they knew which children came from homes receiving welfare aid; they had met the mothers during preenrollment interviews; and they had heard about the experiences of other teachers with the children's brothers and sisters. None of this information, Rist notes, necessarily had anything to do with the talent or ability of the new kindergartners. But it did help create a certain set of expectations in the teacher's mind before the first day of class.

Rist observed that by the eighth day of kindergarten, the teacher in the class he was following had made permanent seating arrangements for each child. At the table closest to her (Table 1) were the well-dressed children who were not from welfare families, who seemed comfortable with classroom routine, and who spoke "school language" at all times (in other words, they spoke like the teacher). At the two remaining tables, farther away from the teacher's desk, sat children dressed in old, worn clothing. The Table 2 and Table 3 children were from welfare homes, seemed ill-at-ease in their surroundings, and rarely spoke. When they did speak, they often used a street dialect rather than "standard English."

The children at Table 1 were not only seated closest to the teacher; they also received most of her verbal and physical attention. Moreover, they were given special privileges and responsibilities by the teacher. Table 1 children were chosen to recite the Pledge of Allegiance, to read the weather calendar, to pass out class materials, and to take messages to the office.

Noting these seating arrangements and the positive treatment being accorded Table 1 children, Rist asked the teacher what was going on. The teacher told him that "the first table consisted of her 'fast learners' while those at the last two tables 'had no idea what was going on in the classroom.'"[33] Thus, by the eighth day of school, a process of labeling was already underway. On the basis of class bias, the teacher had effectively written off two tables of kindergartners as being uneducable.

Over time, Rist saw indications that the children at Table 1 were adopting the attitudes of their teacher. The so-called fast learners began to ridicule and belittle the Table 2 and Table 3 children. Within a few weeks, the low-income children had begun to sense that both the teacher and their more affluent peers were against them. In response, some of them became withdrawn, and others engaged in verbal and physical outbursts. This behavior confirmed the teacher's view that these children were different, troublesome, and not interested in learning. In reality, as Rist observed, the teacher herself had set the situation in motion, and the children's behavior was simply an outcome of her own.

[33]Rist, "Student Social Class and Teacher Expectations," p. 422.

Public Problem, Private Pain
A CHILD IN THE LOWEST TRACK

Social psychologist Thomas J. Cottle has written extensively on children and youth. In pursuing research on how and why many poor children are excluded from receiving a quality education, Cottle recorded the following statement by a student attending elementary school. This youngster has just learned that he is being placed in the lowest academic track and that school officials consider his placement justified by his scores on so-called intelligence and capability tests. The child's words reveal his hurt and anger over this attack on his self-worth. According to Cottle, testing and placement in the lowest track contribute to poor performance, absenteeism, and high suspension and dropout rates among low-income children.

They told me in school that I'm stupid. I didn't know what they were talking about but they just kept saying it. Told me there was no use talking back to them because they had it in their tests, everything they wanted to know about me. I said I should be in the other group, because those kids were learning more and besides, they were getting all the best teachers in their classes. I didn't want them to put me in the class which they put me in. But they said it was what they *wanted* to do, it was what they *had* to do 'cause they don't decide what classes to put the student in, the tests decide that for them. People don't decide.

I was thinking that maybe I should take a rest from school because if they're putting me in that worst class then I don't see any reason why I should be there at all. When you're in that class they don't even care if you go to school or not. All they care about is that their records are right. They got me tested the way I'm supposed to, 'cause you can't refuse it, you got to be tested if they say so. So now I'm tested. So now they know. They think I'm stupid. If they don't think so then all they have to do is go into that office and look inside my folder and then they can see. "We know you're a real smart guy," they'd say, "but the test knows better. We test everybody, and you're dumber than everybody except for all the nobodies we're putting in the same class with you."

I think you should be able to tell them whether you want to take those tests. Maybe if I said no way man, no way I'm going to answer any of your questions except the ones my teacher asks, maybe I could go and be with those other kids in the better class. I saw them testing one girl yesterday. They asked her politely, and she went with them. I followed them. You know why they were testing her? Because she talked too smart to be in the same class with the rest of us. She did talk smart too. I was thinking she was real smart, smarter than me.

They tested her 'cause they *wanted* to get her out of that class. That's why they did it. They wanted her to get out of there with us. But they don't want that with me. They don't want to teach me nothing at that school. They don't want me to get smarter 'cause if I get too smart they'll have to put me in a higher group like they did with that girl. They ain't helping me to read better or faster. All they do is keep testing me to see if I'm doing things any better. But how can anyone get smarter if nobody's teaching 'em nothing. How'm I suppose to read faster and then remember everything I'm reading too if everybody's running around testing everybody. Teachers are supposed to teach, not test! If they spent their time teaching they wouldn't have to test us all the time. Even if they don't teach us they could spend more time with us so if somebody asked them is that kid smart, they'd know. They'd know even without testing.

Thomas J. Cottle, *Barred from School: 2 Million Children!* (Washington, D.C.: New Republic Books, 1976), pp. 116–17.

The process Rist observed has often been called a *self-fulfilling prophecy*. Put simply, if one acts as if a situation is real, the situation may indeed become real. In this case, the teacher acted as if the low-income children could not learn, and as a consequence they did not learn. By her actions, the teacher's prophecy that the children were uneducable was fulfilled.

Most of the kindergarten children went on to the first grade. The kindergarten teacher had already given a dossier on each child to the first-grade teacher, who used the dossiers to make permanent seating arrangements. Not surprisingly, the seating plan closely resembled that of the kindergarten classroom. In the first grade, Table 1 children made rapid progress in reading—the kindergarten teacher had prepared them well. The first-grade teacher spent a good deal of time trying to teach the Tables 2 and 3 children the basics they should have learned earlier. Differential teacher expectations had become translated into differential academic performance, through no fault of the low-income children.

Almost all the children moved on to the second grade a year later. There, according to Rist, students were assigned seats on the basis of their scores on reading tests. The second-grade teacher thus had a "scientific" basis on which to predict each child's performance in the classroom. Tables 1, 2, and 3 were almost totally reproduced in the second grade, but with a new element added. The best readers were the Tigers, the next best were the Cardinals, and the slowest readers were the Clowns. A number of the Clowns were repeating second grade.

The kinds of distinctions made among these children, the teachers' expectations for them, and their treatment by the teachers all fed into a system of tracking and testing. Academic retardation or failure, for the poorer children, quickly became cumulative. It seems reasonable to assume that when these children reach high school they will be persuaded that they deserve to enter a nonacademic track—assuming they have retained interest in education at all. As Rist concluded:

> The public school system, I believe, is justifiably responsible for contributing to the present structure of society. . . .The picture that emerges from this study is that the school shares in the complicity of maintaining the organizational perpetuation of poverty and unequal opportunity.[34]

The High-School Level

Tracking in other public elementary schools may be more subtle and informal than in the school Rist studied. But by the time a student gets to high school, the process typically becomes quite blatant and rigidified. Walter E. Schafer and his colleagues studied two typical high schools, located in the Midwest, in an effort to document the impact of tracking in

[34]Ibid., p. 447.

the higher grades.[35] One school was located in a middle-class, academic community, the other in a working-class, industrial area. Both high schools divided their programs into "college-prep" and "general" tracks. Students were assigned to one of the tracks upon entering the ninth grade.

The researchers had difficulty determining exactly *why* a student was assigned to a particular track, though they felt the guidance counselors played a key role. It became clear that: "Socioeconomic and racial background had an effect on which track a student took, quite apart from either his achievement in junior high or his ability as measured by I.Q. scores."[36] Students attending the high school located in the middle-class community and those from white-collar families in the working-class high school tended to enter the college-prep track. Students from blue-collar families, particularly if they were black, most often entered the general track. For the most part, the decision was permanent; students generally stayed in the same track through all four years of high school.

Track position was correlated with students' success in school. College-prep students had the highest grade average by senior year, and grade differences between this group and the general track students increased between grades nine and twelve. General track students were likely to graduate toward the bottom of their class. The dropout rate was 36 percent for general track students, but only 4 percent for those in college prep. Finally, records indicated higher rates of delinquency and violation of school rules for youngsters in the general track than for college-prep students.

The problem facing the researchers was one of explaining these differences. Scores on the school achievement and IQ tests the students took in elementary school did not seem to be related to high-school performance. The researchers finally reached a conclusion that seems to confirm Rist's findings—that differential academic performance and dropout rates were actually *promoted* by track assignment. That is, being placed in the general track or the college-prep track to some extent caused student behavior.

Probing further, Schafer and his colleagues found that students felt stigmatized by not being assigned to college prep. Their placement in the general track negatively affected their self-esteem and eroded their belief in their own abilities. As a result, they did not work hard in school. Furthermore, the teachers and administrators expected little of general track students, and the students tended to respond accordingly. The self-fulfilling prophecy, mentioned earlier, was at work. The teachers felt justified in awarding low grades for the work performed by general track students, no matter how well the work was done. This practice contributed to low student motivation and a lack of commitment to school atten-

[35]Walter E. Schafer et al., "Programmed for Social Class," *Trans-action,* 7 (October 1970): 39–46.
[36]Ibid., p. 40.

dance—factors reflected in high dropout rates. General track students created a peer-group society in opposition to authority, leading to rule violation and delinquent acts in the community. Such phenomena were found in both high schools, despite the fact that they were located in quite different kinds of communities.

Once again, the outcome of differential treatment seems clear. Students from more affluent backgrounds, having been given preferential treatment in high school, will typically enter college. They will most likely get well-paying jobs and occupy a class position much like that of their parents. The students from low-income backgrounds, many of whom are black, have had their sense of self-worth attacked. They have been told by their track placement, by their treatment by teachers, and by the evaluation of their performance that they are not destined for success. It is unlikely that they will attend college. In such ways, the American system of education produces self-defined losers who, whatever their real talents and abilities, are likely to relive the experiences of their low-income families.

Higher Education

As we have seen, the American system of education does a good deal of sifting and sorting. Education also functions as a gatekeeper on the college and university levels. The question of who goes on to higher education is easily answered. If you have money, you go. Ability counts less than dollars.

Since the end of World War II, an increasing percentage of high-school graduates have gone on for further years of schooling. An important reason for this is that employers have progressively escalated their requirements for entry-level positions.[37] As Figure 3.3 indicates, the educational attainment of the labor force has moved steadily upward. Another reason is the shortage of jobs. Many young persons have found enrolling in higher education—when they can afford it—preferable to being unemployed. Furthermore, there is more opportunity for students to continue their education, for the number and size of colleges and universities have (until quite recently) been undergoing substantial growth. Most noteworthy has been the creation of a massive network of two-year colleges. Today, over half of all high-school graduates go on to some form of higher education each year, mostly to publicly supported institutions.

The gatekeeper function in higher education is seen most clearly in an analysis of which students go on to what kinds of institutions of higher learning.[38] High schools not only channel students to or away from

[37]See Ivar Berg, *Education and Jobs* (New York: Praeger Publishers, Inc., 1970).
[38]See Samuel Bowles, "Contradictions in U.S. Higher Education," in *The Capitalist System*, Richard C. Edwards et al., eds. (Englewood Cliffs, N.J.: Prentice-Hall, Inc., 1972), pp. 491–503; and Jerome Karabel, "Community Colleges and Social Stratification," *Harvard Educational Review*, 42 (November 1972): 521–62.

Figure 3.3. Changing Educational Attainment

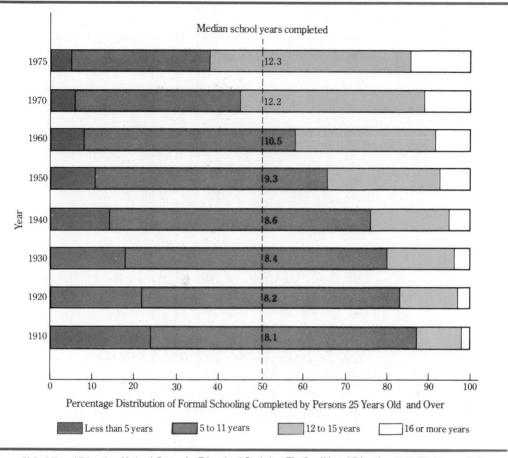

Source: U.S. Office of Education, National Center for Educational Statistics, *The Condition of Education, 1977* (Washington, D.C.: U.S. Government Printing Office, 1977), p. 103.

further schooling; they also channel students to particular rungs on the status ladder of higher education. Again, class background of a student plays a determining role.

State systems of higher education are ordinarily made up of large universities, four-year colleges, and two-year ("community" or "junior") colleges. As one moves from the community college up to the university level—the most prestigious—the income backgrounds from which most students are drawn increase demonstrably (see Table 3.1). Since the level at which one enters the labor force is linked with the type of educational credential one is able to gain, the multitiered system of higher education may be viewed as a part of the tracking process.

Class background also influences a student's chances of completing college. Since attendance at any institution of higher education costs money, the least affluent have the most difficult time remaining. Though public institutions tend to cost less than private ones, and though numerous grant and loan programs have been created to help out needy students, costs continue to escalate. Those most likely to drop out completely, or to interrupt their studies for a period of time, come from low-income backgrounds.

Children from economically advantaged families are most likely to enter universities, not community colleges. Many will attend private elite institutions. From there they are likely to go on to graduate or professional schools. Because they, not the low-income students, stay in school longest, attend universities where per pupil costs are high, and go on to even more expensive graduate training, the affluent capture a disproportionate amount of the tax funds that go to support higher education. One might say that this is a special public subsidy available only to the children of upper-income groups, one that helps them remain at the class level of their families.

The Special Role of the Community College

Over 11 million students were enrolled in college in 1975—more than two and a half times as many as in 1960. This substantial rate of growth is largely a result of the new importance of two-year colleges. Community-college enrollment was five times larger in 1975 than in 1960. On the one hand, community colleges are evidence of the democratization of higher education; access to higher education has been made available to ever more people. On the other hand, community colleges have themselves been accused of playing a gatekeeping role.

Community colleges seem to have taken on two major tasks. First, they prepare students to go on to a four-year degree program at a state college or university. Second, they offer vocational programs for those who wish to (or must) pursue a two-year terminal degree. Vocational

Table 3.1.   Estimated Parental Income of First-Time Students in Institutions of Higher Education, 1974

| Parental Income | Percentage Distribution | | | |
	All institutions	Universities	Four-year colleges	Two-year colleges
Less than $4000	6.0%	3.2%	5.9%	7.8%
$4000–9999	18.3	13.1	17.8	21.7
$10,000–14,999	29.0	26.6	27.3	32.0
$15,000–19,999	16.6	17.8	16.7	15.7
$20,000–24,999	12.0	14.2	12.2	10.4
$25,000 and above	18.2	25.1	20.1	12.4

Source: U.S. Office of Education, National Center for Educational Statistics, *The Condition of Education, 1976* (Washington, D.C.: U.S. Government Printing Office, 1976), p. 231. Data from American Council on Education, *The American Freshman: National Norms* (Washington, D.C.: American Council on Education, 1974).

Pleasant university surroundings like this are more likely to be experienced by students from affluent backgrounds than by those from low-income or minority families. Economically disadvantaged students—if they are able to attend college at all—generally must attend two-year or state colleges.

programs range from health services to data processing. Admission standards are usually very liberal, and students whose formal educational preparation might be cause for rejection by more exclusive institutions can easily get in. Unlike most four-year institutions, community colleges use a system of *open enrollment*, which means that they are consciously open to almost all comers.

Yet, while many of the students who enroll in community colleges may aspire to transfer to four-year schools, relatively few end up doing so. It has been suggested that many students who enroll in two-year schools are subjected to a "cooling out" process.[39] That is, testing and counseling practices may influence community-college students into lowering their academic aspirations by making these students doubt their ability to succeed in a four-year college or university. However, it could also be argued that the high costs of attending college, coupled with highly selective admissions practices at many four-year institutions, are what really lower aspirations. Those who place the blame on community colleges may simply be ignoring other factors that the staffs of such schools have no way of controlling.

According to Jerome Karabel, "community colleges are, in reality, a

[39]Burton R. Clark, "The 'Cooling Out' Function in Higher Education," *American Journal of Sociology*, 65 (May 1960): 569–77. See also Bowles, "Contradictions in U.S. Higher Education," p. 494.

vital component of the class-based tracking system."[40] But in the absence of such institutions, far fewer persons from low-income backgrounds would have the chance of receiving any higher education.

ALTERING THE EDUCATIONAL SYSTEM

Organized schooling both reflects and responds to the prevailing economic and political order. By preparing people to enter an adult world that already is, America's system of education plays socialization functions that help conserve the status quo. Though empirical evidence is scanty, research suggests that the schools fail to liberate children's minds and are as likely to deaden as to enliven human sensibilities. The bureaucratic nature of the school experience, together with the political indoctrination that goes on, may not produce robots. But neither does it produce people who are prepared to critically analyze American society and act collectively to bring about change. Economic inequality and concentrated political power cannot be blamed on public education. But to the degree to which socialization by schools fails to do more than legitimate the prevailing order, the schools cannot escape at least partial responsibility for the harm done to people within this order.

The gatekeeping function of organized schooling is both more complex and more obvious. On the one hand, America's system of education tends to affirm already existing inequalities. On the other hand, one must wonder whether our system of education could bring about a reduction of inequality in the absence of more fundamental changes in the prevailing order. Is education the "weak link" in the chain?[41] In other words, could the problem of inequality be best attacked through education? Or must economic inequality and the concentration of power be taken care of before we can hope to radically improve the organization and operation of education? In the long run, we believe the latter is the case. But in the short run, it is worth pushing the schools, those who run them, and the students who must survive in them toward changes that will minimize the harm being done to millions of children and young adults.

The first, and most basic, change goes to the heart of the American system of education. In a society dedicated to protecting the rights and well-being of individuals, we must alter compulsory school attendance laws. Parents or guardians should have a voice in deciding whether, when, and how their children will be educated. More specifically, whenever it becomes manifestly evident that a school is failing to teach, parents must be able to demand their children's placement in an alterna-

---

[40]Karabel, "Community Colleges and Social Stratification," p. 555.

[41]This is the position taken by Ivan Illich, *Deschooling Society* (New York: Harrow Books, 1971). See also Alan Gartner et al., eds., *After Deschooling What?* (New York: Harper & Row, Publishers, Inc., 1973).

If the schools are to liberate children's minds and enhance their lives, the bureaucratic rules that restrict freedom of speech and physical movement will have to be revised.

tive program of their choice. As it now stands, compulsory attendance laws can be used to force school enrollment even when the educational interests of children are not being met. The issue of compulsory attendance would be less critical if all schools were performing in ways that enhanced the development of children's human potential.

Changes are also long overdue in the organization of schools, specifically their bureaucratic and hierarchical nature. Obviously, rules are required to guide behavior whenever people must function in a group situation, but in many schools rules are used primarily to control and inhibit the freedom of children and youth. While such rules may serve the interests of the administrators and teachers who create and enforce them, they are not always in the best interests of students. Among the rules that should be revised are those restricting students' freedom of physical movement, use of school facilities during and after school hours, and exercise of the rights of freedom of speech and of the press.

The past decade has seen some movement away from the extreme bureaucratization of the school. Among the innovations are:

1. Open classrooms, which typically allow children some freedom to

    move and talk within the classroom and provide a range of choices of learning tasks during at least part of the school day;

2. Individualized instruction, wherein curricular materials permit each child to work at some learning tasks at his or her own pace, and allow teachers to monitor the progress of individual children; and

3. Affective education, through which children are encouraged to recognize and understand their own and others' feelings, and their manner of relating to others.

The extensiveness of these innovations remains limited and their impact remains open to debate.[42] On the face of it, they would seem to be steps in the right direction. However, such classroom programs have been introduced *within* what remain bureaucratically organized institutions, dominated by educational authorities and subject to a wide array of rules and regulations.

What is needed is the democratization of educational institutions—itself an educational experience for those it would involve. Persons with a stake in school functioning—students, staff, and community representatives—should all freely participate in the formulation of rules. They should also collectively determine the division of labor and responsibilities that are to exist among those who fulfill different roles in the school setting. The point is to activate responsible involvement on the part of children and young people in shaping the decisions that affect them.

The implication is that schools must move toward becoming nonauthoritarian institutions, rather than settings for differential power and prestige. Along with this, schools should also become arenas for cooperation among all participants in the interests of meeting collective goals. The fear of failure is but one way—and a destructive one at that—to motivate young people to learn. Rather than encouraging children to compete, the schools should encourage them to cooperate. Individual learning experiences must be balanced by group efforts, to which all may contribute. Only in this way can the nightmare of personal obsolescence that competitive environments nurture be undercut.

Curricular changes that open up classrooms to the outside world must be implemented. Insulation from the world of work, from community problems, and from alternative political views runs counter to the ideal of human development through education. To function intelligently as adults, workers, voters, and taxpayers, students must be directly exposed to situations and issues with which they will have to deal. Rather than only reading about the world of work, students should be out talking to workers, union organizers, managers, and professionals. Instead of discussing current events, students should be creating or otherwise participating in political campaigns and social change movements. Any gap

---

[42]For an assessment of the conflicting findings on the impact of open classrooms, see Hurn, *The Limits and Possibilities of Schooling*, pp. 237–47.

between the school and the real world is an artificial one, and there is no reason to permit it to exist.

Thus far we have dwelt upon changes in the organization of schools and in the kinds of socialization experiences to which students are exposed. An equally important feature of American education that must be altered is its gatekeeping function. Existing economic inequalities must neither be reflected in or reinforced by the educational process.

The immediate goal is equality of opportunity for all children to develop their personalities, intellects, and manual skills to their fullest potential. Stark differences in the resources possessed by school systems must be minimized by reducing their financial reliance on local property taxes. Mechanisms to promote equitable funding of all systems through federal and state treasuries should be a top priority.

Within school systems, tracking must be abolished. More advanced students should routinely help less advanced students. The barriers between academic and vocational learning must also be abolished. All students should be developing interests and experiencing accomplishments that require skill with both head and hands. Testing, if used at all, should be used to diagnose progress, not as a device to channel students away from opportunities.

Educational professionals must be held accountable for their expected contributions to students during their careers in school. Those who are not making a meaningful contribution to school programs should either be retrained or aided in finding some other line of work.

Finances should be no barrier to individuals who wish to go beyond high school—no matter at what point in their lives this decision is made. Free or low-cost tuition and flexible admissions policies can make higher education available to more people and can help meet the changing educational needs of people of all ages. Open enrollment must be implemented at all educational institutions that in any way benefit from public tax funds. That way, anyone who meets minimum educational requirements and who shows evidence of motivation will be assured entry into programs of his or her choice.

Rich educational opportunities from cradle to grave can be made available to all—but only if we are willing to press for change rather than moan about the existing system.

SUMMARY

Historians of education have tended to celebrate the positive contributions of America's system of mass public education. They have claimed that education has contributed to political democratization, economic growth, and the minimization of class inequalities. So-called revisionist historians have recently presented evidence that is somewhat contrary to such positive claims. The revisionists suggest that education has been looked to as a means of political indoctrination and social control, as a device to create a docile and compliant labor force, and as a mechanism to ensure that children of the affluent will retain their families' class position.

While we possess only limited knowledge about the impact of schooling on children today, a number of studies suggest that schools are important agents of socialization. Case studies point to the demands for conformity imposed on school children within bureaucratically organized institutions. It has been suggested that schools foster competition and fear of personal failure. And it is thought that schools function to render children politically unknowledgeable, unprepared for political struggle, and open to manipulation by elites. While the success of such socialization remains open to question, it appears that the momentum of schooling lies in such a direction.

Though mass public education has made schooling possible for everyone, it also performs a gatekeeping function. The resources of the affluent allow them to provide educational opportunities for their children that are qualitatively and quantitatively superior to those available to lower income groups. Moreover, systems of tracking and testing within school settings operate to place the less affluent in a position of educational disadvantage. A self-fulfilling prophecy operates when nonaffluent children are not expected to learn, are not taught, and thus do not perform at a level with their more affluent peers. Differential treatment in school translates into differential academic outcomes and helps keep class inequalities intact.

The gatekeeping function also operates at the level of higher education. Economically privileged families are best able to ensure that their children will attend college and remain until completion. Children from low-income families are less likely to attend and complete college. Those who do enroll are frequently forced to attend community colleges. Since where one enters the labor force is frequently linked to the type of educational credentials one possesses, children of the affluent possess a competitive advantage.

America's system of education can be altered in many ways. Parents must have the right to demand alternative school placement for their children when it is clear they are not being taught. Bureaucratic rules and regulations that are not in children's interests should be abolished, and efforts must be made to democratize educational institutions. Students must have a say in the decisions and policies affecting them. Moreover, schools must be turned into arenas of cooperation instead of competition. They must be opened up to the outside world, so that children can learn about the realities they will confront as adults.

Such changes must be accompanied by the abolition of practices that maintain the gatekeeping function of schools. Educational systems have to be equitably financed, and systems of tracking and testing that perpetuate differential treatment by class origin must be eliminated. The barriers between vocational and academic learning should be dropped, so that all students are able to maximize learning with their heads and hands. Educators must be held responsible for making a meaningful contribution to students throughout their school careers.

Finally, finances should be no obstacle to anyone who wishes to go beyond high school. Institutions of higher education must move toward open-enrollment policies and the elimination of tuition costs. Those who are motivated and possess the basic skills should be assured entry into programs of their choice.

DISCUSSION QUESTIONS

1. In what ways has going to school had an impact on your attitudes and behavior? Give examples.
2. What kinds of in-school behavior have you engaged in that was in violation of rules and regulations? Looking back, why do you think you engaged in such behavior?
3. What aspects of your school experience involved you in competition with others? How did you feel when winning or losing?
4. To what degree has your schooling provided you with the ability to analyze political issues and take a stand? Give examples.
5. Was there a tracking system in the schools you have attended? How was placement accomplished? How did students in different tracks view one another? What impact did being placed in a track have on you?
6. What alterations would you like to see in the organization and operation of the educational system? Why? Who or what stands in the way of such alterations?

4 Institutional Racism

There must be no personal and institutional discrimination against individuals on the basis of race and ethnicity.

F rom the time the Plymouth settlement was founded by English colonists, the United States has been run by and in the interests of white people—and consciously so. Though men and women from a variety of other racial and cultural backgrounds have been major participants in the shaping of American history, most whites know little and care less about their roles. Alternately used, abused, and ignored by the white majority, Native Americans (Indians), black Americans, Spanish-surnamed Americans, Asian Americans, and other minority peoples have had a history of racial oppression.[1] Not only have the rights to "life, liberty, and the pursuit of happiness" historically been distributed along color lines; to a large extent, this is still the situation today.

Today, for example, there are over eight hundred thousand Native Americans. This group has suffered enormous injustice. Shortly after the European settlers arrived on this continent, they found it expedient to clear out the native peoples whose tribal societies stood in the way of territorial conquest and colonial expansion. The firm belief of whites in their own racial and cultural superiority (a belief without any real foundation) provided a ready rationale for their vicious treatment of "Indians." Native Americans were subjected to a continuing series of attacks: the takeover of ancestral lands, racially inspired killings, confinement on white-controlled reservations, bureaucratic manipulation by governmental agencies, and so on. Now, after generations of white domination, Native Americans are among the poorest and most oppressed minority groups in the United States. Their traditional patterns of living have been largely destroyed, and their life chances are almost completely subject to the whims of white-controlled institutions.[2] They were, and are, victims of racism.

The immediate territorial expansion of white American society involved pushing Native Americans back, aside, and under. And its early economic development to a large extent revolved around the wholesale purchase of human beings, their enslavement, and the use of their forced labor. Kidnaped and transported from the African continent, black men and women—like Native Americans—were forced to become a part of American society. Bought and sold, assaulted and bred, black slaves were worked relentlessly under a system of subjugation that was based on the assumption that they were not really human. When slavery in a society with democratic ideals began to present irreconcilable moral dilemmas (and, more importantly, when slavery became politically and economically questionable to maintain), it was cast aside as one outcome

[1]For a history of racism in the United States, see Paul Jacobs and Paul Landau (with Eve Pell), *To Serve the Devil* (New York: Random House, Inc., 1971). Though many white groups (for example, Eastern and Southern Europeans) have also experienced discrimination, this chapter focuses on those who are victims of discrimination based on race—or *racism*.

[2]See Dee Brown, *Bury My Heart at Wounded Knee* (New York: Holt, Rinehart & Winston, 1970); and Vine Deloria, Jr., *Custer Died for Your Sins* (New York: Avon Books, 1969).

of a bloody Civil War. Yet the ingrained belief of whites in their own racial and cultural superiority did not significantly wither. Formal enslavement of black people was replaced by conscious racial segregation and other forms of discrimination that have functioned to keep black Americans "in their place." More than a century after the abolition of slavery, imposed inequalities continue to weigh upon many of the more than 22 million blacks living in the United States.[3]

Westward expansion was carried out at great cost to another group that was also made a part of the United States against its will. Prior to 1848 the southwestern portion of the United States was a part of Mexico. The people of Spanish and Native American ancestry occupying the territory had been there long before the colonists landed near Plymouth Rock. When white settlers began to "open up" the western frontier, the government of the United States precipitated a war against Mexico to "liberate" the rich agricultural lands and natural resources of the Southwest. Upon winning the war, the United States proceeded to annex half of Mexico's sovereign territory. Natives of Mexico who had occupied the lands for many generations were considered to have been conquered, and most landholdings were subsequently transferred into the hands of the victorious "Anglos." Once again the belief of whites in their own racial and cultural superiority came into play, conditioning the treatment of persons of Mexican ancestry. Today over 6 million Mexican-Americans, most of whom reside in the Southwest, continue to struggle under Anglo control and domination.[4]

The American government's historical willingness to pursue territorial acquisition through conquest was responsible for pulling yet another group into this society's collection of minorities. Not too long after the annexation of the Southwest, the United States initiated a war against Spain—ostensibly to end Spanish colonial excesses in Cuba. After winning the war, the United States went on to claim the small Caribbean island of Puerto Rico. Spain ceded Puerto Rico to the United States, whereupon it fell—and remains today—under this society's political and economic control. Particularly in the years since World War II, Puerto Ricans—people whose ancestry includes mixtures of Spanish, African, and Taino Indian—have taken advantage of their American citizenship to migrate from the poverty-ridden island. Members of this group have settled primarily in the cities of the Northeast, especially in New York City. Mainland businesses, seeking cheap unskilled or semiskilled labor, have encouraged this migration. Once on the mainland, Puerto Ricans are just another racial minority so far as the dominant white population is concerned. The socioeconomic status of the almost 1.5 million Puerto

[3]See John Hope Franklin, *From Slavery to Freedom,* 3rd ed. (New York: Alfred A. Knopf, Inc., 1967); and Lerone Bennett, *Before the Mayflower,* 4th ed. (Chicago: Johnson Publishing Co., Inc., 1969).

[4]See Rodolfo Acuña, *Occupied America* (San Francisco: Canfield Press, 1972); and Tony Castro, *Chicano Power* (New York: Saturday Review Press, 1974).

Ricans on the mainland is severely depressed, and many are the victims of poverty and unemployment. Movement to and from the mainland is constant, as members of this group struggle for ways to deal with their difficult situation.[5]

In this chapter we shall examine the major manifestations of racism that such minorities face, to one degree or another, in American society today.[6] We shall point to reasons why racism exists, and we will look at the mechanisms by which the white majority systematically subordinates minorities. Finally, we will spell out some of the consequences of this macro problem and point to the need for change.

THE MEANING OF RACISM

The term *racism* is more than an abstract concept. It refers primarily to practices that harm people. There are two different types of racism.[7] The first type is *personal racism,* wherein individuals express negative feelings toward persons who are members of a minority group. Second, there is *institutional racism,* wherein the routine operations of such institutions as business and the political system work to the disadvantage of minorities in general. We will examine both types of racism in this section. However, much of the remainder of this chapter will focus on institutional racism.

Personal Racism

Personal racism occurs when individuals hold attitudes of prejudice and/or engage in discriminatory or similar behavior. Among the manifestations of personal racism are stereotyping individuals on the basis of alleged racial differences; the use of derogatory names and references; discriminatory treatment during the course of interpersonal contacts; and threats and acts of violence against members of a group that is alleged to be racially and culturally inferior. It is at the personal level that the expression of racism is most visible and easily detected.

For example, in the fall and winter of 1974 a group of white parents

---

[5]See Juan Angel Silén, *We, the Puerto Rican People* (New York: Monthly Review Press, 1971); and Michael Abramson and the Young Lords Party, *Palente* (New York: McGraw-Hill, Inc., 1971).

[6]The focus of this chapter will be on Native Americans, black Americans, and Spanish-surnamed Americans. This is not to say that other groups, such as Asian Americans, have not been or are not today confronted with racism. See, for example, *The Journal of Social Issues,* 29, No. 2 (1973), entitled, "Asian Americans: A Success Story?"

[7]See Louis L. Knowles and Kenneth Prewitt, eds., *Institutional Racism in America* (Englewood Cliffs, N.J.: Prentice-Hall, Inc., 1969).

The violence occasioned by a court-ordered school busing program in Boston during the mid-1970s demonstrates the extremes that expressions of personal racism can attain. Ironically, people who express personal racism often make use of the very symbols (the American flag, the U.S. Constitution) of the equality they are attempting to deny members of minority groups.

vigorously objected to a court-ordered school transportation program intended to help end illegal patterns of racial segregation in the Boston school system.[8] According to news reports, some members of the white community threw rocks and shattered the windows of buses carrying black children to schools in white neighborhoods. A number of individuals chanted obscenities and slogans, such as "Niggers Go Home!" while jumping around the buses making exaggerated apelike gestures at the

[8]See "North's Worst Rioting over Forced Busing," *U.S. News and World Report,* October 21, 1974, pp. 32 ff.; and "Bleeding Boston," *Newsweek,* December 23, 1974, p. 23.

children. These efforts by individual whites to communicate the contempt they felt for persons with black skin is perhaps an extreme example. Expressions of personal racism range in intensity and visibility, but all have the same intent—the denigration of persons on the basis of their group membership.

It is not surprising that individual minority group members sometimes respond to white racism by developing attitudes and/or engaging in actions that could be considered racist. For example, survey research conducted during the 1960s revealed that a substantial sector of the black population held antiwhite attitudes.[9] Occasionally, the newspapers report criminal activities—including acts of violence against whites—that are alleged to be racially based. In general, however, it has been too dangerous for minority individuals subjected to personal racism by whites to fight back in like manner. The power to apply negative sanctions in response to personal affronts or threats (not to mention violence) is, as we shall see shortly, overwhelmingly monopolized by the white majority. As a consequence, whites have had far freer rein in expressing personal racism overtly than have those who would try to turn the tables.

Institutional Racism

The second type of racism, institutional racism, is our major concern in this chapter. The term *institution,* as used here, refers to an organizational structure created to perform certain services or functions within a society. Business and industry, unions, the political system, education, the mass media, the legal system—all may be thought of as institutions. Ideally, such organizational structures can be made to function so as to take the interests of all social groups into account. In reality, of course, they can be made to perform so as to provide advantages or benefits to some groups over and above others. We have already seen in earlier chapters how a few of these institutions operate to the distinct advantage of the economically affluent and to the disadvantage of those who lack economic power. Institutional racism involves the treatment accorded specifically to minority peoples at the hands of such institutions.

The term *institutional racism* draws attention to the fact that Native Americans, black Americans, and Spanish-surnamed Americans—by virtue of their historical exclusion from key institutional policy-making and decision-making roles—frequently find themselves victimized by the routine workings of such organizational structures. Unlike personal racism, the racism that occurs through the day-to-day and year-to-year operation of large-scale institutions is often difficult to detect without careful investigation. It is a form of racism that *only* powerful whites can express, since it is they who fill command positions in such institutions.

[9]Gary T. Marx, *Protest and Prejudice* (New York: Harper & Row, Publishers, Inc., 1967).

Institutional racism was involved in the Boston school system example mentioned earlier. The illegal segregation of children by race, which the courts were persuaded to move against, did not suddenly occur in 1974. Nor did it occur by accident. The racial segregation of schools in Boston was a result of decisions made by white school officials over a period of many years—decisions on such matters as where new schools should be built and for whom, and how school boundaries should be drawn in the city. In Boston, as in many other urban centers, such decisions were made on the basis of, among other things, established patterns of residential segregation. Residential segregation, in turn, is typically traceable to years of decisions made by white property owners, landlords, real estate firms, urban renewal authorities, banks and lending institutions, and housing developers. The isolation of racial minorities is enforced by official school system policies—ostensibly designed to support the concept of a "neighborhood school" for the convenience of every child—that add to the effect of segregation in housing.

White domination of Boston's school board and administration has long meant that blacks have had no voice in important decisions regarding education. The very existence of a dual school system in Boston—along with doubts about the quality of education being made available to their children—serves to remind many black parents of the inferior status to which racial minorities have historically been relegated in American society. Petitioning the courts has proven to be, in this and many other segregation cases, one way that white-imposed racial isolation may be fought. White violence simply underscores the importance to many whites of maintaining the institutionalized color line.

Thus, institutional racism is a societal phenomenon that only powerful whites can set in motion and sustain. The key element is *power* over organizational structures and their operations. Since minority group members generally lack access to positions of power in the key institutions that affect them, they are incapable of discriminating against whites at this level. One can talk about incidents of "black racism"; but it should be remembered that minorities have never had, and do not have today, the means to practice racism on the same scale and with the same broad effects as have whites.

The Myth of Innate Racial Inferiority

As we mentioned earlier, white domination over Native Americans, black Americans, and Spanish-surnamed Americans has long been accompanied by beliefs in the racial and cultural superiority of whites.[10] Such beliefs have frequently taken the form of so-called scientific theories that postu-

[10]Thomas F. Gossett, *Race: The History of an Idea in America* (New York: Schocken Books, Inc., 1965). These beliefs are closely related to the beliefs behind the social pathology approach discussed in the Introduction to this text.

late the innate inferiority of racial minorities due to genetic factors. Such theories have not only purported to explain why minorities, on the whole, lag behind whites in terms of educational achievement and economic success; they have also served to justify *actions* against minority peoples by whites. Thus, theories of genetic inferiority are more than abstract systems of ideas or academic exercises. They provide an intellectual climate for the perpetuation of personal and institutional racism.

A few psychologists and other academicians recently rekindled the long-standing controversy over the bases of human intelligence: the "nature versus nurture" debate.[11] The theories they have put forth rest on the claim that intelligence is primarily determined by genes rather than by environmental influences on learning. These theorists have based many of their conclusions on the results of IQ tests, which they consider devices capable of measuring intelligence. (We mentioned the biases of such tests in Chapter 3.) Since, in terms of group averages, minorities lag behind whites on test results, the theorists suggest that the genetic characteristics of members of racial minorities limit their learning potential. Innate genetic differences, it is alleged, interfere with achievement in schooling. The obvious implication of such theories is that the money spent on the education of minorities is wasted. To the degree to which these kinds of ideas receive acceptance by the whites who are in charge of political and educational institutions, the stage is set for cutbacks in the already inadequate educational opportunities provided minority children.

Such theories and their policy implications are in and of themselves racist. They are forms of ideological thinking that support inequalities along color lines as natural and, therefore, inevitable. That such theories are based on unproven assumptions and faulty premises renders them even more distasteful.

The claim that human intelligence is primarily determined by genes is just that—a claim, not a fact.[12] Most geneticists will readily admit that little is known about the relationship between genes and human behavior, and that there is no scientific evidence that genes play the major role in determining intelligence. In fact, there is not even agreement today about what the concept *intelligence* really means. Thus, there is no consensus on how to validly measure it. If there is any explanation for the economic, political, and educational subordination of minority peoples in American society, it does not rest with genes. Subordination is imposed by racism.

[11]See, for example, Arthur R. Jensen, "How Much Can We Boost I.Q. and Scholastic Achievement?" *Harvard Educational Review,* 39 (Winter 1969): 1–123. Critiques of this position may be found in the Spring and Fall 1970 issues of the *Harvard Educational Review.*

[12]See Leon J. Kamin, *The Science and Politics of I.Q.* (Potomac, Md.: L. Erlbaum Associates, 1974); and Allan Chase, *The Legacy of Malthus* (New York: Alfred A. Knopf, Inc., 1977).

Institutional racism in education and the economic system helps explain the fact that whites generally hold higher paying, more secure, and more desirable jobs, while members of minority groups are most likely to work at lower paying, least secure, and most undesirable jobs. Though individual minority members do have good jobs, in group terms, minorities have been unable to move upward in the occupational structure.

ECONOMIC DEPRIVATION AND EXPLOITATION

In Chapter 1, "Economic Inequality and Poverty," we saw that the United States is a class society, divided along economic lines. Political and economic power and the privileges of material affluence are closely tied to property ownership and high income. Native Americans, black Americans, and Spanish-surnamed Americans generally do not own income-producing property. And only a small percentage of each of these groups has been able to gain entry into occupations and professions that pay well. These facts, along with the disproportionate presence of racial minorities in the poverty and low-income sectors of the American population, can best be explained by institutional racism.

Employment and Income

Native Americans, black Americans, and Spanish-surnamed Americans are far more likely to be unemployed or sporadically employed than members of the white majority. They are far more likely to be underemployed—that is, to be overqualified for the jobs they hold. And they are far more likely to occupy positions with the lowest income, benefits, security, and status. How does one explain the marginal occupational situation of racial minorities as compared to the general white population? Though there are many reasons, institutional racism plays a key role.

First, the handicap of inadequate schooling must be examined. Census data shows that dominant group/minority group differentials in years of education completed have been narrowing, particularly during the last decade. Black Americans especially have made some notable gains.[13] But aggregate statistics on years of school completed do not say anything about the *quality* of educational experiences to which many minority children and teenagers continue to be subjected. Some limited insight may be gained by examining performance on nationwide achievement tests (in reading, mathematics, etc.). Scores on such tests continue to indicate that whites, on the average, are being taught more.[14]

Achievement or "aptitude" tests are often used as screening devices by public and private employers. The failure of educational systems to prepare many minority students—even high-school graduates—to compete on an equal basis with whites on such tests directly limits their occupational opportunities. The use of such tests especially affects groups whose native language is not English—e.g., Puerto Ricans and Mexican-Americans. Employers have claimed that the use of such tests is fair and nondiscriminatory (although there are obviously cases in which the tests have little to do with the work to be done). Yet, insofar as such screening devices function to the direct disadvantage of minorities, the tendency toward discrimination along racial lines is institutionalized.[15]

Nor does high performance on tests necessarily guarantee employment and occupational mobility for minority persons. White employers often react negatively to distinguishing physical features, dress, accent, and other characteristics associated with minority background and culture. They prefer employees who will "fit in." In a predominantly white establishment, this renders minority membership a deficit in and of itself.

Direct discrimination means that even objectively qualified minority candidates have often needed far more in the way of educational credentials than whites in order to get the same kinds of jobs. (This situation is now breaking down under the pressure of antidiscrimination laws.) If statistics on employment can be believed, many employers routinely pay minorities less than whites for similar work and block the advancement of minority group members (with the exception of "token success mod-

---

[13]U.S. Bureau of the Census, *Social and Economic Status of the Black Population, 1974* (Washington, D.C.: U.S. Government Printing Office, 1975), p. 91.

[14]The most comprehensive national survey to date is James S. Coleman et al., *Equality of Educational Opportunity* (Washington D.C.: U.S. Government Printing Office, 1966). Findings regarding white-minority achievement test score differentials continue to remain valid.

[15]See James J. Kirkpatrick et al., *Testing and Fair Employment* (New York: New York University Press, 1968).

els"). [16] In business and in government, white monopolization of positions with the highest pay and the most authority remains largely unchallenged. Moreover, many of the very top institutional positions in the public and private sectors (e.g., boards of directors, cabinet and agency heads, judgeships) are typically gained through appointment. Those in a position to do the appointing are likely to be white, and they tend to choose persons like themselves.

Minority group members who aspire to move upward have also found that denial of their cultural backgrounds—i.e., becoming operationally "white" on the job—may be a prerequisite to employment security and success. The conflict between "selling out" and freely maintaining and expressing consciousness of minority identity is a forced one. It stems primarily from the need to please white superiors in order to gain acceptance and get ahead in majority-dominated institutions. [17]

In the labor market as a whole, according to social scientists, there is a division along racial lines. [18] The *primary labor market* consists of the higher paying, more secure, and most desirable occupations for which employers recruit white workers. For example, as Table 4.1 indicates, white-collar jobs are predominantly filled by white workers. The *secondary labor market* consists of the lower paying, least secure, and most undesirable jobs. It is within this secondary market that most minority group members are likely to find work. For example, within the blue-collar job market, blacks are mostly found as nonfarm laborers and operatives. They also make up a high percentage of service workers (see Table 4.1). A competitive threat occurs when minority groups attempt to move up and out of the sector of the labor market in which they have long been believed to "belong"—a threat felt whenever equal treatment is demanded in employment practices. To the degree to which Native Americans, black Americans, and Spanish-surnamed Americans fall or are pushed aside in the competition for primary labor market positions, whites have an open field.

Minority group members have made their greatest gains in the American occupational structure when there has been a labor shortage, as during periods of war. When there is work to be done, when there is no other way to get it done, employers have dropped some of their normal procedures for screening, hiring, and promoting employees—a situation that provides opportunities otherwise unavailable. On the other hand, during a period of labor surplus—e.g., an economic recession and slowdown—minority group members tend to be the hardest hit. In many

[16]Bennett Harrison, *Education, Training, and the Urban Ghetto* (Baltimore: The Johns Hopkins University Press, 1972).

[17]See, for example, Nathan Hare, *Black Anglo-Saxons* (New York: Collier Books, 1965).

[18]See Harold Baron and Bennett Hymer, "The Negro Worker in the Chicago Labo Market," in *The Negro and the American Labor Movement,* Julius Jacobsen, ed. (Garden City, N.Y.: Anchor Books, 1968), pp. 232–85.

Table 4.1. Occupation of the Employed Population, 1974

Occupation	Number in Thousands			Percent Black
	Total	Black	White	
Total employed	**85,936**	**8,112**	**76,620**	**9%**
White-collar workers	**41,738**	**2,302**	**38,761**	**6**
Professional and technical	12,338	710	11,368	6
Engineers	1,168	14	1,114	1
Medical and other health	2,082	138	1,866	7
Teachers, except college	2,957	252	2,683	9
Other professional and technical workers	6,131	306	5,425	5
Managers and administrators, except farm	8,941	277	8,562	3
Salaried workers	7,131	205	6,858	3
Self-employed workers	1,810	72	1,703	4
Sales workers	5,417	158	5,203	3
Retail trade	3,072	112	2,917	4
Other industries	2,344	47	2,286	2
Clerical workers	15,043	1,202	13,629	8
Stenographers, typists, and secretaries	4,330	257	4,015	6
Other clerical workers	10,713	864	9,613	8
Blue-collar workers	**29,776**	**3,411**	**26,029**	**12**
Craft and kindred workers	11,477	769	10,603	7
Carpenters	1,073	52	1,008	5
Construction craft workers, except carpenters	2,353	197	2,133	8
Mechanics and repairers	2,955	172	2,756	6
Metal craft workers	1,206	73	1,128	6
Blue-collar worker supervisors, n.e.c.	1,457	95	1,350	7
All other craft workers	2,433	180	2,228	7
Operatives, except transport	10,627	1,421	9,075	13
Transport equipment operatives	3,292	459	2,805	14
Drivers, motor vehicles	2,787	369	2,394	13
All other	506	90	411	18
Nonfarm laborers	4,380	763	3,547	17
Construction	808	159	643	20
Manufacturing	1,111	227	873	20
Other industries	2,461	377	2,031	15
Service workers	**11,373**	**2,130**	**9,037**	**19**
Private household	1,228	458	755	37
Service workers, except private household	10,145	1,672	8,282	17
Cleaning service workers	2,136	579	1,529	27
Food service workers	3,538	400	3,026	11
Health service workers	1,612	361	1,234	22
Personal service workers	1,606	196	1,383	12
Protective service workers	1,254	135	1,110	11
Farm workers	**3,048**	**225**	**2,793**	**7**
Farmers and farm managers	1,643	51	1,579	3
Farm laborers and supervisors	1,405	174	1,214	12

Source: U.S. Department of Commerce, Bureau of the Census, *The Social and Economic Status of the Black Population in the United States, 1974* (Washington, D.C.: U.S. Government Printing Office, 1975), p. 75.

sectors of the economy, layoffs are carried out on the basis of seniority: the last to arrive leave first. This process at least partially accounts for the extraordinary unemployment rates among minorities during economic slumps.

In recent years, individual minority members have been permitted to move upward in the occupational structure as pressures have increased against blatant discrimination. These individuals tend to be highly visible, giving the impression that great gains are being made. But in *group* terms, Native Americans, black Americans, and Spanish-surnamed Americans have remained "in place," a situation verified by their continuing lag in income (see Figure 4.1).

Figure 4.1.   Median Income of Families, 1950–74

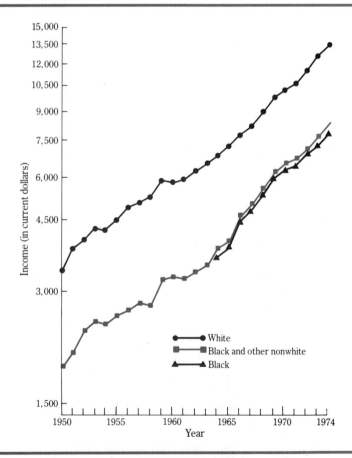

Source: U.S. Department of Commerce, Bureau of the Census, *The Social and Economic Status of the Black Population in the United States, 1974* (Washington, D.C.: U.S. Government Printing Office, 1975), p. 21.

Other factors also influence the occupational situation of many minority group members. Minorities have become residentially concentrated in central city areas, while business and industry have been migrating out of large cities to suburbs and smaller cities that offer attractive tax rates and white labor pools. Locked into central city areas by housing segregation, the expense of alternative housing, and the inadequacy or cost of transportation to outlying jobs, urban-dwelling minorities have found it increasingly difficult to find satisfactory employment. The "white flight" of business and industry, while not necessarily intended to work to the disadvantage of minorities, effectively does so.

Technological changes, which have altered the makeup of parts of the occupational structure, also work against minority employment. In recent years, new job areas calling for training and skills of an extensive and often esoteric nature have been created. Since educational resources and opportunities are disproportionately available to whites, whites are in a privileged position to compete for such jobs. At the same time, technological advances have enabled some employers to cut back on or even eliminate certain positions, typically those that require limited skills. One sociologist has argued that automation, for example, will render much of the labor performed by minorities obsolete and exacerbate their employment problems.[19]

Just as neither business nor government has seen fit to eliminate the employment difficulties facing minorities, so has organized labor served as an impediment.[20] Union membership and long apprenticeships are requirements for entry into many occupations—particularly the higher paying skilled crafts and trades. But members of racial minority groups often have been—and still are—denied membership in white-dominated unions. Discrimination in this area has meant that minority individuals, even if they possess the skills, are locked out of contractual opportunities that would enable them to demand as much for their time and labor as unionized whites. Union resistance to minority enrollment is by no means total. In fact, a higher percentage of black workers than white workers belongs to a union today. But for the better paying, more highly skilled jobs, exclusionary practices by organized labor are another form of institutional racism.

The United States has a work force of over 90 million people. As one moves down the occupational and professional hierarchy, the percentage of persons with dark skin increases. As one moves up, it decreases. If we look only at the very top positions in business and government, we could hardly think that ours is a multiracial society. Through institutional racism, minorities are effectively kept at and toward the bottom of the employment ladder.

[19]Sidney Willhelm, *Who Needs the Negro?* (Cambridge, Mass.: Schenkman Publishing Co., Inc., 1970).

[20]Ray Marshall, *The Negro Worker* (New York: Random House, Inc., 1967).

Minority business ownership has been viewed as a means of improving the economic situation of minority groups. However, this has not worked out in practice. Members of minority groups own proportionately few business enterprises, most of them small. And, with the exception of a handful of top companies, minority-owned businesses tend to be under-financed due to institutional policies that discriminate against smallness and inexperience.

Business Ownership

As a result of white domination of high-level positions, the concentration of members of minority groups at the bottom of the economic ladder, and the reluctance of white employers to hire them, there has been much interest in setting up minority-owned businesses as a means of improving the economic situation of minorities. After all, one way to make money and to struggle toward an improved economic position is through the ownership of a business. Minority business owners, so the theory goes, could hire minority workers and thus improve the situation of the entire group.

But despite the interest in and excitement about minority-owned business, business ownership has not resulted in *group* improvement. When we examine business ownership in the United States, it quickly becomes evident that whites prevail. Surveys by the U.S. Department of Commerce, conducted periodically since the late 1960s, continue to substantiate the same facts.[21] In terms of their percentage representation in the population, Native Americans, black Americans, and Spanish-surnamed Americans own few businesses. Moreover, minority-owned enterprises are likely to be small and to employ few people. All such enterprises taken together account for about 2 percent of the nation's total annual business income.

A number of explanations have been offered to explain the relative absence of minority entrepreneurs and the economic insignificance of

[21]The first nationwide study was U.S. Bureau of the Census, *Minority-Owned Businesses: 1969* (Washington, D.C.: U.S. Government Printing Office, 1971).

most of the firms owned by minorities. Some of these explanations blame the victim, suggesting that minority group members lack the interest and motivation necessary to succeed in the competitive world of profit-making. Such explanations are clearly inadequate. It is not minority inability but instead institutional racism that has been responsible for the low rates of minority business ownership.[22]

Starting a new business or expanding an ongoing one requires cash and credit. Unless an individual has a very substantial income and a large amount of savings, it becomes necessary to deal with banks. In the American economy, the financial sector has always been overwhelmingly controlled and staffed by whites. The aspiring minority entrepreneur may be faced with direct rejection by unsympathetic banking officials, simply on the basis of group membership. But institutional policies—which are said to be totally unrelated to discrimination against minorities—often result in the same kind of negative outcome. Banks and other lending institutions have a plentiful supply of competing white and minority applicants. They are most likely to extend loans to individuals whose economic success in the past renders them excellent credit risks, to those to whom money and credit have successfully been extended before, to those who possess property that can be put up as collateral against loans, and to those who can most easily demonstrate the probable profitability of their business project. On the average, these criteria are met more readily by whites than by nonwhites.

In recent years, the federal government's Small Business Administration has worked with members of the corporate and banking communities to aid minority entrepreneurs. The government has also made limited attempts to purchase more products and services from minority businesses and has urged its large corporate suppliers to do so as well. But these forms of aid, while receiving a great deal of publicity, have not resulted in any dramatic change in the magnitude of minority business ownership.

In the absence of a first chance to become involved in the business world, minorities are likely to remain shut out. It is like being turned down for a job because of lack of formal experience when one can only gain such experience by getting the job. The effect is that one goes nowhere, an experience many minority group members have grown to anticipate in dealing with financial institutions.

POLITICAL POWERLESSNESS

In Chapter 2, "Concentration of Power," we stressed the close relationship between economic power and political clout on the national level. As we have seen, minority groups are economically disadvantaged in com-

---

[22]See, for example, William F. Haddad and G. Douglas Pugh, eds., *Black Economic Development* (Englewood Cliffs, N.J.: Prentice-Hall, Inc., 1969).

parison with the overall white population. And, even more than most whites, they are light-years away from competing with the economic and political power wielded by the ownership class—the small segment of the population among whom wealth and income are concentrated. If, as we saw in Chapter 2, many members of the white majority feel powerless to affect national decision-making, minority group members must feel even more helpless. Nonwhites are almost totally dependent on white power-holders for the initiation and enforcement of policies that might improve their life chances. To varying degrees, this situation of political power-lessness prevails right down to the state and local levels of government.

Government Employment

At the national level, blacks and members of some other minority groups are currently well represented in terms of government employment. But whether we are speaking of the executive, legislative, or judicial branch of the federal government, this representation lies primarily in the lower paying, nonpolicy-making positions. In 1974, for example, blacks held 16 percent of all full-time federal jobs, but less than 3 percent of the top-level posts.[23] Other minority groups have not fared nearly as well. Periodically, the U.S. Commission on Civil Rights (an independent federal watchdog agency) has castigated various bodies of the national government for discrimination in the operation of their programs and in their hiring and promotion practices.

Minorities are underrepresented in key elected positions at the national level. All American presidents have been white, and white-dominated political parties have persistently avoided any attempts to alter that trend. As of 1978 only four blacks had been appointed to the presidential cabinet. There are few minority members of the U.S. Senate or House of Representatives (see Table 4.2); the handful who are there find that their numbers are far too small to allow them to wield much influence in the face of an overwhelmingly white majority of lawmakers. While often expected to represent minority concerns, there is little they can do without the support of their white colleagues.

The situation is similar on the state and local levels (Table 4.2). For example, in 1975 less than 1 percent of all elected officials in the United States were black.[24] This percentage is undeniably a significant improvement over past figures. But most of these officials serve in small, southern communities in which the black population is numerically predominant. The situation facing other groups—e.g., Native Americans and Spanish-surnamed Americans—is even worse.

[23]U.S. Bureau of the Census, *Social and Economic Status of the Black Population, 1974*, p. 77.
[24]Ibid., p. 4.

Table 4.2. Black Elected Officials, by Type of Office

Office and Area	1964	1971	1973	1975
Total	**103**	**1,860**	**2,621**	**3,503**
United States Senators				
United States	0	1	1	1
South	0	0	0	0
House of Representatives				
United States	5	13	15	17
South	0	2	4	5
State legislators and executives				
United States	94	198	240	281
South	16	70	90	124
Mayors				
United States	NA	81	82	135
South	NA	47	48	82
Other elected officials				
United States	NA	1,567	2,283	3,069
South	NA	763	1,239	1,702

Source: U.S. Department of Commerce, Bureau of the Census, *The Social and Economic Status of the Black Population in the United States, 1974* (Washington, D.C.: U.S. Government Printing Office, 1975), p. 151. Figures for 1964 represent the total number of elected blacks holding office at that time, not just those elected in that year. The 1971, 1973, and 1975 figures represent the number of elected blacks holding office as of the end of March 1971, March 1973, and May 1975, respectively. NA = not available.

The findings of a major sociological study conducted in 1965 still seem applicable across the country.[25] This study focused on black representation in key policy-making positions in Cook County, Illinois, which includes Chicago and much of the surrounding suburban area. In 1965, 20 percent of the population of Cook County and 28 percent of Chicago itself were black. But blacks occupied only 5 percent of the governmental policy-making positions identified by the researchers. This 5 percent included elected officials, appointees to various boards, local administrators, and federal jobholders. When the researchers expanded their study to include key positions in the private sector as well (e.g., business, law, higher education, organized labor) the percentage of black representation fell to 2 percent. Then, when all institutional policy-making posts were ranked in terms of the amount of power vested in them, the meaning of black representation was diluted even further. Blacks were less likely than whites to be occupying those posts considered to be powerful.

This brief overview suggests the kinds of problems minorities confront in getting their concerns expressed and dealt with. Yet we have left aside the whole question of the *quality* of the representation minorities have achieved. As in the area of employment generally, at least some of those who manage to make their way into key political positions progressively

[25]Harold Baron, "Black Powerlessness in Chicago," *Trans-action,* 6 (November 1968): 27–33.

lose identification with their minority constituencies. Fearing that failure to adapt to majority views or practices will result in the loss of newly achieved power and prestige, they often let themselves become co-opted by or assimilated into the white-dominated political and governmental system. Minority officeholders may find themselves forced to mute their race-related concerns in the interests of accommodation and compromise with more powerful representatives of the white majority. If they press minority concerns too vigorously and are too unyielding, they may see their overall political effectiveness jeopardized. This too contributes to the dilution of minority political power.

Voter Participation

The forces generating political powerlessness also include the lack of voter participation. For years exercise of the franchise by minority group members has lagged behind that considered normal for whites. A common explanation of this fact involves blaming the victim. Persons of low socioeconomic status and limited formal education—minority or not—tend to have little desire and energy to get involved in institutionalized political activity, especially because they believe that it is dominated by the more affluent and highly educated. This common phenomenon is exacerbated in the case of minorities, whose members disproportionately fall in the lower depths of the class structure.

More to the point is the fact that many minority group members have been faced with extraordinary resistance to their participation in the political system at any level—including voting. We have already discussed the denial of black political rights, most notably but not exclusively in the southern states, in the Introduction to this book. Blacks and others have faced white-controlled election laws and rules designed to impede voter registration and the exercise of the franchise. Among these rules have been insistence that Native American and Spanish-surnamed people take literacy tests in English, the imposition of poll taxes on people who cannot afford to pay them, and threats and acts of economic reprisal. Gerrymandering has also been common—that is, white decision-makers have altered district boundaries so as to keep minority peoples from making up a majority of voters and thus influencing the outcome of elections. Federal voting rights laws have, in recent years, eliminated many such formal practices.

As a consequence, many minority group members have long approached the idea of voting with cynicism. Only recently have representatives of numerically large, urbanized groups—such as black Americans and Mexican-Americans—successfully attempted to get more minority candidates into elected office. And only recently have agencies of the government provided protection for those who had been manipulated or harassed out of the franchise for many years.

In sum, important decisions affecting the life chances of minorities are made *for* them, not *by* them. One outcome of institutional racism in the political structure is the continuing, sporadic outburst of militant discontent directed against the abuses of the white power structure. Such outbursts can be seen as indications of the failure of this structure to incorporate or adequately respond to minority concerns.

Minorities and the Law

Existing laws, and provisions for the enforcement of these laws, have all been created by representatives of the white majority. In the past, law has actually been used to deprive minorities of rights taken for granted by white citizens. Discriminatory practices have continued even as such laws have slowly been repealed, and it has taken years of struggle by minorities and their allies to get new laws guaranteeing protection of their rights passed. The struggle is still going on in such areas as education, employment, and housing discrimination. It is no wonder, then, that many minority group members have little confidence in law as a facilitator of their interests.

Minority discontent has been especially noteworthy in the area of criminal law and its enforcement. State and local police forces are overwhelmingly controlled by whites. Discrimination in police recruitment, hiring, and promotion has been rampant. (This situation has slowly begun to change as minorities press for enforcement of antidiscrimination laws passed in the 1960s.) Furthermore, members of racial minorities have long felt themselves to be the prime victims of police misconduct and brutality. Most police forces are not under the supervision of civilian review boards through which allegations of misconduct and brutality could be investigated by concerned citizens. The police investigate themselves when charges are levied, and in most cases this accomplishes little. Hence, predominantly white police forces have an inordinate amount of freedom to exercise power over minorities—including the indiscriminate use of force—without a great deal of accountability.[26]

Discriminatory treatment of minority persons by white police officers may involve both personal and institutional racism. Personal contact with police in ghettos, barrios, and reservations has led to widespread hostility and distrust on the part of minorities. For example, in the aftermath of the black urban rebellions of the 1960s, investigators found that the major grievance voiced by ghetto residents was police brutality and harassment.[27] Similar complaints were documented in U.S. Civil Rights Commission investigations of the treatment of Mexican-Americans.[28]

[26]Paul Chevigny, *Police Power* (New York: Pantheon Books, Inc., 1969).
[27]*Report of the National Advisory Commission on Civil Disorders* (Washington, D.C.: U.S. Government Printing Office, 1968), Chapter 11.

The problem is not limited to the actions and attitudes of individual police officers. Racism in the administration of justice, as elsewhere, is an institutionalized process. Prosecutors, judges, juries, prison personnel, members of parole boards—all tend to be white. Minority individuals are accused of crimes, placed under arrest, detained in jail before trial, forced to rely on public defenders for legal assistance, prosecuted, found guilty, given severe sentences, and denied early parole more than whites. While in prison, minorities may be subject to racial denigration by guards and other staff. Once out of prison, they are handicapped not only by an arrest record, but also by the extra burden of discrimination in the labor market that even those minority group members who have never been arrested must face. All of this is made possible by minority political powerlessness and the continued exclusion of minorities from institutional positions from which more just and equitable policies could be fashioned.

EDUCATIONAL DEPRIVATION

Formal education is not a guarantee of employment or security in our competitive, hierarchical society. But the lack of quality formal education, coupled with experiences of denigration and school failure, is likely to leave an individual in an untenable economic position. This is true both for whites and minorities, but more so for the latter, given discrimination in the world of work. The burden of school failure disproportionately falls on minority children. Political powerlessness also means that minority parents have little or no control over how, what, and how much their children are encouraged or permitted to learn.

In considering institutional racism in education, we again come back to the question of power. Who holds the command positions through which decisions about education are made and resources allocated? In general, at the federal, state, and local levels, decisions regarding education are made by representatives of the white majority. Minorities thus find it enormously difficult to pressure educational systems to make them provide learning experiences commensurate with their children's needs. School segregation, limited educational programs and teaching resources, alienating curricula, and racist practices by school personnel contribute to the poor education of millions of minority children.[29]

[28]U.S. Commission on Civil Rights, *Mexican Americans and the Administration of Justice in the Southwest* (Washington, D.C.: U.S. Government Printing Office, 1970).

[29]U.S. Commission on Civil Rights, *Racial Isolation in the Public Schools* (Washington, D.C.: U.S. Government Printing Office, 1967); U.S. Congress, Committee on Labor and Welfare, *Indian Education: A National Tragedy—A National Challenge* (Washington, D.C.: U.S. Government Printing Office, 1969); and U.S. Commission on Civil Rights, *Ethnic Isolation of Mexican Americans in the Public Schools of the Southwest* (Washington, D.C.: U.S. Government Printing Office, 1970).

The Battle Against Segregation

Until a little more than twenty years ago, racially segregated public schools were maintained by whites with support from this society's legal system.[30] Tens of millions of minority children passed through "their own" schools, while whites went elsewhere. Typically, fewer resources were allocated to the schools that served minority children, since it was not expected that they would go on to higher education or get jobs that required education. North and South, East and West, rural and urban, inequalities in school expenditures operated in the interests of children of the white majority, particularly the more affluent whites.

In 1954, after decades of legal battling by minority representatives, the nation's courts were persuaded to address the question of whether school segregation was a denial of equal rights under the law. Court decisions calling for an end to dual school systems were followed up by civil rights legislation in the 1960s. The focus was primarily on educational systems in the southern and border states. Since then, white and minority children are slowly being brought together under the same school roofs.

At first, court decisions and antisegregation legislation had little impact in the northern and western states. Only recently have the courts begun to move against segregation in these regions, and there has been less progress than in the South. Where dual school systems have been found to exist, particularly in urban areas, white school officials have blamed this on uncontrollable population shifts and the movement of minorities into racially homogeneous ghettos and barrios. In most central city school systems, segregation has noticeably *increased* since 1954. Urban minority populations have grown; many whites have fled to the residentially segregated suburbs; and city "neighborhood school" policies have continued to perpetuate the racial isolation of minorities. Cities in the southern and border states have begun to develop in similar directions, even while denying intentional segregation practices.

Obstacles to Equal Education

Segregation is an important concern not only because it separates white and minority children into two different worlds. The real problem regarding segregation involves the quality of education received by minorities as compared with whites. As we saw in Chapter 3, "Schooling and Unequal Educational Opportunity," public school systems rely mainly on local property taxes for most of their money. The flight of affluent families to the segregated suburbs, the failure of government to take

---

[30]Meyer Weinberg, *Race and Place* (Washington, D.C.: U.S. Government Printing Office, 1967).

steps to control urban blight, and the movement of business and industry out of central city areas have all contributed to school fiscal crises. Educational costs—like everything else in recent years—have steadily gone up, and the revenues needed to meet these costs have failed to keep pace. Thus the city schools that serve minority children often find that they cannot afford the kinds of programs and services commonly available in affluent white suburbs. Instead, they must make do with outdated physical plants and equipment, overcrowded classrooms, and limited curricular offerings.

Despite the increasing minority enrollment in central city schools, whites predominate in the running of most schools. From the school board, to superintendent, to principals, and often on down to teachers and counselors, minorities are underrepresented, and procedures for input from minority groups are the exception rather than the rule. Members of the dominant white majority administer education to children whose backgrounds, cultures, and everyday life experiences in racially isolated communities are little understood and viewed as alien. Learning is unlikely to take place when understanding and respect are lacking, if the numerous case studies of schools published in the last decade are any indication, and white school personnel are likely to evoke indifference, if not hostility.[31]

Until quite recently, textbooks and other curricular materials were produced primarily for the children of the white majority and did not reflect the multiracial character of American society. Social studies texts either ignored the history and present status of minorities or implied that such topics were unimportant by their brevity of coverage. The implication was that only whites have said or done anything worth learning about. This encouraged and reinforced minority feelings of racial isolation and even of inferiority. Shortcomings in curricula have also extended to the ways in which peoples who live outside the white, Western world are treated. The history and cultures of the predominantly nonwhite Third World, for example, are still rarely dealt with fully and equitably, thereby again suggesting the notion of white superiority.[32]

As we saw in Chapter 3, the commonly used IQ tests favor those students who have best mastered the vocabulary common in white, middle-class homes. Yet minority children are often channeled into one or another school program on the basis of their performance on such tests. Testing is used to place children in ability groups. On the average, minority children tend to perform less well on the tests than do those whites for whom they were originally designed, so minority children are generally shunted into groups set up for those with low ability.

---

[31]See, for example, Herbert Kohl, *36 Children* (New York: World Publishing Company, 1967); Jonathan Kozol, *Death at an Early Age* (Boston: Houghton Mifflin Company, 1967); and Gerald E. Levy, *Ghetto School* (New York: The Bobbs-Merrill Co., Inc., 1970).

[32]Michael Kane, *Minorities in Textbooks* (New York: Quadrangle Books, 1971).

Ability groups are no secret to the children placed in them. Minority children are likely to take their placement seriously and doubt their own potential and intelligence. School personnel also tend to view children in low-ability groups as inferior. Such a view may be expressed through attitudes toward the children or through the use of curricular materials that demand very little of them. The result is a self-fulfilling prophecy (see Chapter 3), as white school personnel demand little from minority children, teach little, and find that their students learn little.[33]

Institutional racism in education fosters failure. The performance of minority children, on the average, tends to be below grade level when compared with children of the white majority. Minority children have higher suspension, expulsion, and dropout rates than their white counterparts. Proportionately fewer minority students go on to higher education. The inadequate educational preparation many receive contributes to lower rates of college completion for those who do manage to go on. All these outcomes, in turn, intensify the economic disadvantage that minority group members face in the labor market, and the circle closes.

RACISM AND SOCIETY

The economic deprivation, political powerlessness, and educational inequality fostered by institutional racism have consequences for the society as a whole as well as for members of racial minorities. In this section we shall spell out some of the costs white America pays for its institutionalization of racism. We shall then look at minority responses to racism and their effect on American society. Finally, we will consider some proposals for change.

The Costs of Racism

It is obvious that institutional racism makes it extremely difficult for members of racial minorities to achieve in economic, political, and educational spheres. But racism also has negative consequences for *whites*, whether they are active practitioners of or allegedly innocent bystanders to minority subordination.

Because of institutional racism, minorities have been regularly denied resources and excluded from opportunities through which they could more fully develop and display their human capabilities. That is, racism arbitrarily restricts the development and utilization of vast amounts of human talent. This talent could be mobilized in the interests of society as a whole, and its restriction means a loss to us all.

[33]Morris Rosenberg and Roberta G. Simmons, *Black and White Self* (Washington, D.C.: American Sociological Association, 1971).

The personal and societal costs of institutional racism are numerous and serious. Minority unemployment created by discrimination in educational and economic institutions, for example, not only leads to increased taxes for unemployment compensation and welfare benefits; it also restricts the development of human talent that could improve everyone's life. In a society that equates high income with success, joblessness also can create feelings of depression and guilt on the part of the unemployed.

Racism ultimately translates into monetary costs as well. Much of the tax money paid by both whites and minority peoples is used to improve or otherwise deal with conditions that institutional racism has helped create and perpetuate. Since unequal educational opportunities and employment discrimination have meant high levels of joblessness and depressed wages for minorities, tax money must be diverted to pay for welfare benefits and other forms of aid. The ghettoization of minorities and the abandonment of central city areas by whites are components of what has been called the urban crisis. A great deal of tax money must go into central cities just to keep them functioning. Despite their flight, whites cannot escape paying for the urban stagnation afflicting cities across the country.

Then there are the unmeasurable psychic costs to whites. Historians of slavery have commented that the slaveholder's own sense of security and freedom was circumscribed so long as he restricted the freedom of others. Knowing that rebellion and acts of retribution were constant possibilities, he always had to look over his shoulder and remain ready to protect himself or his property. More than a century after the formal abolition of slavery, majority-minority relations in this society still give rise to white anxiety and fear. Racial conflict—and the possibility of racial conflict—has led to massive investments in police forces and other instruments of social control.

Racism divides our society. It provides a channel through which members of the white majority can release their frustrations. Minority groups have been said to play the role of lightning rods for the dissatisfactions that whites feel they must somehow express. Since minorities are disadvantaged in terms of ability to fight back freely, they provide a relatively easy target. But the problems that frustrate many members of the white majority—economic difficulties, political powerlessness, and so on—are similar to those minorities face. Racism prevents whites from seeing how much they have in common with minorities; it obscures the fact that all might gain by cooperating and uniting. Intergroup conflict and distrust along racial lines means that the dissatisfactions of many whites are expressed downward—toward powerless groups that are not responsible for the problems. In the meantime, the handful of whites who hold economic and political power and who make decisions affecting *all* those below them benefit from racial disunity. Through a conscious or unconscious divide-and-conquer strategy, societal elites can use racism to the disadvantage of everyone else.

The Inspiration of Minority Responses

Americans have long believed that "white is beautiful." People who neither look nor act as if they are full-fledged members of the dominant white majority have continuously been kept aware of their "disability." To be permanently stigmatized by virtue of color and culture, to be dealt with as inferior and systematically subordinated, may easily cause individuals to doubt their own self-worth. If such doubts are internalized, they lend support to white dominance by making nonwhites believe that they deserve inequitable treatment.[34]

In recent years social science literature has portrayed minority peoples as mentally crushed by racism.[35] In many individual cases, this is no doubt true. But the portrayal of nonwhites as mentally or spiritually crushed is a distortion of reality when applied to minority groups as a whole. It is another version of blaming the victim—of considering racially oppressed groups as incapable and thus responsible for their continuing economic, political, and social disadvantage vis à vis whites.

[34]See Thomas F. Pettigrew, *A Profile of the Negro American* (Princeton, N.J.: D. Van Nostrand Company, 1964), Chapter 1.

[35]One of the best examples of this literature is William H. Grier and Price M. Cobbs, *Black Rage* (New York: Basic Books, Inc., 1968).

Public Problem, Private Pain
BLACK, AMERICAN, AND UNEQUAL

Seeking to probe the experiences and attitudes of black Americans living in northern urban ghettos, Frank L. Keegan conducted in-depth interviews with ghetto dwellers. The statement that follows was made by Elizabeth Young, who is married to an engineer and has three small children. Mrs. Young's parents came North some years ago in search of better job opportunities. Her father had no formal education, and Mrs. Young worked hard to achieve a college degree. Her answer to the question, "Do you think of yourself as an American?" reveals the nonacceptance and exclusion that America's minority people continue to feel. While Mrs. Young prefers to live in a black community, she expresses anger that those who would choose otherwise must confront limited options and white hostility.

We love this country perhaps more than anybody else here because only we see this country being saved by giving us our share of the action. Now most of the time when we say "share of the action" white people think in terms of me visiting them, playing with their children, going to their churches and bars, joining their country clubs and having my daughters come out in their debutante parties. But these are not the things we are asking for.

We are asking for that collective thing I was talking about. Individually, we have never had any problems going up the ladder. Collectively, black people have never been totally accepted. Now let's face it. We are an ethnic group. We are the largest ethnic group in the United States. And that gives us a certain amount of power right there. But even though we are the largest ethnic group in this fantastic country, all other kinds of ethnic groups can go up the ladder but we can't collectively go up the ladder—even though we are all raised in the same environment.

For example, white people go to school and I go to school. Now it comes time to get our little jobs and get into the middle income bracket. But your middle income and mine are two different things. The more money you make, the further up the ladder you go. We're going up the same ladder, and let's say we have equal intelligence and equal everything, okay? But my middle income is less than yours and I go up more slowly.

If a white family moves into a nice little neighborhood nobody is going to scream. Nobody will ask how much they make, nobody will ask what their religion is—all that irrelevant garbage. But the minute the Youngs move into that neighborhood, the first question is "What does your husband do?" The next question is "How much does he make?" Then, "Do you go to church?" I'm not saying we want to move there, but we don't have a choice and that is what it's all about.

I'm not saying that if all the doors in the United States were equal that we wouldn't still live as a group because most ethnic people live in groups. Basically, people are more comfortable with their own kind. I'm a hard segregationist myself. Wallace and I agree one hundred percent on that. But my thing is that if the Youngs want to move into another neighborhood, they should have the choice. The fact is that we don't have the choice. My man can't say to his son, "You can be President," because in all honesty he can't be President. And he can't be senator or a leader of people, not of black people, green people or yellow people, but a leader of people. So what does he have to tell his son? "Find a way for your people. Find a way for your people."

Frank L. Keegan, *Blacktown, U.S.A.* (Boston: Little, Brown and Company, 1971), pp. 76–7.

In fact, of course, we can hardly help but be inspired by the emotional and spiritual health of members of racial minorities in the face of racism. Millions of men, women, and children have revealed the extraordinary ability of human beings to endure imposed hardships. Though many individuals have been crushed by these hardships, overall Native Americans, black Americans, and Spanish-surnamed Americans have survived generations of subordination, denigration, and material disadvantage and have organized and struggled to assert their worth. Despite all that has been done to them historically, such groups have continued to battle for even the smallest gains toward equality with whites.

Ironically, one rarely considered consequence of racism in the United States has been the development of social movements that continue to inspire many persons who suffer under imposed inequalities, no matter what their color. The contemporary women's movement and environmental movement, for example, have drawn inspiration from minority struggles for civil rights, as did the antiwar movement of the late 1960s and early 1970s.

The Civil Rights Movement

The most famous minority struggle against racial discrimination is the black civil rights movement of the 1950s and 1960s.[36] In 1954 the efforts of such groups as the National Association for the Advancement of Colored People (NAACP) culminated in a Supreme Court decision outlawing segregated public schooling. While it would be years before the decision would begin having any substantial impact on the education of racial minorities, it did signal in a new era in American race relations. Once the Supreme Court ruled that segregated schools denied blacks their constitutional rights, it was obvious that discriminatory voting laws and segregated public facilities, housing, transportation systems, and workplaces had to go.

One day in 1955, in Montgomery, Alabama, a seamstress named Mrs. Rosa Parks refused to give up her seat in a segregated city bus so that a white man could sit. Inspired by her arrest, over fifty thousand blacks soon joined a boycott of segregated public transportation in that city; and after a year-long struggle, the buses were desegregated. This protest demonstrated that segregation could be fought by grass-roots collective action. And it turned a leader of the Montgomery protest, Dr. Martin Luther King, Jr., into a national civil rights figure.

Inspired by the success in Montgomery, groups of blacks and their white supporters slowly began to test resistance to desegregation both in the South and in the North. By the early 1960s, this testing had begun to take on the characteristics of a national social movement, led by such

[36]See Franklin, *From Slavery to Freedom.*

The civil rights demonstrations of the early 1960s dramatized the goals of the movement and helped speed the desegregation of public facilities. Marches like this one in Selma, Alabama, in 1963 also helped inspire other minority groups to organize and press for improvements in their positions.

groups as the NAACP, the Congress of Racial Equality (CORE), the Student Non-Violent Coordinating Committee (SNCC), and Dr. King's Southern Christian Leadership Conference (SCLC). Peaceful marches, boycotts, and sit-ins against segregationist practices captured public attention nationwide. The response to civil rights demonstrations was frequently violent. Incidents of harassment and terrorism were directed at both black and white civil rights advocates, in some cases resulting in tragic deaths. Many Americans were outraged, and the incidents thus resulted in increased public support for civil rights.

In 1963 over a quarter million supporters of the civil rights movement staged a dramatic march in Washington, D.C. There, movement leaders such as Dr. King called on the American people and federal officials to support new legal measures that would force an end to segregation. The immediate outcome was the passage of new federal civil rights legislation—most notably the Civil Rights Act of 1964 and the Voting Rights Act of 1965. Blacks could now appeal to the law when faced with discrimination.

Unfortunately, the new legislation did little for blacks who resided in the nation's urban ghettos. If anything, the sense of isolation and hopelessness among many ghetto blacks was inflamed. It had become clear to many that outlawing discrimination was not the same as upgrading ghetto schools, eliminating poverty and inferior housing, reducing police brutality, and providing decent employment opportunities. In the mid-1960s ghetto communities began to erupt in riots. America's "race problem" took yet another turn as the civil rights movement began to splinter.

Groups that had long battled for desegregation and integration, such as the NAACP, maintained their commitment to such goals and continued to solicit white support. CORE and SNCC, on the other hand, began to reject white participation in their activities and called for "Black Power."[37] Basically, this meant that black people should collectively strive to take over those white-dominated institutions that directly affected their lives. It meant community control of schools, local political apparatus, police departments, economic endeavors, and social services. As CORE and SNCC began to mobilize support for Black Power, more militant black organizations began to emerge in ghetto areas. The most well known was the Black Panther party. To the Panthers, racism was the immediate enemy, but its roots were to be found in the capitalist makeup of American society. The ultimate goal to be pursued was not desegregation or even community control. The goal was the abolition of capitalism and the creation of a socialist alternative.[38]

The ghetto rebellions that rocked the nation each year from 1965 to 1968 and the growing political militancy of segments of the civil rights movement alienated many whites. At the same time, the more moderate elements of the movement lost the one charismatic leader with white support. Dr. Martin Luther King, Jr., was assassinated in 1968. In the wake of his death, the already segmented civil rights movement began to founder.

Between the mid- and late 1960s, the federal government used a carrot-and-stick approach to ghetto discontent. Limited funds were poured into new federal programs, like the War on Poverty and the Model Cities Program, that were designed to foster the impression that ghetto problems were being addressed in concrete ways. Simultaneously, federal agencies such as the FBI—along with local police de-

[37]Black power and other outcomes of the 1960s civil rights movement are critically analyzed in Robert L. Allen, *Black Awakening in Capitalist America* (Garden City, N.Y.: Doubleday & Co., Inc., 1969). See also Stokely Carmichael and Charles V. Hamilton, *Black Power* (New York: Random House, Inc., 1967).

[38]Philip S. Foner, ed., *The Black Panthers Speak* (Philadelphia: J. B. Lippincott Company, 1970).

partments—began to systematically harass and disrupt both the militant and moderate civil rights groups.[39]

By the early 1970s the civil rights movement was in a state of disarray. Members of the white majority had lost interest in the continuing plight of racial minorities. Other national issues, such as military involvement in Southeast Asia and the economic recession, overshadowed racism. The gains of the civil rights movement were substantial—especially when measured against the harsh treatment of the recent past. But since the early 1970s, little has been done to further improve the life chances of minorities.

In the last few years, civil rights organizations that remain committed to desegregation have concentrated on two key issues, neither of which have drawn a great deal of support from whites. Attacks on employment discrimination through legal efforts to bring about "affirmative action" in hiring have proven threatening to many whites, especially since these efforts have taken place during a period of economic slowdown. Attacks on urban school segregation have also aroused white concern, if not outright resistance, as we saw earlier in this chapter.

After an era of conflict and minority advance, black-white relations seem to have settled into an uneasy holding pattern. The subordinate position of the black population has only been eased by the successes of the civil rights movement, not eliminated.

Toward a More Equal Society

The elimination of personal and institutional racism will benefit racial minorities and the white majority. Racism and its consequences ultimately harm everyone.

Attacks against racism must take place on two levels. First, racist ideas must be attacked and discredited. Ideas alleging the inferiority of nonwhites, no matter how subtly they are stated, are inevitably used to justify the denigration of minorities or to rationalize minority disadvantage.

Second, attacks must also be made on practices that—whether intended to do so or not—contribute to the subordinate status of nonwhites. This means fighting discrimination and exploitation wherever they appear and pushing for affirmative institutional practices that will upgrade and enhance opportunities for minority group members. Movements to end school and housing segregation and to put an end to discrimination in employment must once again become as energized as the 1960s civil rights movement. More people must join or create collective

[39]Nelson Blackstock, *Cointelpro: The FBI's Secret War on Political Freedom* (New York: Vintage Books, 1976).

efforts against racism, if only out of a self-interested desire to avoid sharing in its costs.

We must not lose sight of the fact that many of the problems facing minority group members are matters afflicting tens of millions of white people as well. Poverty, substandard schooling, unemployment, and poor housing are not solely minority problems. By pushing for large-scale societal changes, such as a reduction in economic inequality and the expansion of free or low-cost services, the plight of many whites as well as minorities can be measurably improved.

Under the prevailing order, improvement in the economic and political position of minorities is often seen as a threat to whites. The assumption is that whites will sustain losses if nonwhites make gains in employment, education, and politics. This will continue to be a problem so long as we believe that competition for existing resources and opportunities is part of the "natural order." We need to begin ignoring the color line, so that all people with common wants and needs can develop strategies for change through which all can gain. The only losers should be those whose inordinate power and privilege depend on maintaining racial antagonisms and preserving the status quo.

SUMMARY

Native Americans, black Americans, and Spanish-surnamed Americans are among the minorities that have been subjected to harm by the dominant white majority. Members of such groups have experienced personal racism, as expressed by individual whites. And they have been victimized by institutional racism. The routine operations of white-dominated institutions continue to function to minority disadvantage. This treatment of minorities has often been rationalized by so-called scientific theories that allege minority genetic inferiority. Such theories have no basis in fact, but they provide an intellectual climate for the perpetuation of personal and institutional racism.

Institutional racism operates in the area of employment. Hiring and promotion practices are often subtly discriminatory—e.g., the use of tests that favor whites (due to the educational advantages the latter enjoy). Those who hire or appoint people to key positions are usually white, and they tend to choose people who are like themselves and who will "fit in." Consequently the labor market is divided along racial lines. The primary labor market, consisting of the more desirable occupations, is largely populated by whites. The secondary labor market, where wages are low and jobs least secure, is the one in which minorities are most likely to find work.

As antidiscrimination laws have begun to bring blatant discrimination to an end, individual minority group members have been permitted to move upward in the job hierarchy. But in *group* terms, Native Americans, black Americans, and Spanish-surnamed Americans have not made significant gains. Factors other than those mentioned help account for this. The white flight of business and industry out of central cities has made it increasingly difficult for ghettoized minorities to find satisfactory employment. Technological changes threaten the existence of unskilled and semiskilled jobs in which minorities are concentrated, while opening up jobs requiring specialized skills for which whites are disproportionately prepared. Exclusionary practices by white-dominated unions have helped keep minority group members out of the better paying skilled crafts and trades. Finally, minorities who want to open their own businesses have been subjected to discrimination by banks and other financial institutions. The limited efforts to aid minority entrepreneurs in recent years have not resulted in any dramatic improvement in minority business ownership.

Institutional racism also operates in the political sphere. Minority employment in government is primarily in the lower paying, nonpolicy-making positions. At the national level, few minority members have been appointed to public office, and few hold elected office. Minority political officials find themselves outnumbered and pressured to limit expression of race-related concerns. Some progressively lose identification with their minority constituencies, thus further diluting minority political power. Until quite recently, minority group members were even discouraged from voting by racist practices. Now that voting rights are protected by law, minority voter activity has been on the increase. But important decisions affecting the life chances of minorities continue to be made *for* them, not *by* them.

In comparison to the dominant white majority, minorities are educationally deprived. Segregated schooling continues, and urban fiscal crises exacerbate the problem of financing education for the ghettoized on a level with that of white suburbs. Whites continue to dominate in the administration of educational programs at the federal, state, and local levels. Within educational systems, minority children are often taught by persons who have little understanding of or respect for their culture and experiences. Curricular materials have suggested white superiority by their failure to reflect the multiracial character of society, a situation only recently undergoing change. Testing practices that favor the environmental advantages experienced by many whites have been used to assign minorities to low-ability classes. Once there, differential treatment leads to differential learning and performance. School failure intensifies the disadvantages that minority members face in the labor market.

Institutional racism harms minorities, and it hurts whites as well. Racism restricts the pool of talent from which society as a whole could benefit. It forces up tax expenditures to counter the effects of unequal educational opportunities, unemployment, and poverty. Racism leaves whites with anxiety and fear in relating to minority group members, and stirs the possibility of racial conflicts against which investment in police forces and other forms of social control must be made. Finally, racism divides our society. The common problems both whites and minorities face tend to be obscured. Those whites who hold economic and political power benefit from racial disunity, consciously or unconsciously using a divide-and-conquer strategy to the disadvantage of everyone else.

Despite the harm done them, minorities have not been mentally or spiritually crushed. Indeed, their historic struggles for survival and equality with whites have revealed the extraordinary ability of human beings to endure imposed hardships. One consequence of racism has been the development of social movements—e.g., the civil rights movement of the 1950s and 1960s—that have inspired many persons who suffer under imposed inequalities, no matter what their color. The gains of the civil rights movement were substantial when measured against the past, but much more effort is needed to eliminate the subordination of minorities.

Attacks must be made against racist ideas, as these are inevitably used to justify the denigration of minorities or to rationalize their situation of disadvantage. Moreover, attacks must be made on personal and institutional practices that—intended or not—subordinate minorities. Many of the problems facing minority group members are faced by millions of whites as well. Efforts to deal with poverty, substandard schooling, unemployment, and poor housing will relieve the plight of many whites—not just minority group members. The only whites who stand to lose from attacks against racism are those whose power and privilege depend on maintaining racial antagonisms and preserving the status quo.

DISCUSSION QUESTIONS

1. A childless white couple wishes to adopt a child. The demand for healthy white infants has outstripped the supply, but several children from minority backgrounds are available. What arguments could be made for and against the adoption of a minority child by whites?

2. Two applicants—one white and one a minority group member—are equally qualified for a professional job opening. What arguments could be made for and against giving preference to the minority applicant? If preference is not given, how will minority underrepresentation in the professions ever be altered?

3. If you are white, discuss your feelings about being in a social situation in which you are the only white present. If you are of minority background, discuss your feelings about being in a social situation that is wholly white. In both cases, discuss the sources of your feelings.

4. At predominantly white campuses across the country, it is common to see

minority students clustered among their racial peers. For example, all-black tables in cafeterias are not uncommon. How does one account for this informal segregation? Is it desirable or undesirable? How so?

5. Several years ago, a movie depicted changes in the life of a white man who woke up one morning and found he had turned black. If you are white and this were to happen to you, what would your reactions be? If you are a minority group member and you were to wake up white, what would your reactions be? In both cases, discuss the change in life chances and opportunities that your color alteration could entail.

6. If, as we noted in this chapter, racism harms whites, why do not more whites see the struggle against personal and institutional racism as in their self-interests? Under what conditions could this situation change?

5 Institutional Sexism

There must be no personal and institutional discrimination against individuals on the basis of sex.

I n previous chapters we examined several distinct patterns of inequality, each of which is an integral feature of the overall structure of this society. We saw that the unequal distribution of wealth, income, and educational opportunity divides Americans into separate classes. Political power is concentrated in the hands of a few, and decisions about the nature and course of American society generally serve the interests of the dominant economic class. Institutional racism creates further cleavages within the population, subordinating minority peoples and obscuring the problems many different groups have in common. Such macro problems adversely affect the life chances of millions of persons, young and old.

Yet another pattern of inequality limits life chances—the pattern of sex inequality. Women are a majority in numbers, comprising slightly over 50 percent of the American population; but they are a minority group in treatment, in that they are socially, economically, and politically disadvantaged in comparison to men. The fact that women are collectively disadvantaged and are thus a minority group is still not fully accepted.[1] Many men and some women greet this idea with derision, even while acknowledging that there are certain costs associated with being born female.

In this chapter we will look at the minority status of women in America. We will first consider the phenomenon of sexism and the myths that back it up. The chapter then goes into the economic and political effects of sexism—for both women and men. Finally, we will consider the goals, gains, and future hopes of the women's movement as it attempts to liberate women from their subordinate status.

THE MEANING OF SEXISM

Sexism is the systematic subordination of persons on the basis of their sex. In the United States, sexism defines women's place as being in the home, and it bases this definition on the belief that biology is destiny.[2] This belief has been perpetuated and instilled in women through traditional socialization practices.

Male Chauvinism Versus Institutional Sexism

In Chapter 4, we drew a distinction between personal and institutional racism. A somewhat parallel distinction can be drawn between male chauvinism and institutional sexism. *Male chauvinism* is exhibited at the

[1]The idea that women comprise a minority group was voiced in sociology about thirty years ago, but it went largely ignored until the late 1960s. See Helen M. Hacker, "Women as a Minority Group," *Social Forces* 30 (1951): 60–69.

[2]A sophisticated statement of biology is destiny is Steven Goldberg, *The Inevitabil-*

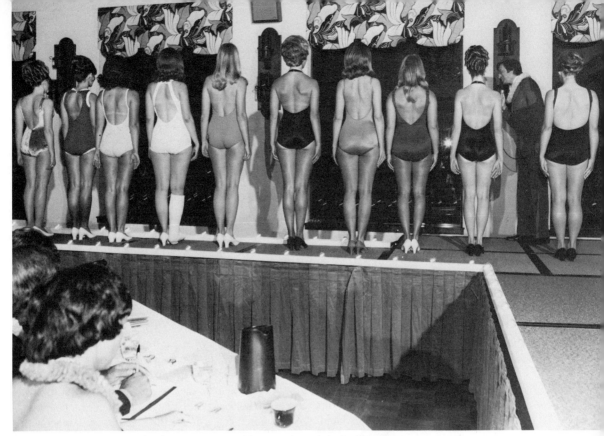

Male chauvinism finds expression in the many annual beauty contests that take place in communities across the nation. In these contests, women are paraded across a stage, where they are rated on their physical attractiveness. Many men and some women do not understand why feminists object to the idea of women's competing against one another on the basis of their looks.

level of interpersonal relationships. The term refers to attitudes and actions through which individual males display their sense of superiority over women. For example, by using such slang terms as "chick," "fox," and "bitch," men place women metaphorically on the level of animals. Other terms, like "broad" for woman, refer to things, or property, rather than human beings. Statements like the male-to-male query "Are you getting any?" segment human relations into genital relations, a process more directly expressed when women are entertained (or paid) for the sole purpose of sexual exploitation.

. Within the home, male chauvinism is expressed in other ways. Many men refuse to perform routine housekeeping tasks, such as cooking and cleaning. After all, they worked hard all day (the implication is that their wives or lovers did not), and besides, such activities are women's work. Women who work outside the home frequently find that they are ex-

ity of Patriarchy (New York: William Morrow & Co., Inc., 1973). The phrase *biology is destiny* is used by Kirsten Amundsen, *The Silenced Majority* (Englewood Cliffs, N.J.: Prentice-Hall, Inc., 1971), p. 108.

pected to bear the burdens of home duties as well. It is not uncommon for a man to insist that a woman bear full responsibility for contraception, or that she be at her mate's beck and call to satisfy his whims. In our culture, "a man's home is his castle," and since few households have paid servants, the "little woman" must often suffice.

Women who work outside the home are often expected to be cheerful coffee-brewers and desk-top straighteners for busy men. Working women may have to put up with being eyed and ogled or subjected to pats and chucks under the chin by friendly males. At annual office Christmas parties, the real reason behind the year's paternal or playful pats is sometimes expressed more directly. To refuse to play along or to get upset can put a woman's job in jeopardy. Men may dismiss a woman's outbursts of fury and resentment over being subjected to these indignities (which few men would silently endure) with the cavalier explanation: "It's just like a woman," or "It must be that time of the month." Women who aggressively challenge expressions of male chauvinism are likely to be considered sexually frustrated, frigid, or lesbians.

Chauvinist attitudes and actions reduce women to objects or to servants catering to the self-defined physical and emotional needs of men. Not all men are chauvinists. Some chauvinists do not recognize themselves as such. Others freely admit their chauvinism, but seem not to understand that their attitudes and actions degrade women as people. On the other hand, not all women chafe under the separate and unequal role into which chauvinists place them. The definition of male chauvinism as sexist (and, indeed, the term itself) is a relatively recent phenomenon. It is attributable largely to the consciousness-raising effects of the women's movement, wherein women sensitive to sexism have encouraged such sensitivity among others.

As annoying and difficult as male chauvinism is, *institutional sexism*—the subordination of women built into societal institutions—has far greater implications. Institutional sexism has proven to be just as, if not more, pervasive than male chauvinism. While male chauvinism operates at the level of interpersonal relations, institutional sexism is more on the level of ongoing, organizational routine. In the economy, in politics, and in education, women are systematically treated in a manner that institutionalizes and increases their disadvantage vis à vis men. Often quite subtle, institutional sexism is less amenable to direct confrontation and attack than is chauvinism.

Is Biology Destiny?

Both male chauvinism and institutional sexism are based on and justified by the ideology that biology is destiny. According to this ideology, basic biological and psychological differences exist between the sexes. These differences require each sex to play a separate role in social life. Women are the weaker sex—both physically and emotionally. Thus they are naturally suited, much more so than men, to the performance of domestic duties. A woman's place, under normal circumstances, is within the protective environment of the home. There, biologically determined physical limitations and emotional sensitivity are not deficits. Nature has decreed that women play nurturant, caretaker roles such as wife and mother, homemaker and confidante. On the other hand, men are best suited to go out into the competitive world of work and politics, where serious responsibilities must be borne. Men are to be the providers; women and children are "dependents."

The ideology also holds that women who wish to or must venture outside the household should naturally fill those jobs that are in line with the special capabilities of their sex. It is thus appropriate for women, not men, to be employed as nurses, social workers, elementary schoolteachers, household helpers, and clerks and secretaries. These positions are simply an extension of women's domestic role as a supportive adjunct to men and their labor. Informal distinctions between "women's work" and "men's work" in the labor force, according to the ideology, are simply a functional reflection of the basic differences between the sexes.

Finally, the ideology suggests that nature has worked her will in another significant way. For the human species to survive over time, its members must regularly reproduce. Sexual attraction between potential mates is the first step in this necessary process. Thus, women must strive to fill the role of sex object. Whether at home or in the labor force, women must make the most of their physical appearance. The role of sex object (and, ultimately, mother) is biologically allocated to women and cannot be lightly dismissed.

So goes the ideology. It is, of course, not true that basic biological and psychological differences between the sexes require each to play such sex-delineated roles in social life. There is ample evidence that sex roles vary from society to society, and those role differences that do exist are largely learned.[3]

But to the degree people actually believe that biology is destiny and that nature intended for men and women to make different contributions to society, sex-delineated roles will be seen as totally acceptable. Expecting women to remain in their place in the home, to limit their aspirations to "women's work" in the labor force, and to preoccupy themselves with sexual attractiveness will not be seen as oppression. Instead, such matters will be viewed as part of nature's grand design. Women who question their biological fate—who demand liberation from the roles they are given on the basis of sex—are likely to be seen as deviants.

---

[3]The ideology is analyzed and critiqued in Elizabeth Janeway, *Man's World, Women's Place* (New York: Dell Publishing Co., Inc., 1971). For sex-role origins and their variation among societies, see M. Kay Martin and Barbara Voorhies, *Female of the Species* (New York: Columbia University Press, 1975).

Public Problem, Private Pain
TRYING TO LEAVE WOMAN'S PLACE

Naomi Weisstein's adventures in her pursuit of a Ph.D. in experimental psychology dramatically illustrate the workings of institutional sexism in the academic world. Her experiences also demonstrate the ways in which institutional sexism is buttressed by male chauvinism. Dr. Weisstein's statement underscores obstacles that millions of working women—not only the relatively few female professionals who want jobs that have been reserved for men—frequently confront. Potential employers often express doubt about women's capabilities and potential. Women who are willing to compete with men for advancement on the men's own terms are often met with hostility. They are told that women who assert their intelligence and strive for achievement are less than feminine and are wandering outside their "natural" sex roles. Women are excluded from the male social networks that are often crucial for advancement in the labor force. All this leads to the segregation of women into work positions wherein their true abilities may never be realized.

While antidiscrimination laws and the women's movement have begun to combat the kind of blatant sexism described by Dr. Weisstein, the statistical picture of women's position in the labor force presented elsewhere in this chapter indicates that, blatant or subtle, sexism continues to keep women "in their place." Dr. Weisstein's adventures help sensitize us all to the battles being fought daily by women who aspire to use their talents and education in the pursuit of a career.

I am an experimental psychologist. I do research in vision. The profession has for a long time considered this activity, on the part of one of my sex, to be an outrageous violation of the social order and against all the laws of nature. Yet at the time I entered graduate school in the early sixties, I was unaware of this. I was remarkably naive. Stupid, you might say. Anybody can be president, no? So, anybody can be a scientist. Weisstein in Wonderland. I had to discover that what I wanted to do constituted unseemly social deviance. It was a discovery I was not prepared for: Weisstein is dragged, kicking and screaming, out of Wonderland and into Plunderland. Or Blunderland, at the very least. . . .

As I mentioned, I was not prepared for the discovery that women were not welcome in science, primarily because nobody had told me. In fact, I was supported in thinking—even encouraged to think—that my aspirations were perfectly legitimate. I graduated from the Bronx High School of Science in New York City where gender did not enter very much into intellectual pursuits; the place was a nightmare for everybody. We were all, boys and girls alike, equal contestants; all of us were competing for that thousandth of a percentage point in our grade average that would allow entry into one of those high-class out-of-town schools, where we could go, get smart, and lose our New York accents.

I ended up at Wellesley, and this further retarded my discovery that women were supposed to be stupid and incompetent: the women faculty at Wellesley were brilliant. (I learned later on that they were at Wellesley because the schools that had graduated them—the "very best" schools where you were taught to do the very best research—couldn't, or didn't care to, place them in similar schools, where they could continue their research.) So they are our brilliant unknowns, unable to do research because they labor under enormous teaching loads, unable to obtain the minimal support necessary for scholarship—graduate students, facilities, communication with colleagues. Whereas I was ignorant then about the lot of women in the academy, others at Wellesley knew what it was like. Deans from an earlier, more conscious feminist era would tell me that I was lucky to be at a women's college where I could discover what I was good at and do it. They told me that women in a man's world were in for a rough time. They told me to watch out when I went on to graduate school. They said that men would not like my competing with them. I did not listen to the deans, however; or, when I did listen, I thought what they were telling me might have been true in the nineteenth century, but not then, in the late fifties.

So my discovery that women were not welcome in psychology began when I got to Harvard, on the first day of class. That day, the entering graduate students had been invited to lunch with one of the star professors in the department. After lunch, he leaned back in his chair, lit his pipe, began to puff, and announced: "Women don't belong in graduate school."

The male graduate students, as if by prearranged signal, then leaned back in their chairs, puffed on their newly bought pipes, nodded, and assented: "Yeah."

"Yeah," said the male graduate students. "No man is going to want you. No man wants a woman who is more intelligent than he is. Of course, that's not a real possibility, but just in case. You are out of your *natural* roles; you are no longer feminine."

My mouth dropped open, and my big blue eyes (they have since changed back to brown) went wide as saucers. An initiation ceremony, I thought. Very funny. Tomorrow, for sure, the male graduate students will get it.

But the male graduate students never were told that they didn't belong. They rapidly became trusted junior partners in the great research firms at Harvard. They were carefully nurtured, groomed, and run. Before long, they would take up the white man's burden and expand the empire. But for me and for the other women in my class, it was different. We were shut out of these plans; we were *shown* we didn't belong. For in-

stance, even though I was first in my class, when I wanted to do my dissertation research, I couldn't get access to the necessary equipment. The excuse was that I might break the equipment. This was certainly true. The equipment was eminently breakable. The male graduate students working with it broke it every week; I didn't expect to be any different.

I was determined to collect my data. I had to see how the experiment I proposed would turn out. If Harvard wouldn't let me use its equipment, maybe Yale would. I moved to New Haven, collected my data at Yale, returned to Harvard, and was awarded my Ph.D. in 1964, and afterward could not get an academic job. I had graduated Phi Beta Kappa from Wellesley, had obtained my Ph.D. in psychology at Harvard in two and one half years, ranked first in my graduate class, and I couldn't get a job. Yet most universities were expanding in 1964, and jobs were everywhere. But at the places where I was being considered for jobs they were asking me questions like—

"How can a little girl like you teach a great big class of men?" At that time, still unaware of how serious the situation was, I replied, "Beats me. I guess I must have a talent."

and

"Who did your research for you?" This last was from a famous faculty liberal at another school, who then put what I assume was a fatherly hand on my knee and said in a tone of deep concern, "You ought to get married."

Naomi Weisstein, "'How Can a Little Girl Like You Teach a Great Big Class of Men?' the Chairman Said, and Other Adventures of a Woman in Science," in *Working It Out: 23 Women Writers, Artists, Scientists, and Scholars Talk About Their Lives and Work*, Sara Ruddick and Pamela Daniels, eds. (New York: Pantheon Books, 1977), pp. 242–44.

Socialization and Self-Concept

The treatment of women in the United States is similar to the treatment received by racial and ethnic minority groups. But women make up a numerical majority in American society. Why have they, in general, accepted this treatment and allowed its ideology to be perpetuated? The answer lies in traditional patterns of socialization.

Early personality development hinges largely on experiences in one's family, and the meaning attached to sex group membership—both for men and women—begins in the home.[4] At birth, children typically are dressed in either pink or blue—the initial uniform that sets girls and boys apart. Although infants cannot discern the message of these colors, adults. can, and it is at this point that sex-role differentiation begins. Parents actively impart their own sense of what it means to be male or female to their children, thereby *creating* many personality and behavioral differences that would not otherwise exist. These differences, as they receive subsequent reinforcement through school and exposure to the mass media, help both men and women define their "place" in adult society.

Even such mundane aspects of the child's world as toys and games promote separate sex roles. Girls usually receive dolls (which they can "mother"), cooking and tea sets (to practice "housework"), and cast-off handbags and cosmetic kits (to practice being a "sex object"). Most parents encourage their daughters to develop traits associated with femininity. Aggressive behavior and fighting are discouraged; crying is acceptable. It is all right to be cute, coy, and flirtatious—an operational definition of what it means to be "daddy's little girl."

Conversely, boys are typically given tool kits and building equipment (to practice "work") and sports paraphernalia (so that they might develop masculine "toughness"). So-called feminine traits, such as emotional sensitivity, are discouraged. Aggressiveness, competitiveness, and a drive to excel are prized. The worst insult to a little boy is to say that he acts, sounds, looks, or smells like a girl. Most boys (and girls, for that matter) find it easier to live up to their parents' sex-role expectations than to question or resist them. Fortunately, many parents are themselves becoming conscious of the negative impact of sex-role stereotyping.

Parental influence is quickly supplemented by the experience of schooling. It is in school that children will have their first in-depth exposure to segregated toilet facilities and single-sex team sports (softball for girls, baseball for boys). In many schools, girls get lessons in home economics, while boys take shop. In the upper grades, girls wave pompoms in support of the team, while the boys bear the responsibility of fighting for athletic glory.

[4]See Judith M. Bardwick and Elizabeth Douvan, "Ambivalence: The Socialization of Women," in *Woman in Sexist Society*, Vivian Gornick and Barbara K. Moran, eds. (New York: Mentor Books, 1971), pp. 225–41.

From childhood, boys are encouraged to compete against one another and to engage in physical activity, so that they will develop their physical capabilities and be "strong." On the other hand, girls have traditionally been required to play more sedate games. These traditional patterns are slowly changing, however, and girls growing up today have more opportunities than their older sisters to engage in strenuous exercise and games.

Throughout the schooling experience, curricular materials remind children of sex-role differentiation.[5] Numerous studies of sex stereotyping in children's books and school texts have found women portrayed as mothers and housewives to such an extent that one would never guess that there are over 40 million women in the labor force. History tends to be the history of men's accomplishments; social studies, the story of how men govern; and English, the literature and poetry of men. Girls cannot help but get the impression that women are not very important, at least not outside of the home.

By adolescence, girls—having been sensitized to their sex identity by their parents and their school experiences—begin to have their first fears of human obsolescence.[6] They begin to ask: "Will/do/why don't boys like me?" The drive for social acceptability, popularity, and recognition is constantly tempered by concern with what boys will think. Looks attract.

[5]See Carol Andreas, *Sex and Caste in America* (Englewood Cliffs, N.J.: Prentice-Hall, Inc., 1971), Chapter 2. See also Nancy Frazier and Myra Sadker, *Sexism in School and Society* (New York: Harper & Row Publishers, Inc., 1973). This has been changing as educators, authors, and publishers have become more concerned about sexism.

[6]See Bardwick and Douvan, "Ambivalence: The Socialization of Women," pp. 225–41.

But competitive accomplishments—physical or intellectual—can be interpreted as masculine and are likely to repel. It seems safest just to be a woman, a member of the "weaker sex"—a sexually attractive, sensitive, nurturant, supportive companion. Girls thus slip into "woman's place" as defined by the biology-is-destiny ideology. Since successful performance of the female sex role requires them to avoid competing with men, they can only see themselves as something less than men.

THE ECONOMIC EFFECTS OF SEXISM

If advertisements, commercials, and television programs are indeed a reflection of popular beliefs and ideas, then most people must think of the typical American woman as an industrious, happy housewife concerned only with laundry, dishes, children's snacks, and personal cleanliness. But this image distorts contemporary realities. Over the last several decades an ever increasing percentage of the adult female population has been taking on part-time or full-time employment outside the home. By ate 1977, 49.2 percent of all women aged sixteen or above—more than 40 million women in all—were in America's labor force.[7] Millions more wished to work but could not find jobs. Many of the women working part-time were doing so because of an absence of full-time employment opportunities.

For the most part, women work outside the home because of *economic necessity*. In 1976, 45.3 percent of all married women were in the labor force. Most of these women were working in order to supplement their husbands' earnings and provide for adequate family support. This was particularly the case for minority women, whose families are, as we saw earlier, disproportionately represented in low-income categories. Among women who were widowed, divorced, or separated from their mates, 40.5 percent were in the labor force. Most of them had no choice but to become breadwinners for themselves and their families. Finally, 61 percent of all single women were in the labor force; they needed some means of self-support or had to contribute to their families' earnings. Thus, the beliefs that American women are not serious participants in the labor force and that they work primarily for "pin money" are clearly erroneous. The labor performed by women outside the household makes a significant contribution to our capitalist economy.

Nor has having children blocked millions of women from seeking work,

---

[7]Statistics in this section are from U.S. Department of Commerce, Bureau of the Census, *A Statistical Portrait of Women in the U.S.* (Washington, D.C.: U.S. Government Printing Office, 1976); U.S. Department of Labor, Women's Bureau, *Handbook on Women Workers, 1975* (Washington, D.C.: U.S. Government Printing Office, 1976); and issues of *Employment and Earnings* and *Monthly Labor Review* (periodicals published by the federal government).

despite the responsibilities of motherhood. Most working mothers have had families still living at home. In early 1976, almost 12 million married women with children under eighteen were either working or looking for jobs. It seems silly to argue about whether mothers should be in the labor force—for they are there. Almost 30 million children, roughly 48 percent of those under eighteen, had mothers in the labor force by early 1977; the majority of such mothers were working full-time. The number of mothers employed would probably be higher if many women did not feel guilty about leaving the home (because they have internalized the biology-is-destiny ideology), if there were more employment opportunities for women, and if adequate and inexpensive child-care facilities were more widely available. The latter two factors particularly hamper women who are heads of households, forcing reluctant dependence on poverty-level public welfare programs.

A number of forces promise to propel more and more women into the search for employment in future years. Women are marrying later, so it seems likely that a higher percentage of single women will be looking for means of support. More effective means of contraception and the conscious limitation of family size mean that a higher percentage of married women will find it possible to break away from home and/or extend their stay in the labor force. Since divorce and separation rates have continued to rise in recent years, and since women, on the average, outlive men, an increasing percentage of women will find themselves living without a mate at some period during adult life. Many will require employment in order to sustain themselves and their children. In sum, women's involvement in the American labor force is not only here to stay; it can be expected to grow—despite the ideology that woman's place is in the home.

Earnings and Job Opportunities

By 1977 over 90 million persons were in the American labor force, some 40 percent of whom were women. What do women receive in return for their labor? By all indications, they get much less in return than do men.

We can, for example, examine the median annual incomes of full-time, year-round workers. When workers' incomes are broken down in accordance with sex, we find that women, on the average, earn only $3 for every $5 earned by men. This huge gap between the median earnings of full-time male and female workers has actually been *growing* since World War II (see Figure 5.1). Thus, at the same time women's participation in the labor force has been on the increase—primarily out of economic necessity—their economic standing has been eroding.

A further indication of the vast discrepancy between the earnings of the sexes arises if we group full-time workers by earning levels. In 1975, 43 percent of women workers earned less than $7000 for their year's

Figure 5.1. The Earnings Gap Between Men and Women

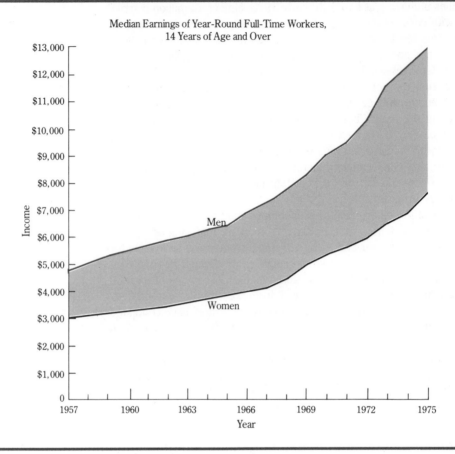

Median Earnings of Year-Round Full-Time Workers,
14 Years of Age and Over

Sources: U.S. Department of Labor, Women's Bureau, *Handbook on Women Workers, 1975* (Washington, D.C.: U.S. Government Printing Office, 1976), p. 129; U.S. Department of Commerce, Bureau of the Census, *A Statistical Portrait of Women in the U.S.* (Washington, D.C.: U.S. Government Printing Office, 1976), p. 47; and Anne McDougall Young, "Year-Round Fulltime Earnings in 1975," *Monthly Labor Review*, 100 (June 1977): 36.

labor, as compared with less than 12 percent of men. Women work, but they get little in return.

For the most part the low incomes of women are a result of the *types* of positions women hold. U.S. Labor Department statistics regularly show that women are grossly overrepresented in low-status, low-paying jobs—for example, clerical work and service occupations (see Figure 5.2). In 1975, for example, 55 percent of all full-time women workers were in jobs with the lowest median earnings. Conversely, women are underrepresented in the better-paying occupations. In 1977 only 20 percent of employed women held technical and professional jobs.

Even within the broad occupational categories, women receive less in return for their labor than do men. In 1975 the income of full-time female professional and technical workers averaged $10,500, two thirds that of the income of similarly employed males. The gap was even larger in other occupational categories. This seems to suggest that within such broad categories women hold less responsible positions than men and/or that even when both hold similar jobs there is not equal pay for equal work.

The situation of female sociologists is a case in point. One study examined sociology departments that offered graduate degrees. In these departments, women made up only 5 percent of the full professors (the highest academic rank) on the faculty. By contrast, 59 percent of the instructors and lecturers (the lowest academic ranks) were women.[8] Since rank is directly linked to income, the median income of female sociologists is much lower than that of their male colleagues.

The high concentration of women workers in low-paying and often menial positions and the gap between their earnings and that of men holding similar jobs are not consequences of female biology. Clearly, not all women in the United States perform menial work at discriminatory wages. And in other countries women are far better represented in so-called men's occupations. Nor can these matters simply be attributed to differences in the educational attainments of women as compared with men. For it seems that women in the labor force have, as a group, completed approximately the same number of years of schooling as men.

The disadvantaged position of women workers can only be explained in terms of institutional sexism. Women are the losers in a labor market that is divided along sex lines. Employers—for the most part men—have taken advantage of the biology-is-destiny ideology, treating women differently than men. Direct discrimination in employment, promotion, and pay works to keep women down, often despite their capabilities. According to the President's Task Force on Women's Rights and Responsibilities: "Sex bias takes a greater economic toll than racial bias. . . . Women with some college education, both white and Black, earn less than Black men with eight years of education."[9] There is no need to get into the useless argument over which hurts worse, racism or sexism. Both harm people, economically and in other ways.

Forces Favoring Economic Subordination

The inferior economic position of women workers is obviously not to their advantage. On first glance, however, it appears to work to the advantage of men in the labor force. The direct employment discrimination that channels women into low-status, low-paying jobs and/or re-

[8]Helen MacGill Hughes, ed., *The Status of Women in Sociology* (Washington, D.C.: American Sociological Association, 1973), p. 31.

[9]President's Task Force on Women's Rights and Responsibilities, *A Matter of Simple Justice* (Washington, D.C.: U.S. Government Printing Office, 1970), p. 18.

Figure 5.2.   Employment in Different Occupational Groups, by Sex

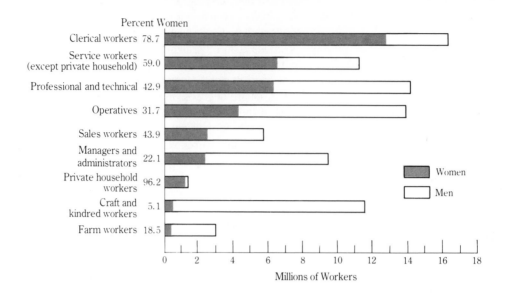

Source: *Employment and Earnings,* 24 (November 1977): 34.

stricts their job mobility also lessens the competition men face for the better positions. In the absence of unlimited occupational opportunities (an absence exacerbated in periods of economic slowdown), there simply is not room for all at the top.

But it is more likely that men are hurt by institutional sexism in the world of work.[10] For example, discrimination against married women with children reduces family income potential and sustains the pressures on men to achieve economically. In this situation, men are certainly not benefiting from the continuation of sexist employment practices. Neither do they benefit when they must pay their divorced wives child support and/or alimony because the wives cannot earn enough to support themselves and their children. Such payments are a source of economic hardship for many men.

The presence of a large pool of low-paid women who could replace men for cheaper wages acts as a depressant on men's wages. Male workers are aware that they are not totally indispensable; if they are threatened with displacement by women who—out of financial need—are willing to work for less, they must temper their own wage demands. In addition, men who enter occupations presently dominated by women—e.g., nursing, secretarial work, elementary school teaching—are likely to find

[10]See Kirsten Amundsen, *The Silenced Majority,* pp. 55–61.

themselves forced to accept the going rates for women's work. Thus, while on one level men generally enjoy benefits from restricted job competition and the subordination of women within the labor market, on another level they must pay the price for sexist practices.

But some men do benefit in this situation. By channeling women into certain types of jobs, restricting their mobility, and keeping their pay low, employers can keep their labor costs down. Insofar as the costs of labor can be kept down, profits are enhanced. Since profit is the key objective requirement of economic institutions operating within America's capitalist economy, the exploitation of women's labor (like that of other minorities) cannot simply be ended without disrupting many businesses and industries. Employers thus have a positive incentive—aside from whatever feelings they may have about women—to perpetuate sexist practices.

The fact that so many women work out of necessity also plays into the hands of employers. In the absence of full-time work opportunities and/or because they must care for their children, millions of women must take

Though the occupation of registered nurse requires considerable training and skill, and though it has a great deal of importance to our society, nursing carries relatively low wages and relatively little prestige. This is a result of the belief that nursing is "women's work." Women have generally been forced to compete against one another in the handful of job categories open to them, and wages for these occupations have generally remained low.

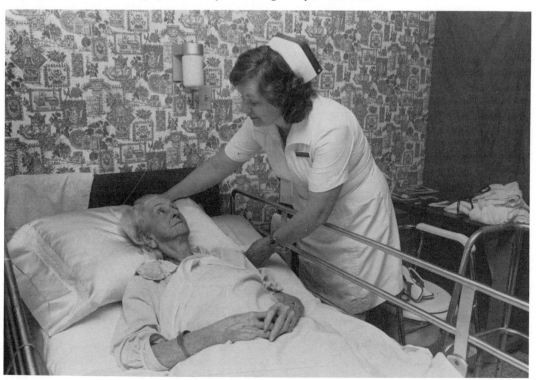

part-time jobs. This means being dependent on periodic, temporary, and often seasonal jobs, for which it is too costly to maintain a ready reserve of full-time workers. In hiring women on a part-time basis, employers save money on such employee benefits as vacation pay, sick pay, and pension plans that full-time workers expect almost as a matter of right. They are thus able to exploit the fact that women comprise a large reserve labor pool, to be drawn upon at will and sent home when not needed.

In sum, institutional sexism in the labor market is an important force sustaining the success of our economy. As we have seen in past chapters, the benefits of this economy are appropriated to a disproportionate degree by the dominant economic class—primarily those who own and control business and industry. Sexism, then, harms women and has dubious advantages even for most male workers. But it is profitable to the dominant few, who are an important obstacle to its elimination.

Laboring in the Home

Though married women have been entering the labor force at an increasing rate in recent years, about 43 million, or 55 percent, still remain at home during the work week. In some cases, women prefer not to work, believing that a woman's place is in the home. But many of the millions of women who call themselves "just a housewife" do not do so out of preference.

We are all familiar with the television version of being a housewife. TV commercials typically show young, fresh-faced, fashionably dressed starlets exuding enthusiasm over a product that has perfected the already immaculate state of their beautifully decorated homes. Mothers are shown in total control of their well-behaved, healthy children, blissfully enjoying their biological mission and accomplishing light tasks with playful ease (and the occasional help of a quick-acting drug). The imagery tells us that work is really something that takes place outside the home.

What this imagery ignores is the labor entailed in housework and its unrecognized value to the American economy.[11] We can get a good idea of what is involved by imagining how much a husband would have to pay persons to perform the tasks that a wife and mother does for free. He would probably have to hire a cook, a cleaning person, a chauffeur, and a baby-sitter or other child-care worker. He might require the services of a nurse, a psychologist, or an accountant. This husband would quickly find that his take-home wages were rapidly depleted when payday came for all his employees. He would have to conclude that his wife's work has monetary value when someone other than a wife does it.

[11]Margaret Benston, "The Political Economy of Women's Liberation," *Monthly Review* (September 1969): 4, 13–27.

Domestic and child-care workers get paid for such tasks because, contrary to television imagery, they are not much fun. Most persons do not dream of being domestics—and for good reason. In the labor market, household workers are of low social status and receive the minimal economic rewards associated with the performance of "dirty work."

Husbands who do not think of housework as a form of labor usually change their minds when, for some unexpected reason, they must temporarily take over the "little woman's" role. For it is not that housewives do not work. Rather, they labor *outside* the mainstream economy within which work is defined as an activity you are paid to do. Women who call themselves "just a housewife" implicitly recognize the secondary importance attributed to their labor.

In essence, housewives are contributing unpaid labor to the economy. This unpaid labor is a boon to employers. In its absence, husbands would be forced to demand far higher wages than they presently receive in order to pay for housekeeping and child-care services. They would have to take more time off work, and they would be unable to work overtime. They would be unable to travel frequently, if their jobs demanded travel. So long as wives perform household and child-care tasks for free, employers directly benefit. By maintaining that housewives do not really perform useful work, and certainly not work that deserves wages, employers effectively get *two* employees for the price of one. Should housewives demand wages for the work that allows business and industry to have their husbands each day, the pursuit of profit would be seriously undercut. Again, economic success is sustained by women's separate and unequal status, a status celebrated by the biology-is-destiny ideology.

The Consumer Role

It has been estimated that women are responsible for 75 percent of consumer expenditures annually. Business and industry recognize this and gear billions of dollars in investments toward the production of commodities it is hoped women will buy. Commercial advertising is used to stimulate and elicit consumption, to convince women that they and/or their households simply cannot do without "Product Z."[12] Whether women really need these commodities, or if instead they are being manipulated into wanting them, is not a concern of business and industry. No matter what the reason, business and industry profit when commodities sell.

Sales appeals to women take place on two levels: subtle attacks on their sense of personal adequacy and messages designed to suggest ways

[12]See Lucy Komisar, "The Image of Women in Advertising," in *Woman in Sexist Society,* Gornick and Moran, eds., pp. 304–17. See also Alice Embree, "Media Images I: Madison Avenue Brainwashing—the Facts," in *Sisterhood Is Powerful,* Robin Morgan, ed. (New York: Vintage Books, 1970), pp. 175–91.

to relieve the burdens of housework and further adorn the home. The appeals tend to be written by men and to play upon the roles allocated to women by the biology-is-destiny ideology.

Attacks on women's sense of personal adequacy revolve around the idealization of the role of sex object. Advertisers encourage women to worry about their skin, eyes, lips, hair, weight, shape, clothing, and odor. Commercial appeals both create and exploit women's doubts and fears regarding loss of sexual attractiveness. Simultaneously, manufacturers and advertisers provide solutions to the anxieties to which they contribute: purchase more beauty aids and appliances, clothing, rejuvenating drugs, diet foods. Immense profits ride on the comparisons women make between themselves and other women. For the woman who sees herself as "just a housewife" or who is functioning as a near-robot in the labor force, consumption promises a way to gain a sense of self-worth and identity—at least she can try to emulate commercial standards of sexual attractiveness. If women were to discard such concerns and ignore commercial appeals, a whole sector of the economy would be disrupted.

The dissatisfactions caused by the burdens of housework provide another basis for consumption in the interests of private profit. By promoting doubts about the adequacy and efficiency of products and appliances currently in use and by singing the glories of new home commodities, advertisers take advantage of the wish to reduce housekeeping time and effort. They also push the idea that "other people do not live like you do" ("Whose wash is whiter?"), suggesting that women can gain self-esteem through improved performance of household labor or the purchase of home adornments that everyone supposedly has.

Advertising does not itself create roles for women. Rather, it serves to reinforce stereotyped sex roles and to then take advantage of the roles. Women are not the only targets of sexist advertising. The "macho" appeals to purchase "men's products" both promote and exploit male chauvinism. Such products are often sold by using women as sex objects to capture attention, implying to men that they can overcome doubts about their sex-role performance through acts of consumption.

THE POLITICAL EFFECTS OF SEXISM

The exploitation of women at work and at home, wherein they are cast into separate and unequal sex roles, is closely linked with women's collective exclusion from political power. We have seen in past chapters that political power is associated with wealth and economic influence and with being white. In this section we shall see that political power is also associated with being male.

Women and Law

The American legal system only peripherally recognizes women's economic plight and their rights as citizens. A case in point is the Civil Rights Act of 1964. This piece of federal legislation was introduced into Congress in order to put the approval of the national government behind efforts to end discrimination against persons on the basis of race. Before the act was passed, a Congressman who hoped to sabotage the bill jokingly added the word *sex.*[13] His effort to defeat the bill by making it ludicrous failed, and the provision against discrimination on the basis of sex became law. That a bill pertaining to civil rights should almost *accidentally* include women is an indication of how little lawmakers cared about the status of women even as late as the mid-1960s.

The difficulties women face in gaining legal recognition of their rights through the political system are most obvious in the efforts to add the Equal Rights Amendment (ERA) to the U.S. Constitution. The Fourteenth Amendment to the Constitution has long guaranteed all American citizens—regardless of race, creed, or color—equal rights under the law (the extension of these rights in practice is another question). But the Constitution does not protect persons who are treated differently under the law just because of their sex group membership. After fifty years of effort by women's rights groups, ERA was finally proposed by Congress in 1972. In order to become law, it must be ratified by thirty-eight states by 1979. Organized resistance to ERA has been widespread, and ratification by the required number of states has been slow in coming. Quite a few women are against ERA, fearing that it means an end to alimony and the start of drafting women in times of war. As of this writing, the U.S. Constitution guarantees equal rights under the law to all Americans, so long as they are male.

Laws that specify different treatment for men and women remain in force in states and localities across the country. Many of these laws deal with employment and allegedly exist as forms of protective legislation—e.g., there are laws restricting the hours and working conditions for women. Such laws contribute to the economic subordination of women discussed in the previous section.

In the last few years, two topics directly affecting women's legal rights have generated a great deal of discussion—rape and wife battering. Both involve the infliction of physical and psychological damage upon women, as men seek to demonstrate power over them in the rawest terms. Legal obstacles with sexist overtones often make it difficult for women to prove they were raped—men usually claim women invited and/or willingly participated in the sex acts in question. The law also provides little protection to a woman who is physically abused by her husband, short of placing

[13]Caroline Bird, *Born Female* (New York: Pocket Books, 1969), Chapter 1.

Because existing laws and court orders have made it possible for some women to enter occupational fields that have long been reserved for men, many Americans believe that economic discrimination against women no longer exists. But the presence of a small number of female air controllers, corporate executives, and truck drivers, among others, does not change the fact that inequitable laws and sexist employment practices are still the norm in many fields.

the husband in jail and thus eliminating the family's means of economic survival. The inability of women to count on legal protections against such treatment stands as yet another indication of their collective powerlessness.

Political Participation

The failure of this society's legal system to fully protect women from discrimination and the excruciatingly slow enforcement of the antidiscrimination legislation that does exist are consequences of institutional sexism in the political system.[14] We need only examine the composition of key political institutions to see one reason why the momentum of sexism continues.

On the federal level women fare poorly in terms of representation in those institutional positions through which the collective interests of women could be pursued. There has never been a woman president, nor

[14]An excellent discussion of the political powerlessness of women on all levels is found in Amundsen, *The Silenced Majority,* pp. 62–86. See also Center for the American Woman and Politics, Rutgers University, ed., *Women in Public Office* (New York: R. R. Bowker Company, 1976), for recent statistics.

have the Democratic and Republican parties ever seriously considered a female candidate. The vice-presidency has also steadfastly remained a male post. Throughout American history, only a handful of women have been appointed to cabinet-level positions. No woman has ever served on the U.S. Supreme Court, nor has a woman ever been nominated.

In the House and Senate women are grossly underrepresented in terms of their proportion of the American population. In 1976, there were no women senators and only nineteen women representatives. The few women who manage to get elected to Congress find themselves handicapped by the informal "male locker-room" nature of legislative wheeling and dealing, from which they are easily excluded. Most women in Congress have served relatively short terms (many temporarily replacing husbands who died in office); their lack of seniority has blocked them from attaining such powerful positions as heading important committees.

At the lower levels of the federal government, the picture remains similar to that of racial and cultural minorities. Both in appointed offices and high-level, career civil service posts, women are most notable for their absence. As might be expected, they are more than fully represented in the lowest employment positions.

One cannot expect a male-dominated federal government, which *itself* appoints, hires, and advances men over women, to be deeply concerned about women's social and economic position in the society at large. The exclusion of women from central positions in the national political system renders them the weaker sex when it comes to having their concerns taken seriously and acted upon.

The conspicuous absence of women continues to evidence itself on the state level. Only five women have ever been governors. Three of the five succeeded their husbands, and thus did not gain the post solely in recognition of their own merits. When Ella T. Grasso was elected governor of Connecticut in 1974 and Dixy Lee Ray became governor of Washington shortly thereafter, these unusual events drew national and even international attention. Today women hold less important elective and appointed posts in state executive branches, but nowhere near their representation in the population. The same can be said with regard to state legislatures and judicial bodies. In 1975 women made up only 4.5 percent of state senators and 9.3 percent of state representatives. But when there is typing to be done, there are plenty of women in evidence.

Finally, on the local level, the political presence of women improves somewhat. While, as of 1975, only 4.4 percent of the nation's mayors were female and female representation in local legislative bodies was akin to that on the state level, some posts have been "reserved" for women. For the most part, these are the poorly paid or volunteer positions on local boards deemed "appropriate" for women and found unattractive by many men.

But women do vote; the right was extended to them in 1920, after a long battle. Unfortunately, women are still not using the franchise to the fullest possible degree. Indeed, only in the last few years has the percentage of eligible women voting become similar to that of men.

Racial minorities and the poor tend to view politics as being dominated by the white and affluent (a realistic assessment); thus many have avoided political activity, including voting. In a somewhat parallel vein, women have been encouraged to view politics as part of man's world, and many have restricted or narrowed the range of their involvement in it. But given the fact that women make up 53 percent of the voting population, the possibility of their making some impact through electoral power far exceeds that of other minority groups. It remains to be seen whether women can successfully mobilize this power by putting forth and electing candidates for office who will be more responsive to women's needs—particularly at the national level.

THE WOMEN'S MOVEMENT

With the development of the women's movement, women's economic and political subordination has come under attack. Earlier in this chapter, we saw some of the reasons why this attack has been so long in coming. Women have tended to see themselves as separate and unequal. Attainment of economic and political equality with men requires the mobilization of personality traits and behaviors that girls have been taught are unwomanly. Women have, in effect, been participants in their own oppression. But in the last decade, under the stimulus of the women's movement, sex-role differentials have begun to be questioned by increasing numbers of women.

The Development of the Women's Movement

Viewed historically, there have really been two women's movements in the United States.[15] The first movement essentially entailed a seventy-year struggle for the right of women to vote, culminating in 1920 with the passage of the Nineteenth Amendment to the Constitution. The women who led that protracted struggle often differed over other issues concerning women's place in a male-dominated society, including the treatment of women within the institution of marriage and within the world of employment. The one issue they were able to coalesce around and agree on was the desirability of women's suffrage. Once the vote was won, this first manifestation of collective political activism among women died off, leaving a period of quietude that lasted all the way up to the mid-1960s. The contemporary women's movement, of which we shall take note

[15]See Eleanor Flexner, *Century of Struggle* (New York: Atheneum Publishers, 1973); and Shulamith Firestone, *The Dialectic of Sex* (New York: William Morrow & Co., Inc., 1970), pp. 16–45.

here, took up an agenda of issues that had been left unresolved in the past.

Analyses of the contemporary women's movement often start by pointing to the stresses that educated, middle-class women had begun to experience by the 1960s. Increasing numbers of women had been going on for higher education in the post-World War II period, but either ended up becoming housewives or taking low-level positions because they were barred from access to men's jobs. Whether at home or at work, women found themselves limited by male dominance—a situation they were expected to endure.

Events in the 1960s helped transform the generalized discontent of many women into overt forms of political expression. In the opening years of the decade, female college students became involved in the civil rights movement, the student movement, and other political change activities. In spite of their energetic contributions, female political activists found themselves routinely relegated to subordinate roles in male-dominated organizations. By the mid-1960s, many movement women had been struck by the irony: here they were participating in struggles for minority civil rights and societal changes that were intended to better the life chances of others, while the conditions under which America's women were forced to suffer were being ignored. Female activists bridled under the gap between the progressive political rhetoric espoused by their male cohorts and the indifference of movement men to their own sexism.

The resentments of politically active women were given impetus by the emergence of a new organization, one primarily aimed at advancing the interests of educated, middle-class professionals. The National Organization for Women (NOW), founded in 1966, became instrumental in focusing nationwide attention on the subject of sexist discrimination. NOW became, if not the voice of a women's movement, a key consciousness raiser of political issues with which women could easily identify.

From the mid-1960s onward, the women's movement has consisted of a wide assortment of groups, ranging from NOW to entirely localized women's organizations. All share common concerns with regard to the treatment of women in American society. But beyond this, such groups reflect a wide spectrum of political perspectives as to just what women should be seeking.

Issues and Goals

In some ways, the term *women's movement* is a misnomer, for there is not one unified movement—rather, there are several.[16] Just as other minorities who have struggled in recent years to fashion goals and strategies for change have often split into different factions, so it is with women.

[16]See Jo Freeman, "The Origins of the Women's Liberation Movement," *American Journal of Sociology,* 78 (January 1973); 792–811. See also Firestone, *The Dialectic of Sex,* pp. 32–40.

The women's rights faction of the contemporary women's movement has combined the techniques of protest marches and demonstrations with political lobbying, legal battles, and educational campaigns in their efforts to awaken people's consciousness and to improve the economic and political situation of women.

There is, first, the *women's rights faction,* perhaps best represented by such organizations as the National Organization for Women. NOW is a predominantly white, middle-class group whose goals revolve around increasing the participation of all women in economic and political life. The focus is on integrating women into existing institutions and opening up more opportunities in education and employment. The women's rights faction accepts the prevailing societal order, but seeks an end to discrimination against women within it. The strategists of NOW, for example, have concentrated their resources on political lobbying, legal battles against discrimination, and educational campaigns to awaken women's and men's consciousness and gain public support.

The *radical feminists* comprise another, much smaller, faction of the women's movement. Here one may identify two distinct groups that see the need for far-reaching changes. The first group consists of women who define men as a collective "enemy" and seek liberation from all roles associated with male dominance. Marriage is considered a particularly oppressive social arrangement for women, placing debilitating restrictions on their potential for human self-realization. Thus one goal of many radical feminists is the redefinition of the meaning of "family," making it possible for women to freely enter into relationships with other adults and children on their own terms. The emphasis is on the conscious creation of new roles by and for women—rather than acquiescence to those imposed by and in the interests of men.

A second group of radical feminists has analyzed American capitalism, not men, as the enemy to be fought. Both women and men are viewed as victims of an economic system that exploits the labor of both sexes and that serves only the interests of the ownership class. From this perspective, to seek integration into the prevailing order is to accept and strengthen an economic system that deserves to be abolished; to see men as the enemy is to divert energies in the wrong direction. Thus, the goal of this group is to call the entire capitalist political economy into question, exposing its faults and encouraging men and women to join in the struggle for a socialist alternative. This goal flows out of the belief that sexism is an integral part of capitalism—in other words, that sexism is a requirement of a society in which those holding power put profit interests before the needs of people. This being the case, sexism cannot be abolished within the prevailing order nor can women truly be liberated within its confines.

The very existence of these factions within the women's movement points out a number of deeply felt concerns among a growing proportion of America's female population. Women are reacting to a sense of economic, political, legal, and social exclusion. Many are highly dissatisfied with present male-female and family relationships, within which women have been made to play separate and unequal roles. And there is a concern with the direction of American society as a whole, a society to which both sexes contribute but from which neither seems to receive full human satisfaction. All told, the women's movement has raised issues that bear on the future roles and well-being of all adults and children—male and female.

The Gains of the Movement

Institutional sexism—the systematic subordination of persons on the basis of their sex—simultaneously has been sustained by and has helped sustain the ideology that biology is destiny. The social, economic, and political disadvantages women face in comparison to men are only beginning to be addressed, and the ideology has only begun to lose its power.

The women's movement has made some notable gains. It has succeeded in making millions of people conscious of sexist ideas and practices. More and more women have become sensitized to the harm done them in a sexist society and have been objecting to the sex-delineated roles in which they have traditionally been placed. Partly as a consequence, male-female relations—both outside of and within marriage—have begun to change. To some extent, socialization practices in the home and in school have begun to reflect this new consciousness of sexism. Finally, the women's movement has produced an ongoing struggle against sexism in the world of work and in the mass media.

But the forces that continue to promote sexism are impressive, and there is some question as to just how much change the existing women's movement can bring about. This question is particularly relevant with regard to the position of women in the economy, within which sexist practices thrive under the incentive of the pursuit of profit. Insofar as concentrated economic power is crucial to the exercise of political power at the national level, the subordinate position of women in the economy is a major political handicap—just as it is for racial minorities.

In response to the women's movement, women may well have gained increased verbal support of their rights. But this is not the same as granting an end to their collective subordination. Again, the struggle of racial minorities is instructive: laws and constitutional amendments have done little more than legitimate their right to struggle for improved life chances; they have not granted such groups control *over* their life chances.

Once more we return to the variable of power. Insofar as economic and political power continue to be concentrated in the hands of a few; insofar as women's separate and unequal position serves, for example, profit interests; and insofar as women are unable to conquer those who benefit from their disadvantage—the movement to eliminate sexism from American society is unlikely to go very much further than it now has.

But unlike the civil rights movement, the women's movement has not yet withered away, even though its limited successes are far outweighed by the continuing presence of institutional sexism and male chauvinism. Since women comprise over half the American population, there remains a large pool of uninitiated recruits available to become future movement activists. And because the women's movement embraces a lengthy agenda of issues, it maintains the potential of offering an outlet for the expression of grievances by women from all walks of life.

The Question of Men's Liberation

Criticisms of male chauvinism and institutional sexism have also, if somewhat belatedly, brought a number of men to question their own sex-related roles.[17] According to the biology-is-destiny ideology, men are supposed to be aggressive, competitive, achievement-oriented, and decisive. They are expected to hide their emotions in favor of an impression of strength and toughness. As we have seen, socialization in the family and in school tends to encourage the development of personality traits and behavioral orientations appropriate to the male sex role.

But, despite the opportunities and benefits that accrue to men in a sexist society, the role-playing expected of them can be highly demanding. Not all men are equally capable of fulfilling the demands; not all men feel comfortable when playing the role. The responsibilities associated with "manhood" can be a source of stress, and many men feel doubts

[17]See Herb Goldberg, *The Hazards of Being Male* (New York: Signet, 1976).

about their adequacy as lovers and providers. The requirement that they bottle up their fears, anxieties, and emotionality means that the tensions accompanying the male sex role may be difficult to dissipate.

Hence, while some men may find themselves threatened by the changing consciousness and more positive self-concepts being promoted by the women's movement, others would no doubt be relieved to give up acting out the pretense of male superiority. More equalitarian interpersonal relationships, in which both sexes share in confronting the problems of living in American society, should ideally *reduce* the burdens of being a man—not increase them.

Hopes for the Future

Any approach to the elimination of sexism in America must be multifaceted. Not only must more women get involved in attacking sexism, men must also join the battle, if only to reduce the costs that sexism exacts from them.

Though experts disagree over whether American men are sharing household chores more than in the past, all agree that women still carry the major responsibility for cleaning, cooking, shopping, and child care. The problem of household responsibility promises to become a major issue in the future, as more women hold full-time jobs outside the home and come to resent bearing the entire burden of housework.

The economic disadvantages suffered by women still remain to be aggressively addressed. Women, along with racial minorities, have historically made their greatest gains in the work force during periods of labor shortage (unfortunately, this has tended to be during times of war). Revamping the American economy through governmental strategies to expand nonhousehold job opportunities is imperative. Expanding job opportunities would also mean a reduction of men's fear of competition as more and more women enter the workplace.

Accompanying these expanded opportunities must be an expansion of the availability of low-cost child-care facilities. Critics have argued that access to such facilities would contribute to family breakup by encouraging women to abdicate their motherly responsibilities. This is nonsense. Family well-being is more likely to be threatened by the inability of women to make use of child-care facilities so that they can help relieve economic burdens facing their families or so that they can escape the monotony of housework. Moreover, the lack of child-care facilities places an enormous burden on women who are already heads of broken households and who must either work or live in poverty on welfare assistance.

The contribution of those women who must or wish to remain in the home must be recognized—in a more material way than simply celebrating Mother's Day once a year. It would not be unreasonable to alter the tax structure to provide annual family allowances to women, based perhaps on the full-time versus part-time nature of women's household responsibilities and the number of persons being cared for. It has recently been proposed that we recognize housework as an occupation for the purpose of bringing women who are laboring in the home into America's social security system. This alone would be a major step toward recognizing housewives' economic contributions. It would also help women of advanced age who cannot live on the benefits accrued by their husbands.

Expanding job opportunities and child-care facilities will not automatically end discrimination against women in the labor force. As with other minorities, a much more aggressive attack on discrimination and exploitation is required. At the national level, the U.S. Equal Employment Opportunities Commission has the responsibility for handling complaints from around the country from both women and nonwhites. The resources allocated to this commission are so meager that aggrieved persons may have to wait *years* before any actions are taken. There are also heavy backlogs of cases in state equal employment commissions. There is no point in having antidiscrimination laws if they are not going to be enforced quickly and effectively. The current situation ultimately discourages women, since those suffering discrimination may assume that little good is likely to come from complaining about it.

The foregoing economic questions are clearly political ones as well, and it is thus important for more women and men to press for greater representation of women in America's political institutions. For starters, pressure must be placed on federal and state governments to practice what they preach and to ensure that women are appointed to top-level decision-making positions. More tax money (increasingly provided through women's labor force participation) must be allocated to programs for the improvement of the status of women. Over half the American population is female, and women's collective disadvantage is surely significant enough to justify the allocation of such resources.

The relatively few women who run for public office at the state and national levels often seem hesitant to stress the issue of sexism in their campaigns. Thus, an important opportunity to generate discussion and further educate the public is being missed. In the long run, underplaying what must be done by and for women contributes to the maintenance of institutional sexism. More discussion of the issue of sexism could also help persuade male candidates and incumbent politicians to take a more positive stand on women's rights.

America's schools and colleges are an important source of knowledge about and attitudes toward sexism. Though more and more children and youth are being taught that biology is not destiny, students are not being taught how to struggle against sexism. Schools could be part of the women's movement, but they are not. Struggling to make them so will, at the very least, rejuvenate and stimulate discussion of sexism—a prerequisite to change.

SUMMARY

While women are a majority in numbers, they are a minority group due to their social, economic, and political disadvantage in comparison to men. Women are victims of *sexism*—the systematic subordination of persons on the basis of their sex. Sexism is displayed on one level through *male chauvinism*. This term refers to attitudes and actions through which males display their sense of superiority over women. On another level is *institutional sexism*, wherein the subordination of women is built into societal institutions. Institutional sexism involves ongoing organizational routine in such areas as the economy, politics, and education.

Male chauvinism and institutional sexism are justified by an ideology that says that biology is destiny. This ideology holds that there are basic biological and psychological differences between the sexes which require that men and women play quite different roles in social life. Women, allegedly the weaker sex, belong in the home or performing women's work in the labor force. In order for the human species to reproduce, they must strive to fulfill the role of sex object. Despite the claims of this ideology, it is not true that differences between men and women require each to play such sex-delineated roles in social life. Sex roles vary from society to society, and role differences are largely learned rather than being biologically based.

Women's acceptance of unequal treatment and the biology-is-destiny ideology has primarily been due to traditional socialization practices. From birth, girls and boys are treated differently in the family as parents impart their own sense of what it means to be male or female. Sex-role differentiation by parents helps create personality and behavioral differences that would not otherwise exist. Parental influence is supplemented by the experience of schooling. From sports activities to curricula and textbooks, children are reminded of sex-role differences. In the classroom and in dating relationships, girls are likely to find that successful performance of the female role requires them to avoid competing with men and to see themselves as something less than men.

Institutional sexism has economic effects. More and more women have been entering the labor force. Many are married; some have children at home; others are widowed, divorced, separated, or single. Despite their labor-force participation, women earn substantially less than men. They are overrepresented in low-status, low-paying jobs. Even when they are in more desirable professional and technical positions, women earn less than men on the average. The labor market is divided along sex lines as employers take advantage of the biology-is-destiny ideology and treat women differently than men. The main beneficiaries of sexism in this case are employers, who are able to profit by keeping labor costs down.

Millions of women remain homemakers. The economic value of their labor goes largely unrecognized. In the absence of their unpaid labor, men would be forced to demand far higher wages to pay for housekeeping and child-care services and would be more restricted in their hours and work-related travel. Employers benefit from this unpaid labor, for in essence they get two workers for the price of one. Meanwhile, business and industry appeal to the spending ability of housewives (and women working outside the home as well) by stressing consumption. Sales appeals attack women's sense of personal adequacy and play on dissatisfactions imposed by the burdens of housework. Advertising reinforces stereotyped sex roles and seeks to take advantage of these roles. While such activities may be profitable, they contribute to the biology-is-destiny ideology.

Institutional sexism operates in the political system, where women are collectively excluded from positions of power. The American legal system only peripherally recognizes the economic plight of women and their rights as citizens. The composition of the political system helps account for this. At the federal level, women are grossly underrepresented in key policy-making positions—from the White House, to Congress, to the courts. The situation is similar at the state and local levels. The exclusion of women from central positions in politics renders them the weaker sex when it comes to having their concerns taken seriously and acted on.

With the development of the women's movement in the mid-1960s, women's economic and political subordination has come under attack. The women's movement has consisted of a variety of groups and factions, all concerned with the treatment of women but reflecting a range of political perspectives. The women's rights faction has sought increased participation of all women in economic and political life. Some radical feminists see men as the enemy and are concerned with liberating women from roles associated with male dominance—e.g., within marriage.

Other radical feminists hold that sexism stems from and is crucial to the operation of capitalism; they argue that men and women must struggle together for a socialist alternative.

The women's movement as a whole has made many gains, particularly in raising people's consciousness of sexism and encouraging women to struggle against social, economic, and political domination. However, its gains are far outweighed by the continuing presence of male chauvinism and institutional sexism. In recent years a number of men have also begun to question their sex-delineated roles. These roles can be highly demanding, despite the opportunities and benefits that often accrue to men in a sexist society. The responsibilities of manhood can be a source of stress. More equalitarian interpersonal relationships, in which both sexes share in confronting problems, should ideally reduce the burdens of being a man.

Both men and women stand to benefit from joining in the battle against sexism. Women's economic disadvantage must be addressed by expanding job opportunities and child-care facilities. The economic contributions of homemakers must be recognized in material terms. Employment discrimination must be more directly and aggressively attacked, and antidiscrimination laws more quickly and efficiently enforced. Pressure must be put on government to employ and appoint more women to top positions, while women and men should do more to make sexism an issue in election campaigns. Finally, schools and colleges have an important role to play. Though more and more children are being taught that biology is not destiny, they are not being taught how to struggle against sexism. It is worth making schools part of the women's movement.

DISCUSSION QUESTIONS

1. In your experience, what are the most common ways in which male chauvinism is expressed? How do you feel about being subjected to or witnessing expressions of male chauvinism?

2. Make a list of all the advantages of being male that you can think of. Make a list of all the advantages of being female. Which list is longer? Compare and discuss your lists with the lists your classmates made.

3. Two applicants—one male and one female—are equally qualified for a professional job opening. What arguments could be made for and against giving preference to the female applicant? If preference is not given, how will female underrepresentation in the professions ever be altered?

4. Should women be paid for the work they do as housewives? Why? If you think they should be paid, who should pay them, and how should the value of their labor be determined?

5. Obtain a selection of men's, women's, and general circulation magazines from your home, dorm, or library. Examine the advertisements—photographs and texts—and discuss the attitudes they project toward male and female sex roles.

6. If sexism has dubious benefits for, and may even harm, many men, why do not more men see the struggle against sexism as in their self-interests? Under what conditions could this situation change?

6 Militarism and War

None of America's resources should be devoted to military aggression and violence against other peoples of the world. Instead, our nation and others must move toward disarmament and the peaceful settlement of differences.

I n the spring of 1975 the American military officially withdrew from South Vietnam, a small peasant society located eight thousand miles away in Southeast Asia. Vietnam was reunited under a revolutionary government that the United States had failed to defeat in a decade of military action that left fifty-six thousand Americans dead and hundreds of thousands more maimed and disabled. The war in Vietnam caused unprecedented domestic political unrest. It cost American taxpayers an estimated $150 billion and created a cycle of inflation and recession in our overall economy. The devastating impact of the war on the Vietnamese will probably never be calculated in full.

Even after the United States retreated from South Vietnam, the domestic institutional forces that had sustained our military involvement remained intact. The United States government warned the world that the setback in Southeast Asia was not to be interpreted as a sign of weakness. The United States, proclaimed President Gerald Ford, would not hesitate to unleash her military power again. Ford almost immediately proved the truth of this statement by sending military forces to free the merchant ship *Mayagüez* from temporary Cambodian capture.

According to contemporary critics, the United States is a "weapons culture" and a "warfare state."[1] Retired Marine Colonel James A. Donovan has written: "America has become a militaristic and aggressive nation embodied in a vast, expensive, and burgeoning military-industrial-scientific-political combine which dominates the country and affects much of our daily life, our economy, our international status, and our foreign policies."[2] The "combine" to which Colonel Donovan refers is more popularly called America's *military-industrial complex.*[3] It is an ongoing human creation that contributes to this society's predisposition to police the world and to saturate it with the technology of violence. With the rapid proliferation of conventional and nuclear arms here and abroad, the possibility of warfare increases daily. But the military-industrial complex that produces such weaponry continues to grind on.

Why has such a dangerous situation come about? What are the domestic institutional forces that provide the momentum for American militarism? What are the critical "national interests" that must be served, protected, or extended—even in the face of contributing to the possible destruction of the human species? We will address these questions in the sections that follow.

THE MILITARY-INDUSTRIAL COMPLEX

As the Vietnam war began to escalate in 1965, Marc Pilisuk and Thomas Hayden wrote an article that asked, "Is there a military-industrial complex which prevents peace?" Their conclusion—still relevant over a decade later—was that "American society *is* a military-industrial complex."[4]

The complex is usually said to have emerged at the time of World War II.[5] It consists of several components—the uniformed military, the aerospace/defense industry, the civilian national security managers, and the U.S. Congress.

Each component of the military-industrial complex promotes and protects its own interests, while reinforcing the interests of the other components:

> Each institutional component of the military-industrial complex has plausible reasons for continuing to exist and expand. Each promotes and protects its own interests and in doing so reinforces the interests of every other. That is what a "complex" is—a set of integrated institutions that act to maximize their collective power.[6]

The uniformed military jockeys for the resources required to sustain, if not to expand, America's war-making capabilities. The aerospace/defense industry presses for a continuing flow of procurement contracts, under which it can pursue profits at low risk. The civilian national security managers champion the large military expenditures central to their definition of national security and the formulation of foreign policy. And members of Congress provide the tax dollars that keep the military-industrial complex humming, enjoying credit for the impact of this money on the economic life of their states and districts.

The Rise of the Military-Industrial Complex

Before World War II, the United States did not routinely maintain large numbers of men and women in uniform. Nor did it devote much in the way of national resources to the maintenance of massive war-making capabilities. During World War I, for example, people and matériel (equipment and supplies) were mobilized as needed. When the war had been won, the military establishment was virtually dismantled, and war industries were converted back to peacetime operations. With World War II this pattern of mobilization and postwar demilitarization was to change.

[1]Richard E. Lapp, *The Weapons Culture* (New York: W. W. Norton & Co., Inc., 1968); and Fred J. Cook, *The Warfare State* (New York: Macmillan, Inc., 1962).

[2]James A. Donovan, *Militarism, U.S.A.* (New York: Charles Scribner's Sons, 1970), p. 1.

[3]This term was made popular by President Dwight D. Eisenhower in his farewell address in 1961.

[4]Marc Pilisuk and Thomas Hayden, "Is There a Military-Industrial Complex Which Prevents Peace? Consensus and Countervailing Power in Pluralistic Society," *Journal of Social Issues,* 21 (July 1965): 67–117.

[5]The roots of the military-industrial complex actually go back much further than World War II. See Carroll W. Pursell, Jr., ed., *The Military-Industrial Complex* (New York: Harper & Row, Publishers, Inc., 1972), Introduction.

[6]Richard J. Barnet, *The Economy of Death* (New York: Atheneum Publishers, 1969), p. 59. Our analysis of the components and operation of the military-industrial complex is based largely on Barnet.

American fears of the spread of Soviet socialism resulted in political repression within the United States as well as in military buildups to "save the world from communism." Social commentators like political cartoonist Bill Mauldin felt that the hysteria over the "Soviet monster" was leading to the denial of the liberties that formed the basis of the American system.

"MAYBE IT'LL GO AWAY IF WE PUT OUT THE LIGHT."

During the Second World War, the United States became a highly efficient war machine. The American economy, which had been unable to break out of years of peacetime depression in the 1930s, boomed as a consequence of wartime production demands. Depression-level unemployment—wherein 10 million people were out of work—ceased to be a problem, given the labor requirements of industry and the uniformed military services. A sense of national purpose and unity grew in response to the challenge of achieving victory overseas. By the war's end, the United States had demonstrated a level of military power unequaled in history. It had developed and shown a willingness to use nuclear arms. And it had escaped the war intact and (unlike many of its European allies) virtually unscathed.

At the end of World War II, the war machine was not wholly dismantled. High-ranking military officers, having gained great public honor from the victory and enjoying command over an unprecedentedly huge military establishment, campaigned to keep their powers and responsibilities intact. Governmental and corporate elites feared that a full-scale military demobilization and industrial conversion would lead the United States back into an economic depression. Moreover, corporate chieftains had learned that a lot of money could be made from government contracts for military weapons, equipment, and supplies.

A further justification for maintaining a permanent war economy was simultaneously provided by the outbreak of the cold war with the Soviet Union—a war in which both nations have jockeyed for world dominance without actually using their enormous military arsenals against one another. After World War II, American elites saw the Soviet Union as constituting a political and military threat. They pointed to the spread of Soviet domination within Eastern Europe as evidence of that threat. Further, they warned that Soviet socialism posed a real danger to all governments committed to maintaining capitalist economies. When the Soviet Union demonstrated its potential as a nuclear power in the 1940s, and when mainland China moved toward building a socialist society in 1949, it seemed clear to elites that socialism could only be held in check by the threat or use of military power.

For over thirty years now, this society's military-industrial complex has continued to ride on the fears of expanding socialism. During these three decades we have witnessed American military and paramilitary (e.g., CIA) interventions across the globe and a spiraling nuclear arms race with the Soviet Union. At the same time, more and more nations, particularly those in the economically underdeveloped areas of the world, have moved toward socialist economic and political systems. It remains to be seen just how our military-industrial complex will react to the noncapitalist world in the future.

The Uniformed Military

Among the institutional components central to the military-industrial complex is the uniformed military. The United States Air Force, Army, Navy, and Marine Corps are all under the authority of a civilian-headed umbrella organization—the Department of Defense (DOD). Since World War II, the military services have developed into vast bureaucracies commanded by professional career officers who make up an *officer class*. The services receive tens of billions of dollars annually from the federal government in order to carry out their domestic and foreign operations.

They control property and weapons systems valued in the hundreds of billions, including networks of military bases and installations around the world. At a signal from the president, who is the commander in chief of the military, the civilian head of DOD can call any or all of the uniformed military into immediate action—to move people and equipment or even to obliterate whole segments of the earth's population. The duty of the uniformed military is to follow orders.

Since the Second World War, each of the military services has carved out its own roles or *missions* in defense and active warfare. Each service is constantly competing with the others for new responsibilities and resources and the "honor" of being used first in military action. Large annual budgets, new weapons systems, and increased personnel are the prizes that the officer class of each service tries to win as they all justify the strategic importance of their activities and plans. In a word, each of the services is continually striving to *sell* the notion of its flexible capabilities and indispensability.

Selling has meant working to persuade governmental civilians and the public that there are serious military dangers for which this society must be prepared.[7] Top-ranking officers pressure their civilian Department of Defense overseers and the White House to prepare budgets that will enlarge the authority and prestige of their respective services. Military personnel join DOD and White House officials in briefing Congress, which provides funds for these budgets. Interservice rivalries revolve around identifying new dangers to be guarded against, whether immediate or potential, to back up fund requests.

As a tribute to the military sales effort, Congress presently allocates billions in tax funds each year for guns, tanks, planes, bombs, missiles, ships, submarines, and communications devices for undersea and outer-space use. Additional funds go for research, development, and production of new weapons systems to enlarge America's military arsenal and to replace the obsolete. Since military threats and weapons technology alter with time, obsolescence is often underway before the new tools of warfare are finished and in place. A quarter of total annual federal expenditures (that is, well over $100 billion) go toward defense (see Figure 6.1). It has been estimated that the United States has spent over $1 trillion on the military since World War II.[8]

Since most Americans take this use of their tax dollars for granted, the uniformed military services are in a position to exploit their institutional self-interests. How many of us are expert enough to judge the importance of missions and the consequent military claims on the federal budget? How many of us can accurately assess the validity and seriousness of military dangers alleged to exist around the world? Even if we were experts, we would find it hard to get the facts, for the uniformed

[7]See J. William Fulbright, *The Pentagon Propaganda Machine* (New York: Liveright, 1970).

[8]Barnet, *The Economy of Death*, p. 5.

Figure 6.1. Federal Budget Income and Expenditures

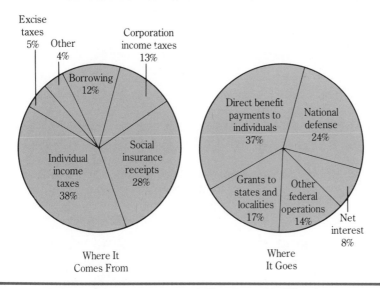

Where It
Comes From

Where
It Goes

Source: "The Budget Dollar, 1978–79," *New York Times,* January 24, 1978, p. 1.

military and its civilian overseers in the DOD and White House attempt to maintain a ring of secrecy around such matters. Even Congress finds this secrecy hard to counter.

The massive resources provided to the uniformed military allow them to wage substantial public relations campaigns. The services remind the American public of their patriotism, demonstrate some of their war-making capabilities, and allude to the nightmares that presumably make American military power deserving of support. Military speakers and seminars are made available to interested citizens' groups around the country. Community leaders are invited to tour military facilities, where they receive VIP (Very Important Person) treatment. Armed Forces Day is celebrated at military bases and installations each year, usually with displays of military hardware for the public to enjoy. Mobile informational displays on military missions and weaponry are installed in shopping centers. Tapes and films dealing with military matters are mass-produced for use by schools and citizens' organizations. Local newspapers regularly receive news releases from military press units. Civilian advertising agencies are hired to promote the virtues of military service. And DOD has cooperated with Hollywood to produce war extravaganzas that reflect well on American military prowess. In sum, millions of tax dollars are used each year to promote the uniformed military and legitimate its activities.

Some observers have claimed that the military is the key element in the military-industrial complex, which they see as a conspiracy orches-

Public Problem, Private Pain
WOUNDED IN BATTLE

Ron Kovic was born on July 4, 1946, to a highly religious and patriotic family. Throughout his childhood, Kovic and his friends played "war" and dreamed of being combat heroes. An all-around high-school athlete, he had an opportunity to try out for the New York Yankees upon graduation. But consistent with his boyhood dreams, he chose to enlist in the Marine Corps where, according to the recruiters, he would become a man and get to serve his country. In this excerpt from his autobiography, Kovic describes his last battle, which began when the Viet Cong fired at his outfit as they walked toward a South Vietnamese village. Kovic, who will spend the rest of his life in a wheelchair, became an antiwar activist shortly after returning to the United States for medical treatment and physical therapy.

I had started walking toward the village when the first bullet hit me. There was a sound like firecrackers going off all around my feet. Then a real loud crack and my leg went numb below the knee. I looked down at my foot and there was blood at the back of it. The bullet had come through the front and blew out nearly the whole of my heel.

I had been shot. The war had finally caught up with my body. I felt good inside. Finally the war was with me and I had been shot by the enemy. I was getting out of the war and I was going to be a hero. I kept firing my rifle into the tree line and boldly, with my new wound, moved closer to the village, daring them to hit me again. For a moment I felt like running back to the rear with my new million-dollar wound but I decided to keep fighting out in the open. A great surge of strength went through me as I yelled for the other men to come out from the trees and join me. I was limping now and the foot was beginning to hurt so much, I finally lay down in almost a kneeling position, still firing into the village, still unable to see anyone. I seemed to be the only one left firing a rifle. Someone came up from behind me, took off my boot and began to bandage my foot. The whole thing was incredibly stupid, we were sitting ducks, but he bandaged my foot and then he took off back into the tree line.

For a few seconds it was silent. I lay down prone and waited for the next bullet to hit me. It was only a matter of time, I thought. I wasn't retreating, I wasn't going back, I was lying right there and blasting everything I had into the pagoda. The rifle was full of sand and it was jamming. I had to pull the bolt back now each time trying to get a round into the chamber. It was impossible and I started to get up and a loud crack went off next to my right ear as a thirty-caliber slug tore through my right shoulder, blasted through my lung, and smashed my spinal cord to pieces.

I felt that everything from my chest down was completely gone. I waited to die. I threw my hands back and felt my legs still there. I couldn't feel them but they were still there. I was still alive. And for some reason I started believing, I started believing I might not die, I might make it out of there and live and feel and go back home again. I could hardly breathe and was taking short little sucks with the one lung I had left. The blood was rolling off my flak jacket from the hole in my shoulder and I couldn't feel the pain in my foot anymore, I couldn't even feel my body. I was frightened to death. I didn't think about praying, all I could feel was cheated.

All I could feel was the worthlessness of dying right here in this place at this moment for nothing.

Ron Kovic, *Born on the Fourth of July* (New York: Pocket Books, 1977), pp. 220–22.

trated by a handful of top-ranking "warlords."[9] We do not agree. Though the officers of the respective services do have personal and institutional self-interests to pursue, the uniformed military is under firm civilian control. The influence of the military within the military-industrial complex is strong, but it appears to be fed by—and feeds—other institutional components, which also have a major stake in keeping the complex going.

The Aerospace/Defense Industry

American militarism is big business.[10] The billions in tax dollars spent annually by the military establishment have been the mainstay of the permanent war economy since the 1940s. Handsome stockholder revenues for members of America's ownership class (see Chapter 1) are one result of such expenditures. In addition, the livelihood of millions of American workers has come to depend on the permanent war economy.

Each year the Department of Defense enters into contracts for the purchase and procurement of weapons, ammunition, equipment, supplies, and services. The recipients of these contracts include twenty thousand principal firms, which in turn are served by approximately a hundred thousand subcontractors. In recent years, however, the lion's share of the DOD procurement budget has gone to a mere one hundred large corporations. A number of these corporations are highly dependent on military expenditures for their continued existence. The aerospace/defense industry has, understandably, developed an outlook on military spending comparable to that of the uniformed services.

Pentagon capitalism.   The relationship between the aerospace/defense industry and the Department of Defense has been characterized as *Pentagon capitalism.*[11] Among other things, this term denotes the rather special relationship between DOD and its contractors. Doing business with DOD is quite different from operating in the civilian marketplace and selling consumer goods to the public.

Corporations that produce goods and services for the civilian marketplace often must compete for customers' attention and dollars. They must adjust their production to actual and anticipated public demand. There is a degree of risk involved in dealing with the public—there will be no profits if goods and services cannot be sold. Errors in production may

[9]See Charles C. Moskos, Jr., "The Concept of the Military-Industrial Complex: Radical Critique or Liberal Bogey?" *Social Problems,* 21 (April 1974): 498–512.

[10]See Richard F. Kaufman, *The War Profiteers* (Garden City, N.Y.: Anchor Books, 1972). The world arms trade is analyzed in Robert E. Harkavy, *The Arms Trade and International Systems* (Cambridge, Mass.: Ballinger Publishing Company, 1975); and Anthony Sampson, *The Arms Bazaar* (New York: The Viking Press, 1977).

[11]The term is Seymour Melman's in *Pentagon Capitalism* (New York: McGraw-Hill, Inc., 1970). The Pentagon is, of course, the Washington, D.C., headquarters of the Department of Defense.

The federal government currently spends over $100 billion on defense. A good part of this money goes toward sophisticated weapons systems, like this B–52 carrier plane.

prove quite costly. Such risks are taken for granted by firms that service the public, though efforts are constantly made to minimize them.

Under Pentagon capitalism, on the other hand, most procurement contracts are issued to principal contractors without requiring competition `among them. Aerospace/defense firms frequently develop their products and services in close cooperation with their military customers. The amounts to be produced are specified in advance, and the demand is guaranteed. In contrast to doing business in the civilian marketplace, production for the military establishment involves few risks and assured profits. Even if the goods and services turn out to cost more than originally anticipated (*cost overruns*), the aerospace/defense contractor can request and usually get supplemental funds. If errors in production occur, or if the time schedule for delivering goods and services cannot be observed, DOD cooperates, waits, and often shoulders any extra costs involved.

The highly dependable and lucrative nature of DOD procurement contracts—under which cost overruns, errors, waste, and assured profits are taken for granted—has made aerospace/defense firms strong backers of American militarism. The aerospace/defense industry serves its own interests by responding to the perceived needs and plans of the officer class, supporting their constant pursuit of new missions, responsibilities, and budgetary resources. On its own initiative, the industry develops products and services that might encourage the military to push for new missions not yet in existence. Under the drive for profits, the industry has engineered a community of interest with the military establishment within which each embellishes the momentum of the other.

The community of interest.   The community of interest between industry and the military has been cemented through the circulation of personnel.[12] Executives from the aerospace/defense industry have, with startling frequency, moved into important civilian positions in DOD. Top-ranking military officers, as well as lesser members of the officer class, have retired and moved into positions in the industry. In the latter case, contractors have been able to exploit the specialized knowledge and skills of former officers as well as their familiarity with people and procedures involved in procurement contracting at DOD. The circulation of military personnel to aerospace/defense corporations raises the concern that some military officers may be tempted to bestow favors on particular firms in order to ensure themselves employment upon retirement from active duty. The same potential conflict of interest exists for persons holding key civilian positions in DOD.

In a 1969 speech, Senator William Proxmire pointed out some of the issues involved in the "community of interest" that has evolved between industry and the military establishment:

> When the bulk of the budget goes for military purposes; when 100 companies get 67 percent of the defense contract dollars; when cost overruns are routine and prime military weapon system contracts normally exceed their estimates by 100 to 200 percent; when these contracts are let by negotiation and not by competitive bidding; and when the top contractors have over 2000 retired high-ranking military officers on their payrolls; there are very real questions as to how critically these matters are reviewed and how well the public interest is served.[13]

The National Security Managers

As we have seen, the military services are under civilian control within the Department of Defense. The ultimate responsibility for safeguarding national security and for formulating foreign policy outside the White House is held by executives in DOD and civilian representatives from such other agencies as the Department of State, the Atomic Energy Commission, and the Central Intelligence Agency.

---

[12]From a Congressional speech by Senator William Proxmire, March 24, 1969. Reprinted in Pursell, *The Military-Industrial Complex,* pp. 253–62.

[13]Ibid., p. 258.

Who are the people who have determined that militarism is in the interest of national security? Richard J. Barnet has attempted to identify the backgrounds and hint at the world view of America's civilian *national security managers,* the top-level civilian executives of the federal agencies mentioned above. When Barnet examined the backgrounds of ninety-one individuals who held key executive posts between 1940 and 1967, he found that seventy "were from the ranks of big business or high finance."[14] Barnet took this to mean that military policy was formulated largely on the basis of business interests:

> Defining the national interest and protecting national security are the proper province of business. . . . For a National Security Manager recruited from the world of business, there are no other important constituencies to which he feels a need to respond.[15]

But despite the fact that the national security managers generally come from the business elite, care must be taken in drawing conclusions about the role of business interests in the process of formulating policy. Nevertheless, at the very least, the fact that the national security managers are usually drawn from business constitutes another case of conflict of interest. Since massive military expenditures are the mainstay of America's permanent war economy, the national security managers recruited from big business and high finance are unlikely to tamper with the status quo. This is particularly so in that national security managers often move in and out of governmental service, using it as a means of enhancing their career chances in the business world. The potential of conflict of interest is highest in the case of executives recruited from the aerospace/defense industry, an industry to which they are likely to return.

As we shall see later, America's business community has progressively taken on multinational dimensions. Many of the economy's largest corporations have increasingly come to depend on profits generated by investments and sales abroad. A global military posture can readily be rationalized as a means of protecting American corporate interests around the world. National security managers who come from big business and high finance can be expected to be sensitive to such matters, insofar as the national interest can be equated with the well-being of the American economy.

The Militarized Congress

The uniformed military, the aerospace/defense industry, and the national security managers are the main institutional components of the military-industrial complex. But in order for this complex to exist, billions of tax dollars must be given it every year. The national security managers and

[14]Barnet, *The Economy of Death,* p. 88.
[15]Ibid., pp. 89 and 100.

the uniformed military prepare annual budget requests and justifications for proposed expenditures. These are then presented to Congress, which alone has the authority to appropriate the funds requested. As the controller of the purse strings that must be loosened for American militarism to continue unhampered, Congress has virtually become an institutional component of the complex.

In past years the United States Senate and House of Representatives have, almost without exception, responded favorably to requests for funds to support the military establishment and its procurement contracts. Periodic investigations by Congressional committees and individual senators and representatives have resulted in criticism of the costs of military procurement and errors and waste on the part of contractors. But when it comes time to vote on military budgets, most members of Congress support the high spending levels. An annual ritual in Congress involves hearings on the military budget. During these hearings a few legislators pose some harsh questions, pare some money off the requests, and end up approving most of the funds requested.

There are several reasons for Congressional support of the permanent war economy. Many members of Congress are themselves veterans and retired or reserve officers, so they identify favorably with the military as an institution. Despite their positions of responsibility, many are as uninformed as most citizens when it comes to judging national security needs, the relevance of missions, the necessity for weapons systems, and the dangers against which military power must be poised. There is thus a tendency to accept the authoritative judgments of the national security managers and top-ranking military officers.

Most members of Congress are affluent, which means that they are likely to own stock in American corporations, including aerospace/defense firms. And even if they do not, certainly many of those who provide contributions for their campaign expenses do. Hence, their stand on military budget requests may make the difference between being reelected or finding a new job, especially since DOD money is channeled into the states or districts of most members of Congress. There is obviously little political incentive to vote down military expenditures if this means the loss of bases, procurement contracts, and employment for constituents. Rather, there is even more reason to approve such expenditures.

Thus Sidney Lens, author of *The Military-Industrial Complex,* has posed this rhetorical question:

> Who can tell in this game of *quid pro quo* how many legislators vote for a weapons system they don't think is necessary in order to get a contract for their own business community, and how much pork is put into the budget by the Pentagon to lure a congressional vote?[16]

[16]Sidney Lens, *The Military-Industrial Complex* (Philadelphia: Pilgrim Press, 1970), p. 45.

In response to the "pork" (extra proposed expenditures), to lobbying efforts by the various institutional components of the military-industrial complex, and to pressures from such special interest groups as organized labor and veterans' associations, Congress goes along with the game. Only when public outrage becomes intense, as in the later stages of the Vietnam war, does Congress adjust its stance on American militarism.

PROTECTING AMERICAN ECONOMIC INTERESTS ABROAD

America's economic system has often been labeled *corporate capitalism* in recognition of the key role that large corporations have come to play within it. In *Economics and the Public Purpose,* John Kenneth Galbraith has noted that, while 12 million business enterprises operate in the United States, half of all goods and services are produced by only 1000 manufacturing, merchandising, transportation, power, and finance corporations. Moreover, within each of these areas a relative handful of corporate giants dominate. For example, 111 firms—each possessing assets of a billion dollars or more—account for well over half of American manufacturing sales and earnings.[17] The economic well-being of these large corporations is crucial to American society. To the degree they are successful in meeting their objectives of profit and growth, this society's capitalist economy avoids stagnation.

In order to grow and profit, American corporations have found it necessary to extend their activities well beyond the political boundaries of the nation. In the years since World War II, we have witnessed the growth (both in size and numbers) of multinational firms, businesses with plants and offices around the world.[18] Between 1960 and 1976, direct corporate investments in foreign nations grew from $31.9 to $137 billion. Most of this money has been channeled into the developed economies of Canada and Western Europe, where American-owned enterprises cater to markets for manufactured goods. The rest has gone to Middle East petroleum suppliers and to a number of economically underdeveloped nations in the Third World (Latin America, Africa, and Asia). For the most part, investments in the Middle East and elsewhere in the Third World have been for the purpose of obtaining natural resources to be used in production in the United States and other developed economies. Even though corporate investment dollars have primarily gone into Canada and Western Europe, the rates of return on Third World investments have proven to be higher.

[17]John Kenneth Galbraith, *Economics and the Public Purpose* (Boston: Houghton Mifflin Company, 1973), p. 43.

[18]Richard J. Barnet and Ronald Müller, *Global Reach* (New York: Simon and Schuster, Inc., 1974).

Earnings from foreign operations comprise an increasing percentage of the annual net incomes of many of America's largest firms. It seems fair to conclude that the economic health of the United States has come to depend, to a significant degree, on the multinationals' ability to penetrate the economies of other nations. In doing so, the multinationals gain access to and control over valuable raw materials, including many materials utilized by such key industries as aerospace/defense. Many of these raw materials are in short supply or would be too expensive to extract in the United States. In addition, multinational corporations are able to cultivate new markets for products manufactured in this country and in their plants abroad. And, particularly in the Third World, such firms are able to take advantage of large pools of cheap labor, thus cutting costs. The profits from such operations flow back to corporate headquarters in the United States, where they can be used to reward stockholders and/or provide a basis for further investments.

The Corporate-Governmental Partnership

The spread of American economic interests across the globe has been greatly facilitated by the federal government—or, more specifically, by the national security managers.[19] Given their background in business and finance, it is not surprising that these managers have tailored foreign policy to protect corporate operations abroad.

For example, after World War II the government financed what came to be called the Marshall Plan, a program of aid designed to help rebuild the war-torn nations of Western Europe. The Marshall Plan was initiated during the emergence of the cold war, at a time when Soviet socialism was perceived as a growing danger to Western European capitalist nations. At a cost of $13 billion, the aid program succeeded in revitalizing these nations' economies within a capitalist framework. And this revitalization provided immense investment and market opportunities for American corporations, thus helping stimulate their increased involvement abroad.

At the same time, America's national security managers entered into a military pact with these and other friendly nations, a pact calling for mutual cooperation in the event of outside aggression (e.g., by the Soviet Union). This involved the creation of the North Atlantic Treaty Organization (NATO) in 1949. Through NATO, the United States has maintained permanent military capabilities in Europe and elsewhere. This society's involvement in NATO has also served to protect American economic

[19]See Michael Tanzer, *The Sick Society* (New York: Holt, Rinehart & Winston, 1971), pp. 63–93. America's corporate-governmental partnership abroad is also stressed in Felix Greene, *The Enemy* (New York: Vintage Books, 1970); David Horowitz, *Empire and Revolution* (New York: Random House, Inc., 1969); Gabriel Kolko, *The Roots of American Foreign Policy* (Boston: Beacon Press, 1969); and Harry Magdoff, *The Age of Imperialism* (New York: Monthly Review Press, 1969).

interests and has enabled our military-industrial complex to benefit from overseas demands for men and weapons systems.

The national security managers have also provided foreign economic and military aid to many underdeveloped countries of the Third World. Economic aid has often taken the form of loans that require the recipients to purchase goods and services from American corporations. Such aid has also been used to encourage Third World nations to allow multinational corporations access to raw materials and low-wage labor.

Since the Third World has been prone to political upheaval and often to revolutionary change, corporate investments have also required protection. American military aid has enabled the governments of Third World nations to purchase military equipment produced by America's military-industrial complex. The sale of American arms and weapons systems abroad (including those to developed nations) has grown to well over $10 billion per year (see Figure 6.2). Military aid directed into Third World nations has often been designed to help governments contain internal movements for radical change—e.g., toward socialism.

Defending the World Against Socialism

As many of the examples we have discussed indicate, American militarism has often been seen as a means of protecting the world from socialism. Michael Tanzer, in *The Sick Society,* argues that the threat posed by socialism is not wholly, or even necessarily, a military one:

> Once granted that economic interests play the major role in foreign policy, then it makes a great deal of difference whether a country is . . . socialist or capitalist, even if the country is totally incapable of threatening us militarily. Each country that shifts from the capitalist world to the socialist world is a country where the United States loses valuable existing investments as well as potential outlets for profitable future investments (and possibly trade).[20]

After all, the United States has the power to destroy any nation that poses a military threat. Nor is socialism a threat to democratic freedoms and civil liberties in some of the nonsocialist societies the United States is allied with. The American government has often provided economic and military aid to harsh dictatorships, so long as they in turn have been friendly to U.S. corporate interests. Rather, the threat of socialism is largely economic. American militarism is one means by which national interests—so often equated with economic interests—can be served, protected, and extended.

Several different military strategies have been developed in the battle against socialism.[21] In the post–World War II period, when the cold war

[20]Tanzer, *The Sick Society,* p. 66.
[21]See Michael T. Klare, *War Without End* (New York: Vintage Books, 1972).

Figure 6.2. U.S. Arms Sales Agreements

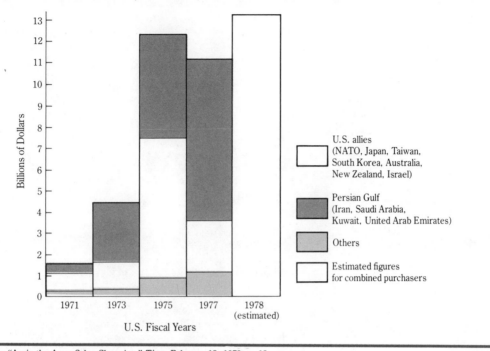

U.S. allies
(NATO, Japan, Taiwan,
South Korea, Australia,
New Zealand, Israel)

Persian Gulf
(Iran, Saudi Arabia,
Kuwait, United Arab Emirates)

Others

Estimated figures
for combined purchasers

Source: "Again the Arms Sales Champion," *Time,* February 13, 1978, p. 12.

was expected to include military aggression by the Soviet Union, the military-industrial complex came up with the means of "massive retaliation." The idea was that American nuclear arms, visibly poised for use, would act as a deterrent against Soviet military adventure. When it became known, shortly after World War II, that the Soviet Union was also developing a nuclear capability, the United States began to strengthen its military arsenal to make possible a "first strike." The idea here was that the Soviet Union would be deterred from using its weapons since the United States could put the nuclear arms to use first. The nuclear arms race has been going on ever since; and the United States and the Soviet Union have progressively escalated their respective destructive capabilities to the point where neither could survive a full-scale nuclear war. In the meantime a score of other nations, both capitalist and socialist, have proceeded to join the "nuclear club"—thereby increasing the likelihood of a future holocaust.

A second type of military strategy has been "limited warfare," the direct use of military power involving conventional, rather than nuclear, arms. American involvements in Korea in the 1950s and later in Southeast Asia were defined as limited wars against the encroachment of socialism. In both, the costs were extremely high in terms of American

Though the war in Vietnam was officially defined as a "limited war" or "police action," it cost Americans approximately $150 billion, took fifty-six thousand American lives, and left hundreds of thousands disabled. Ironically, even at this enormous cost, the American military was unable to achieve its goal of keeping South Vietnam free of socialism.

lives; but both were considered the only acceptable alternative to the use of nuclear force.

A third type of military strategy is "counterinsurgency warfare," utilizing the resources of such paramilitary agencies as the CIA.[22] Here the approach has been to combat the threats posed by socialism through secret, disruptive tactics. In 1953 the CIA organized the overthrow of the government of Iran, where American oil interests had been threatened. The following year the CIA was involved in altering the government of Guatemala, which was encroaching on American investments and hampering explorations for oil. Oil interests were also at stake in the CIA's participation in overthrowing the government of Indonesia in 1958. In the 1960s, before becoming a major participant in the war in Southeast Asia, the CIA participated in organizing the abortive Cuban Bay of Pigs invasion and has since been implicated in attempts to assassi-

[22]David Wise and Thomas B. Ross, *The Invisible Government* (New York: Bantam Books, Inc., 1964).

nate Cuban socialist leader Fidel Castro. The government of Cuba had appropriated a billion dollars worth of American corporate investments shortly after its succession to power in 1959. In 1974, the elected government of Chile, whose socialist program effected a takeover of American-owned copper production, was "destabilized" with the assistance of the CIA. Since the activities of the CIA are supposed to be secret, it is impossible to know when and where other efforts at destabilization have been attempted.

It is not always the absolute dollar value of American economic interests abroad that provokes militaristic responses to socialism. Certainly the United States had no corporate investments in South Vietnam even remotely worth the $150 billion spent on fighting socialism there. Rather, the national security managers have often feared that movements toward socialism in a given country can set an example for others. The so-called domino theory of foreign affairs—still embraced in national security circles—interprets the successful move toward socialism in one part of the world as inviting experimentation elsewhere. Socialism in South Vietnam was viewed as unacceptable, not because that country was a military threat to America or because of corporate investments there, but because of what that could mean in terms of the future of Southeast Asia as a whole. Socialism in Cuba and Chile promised similar developments in the rest of the underdeveloped nations of Latin America.

Hence, from the perspective of America's national security managers, dominoes must not be allowed to fall, because if they do, we might be economically isolated and forced to deal with other nations on less than advantageous terms. Counterinsurgency, limited warfare, and the threat of all-out nuclear annihilation—all made possible by a well-financed military-industrial complex—are used to make the world "safe" for America to do business. The irony behind using war to create peaceful business conditions is rarely questioned within American society, despite the dangers to which it gives rise.

THE EFFECTS OF MILITARISM

American militarism affects more than the nature of our relations with socialist and nonsocialist nations. It has negative influences on the civilian economy of the United States and the quality of life of citizens. It also poses the threat of bringing an end to civilization as we know it.

Military Expenditures and the Civilian Economy

Since World War II, American military, political, and economic elites have claimed that large military expenditures benefit the United States in many ways. Often such expenditures are portrayed as a positive force in promoting domestic economic health—even apart from their relationship to the protection of American corporate interests abroad. In the words of Seymour Melman, "the belief that war brings prosperity has served as a powerful organizing idea for generating and cementing a cross-society political consensus for active or tacit support of big military spending."[23] This belief is just as influential in keeping the military-industrial complex going as are external threats of socialism. But, as Melman and others have come to argue, there are a number of rarely considered negative consequences associated with big military spending. No society can maintain a permanent war economy without some adverse internal effects.[24]

It is frequently estimated that 10 percent of the American work force is, in one way or another, directly dependent on military expenditures. But the goods and services produced through these expenditures do not really serve basic needs of the American population. We cannot consume aircraft carriers, supersonic fighters, submarines, or munitions. The funds spent on maintaining and equipping people in uniform do not enhance the quality of everyday life. Moreover, the vast productive apparatus that military expenditures support—plants, equipment, tools—is isolated from civilian-oriented use. Thus a significant segment of the American economy, from people to matériel, is nonproductive in terms of public well-being.

Another effect of the permanent war economy has been the creation of firms that have little knowledge of business other than their ability to exist on tax funds. As we have seen, many aerospace/defense firms depend on continued military expenditures for their economic survival. They cannot operate successfully in the civilian marketplace, but have instead geared their products and talents toward the security provided by Pentagon capitalism. Their managerial and professional personnel have had no need to gain experience in advertising, marketing, and product planning to meet the needs of civilian consumers. Consequently, many aerospace/defense firms would find it exceedingly difficult to convert over to nonmilitary-related business.

Related to this has been the "brain drain" of technically educated workers, wherein people have been siphoned away from civilian industry into nonproductive aerospace/defense jobs. This brain drain has been encouraged by massive military expenditures that have opened up lucrative employment opportunities in the military-industrial complex. Scientific and engineering talent that could have been put to use in other settings has been usurped. According to Richard J. Barnet, "more than half the scientists and engineers in the country work directly or indirectly for the Pentagon."[25] Moreover, the skills and technical knowledge pos-

[23]Seymour Melman, *The Permanent War Economy* (New York: Simon and Schuster, Inc., 1974), p. 18.
[24]Ibid. See also Melman's *Pentagon Capitalism,* and *Our Depleted Society* (Holt, Rinehart & Winston, 1965).
[25]Barnet, *The Economy of Death,* p. 50.

sessed by many such persons are not easily transferred elsewhere. Even the nation's colleges and universities have been affected, as federal research and development funds—important sources of income for many institutions—have largely gone to meet military-related requirements.

Seymour Melman has argued that, despite the apparent prosperity of the American economy, nonwar-related industries have become progressively underdeveloped—both in terms of their productive potential and in comparison with industries in other nations (e.g., in Western Europe and Japan) that spend relatively little on militarism.[26] With so much of our labor force and productive apparatus engaged in remaining the world's number one military power, our production of peacetime goods and services has begun to suffer. Important sectors of the civilian economy are afflicted with low levels of productivity, inefficiency and the need for modernization, inability to maintain quality, and unnecessarily high production costs that inflate prices. Inflated prices then stimulate worker demands for higher wages, thereby increasing the cost of living.

One result is that the United States is finding it increasingly difficult to compete successfully with other nations in world trade. Many American-made products cannot find foreign buyers, and the United States has begun to import finished goods that formerly had been produced domestically. The United States has become more and more dependent on selling its agricultural products abroad, creating shortages and increasing food prices at home. And it has, as we have seen, become involved in selling billions of dollars worth of military weapons systems and equipment—also to help balance off the value of imported goods.[27]

The deteriorating state of domestic civilian industry has made it necessary for American corporations to invest outside this country in order to keep profits high. By opening up plants elsewhere, corporations can cut transportation and labor costs so as to render their products more competitive with those of other nations. This strategy exacerbates domestic economic problems. Corporate investments abroad mean that these dollars are not being utilized to update and improve deteriorating stateside industries. Moreover, such investments often function to ship jobs abroad, putting more Americans out of work. Finding it difficult to afford higher priced, domestically made goods, unemployed people, and many who are employed, turn to imported products. This then throws more Americans out of work.

One need not be an economic genius to understand that the foreign investments of the last thirty years have been developing a cumulative effect that is just beginning to be felt. By allocating massive societal resources to militarism, other activities that are important to our daily lives have been allowed to go into decline. Military expenditures, in

[26]Melman, *The Permanent War Economy,* pp. 74–104.

[27]See George Thayer, *The War Business* (New York: Simon and Schuster, Inc., 1969).

Seymour Melman's judgment, have "become a major source of corrosion of the productive competence of the American economy as a whole."[28]

The Quality of Life

High military expenditures have also created underdevelopment in the area of social welfare. The money allocated toward military expenditures could be used to improve the quality of life for millions. It should take only a few examples to make the point.

1. According to the President's Council on Environmental Quality, it would cost $105.2 billion to totally clean up the environment of the United States. This is about what is spent by the military establishment in one year. It is far less than was spent in Southeast Asia during the Vietnam war.
2. The Urban Coalition has estimated that hunger and malnutrition among America's poor could be eliminated at a cost of $4 to $5 billion. This is the expected final bill for the new C-5A military transport designed to move more men and equipment into military action at a faster rate than hitherto possible.
3. For approximately $3 billion, physically blighted areas of America's central cities could be rebuilt, according to the League of Cities. This is the purchase price of a nuclear aircraft carrier, fully equipped and escorted. [29]

It is not hard to think of other examples. The areas of education, medical and health care, housing, public transportation, recreation, assistance to the aged, and child care, among others, are all underdeveloped, while talent and resources are skewed toward maintaining the permanent war economy.

Militarism affects the quality of life in more than just economic ways. It also interferes with our democratic rights and civil liberties. It is not surprising that a militarized government committed to a warlike posture toward external enemies should attempt to repress imagined threats from within.

Since the early 1960s, America's military and paramilitary apparatus have been used at times against lawful activities by citizens. Many of the internal "enemies" were individuals and groups who actively protested military expenditures, the uses to which they have been put (particularly in Southeast Asia), and the adverse effects of all this for American society. Among the activities carried out under the rationale of protecting internal security were wiretapping and spying; organized disruption of

---

[28]Melman, *The Permanent War Economy*, p. 260.

[29]Ibid., pp. 358–69. These and other examples of civilian-military tradeoffs were compiled by economist Tom Riddell and were first published in May 1972 in a SANE bulletin entitled "What Could Your Tax Dollars Buy?"

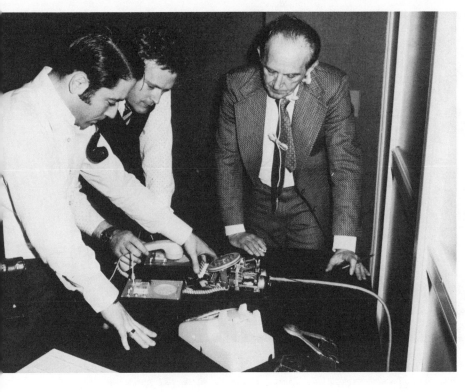

In recent years Americans have learned that paramilitary agencies have spied on citizens who were defined as "internal enemies" by the government. The civil liberties and democratic rights of individuals who had engaged in dissent—in demonstrations, speeches, or published articles—and of people who were known to be friends of dissenters were violated. Scenes like the one in this photograph became increasingly common as Americans who had criticized governmental policy called in experts to check for listening devices in their telephones.

dissident groups; the employment of agent provocateurs; burglary and violation of the mails; infiltration of campuses and classrooms; maintenance of secret dossiers on thousands of innocent people; and legal harassment and intimidation.[30]

The machinery for the violation of democratic rights and civil liberties remains in place, though it is hoped that through exposure of past activities such treatment of citizens will not occur again. But, there is no way to know what the future will bring should a popular assault on American militarism again arise.

The Nuclear Threat

All the macro problems we have considered thus far—from poverty to sexism, from educational inequality to institutional racism—cause harm to and limit the life chances of millions of people. But as tragic and wasteful of human potential as they are, none of these problems can

[30]See Alan Wolfe, *The Seamy Side of Democracy* (New York: David McKay Co., Inc., 1973); Paul Cowan et al., *State Secrets* (New York: Holt, Rinehart & Winston, 1974); and David Wise, *The American Police State* (New York: Random House, Inc., 1976).

Arms limitation talks have made little progress—especially when measured against the destruction that could result from the use of nuclear weapons. The nations involved in the talks doubt one another's good faith. They are reluctant to give up their nuclear and conventional armaments, and they continue to develop even more deadly weapons.

create anywhere near the carnage that would result from the use of nuclear arms.[31] It is amazing that we can go about our daily lives either ignorant of or apathetic to the dangers to which American militarism contributes.

A simple miscalculation of other nations' military intentions or a bravado show of brinksmanship can plunge the American military establishment into an exercise in destruction that few earth-dwellers are likely to survive. Over 116,000 Americans died in World War I, and more than 407,000 were killed in World War II. These figures are nothing in comparison to the likely outcome of a nuclear war. And there is no telling what kind of world the survivors would inherit.

Nuclear weaponry proliferates around the world, and, despite arms limitation talks, the end to America's arms race with the Soviet Union is not in sight. In the absence of adequate safeguards, a deranged political leader could touch off a World War III that will leave no historians to debate its origins. The technical knowledge and even the materials re-

[31]See Robert A. Dentler and Phillips Cutright, *Hostage America* (Boston: Beacon Press, 1963).

quired to construct a nuclear weapon are now relatively accessible; not only other nations but also domestic and foreign bandit groups may gain access to such means of total destruction. Attempts at nuclear blackmail may not be limited to the pseudoreality of nighttime television thrillers. [32]

Despite massive military expenditures, there is no real way this society can be protected from nuclear annihilation. And yet America's national security managers gamble daily with the possibility of a nuclear Armageddon. A strongly sanitized jargon obscures the destructive potential of our buildup of submarines, missiles, bombers, tanks, and artillery pieces equipped with thermonuclear capabilities. What, after all, does Congressional funding of MIRV mean to the average citizen? Stripped of its alphabetical neutrality, MIRV stands for an advance in destructive capability that allows the United States to launch multiple nuclear warheads at different targets from the same single shot. While MIRV enhances America's ability to wipe out every single living thing on the planet a dozen times over, the billions spent on it do not provide a whit of additional security for this society.

Because the choice is between militarism and the existence of the human species, it seems obvious that multilateral disarmament is imperative. War is no longer a viable solution for the problems facing this or any other society, since it may well mean the end of the human species. While we do not know what it will take to stimulate disarmament elsewhere, at home it will mean combating institutional forces whose self-interests are tied up in an economy of death.

CHOOSING HUMAN SURVIVAL

The forces promoting American militarism are formidable. But there are ways to offset them so that the human species can survive. Changes are required in a number of different areas.

Clearly, it is vital for this society to take the lead in promoting worldwide, multilateral disarmament. Annual expenditures on militarism by the United States and other nations run into hundreds of billions of dollars. If such huge sums were directed into peace-oriented activities, this would greatly enhance the well-being of everyone on this planet. Investments in such areas as food production, population control, and environmental cleanup would easily be possible.

In the immediate future, the United States must stop making the world into an unstable armed camp. For example, we can cease selling arms and military-related technology to other nations. An argument for continuing such sales is that if America does not do so, other nations will. But

[32]See Robert L. Heilbroner, *An Inquiry into the Human Prospect* (New York: W. W. Norton & Co., Inc., 1974).

whatever other nations do, this does not diminish our responsibility for the carnage our own contributions help foster.

Another step, one that could directly contribute to our domestic well-being, is the nationalization of the aerospace/defense industry. Assuming that this society must continue to protect itself as work progresses on multilateral disarmament, we will have an aerospace/defense sector for an indeterminate (but, one hopes, brief) period. Nationalization—i.e., federal ownership of this industry—would allow public control over the use of tax funds for defense purposes. Inflated prices and cost overruns could be eliminated, as could the excess costs that now allow private corporations to profit from militarism.

The dollar savings provided by nationalization could be combined with yet another step: an actual progressive reduction in spending on militarism, paced to the progress being made in multilateral disarmament. The funds freed up could be diverted to any of a number of projects, including the upgrading and modernization of underdeveloped areas in the civilian economy and the retraining and placement of workers displaced by reduced military spending. In the 1940s the United States quickly mobilized its productive resources for war; a conversion back to peace is no doubt equally possible.

This and other societies must perfect nonviolent means of resolving conflicts—for example, diplomacy, adjudication of differences by neutral international bodies, techniques of passive resistance designed to make a point and influence world opinion. Nations will always disagree, but there is no reason why such disagreement must be resolved by the continued threat or use of armed force. Nor is there any reason to use covert paramilitary forces (e.g., the CIA and its equivalents) to solve problems. The involvement of intelligence forces in other nations' domestic affairs must be outlawed in the context of multilateral disarmament.

Utopian? Perhaps. But each day that passes makes it that much more difficult for America and the rest of the world to avoid war deaths—and possibly a grotesque end to life as we have come to know it.

SUMMARY

America maintains a large-scale military-industrial complex whose impact is felt in areas ranging from foreign policy to the quality of domestic life. The components of this complex include the uniformed military, the aerospace/defense industry, the civilian national security managers, and the U.S. Congress. Each component of the military-industrial complex, which has existed since World War II, has its own interests to pursue and protect. In doing so, each serves the interests of every other component.

Following the end of World War II, a number of factors contributed to the continued existence of the military-industrial complex. The uniformed military campaigned to keep the powers and responsibilities of the military establishment intact. Governmental and corporate elites, fearful of a return to prewar depression conditions, were reluctant to end the war economy. Corporate elites had found military spending highly profitable. The outbreak of the cold war with the Soviet Union provided a further justification for maintaining a permanent war economy. American elites viewed socialism, and the threat of its spread, as requiring a military response. Fears of expanding socialism have been important to the maintenance of the military-industrial complex for over thirty years.

Each component of the military-industrial complex plays a role in its operation. The uniformed military services have carved out missions in defense and active warfare and work to sell the importance of their role to governmental civilians and the public. The aerospace/defense industry, the second component of the complex, profits from large-scale tax expenditures on militarism. The industry's relation to the U.S. Department of Defense has been characterized as Pentagon capitalism. Military-related products and services are provided by aerospace/defense firms under conditions involving far less competition and risk, and more assured profits, than is the case in production for the consumer public.

The third component of the military-industrial complex consists of the national security managers, governmental civilians who are responsible for safeguarding national security and formulating foreign policy. They are usually drawn from the world of big business and high finance and are thus likely to be sensitive to the economic implications of military spending. Such spending has an impact on the domestic economy, for millions of jobs depend on it. As American corporations have become increasingly involved in doing business in other countries, our military capabilities provide a means of protecting our economic interests abroad.

The U.S. Congress, the final component of the military-industrial complex, provides the tax funds that keep the complex going. Congress typically appropriates most of the money requested by the national security managers and the uniformed military each year. One major reason is that military expenditures have an important economic impact on the home states or districts of senators and representatives.

American corporate investments overseas have grown enormously since World War II, as have the number and size of multinational firms. An increasing percentage of the net incomes of many of America's largest corporations comes from foreign operations. Operating overseas, multinational firms are able to gain access to valuable raw materials, cultivate new markets for their goods and services, and take advantage of low labor costs. The spread of American economic interests abroad has been facilitated by government foreign and military policies. These policies have included efforts to combat the spread of socialism, which elites see as a danger to capitalist economic activities.

Several military strategies have been employed to fight against socialism. These include the threatened use of nuclear arms, conventional nonnuclear warfare, and counterinsurgency warfare involving such paramilitary agencies as the CIA. In addition, America sells over $10 billion in arms each year to friendly governments that allow American corporate involvement in their economies. These strategies—all made possible by a well-financed military-industrial complex—are used to make the world safe for American business.

Critics have pointed to negative effects of militarism on the American civilian economy. That sector of the economy that produces military-related goods and services is said to be nonproductive, in that it does not serve basic needs of the civilian population. Many firms that have grown dependent on producing for the Department of Defense would find it exceedingly difficult to convert to production for civilian consumption. Many technically educated persons have been siphoned away from civilian industry into aerospace/defense jobs, creating a "brain drain" or loss of talent that could have been used in other settings. Finally, investment in militarism is said to have caused the underdevelopment of sectors of the civilian economy, leading to inefficiency and higher production costs. The productive competency of the American civilian economy has become corroded, and this has begun to interfere with our ability to compete in the world market.

Militarism also has negative effects on the quality of life in the United States. Tax funds going to support the military-industrial complex could be used for other purposes—e.g., cleaning the environment, ending poverty and hunger, rebuilding the nation's cities, and so on. The maintenance of a militaristic posture also affects domestic civil liberties. A government oriented toward the use of force against external enemies is prone to repress imagined threats from within. Since the early 1960s, America's military and paramilitary apparatus has at times been used against citizens engaged in lawful activity—e.g., persons and groups protesting militarism.

One final negative effect of militarism is the constant possibility of nuclear warfare. Nuclear weaponry has been proliferating around the world. As more nations join the "nuclear club," the likelihood of nuclear holocaust increases. Should nuclear warfare occur, the carnage would be immense. And there is no way of telling what kind of world the survivors would inherit. Despite our massive military expenditures, there is no real way this society can be protected from nuclear annihilation.

In the interests of human survival, efforts to bring about worldwide multilateral disarmament must take place, and expenditures on militarism must be directed into peace-oriented activities. America must cease selling weaponry to other nations. On the way toward disarmament, the aerospace/defense industry might be nationalized to cut down on the losses due to waste and profiteering. Ultimately, this and other societies must perfect nonviolent means of resolving conflicts.

DISCUSSION QUESTIONS

1. What arguments can be made for and against resolving disagreements through violence? Are there circumstances under which the ends justify violent means?

2. In all past wars, at least some Americans have refused to be inducted into military service. Should people have the right to decide whether they will follow the demands of a government that engages the nation in warfare?

3. In what ways and to what degree is your community or state dependent on military expenditures? Discuss what would happen if these expenditures were to suddenly cease.

4. Who ultimately benefits the most from the maintenance of a permanent war economy in the United States? In what ways?

5. How often have you thought about the possibility of this society's involvement in nuclear warfare? What are your feelings about that possibility?

6. Is the propensity to engage in warfare a part of human nature? Or is it the outcome of socioeconomic and political forces? Give evidence in support of your answer.

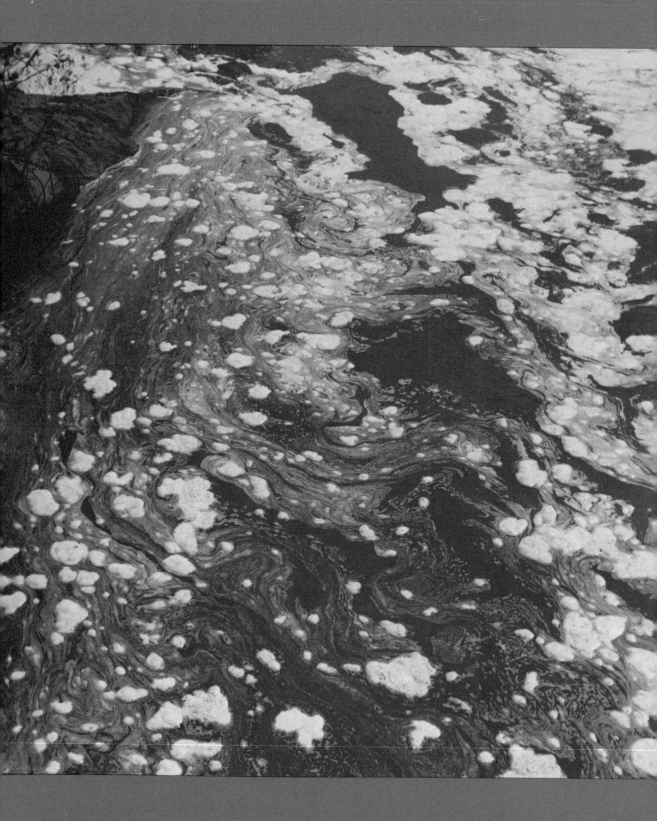

7 Environmental Abuse

Resources must be devoted to the preservation and conservation of the natural environment, and technological decisions must take into account the well-being of future generations.

A mericans have long been abusing their environment. We routinely pour gaseous and solid wastes into the air and water, misuse the land, and use up irreplaceable commodities. We are all aware of environmental abuse—and we all contribute to it. When we drive our cars, discard trash, do the laundry with phosphate detergents, or set thermostats high in winter and low in summer, we are helping abuse the environment. Billboards blocking the view, airplanes roaring overhead, and trucks crowding our highways are some of the kinds of environmental abuse we take for granted.

The term *ecology* is used to refer to "the intricate web of relationships between living organisms and their living and nonliving surroundings."[1] Every action we take within our environment—indeed our very presence—has some impact on the earth. Our environment is not "out there" and apart from humanity. We and our societal institutions are a part of it, whether we think in such terms or not.

The nature of the relationship between human beings and the environment is brought out in the following basic principles of ecology:

1. Living organisms (including people) and their surroundings are mutually interdependent. The earth is one big *ecosystem* in which each part—including human institutions—serves functions that have a bearing on the system as a whole. In turn, the well-being of the whole has implications for the various parts.
2. Every living organism is part of this global ecosystem. All life is, however indirectly and distantly, interconnected.
3. Each species of life carries out its activities in its own environmental niche. Some species have proven to be much more adaptable to changes in their surroundings than others. Adaptability contributes to ecosystem stability.
4. The more species there are, the more stable the ecosystem is likely to be. This is because of the increased probability that some species will take over an important system function if another cannot.
5. Species tend to be dependent on one another and to be interconnected through chains or cycles. For example, we live by inhaling oxygen from the air and exhaling carbon dioxide. Plants, in effect, do the reverse. Thus, people and plants need one another. Likewise, just about every species of life uses another as food and in turn serves as nourishment for an additional species.
6. It is impossible to throw anything away in the global ecosystem. Everything must go somewhere. When something is disposed of, there is an impact on the part of the system from which it is removed and on the part into which it is discarded.
7. No part of the ecosystem is "free." Whenever we use or deplete some part of the system, this affects the functioning of the ecosystem as a whole.

[1]Council on Environmental Quality, *First Annual Report, August 1970* (Washington, D.C.: U.S. Government Printing Office, 1970), p. 6.

8. People and the institutions people create are only one part of the global ecosystem, and perhaps not even the most important part. We are far more dependent on other living species than they are on us. The ecosystem could probably easily survive without humanity.[2]

These principles make it clear that polluting the air and water, spreading radioactivity into the atmosphere, generating increasing levels of noise, creating numerous wastes, and consuming irreplaceable resources change or otherwise affect the global ecosystem. Since human beings are part of the ecosystem, we too are affected by these activities. The phrase *ecocatastrophe* is an apt description of the overall effect such harmful human activities seem to be having. While obviously not all human activities are ecologically harmful, those cited above appear to be undoing millions of years of nature's complex work.

In some cases the damage being done to the air, water, land, and the life they sustain poses a threat to human survival. Since all people are participants in the global ecosystem, this threat goes beyond the political boundaries of the United States. But the United States stands out in terms of its massive contribution to environmental ills. For example, no other nation consumes so much of the world's unrenewable natural resources each year.

In this chapter we will look at the macro problem of environmental abuse. We will distinguish among seven types of environmental abuse, indicating their extent and their implications for the future. Finally, we will examine the causes of and possible solutions to this basic and far-reaching problem, discussing the institutional and individual problems that stand in the way of cleaning up the environment.

NATURE AND EXTENT
OF ENVIRONMENTAL ABUSE

The term *environmental abuse* refers to several varied types of human activities, from dirtying the air to depleting irreplaceable resources. In this section we will look at the major types of environmental abuse. We shall estimate the extent of each type and look at the possible effects on human survival.

Air Pollution

Most of us take the life-sustaining activity of breathing for granted. But threats to this activity have been emerging all around us, most noticeably since the 1960s. Prior to that time, most people saw "dirty air" as a localized phenomenon, not as the national and international threat it is.

[2]These ecological principles are adapted from Alan Bock, *The Ecology Action Guide* (New York: Pyramid Books, 1972), pp. 21–5.

The earth's atmosphere contains a finite amount of air—5 to 6 quadrillion tons of it. Under ordinary circumstances, this air is constantly being recycled and cleansed of contaminants through a complex process involving wind, rain, and changes in temperature. Air pollution occurs when so many contaminants are released into the atmosphere that the recycling and cleansing functions begin to break down.

An estimated 200 million tons of pollutants are released into the air each year in the United States. While this tonnage may seem insignificant in relation to the amount of air in the earth's atmosphere, it is not really the weight of pollutants that counts. More important is the fact that pollution is concentrated in particular geographical areas—most notably in large cities and their suburbs. Since most Americans live in and around cities, air pollution directly affects most Americans. Of course, pollutants even travel into rural areas.

There are five common classes of air pollutants, according to studies by the federal government.[3] *Carbon monoxide* is a colorless, odorless, poisonous gas that constitutes 47 percent of air pollution tonnage. Roughly two thirds of this gas comes from internal combustion engines. *Particulate matter*—that is, solid and liquid substances that may or may not be visible to the naked eye—make up 13 percent of pollution tonnage. Particulates are emitted during industrial operations and the combustion of fuels in stationary sources (e.g., electric power plants). *Sulphur oxides* enter the air as a by-product of the use of sulphur-containing fuels (coal and oil). Industry and generators of electric power are the biggest users. The oxides are released in the form of poisonous, corrosive gases and comprise 15 percent of our annual pollution output. *Nitrogen oxides* represent 10 percent of our pollution tonnage. They are a major component of what is commonly called *smog*. The major contributors are power plants and transportation vehicles. *Hydrocarbons* also play a role in smog formation. Hydrocarbons, which make up 15 percent of pollution tonnage, are primarily emitted by automobiles.

Researchers do not agree about the effects of particular pollutants on the human body, but it is certain that some or all of them do have negative effects. For example, medical researchers have found a correspondence between air pollution and coughing, colds, and other respiratory diseases, lung cancer, cardiovascular diseases, infant mortality rates, death rates among the elderly, and the speed of recovery from illness.[4]

In 1972 the U.S. Environmental Protection Agency estimated that the annual cost of air pollution is at least $25 billion. This includes $9 billion in extra health costs, $8 billion in damage to residential property, and around $8 billion worth of harm to vegetation and materials (e.g., steel,

[3]Council on Environmental Quality, *First Annual Report,* pp. 62–6. A critique of governmental air pollution policies may be found in John C. Esposito, *Vanishing Air* (New York: Grossman, 1970).

[4]See, for example, Lester B. Lave and Eugene P. Seskin, "Air Pollution and Human Health," *Science,* 11 (August 21, 1970): 723–33.

rubber, marble).[5] Millions of hours of work are lost each year as employees deal with the effects of pollutants. No real dollar value can be assigned to the ways air pollution hastens the death of living things—including people.

A number of scientists have warned that air pollution may be creating a *greenhouse effect*—that it might be causing an increase in worldwide temperatures that will melt the polar ice caps. Were this to happen, the oceans would rise an additional twenty-seven feet, causing severe flooding. Other scientists theorize that the temperature of the earth might instead be falling, thereby ushering in a new ice age. We do not know whether these predictions are realistic, but no matter how remote the possibilities are, it seems imperative to work for the complete elimination of all air pollution as rapidly as possible. Instead, this country doesn't appear to be in much of a hurry:

> Which pollution effect will ultimately dominate? Will we indeed drown or will we freeze? Despite firm predictions by some ecologists, we do not know the answers. Careful monitoring and extended research are required if we are to manage our environmental climate wisely. These questions may become critical in the future.[6]

In the meantime, prepare to dress accordingly. And be careful when you breathe.

Water Pollution

Travelers to foreign countries are often warned against drinking anything but sterilized liquids sealed in bottles. Contaminated water is a major problem in the United States as well. Over the years, we have managed to pollute virtually every major body of water in the nation. Rivers, streams, and lakes have been fouled with organic and inorganic chemical wastes. Public water supplies contain substances linked with cancer. Water, like air, is a key life-sustaining feature of our surroundings. We drink it, bathe in it, use it for recreational purposes, eat many of its creatures, and rely on it for use in agriculture and industry. Water pollution constitutes a threat that is just as serious as the abuse of the earth's air. There is a distinct possibility that we could run out of usable water, not only because of pollution but also because of the increasing demand for fresh water. In addition, according to biologist Barry Commoner, pollution of our surface waters "may expose human beings to a host of new and unaccustomed diseases for which immunity may be lacking."[7]

Many pollutants have been found in our water, and there is good

[5]U.S. Environmental Protection Agency, *The Economics of Clean Air* (Washington, D.C.: U.S. Government Printing Office, 1972), pp. 1–11.

[6]Council on Environmental Quality, *First Annual Report,* p. 100.

[7]Barry Commoner, *The Closing Circle* (New York: Bantam Books, Inc., 1974), p. 220.

reason to believe that many others have not yet been discovered. How these pollutants affect one another is unknown.

One of the major contaminants is *industrial waste*. Overall, industry accounts for 60 percent of this society's water pollution. Over three hundred thousand factories discharge water containing wastes, many of which are known to be toxic. Over half the wastes come from the paper, organic chemicals, steel, and petroleum industries.

Thermal pollution is also one of the most serious types of water pollution, and the waste heat problem is expected to grow much worse in the future. The main source of thermal pollution is the electric power industry, which uses great amounts of water for coolant purposes. The used water is then poured back into rivers, streams, and lakes, raising their temperature and adversely affecting aquatic life.

Municipal wastes make up about 25 percent of all water pollution. The treatment of wastes generated in homes, commercial establishments, and industry remains at a primitive level in most urban areas. Only about a third of the nation's population is served by sewer systems and adequate waste treatment plants.

Agricultural wastes include animal and chemical wastes. Each year animals produce the same amount of organic wastes as do 2 billion people. Increasingly, agricultural animals have been reared in centralized feedlots, where their wastes become highly concentrated and are impervious to natural decomposition. Elements of these wastes then seep into underground water channels and surface waters. A similar process occurs as a consequence of the heavy use of chemical fertilizers and pesticides in farm areas.

Our waters are also being widely contaminated by land erosion and sediments. Oil and other hazardous substances are frequently spilled —by accident or on purpose—in waterways. And mine drainage (particularly from strip mining) fills streams and rivers with toxic metals and acids.[8]

Noticeable changes are also taking place in the oceans. For years it was assumed that the oceans could readily dilute and absorb whatever we decided to dump into them. The results of this assault are finally being felt.[9] Since toxic wastes are absorbed by fish and other forms of sea life, the chemicals dumped in the oceans often appear on our dinner plates. In many areas, beaches have been spoiled and recreational activities disrupted. Oil and other substances dumped accidentally or purposely are thought to have implications for our climate. Solid wastes, sludge from sewage, industrial wastes, explosives, radioactive wastes, and dredge spoils (from harbor construction, etc.) threaten to turn the oceans into

[8]Information on types of contaminants is from Philip Nobile and John Deedy, eds., *The Complete Ecology Factbook* (Garden City, N.Y.: Anchor Books, 1972), pp. 221–27. See also Federal Water Quality Administration, *Clean Water for the 1970's* (Washington, D.C.: U.S. Government Printing Office, 1970).

[9]See Council on Environmental Quality, *Ocean Dumping: A National Policy* (Washington, D.C.: U.S. Government Printing Office, 1970).

Atmospheric testing of nuclear weapons was relatively common during the 1950s, causing radioactive debris—or nuclear fallout—to appear far from the remote test sites. Scientists have discovered that atomic radiation can cause cancer and genetic defects in living things.

huge cesspools. In 1968, 48.2 million tons of such pollutants were dumped; experts predict that more will be dumped each year. The pollution problem is likely to be exacerbated as we continue to exploit the oceans' mineral and oil resources.

Nuclear Radiation

Over thirty years ago, a group of American scientists and technicians participated in the secret, federally sponsored Manhattan Project. This wartime effort resulted in the first atomic bombs, which were used in the war against Japan. The explosion of atomic bombs in Hiroshima and Nagasaki in 1945 produced death, injury, and property destruction on a scale never before seen. Scientists throughout the world began working with nuclear power, not only for military uses but also for peacetime needs, particularly to meet growing energy demands.

It was not until the 1950s that some serious dangers of nuclear power began to be discerned.[10] The United States, Great Britain, and the Soviet Union were detonating atomic explosions in remote areas for test purposes. Suddenly, scientists found that the tests were producing radioactive debris that was literally showering down on the earth far away from the test sites. Radioactivity was appearing everywhere—in water, soil, plants, animals. One component of the *nuclear fallout*—strontium 90—was a possible cancer-causing agent. Other radioactive elements were associated with genetic defects. For the first time, atomic radiation began to be seriously appreciated for what it is—a major threat to life. While such atmospheric testing has since been sharply curtailed, radioactivity from the original tests is still around and will be for many years. Persons living in the United States during the 1950s and 1960s may not know it, but they are members of an "atomic generation."

Even the peacetime uses of atomic energy have become a major source of concern in recent years. The United States has joined other nations in an expanding program of nuclear power plant construction. Nuclear plants presently provide only 5 percent of America's energy, but this percentage is expected to grow much higher as the demand for energy continues to escalate and the costs of oil and coal increase.

There are several dangers inherent in nuclear power.[11] Nuclear power plants require enormous amounts of water and produce far more heat pollution than do conventional power generators. They emit radioactive effluents as well, such as krypton-85 and tritium. While only small amounts are involved, a progressive buildup of these elements in the atmosphere could create a serious health hazard. Nuclear power plants also produce extremely dangerous radioactive wastes that must be handled carefully. Problems of waste storage, transportation, and disposal are expected to mount as more and more plants are opened. There is also the constant danger of plant breakdown and the possibility of radiation leakage. Nuclear power plants are susceptible to sabotage and military attack—even a war with conventional weapons could unleash radiation dangers. Unforeseeable accidents or such natural disasters as earthquakes could lead to similar results. Finally, with the increased use, production, and transport of radioactive materials around the country, the possibility of theft increases. It just may be possible for an individual or group to use stolen materials to construct a nuclear weapon.

Presently, all of us are subject to some degree of exposure to radiation. Natural radiation regularly enters the atmosphere from outer space. Radioactive elements can be found in water and mineral deposits. We are often exposed to radiation from X rays, luminous watch dials, color televi-

[10]The story of how these dangers were discovered is told in Commoner, *The Closing Circle*, pp. 45–62.

[11]See Kurt H. Hohenemser, "The Failsafe Risk," *Environment*, 17 (January-February 1975): 6–10.

Table 7.1. The National Trash Can

Kinds of Materials	Material Totals 10^6 tons	Percent	Product Source Categories, Millions of Tons Newspapers, books, and magazines	Containers and packaging	Major household appliances	Furniture and furnishings	Clothing and footware	Food products	Other products
Paper	39.1	31.3%	10.3	20.4	—	*	*	—	8.4
Glass	12.1	9.7	—	11.1	*	*	—	—	1.0
Metals									
Ferrous	10.6	8.5	—	5.4	1.7	*	—	—	3.5
Aluminum	0.8	0.6	—	0.6	0.1	*	—	—	0.1
Other nonferrous	0.4	0.3	—	0.1	0.1	*	—	—	0.2
Plastics	4.2	3.4	*	2.5	0.1	0.1	0.2	—	1.3
Rubber and leather	3.3	2.6	—	*	0.1	*	0.5	—	2.7
Textiles	1.8	1.4	*	*	—	0.6	0.5	—	0.7
Wood	4.6	3.7	—	1.8	—	2.3	*	—	0.5
Food wastes	22.0	17.6	—	—	—	—	—	22.0	—
Product totals	**99.1**	**79.3**	**10.3**	**41.9**	**2.1**	**3.2**	**1.2**	**22.0**	**18.4**
Yard wastes	24.1	19.3							
Misc. inorganics	1.8	1.4							
Total waste	**125.0**	**100.0**							

Source: Citizens' Advisory Committee on Environmental Quality, *Energy in Solid Waste* (Washington, D.C.: U.S. Government Printing Office, 1975), p. 13. *trace.

sion sets, microwave ovens, and radar. Some workers are routinely bombarded at their place of employment. Scientists seem to agree that *all* radiation is harmful, but there is little consensus on the amount we can safely tolerate. Nuclear warfare (even the use of such weapons in a limited war) and/or the long-term effects of nuclear power plant proliferation could provide a tragic answer to the question of tolerance.

Solid Wastes

A key indicator of America's material affluence is its volume of junk, garbage, and other forms of solid waste. Most of it is in the form of agricultural, mineral, and industrial waste.[12] Table 7.1 shows some of the sources and amounts of solid wastes.

Agricultural and mineral waste generally go unnoticed, for they are concentrated in nonurban settings. Industrial waste is far more noticeable, since it often contributes to the waste disposal problems facing highly populated areas. Fly ash from electric utility companies, scrap metals, rags, and bales and drums of industrial by-products must all be thrown away somewhere.

[12]See Nobile and Deedy, eds., *The Complete Ecology Handbook*, pp. 358–59, for a wide-ranging review of our solid waste problems. This is the primary source of our statistics in this section.

Our output of junk is almost mind-boggling:

Among the wastes produced in the United States, Americans annually throw away 30 million tons of paper and paper products, 4 million tons of plastics, 100 million tires, 30 billion bottles, 60 billion cans, and millions of major appliances including cars.[13]

In 1920 each city dweller threw away 2.75 pounds of refuse each day; by 1970 this figure had increased to 5 pounds. The level is expected to reach 8 pounds by 1980.[14]

Where does it all go? The solid waste collected in most municipalities is simply hauled away to open dumps. Only a small percentage gets buried in sanitary land fills or burned in incinerators. Dumping exhausts land space that could be more fruitfully used; it also poses possible health hazards. Incineration (along with fires due to spontaneous combustion in open dumps) contributes to pollution of the air.

To underscore the problems involved, let us look at some examples. By weight, paper and paper products are a major type of refuse. In recent years paper consumption has increased to the point that the average American now uses 576 pounds annually. Much of this is associated with the use of heavily packaged products. Very little paper is recycled in the United States—80 percent is simply dumped or burned. While paper and paper products are bulky and take up space, fortunately they do eventually decompose. When burned, however, they contribute to air pollution.

Plastics are a different matter. The production and use of plastics has grown enormously in recent years. Modern plastics are substances with high durability and resistance to biological decomposition. Plastics thus are being used in the place of wood, metals, and cloth for many products. It is their very properties that render plastics an ecological problem. Since they do not decompose, they simply pile up permanently. If burned, plastics are likely to melt and foul up incinerator operations, while emitting gaseous pollutants that are often poisonous. It has been claimed that plastics pollute the air even in garbage dumps, due to solar heat and the heat processes that lead to spontaneous combustion.

Metal cans and glass bottles are another solid waste problem. Cans decompose too slowly to disappear before even more cans are dumped. Glass is rather invulnerable to natural decomposition. Bottles, along with some metals used in cans, can be reclaimed for use. But little is being done along such lines. Furthermore, corporate producers have moved away from returnable containers (e.g., for beverages) that could help reduce waste volume. Today they try to sell throwaways, which often end up littering our roadways and recreational areas. The throwaway trend may be convenient for consumers, but it is not a sign of ecological sanity. By 1980 it is expected that we will be tossing out 100 billion

[13]Walter A. Rosenbaum, *The Politics of Environmental Concern* (New York: Praeger Publishers, Inc., 1973), p. 41.
[14]Council on Environmental Quality, *First Annual Report*, p. 106.

Part of the millions of tons of solid wastes Americans dispose of simply ends up littering our cities. Junk and garbage create health and safety hazards and also make an area look unpleasant and unlivable.

bottles and cans each year, all of which must go somewhere. Though a number of states have begun to restrict the use of disposable bottles, the waste problem overall continues to grow.

Automobiles, besides being a major source of air pollution, tend to be a rather conspicuous form of solid waste. There are over 100 million vehicles registered for use in the United States, and 9 million go permanently out of service annually. Of these, almost 1 million are simply abandoned. The rest wind up in our 33,000 auto junkyards. Only a small percentage are recycled for scrap; most, having been cannibalized for usable parts, are left in piles where the metal rusts and the plastic parts remain. Between 2.5 and 4.5 million abandoned autos, of little value to junk firms, lie along city streets, in vacant lots, and in rural settings. The millions of auto tires tossed out each year are bulky and difficult to get rid of. When burned, tires pollute the air.

Noise and Visual Pollution

We tend to take the sounds of our surroundings for granted and to consider the noise level as somehow inevitable. The sounds of home appliances, traffic, factory and office machinery, aircraft, boats, lawn

Public Problem, Private Pain
CONTEMPLATING THE ECOCATASTROPHE

Environmental abuse is antinature. It undermines and threatens the earth's natural evolutionary processes and despoils the earth's beauty. The attack on nature began slowly, generations ago; its pace has been steadily increasing in modern times. In the following essay, Allen Planz, the poetry editor of The Nation, *describes a polluted pond, traces its history, and records his reactions to environmental abuse.*

On the west bank of brown river there is a place where the wildness of nature mingles savagely with the wildness of civilization. Bare rocks have shouldered the rain into a sunken meadow, and more than a dozen auto-bodies create a ring of metallic resonance around the small pond, from which all life, even the mosquito wriggler, has been choked by chemical stasis. Sunlight sickens on rust and purpled alloys, glints on the black water and shimmers on oilstained sand. This was a watering place once, a ford, a concourse, and one of many thousands of departure points. Buffalo rested by the rocks, heads to the wind, and geese held back the encroaching swamp for centuries, until guns killed off the geese and later gasoline killed the weeds. The erosion gulley was a stream when lush grasses upcountry sifted the rain through their roots. Now every drizzle means sudden flood. Here Indians made camp near the bank, and watched the fire shape and shadow the waters. The pioneer paused to collect his forces for the plunge farther into the west on the trail which, under moonlight, stirred faintly above the dark. A family settled here, and built a homestead, of which only a few rectangular depressions remain. This land was overgrazed, overfarmed, and abandoned, then assumed a civilized function as a dumping-ground for vandalized carwrecks from the highway a mile off. Though doubtless ti-

tle to it is jealously guarded, nobody possesses it now, nobody watches over it, and it is nameless. One can come across it hiking and descend the rocks to the black pond and rest among the junked cars and among slaughtered beasts. Locusts skid in the sand or sing, entombed, in the sticky sludge spilled from crankcases. The river with its machined flow scours the pocked bank. The shadows inside and under the cars are bruises of blue air. Dustdevils snake in the fine grit, and whirl flakes of rusted metal. One may calculate and possess again all the miles he has traveled, all the cities and towns that he called home and that irresistibly erupted him back on the road. One may calculate all those whom money had bought, or killed. One may do nothing, wish nothing. If the hot breeze stirs, it brings only the hands of buried men, and bears no witness to the riposte of osprey and eagle above terraces of clear water. And the night comes on, upside down, gaining on the earth a darkness it never has in the sky. The air smells of heated iron, rancid oils, and of water thickened with sewage. Voices in the blood begin talking of the blood's cessation. One picks up a theme, then, of the splendor of empire weighted against the dust of the people who built it.

And gives it to the heaviness of the night through which one has lived each night, getting drunk under stars arranged in patterns long since prefigured in the fears of men. And with the geophysics of the night in one hand, a bottle in the other, invokes that theme, so that, when the dawn splays the broken figure of man or beast on a hilltop, the wind may come again, if ever it comes again, singing not requiem but revolution.

Allen Planz, "The Pool," in *Ecotactics: The Sierra Club Handbook for Environment Activists*, John G. Mitchell and Constance L. Stallings, eds. (New York: Simon and Schuster, 1970), pp. 115–16.

mowers, construction projects, and sirens affect Americans daily. Urban dwellers in particular are bombarded by a constant and almost unremitting din. The noise level has doubled in the last fifteen years.[15]

The effects of noise on people have been found to vary, for not all individuals are equally sensitive to sounds. Nevertheless, there is reason for concern about the dangers to human hearing. For example, noisy work environments pose the threat of hearing disability or loss for approximately 16 million workers. Excess levels of noise are known to have a bearing on physiological functioning. In experiments, noise has caused the constriction of arteries, increased pulse and respiration rates, involuntary muscle reactions, and abnormal fatigue. In addition, noise is often just plain distracting and annoying. Extremely loud noises, such as the sonic booms created by jet aircraft, fit into this description. (Sonic booms have also been known to cause physical damage to buildings and other structures.)

We rarely think about visual pollution, except when we are confronted with its most extreme manifestations. One type of visual pollution actually prevents people from seeing their surroundings. Photochemical smog, for example, is more than a health hazard. For drivers and pilots it can be a safety hazard as well. It can also be an aesthetic nuisance, blocking out views that are visually pleasing.

There are aspects of our surroundings that many persons, when given a choice, would just as soon not see. This second type of visual pollution is, one might argue, really a matter of taste. Billboards and signs dot the countryside and proliferate in metropolitan areas. Attention-seeking architecture surrounds us, often in the form of neon-lit commercial "strips." Buildings are often put up with no attention to the views they block. Roads and highways tear up neighborhoods and areas of scenic beauty. Polluted rivers and lakes not only smell bad, they are also ugly. Mining operations denude the countryside in many areas, as soil and timber are stripped away to expose coal seams. Public dumps and auto junkyards are not known for their aesthetic appeal. Despite rather expensive efforts to cope with it, litter continues to assault the eyes. In so many ways, human activities continually alter the color, shape, and context of parts of the ecosystem without regard to taste and sensibility.

Land Misuse

Many of the examples of visual pollution relate to the impact of human activities on America's land. But the environmental abuses associated with land use go far beyond aesthetics and taste. According to the President's Council on Environmental Quality, "Misuse of the land is now one

---

[15]See Henry Still, *In Quest of Quiet* (Harrisburg, Pa.: Stackpole Books, 1970); and Theodore Berland, *The Fight for Quiet* (Englewood Cliffs, N.J.: Prentice-Hall, Inc., 1970).

of the most serious and difficult challenges to environmental quality, because it is the most out-of-hand, and irreversible."[16]

The casual way this nation's 2.3 billion acres of land has been used is indicative of what Gene Marine calls the "engineering mentality." Marine says that the engineering mentality is displayed when public or private landowners tamper with land resources without regard to the well-being of the ecosystem as a whole. Their focus is limited to the financial costs and technical feasibility of projects intended to meet immediate, narrowly defined objectives.[17] As with other mindless assaults on the ecosystem, the cumulative effects of land misuse are coming back to haunt us. Here we shall consider some major examples.[18]

Americans seem to assume that this nation has an unlimited abundance of land for unhindered development and exploitation. But our supply of open land is finite, and shortages are beginning to appear. Among the reasons are urban development and suburban sprawl; the linking of major cities by strips of densely populated, developed land; airport and highway construction; and the creation of reservoirs and large-scale flood control projects. Each year approximately a million acres of rural land is gobbled up. Farmlands are turned over to other uses. Irreplaceable marshes and wetlands—the environmental niches in which many species breed and survive—disappear permanently. Such land misuse spreads pollution of all types and eliminates areas that previously had recreational value.

The construction of dams, canals, and waterways also alters land-use patterns. Dredging, draining, filling, and changing the natural routes of streams and rivers have all been done without concern for the environmental consequences. As a result, the habitats of fish and animals have been destroyed, land has been taken away from other uses, and water pollution has inadvertently been exacerbated.

In the past few years we have become aware of the impact of mining practices on America's land. Surface or strip mining, which has blighted the coal-rich Appalachian region and has spread into a number of western states, involves ripping the natural covering off the land (including hills and mountainsides) in order to get at the mineral seams. This is followed by blasting and gouging so that the seams can be fully exposed for removal. The result is often total destruction of natural land contours. Vegetation and wildlife are uprooted, their niches in the ecosystem destroyed. Drainage from such mining areas, containing acids and sediments, contaminates inland waters to the detriment of aquatic life.

Exploitation of the nation's public and private forest lands is having similar adverse consequences. Commercial operations in timber reserves have increasingly taken the form of *clearcutting*, in which large areas are

[16]Council on Environmental Quality, *First Annual Report,* p. 165.
[17]Gene Marine, *America the Raped* (New York: Simon & Schuster, Inc., 1969), p. 18.
[18]These examples are drawn from Rosenbaum, *The Politics of Environmental Concern.*

Strip mining, in which coal is uncovered by ripping the natural covering off the land, is a supreme example of land misuse. This photograph of an open pit mine in Arizona indicates the extent of damage caused by this form of coal mining.

stripped of all trees, leaving behind nothing but short stumps. Logging roads to remote sections bisect otherwise unblemished wilderness. Clearcutting also negatively alters soil conditions, since removal of forest covering exposes soil to the weather, weakening its nutrient properties. Land erosion increases, and streams become choked with debris and sediments. Again, vegetation and wildlife habitats are despoiled.

Resource Depletion

Our discussion has for the most part focused on what American society puts *into* the ecosystem, rather than what we take *from* it. Obviously these two matters are interrelated, given the basic ecological principle that what we throw away had to be first removed from somewhere. In this section we shall deal with America's need for minerals and other materials. Nothing in the ecosystem is really free for the taking. As we shall see, the costs of resource depletion promise to be extremely high.

The exhaustion of irreplaceable commodities. Not too long ago this society's Gross National Product—the sum value of all the goods and services produced each year—rose to over $2 trillion. The GNP is a rough indicator of a nation's overall economic growth, and that of the United States is the highest in world history. Such unprecedented growth is dependent on, among other things, access to mineral supplies, including those that provide energy. This is not a profound observation, but it is one that few Americans have had to think about until quite recently. The point was most dramatically brought home during the nationwide energy crisis that jarred us in 1973–74, when shortages and increased costs of oil, gasoline, and natural gas forced many people to turn down thermostats, turn off lights, drive less, and pay higher prices for virtually all goods and services. The crisis is not over, and it may never be.

With 6 percent of the world's total population, the United States consumes between 50 and 70 percent of the world's resources. In 1950 we consumed 2 billion tons of energy-producing fuels, ores from which metals and alloys are made, abrasives, sand, gravel, stone, clays, and so on. This came to 26,000 pounds per person. By 1972 our use of such resources had doubled to 4 billion tons or more. By weight, fuels alone accounted for 46 percent of the tonnage. Once processed, all these commodities were worth more than $150 billion in 1972, an amount equivalent to almost one fourth of that year's GNP.[19]

Though most of the minerals and other materials we consume are available domestically, the insatiable demands of the American economy are beginning to sharply endanger our supplies. Of eighty-seven commodities currently crucial to our economic well-being, known domestic reserves of forty-seven will fall short of our needs by the year 2000. We are already dependent on imports in a number of crucial areas (see Figure 7.1). From 90 to 100 percent of such commodities as chromium, aluminum, manganese, and platinum must be sought outside the United States. We import from 50 to 90 percent of our tin, nickel, zinc, mercury, and titanium. Lesser but still significant amounts of iron, lead, copper, and gypsum are also imported. At present, 30 percent of the petroleum we use comes from other nations. Over time the United States has moved from being a resource-rich nation to one that cannot grow economically—or even sustain itself as is—without purchasing key resources from other nations.

This situation, which is expected to grow even worse in coming decades, raises some extremely important issues. The resources necessary for our high GNP—and, indeed, our life-styles—are finite. All of them are probably subject to depletion at some point.[20] At present, the United States, the consumer society par excellence, is making the greatest single contribution to the exhaustion of irreplaceable commodities. We and other consumer societies then restore these resources to the global ecosystem in the form of wastes and other pollutants.

[19]These data and those immediately following are from Council on Environmental Quality, *Fifth Annual Report, December 1974* (Washington, D.C.: U.S. Government Printing Office, 1974), pp. 305–17.

[20]For an attempt to depict the depletion problem on a worldwide scale, see Donella H. Meadows et al., *The Limits of Growth* (New York: Universe Books, 1972). This is the so-called Club of Rome report whose bleak conclusions are still being debated.

Figure 7.1. U.S. Demand for Minerals and Mineral Resources Supplied by Imports, 1972

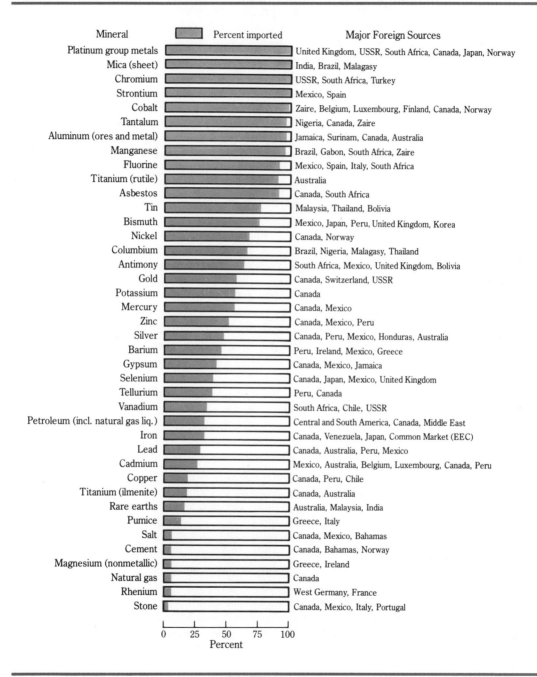

Mineral	Percent imported	Major Foreign Sources
Platinum group metals		United Kingdom, USSR, South Africa, Canada, Japan, Norway
Mica (sheet)		India, Brazil, Malagasy
Chromium		USSR, South Africa, Turkey
Strontium		Mexico, Spain
Cobalt		Zaire, Belgium, Luxembourg, Finland, Canada, Norway
Tantalum		Nigeria, Canada, Zaire
Aluminum (ores and metal)		Jamaica, Surinam, Canada, Australia
Manganese		Brazil, Gabon, South Africa, Zaire
Fluorine		Mexico, Spain, Italy, South Africa
Titanium (rutile)		Australia
Asbestos		Canada, South Africa
Tin		Malaysia, Thailand, Bolivia
Bismuth		Mexico, Japan, Peru, United Kingdom, Korea
Nickel		Canada, Norway
Columbium		Brazil, Nigeria, Malagasy, Thailand
Antimony		South Africa, Mexico, United Kingdom, Bolivia
Gold		Canada, Switzerland, USSR
Potassium		Canada
Mercury		Canada, Mexico
Zinc		Canada, Mexico, Peru
Silver		Canada, Peru, Mexico, Honduras, Australia
Barium		Peru, Ireland, Mexico, Greece
Gypsum		Canada, Mexico, Jamaica
Selenium		Canada, Japan, Mexico, United Kingdom
Tellurium		Peru, Canada
Vanadium		South Africa, Chile, USSR
Petroleum (incl. natural gas liq.)		Central and South America, Canada, Middle East
Iron		Canada, Venezuela, Japan, Common Market (EEC)
Lead		Canada, Australia, Peru, Mexico
Cadmium		Mexico, Australia, Belgium, Luxembourg, Canada, Peru
Copper		Canada, Peru, Chile
Titanium (ilmenite)		Canada, Australia
Rare earths		Australia, Malaysia, India
Pumice		Greece, Italy
Salt		Canada, Mexico, Bahamas
Cement		Canada, Bahamas, Norway
Magnesium (nonmetallic)		Greece, Ireland
Natural gas		Canada
Rhenium		West Germany, France
Stone		Canada, Mexico, Italy, Portugal

0   25   50   75   100
Percent

Source: U.S. Department of the Interior, *Mining and Minerals Policy, 1973* (Washington, D.C.: U.S. Government Printing Office, 1973), p. 22.

Resource depletion and the Third World.   The threat of resource depletion is a real one. But the timetable is unclear because of a number of unpredictable factors: the possibility of new discoveries, the costs of extraction and processing, changes in technology, and the degree to which more readily available commodities can be substituted for scarcer ones. The depletion issue is also related to the fact that many of the minerals and materials on which our economy is dependent, and which we increasingly must import, are located in poor countries of the Third World. As we saw in Chapter 6, "Militarism and War," this society's economic dominance rests on its ability to exploit underdeveloped nations' raw materials cheaply.[21] The gap between rich nations and poor nations promises to be the main political challenge confronting our foreign-policy-makers in the remaining years of this century.[22] In the area of resources, the stakes are great.

Third World nations cannot develop economically or socially without expanded resource consumption opportunities. In practical terms, the advance of these nations—within which most of the world's population lives—can take place in one of two ways. Resources could be distributed away from the United States and other rich nations and to the nations of the Third World. Or, Third World nations could simply join the rich nations on the road to resource depletion. This would involve more intense exploitation of existing commodity supplies. The United States probably won't be willing to give up economic growth in favor of stagnation and a declining standard of living. Pronouncements from the White House presently reflect a definite preference for the second scenario. Third World nations—fearing that choice would not close the rich/poor gap—are not so enthusiastic.

Our growing dependence on key imports from the Third World has produced another issue, one revealed through the Arab embargo on petroleum shipments and the subsequent price increases. The poor but resource-rich countries, by cooperating with one another and forming cartels to control commodity production and prices, may be able to force important concessions from the developed world. Such nations could collectively decide to improve their well-being by forcing a redistribution of consumption opportunities away from the rich nations and to the poor. Should such a stranglehold be placed upon this society (and/or other rich nations in which we hold substantial economic interests), it could well generate a military response. For example, in the aftermath of the Arab oil embargo, as Middle East petroleum prices continued to rise due to cartel action, federal officials and news reporters discussed and/or hinted at the desirability of military action. Given that this society and other

---

[21]See Harry Magdoff, *The Age of Imperialism* (New York: Monthly Review Press, 1969).

[22]This theme runs through Robert L. Heilbroner, *An Inquiry into the Human Prospect* (New York: W. W. Norton & Co., Inc., 1974).

developed nations are steadily arming various Third World nations as a means of "befriending" them (and to boost sagging domestic economies), military aggression against such countries could exact a horrendous toll.

The world is presently facing a tension-filled, no-win dilemma. Irreplaceable resources are being depleted. The United States must bear a large amount of the responsibility for this attack on the global ecosystem. If we try to maintain the status quo, the depletion rate will continue—but so will the misery and political hostility of the poor nations. Cartels and efforts to squeeze greater rewards in return for declining resource supplies will be the order of the day, perhaps calling forth a military solution. If, on the other hand, we attempt to maintain our present growth rates while offering to help poor nations increase theirs, serious conflict may be avoided. But resource depletion rates will escalate, and conflicts are bound to emerge once serious scarcities begin to be felt.

SEARCHING FOR CAUSES

The changes now occurring in the global ecosystem are obviously the consequence of human activities. Our environment is not polluting and depleting itself. But there is little agreement about just what it is about people and their actions that is causing the current ecocatastrophe. A consensus on causes is a crucial first step toward ending environmental abuse. Here we shall highlight some of the different views, indicating which ones make the most sense.

Human Nature

Now and again observers claim that environmental abuse is a result of human nature. People, it is alleged, are basically dirty. Unlike other forms of animal life, we are prone to "fouling our own nests."[23] This being the case, there is really no way to stop the destruction of the environment short of eliminating people from the global ecosystem.

This view is very seductive, perhaps because of its simplicity. But there is no evidence that it is correct. Other animals are "clean" only because they return what they remove from the ecosystem in forms useful to those parts of the system on which they are dependent. They do not violate the chains and cycles on which their survival is based. There is no evidence to suggest that people cannot do the same, even if we cannot match the efficiency of other animal species. Human beings are capable of making conscious, rational choices as to how they wish to relate to the

[23]"Nest fouling" is discussed in Commoner, *The Closing Circle*, pp. 122–23.

rest of the ecosystem. Over time our choices have been ecologically disastrous. But our awareness of environmental deterioration offers the possibility of our choosing to end it—assuming that we can figure out how, that we are willing to bear the costs, and that it is not too late. If we accept the human nature argument, we can only sit back and wait for the Big Collapse or hasten the collapse through an orgy of environmental abuse.

Population and Affluence

An alternative view stresses the significance of the growth in population that is taking place in the United States and around the world. Environmental deterioration, it is alleged, is an inevitable outcome of loading the earth with too many people. The more people there are, the greater the impact they make on the ecosystem as a whole. Increased world population means increased demands on finite resources, along with more waste disposal problems, land misuse, pollution, and so on. [24] The solution to environmental abuse, in this view, is to limit or even decrease the world's population—particularly in the poor countries of the Third World where a "population explosion" is well underway.

This view is also attractively simple: increase the effectiveness of birth control and the ecocatastrophe will go away. Uncontrolled population expansion is primarily a serious problem in nations where food is scarce and/or the productive resources are held by and benefit a small elite. The major perpetrators of environmental deterioration are *not* these poorer societies. Rather, the economically developed nations, such as the United States, which are not experiencing severe population explosions are contributing most to the ecocatastrophe. They consume most of the world's irreplaceable resources, while indiscriminately dumping wastes and harmful contaminants back into the global ecosystem. This is not to say that Third World nations live in harmony with this system or that future developments will not see them playing a more important role in environmental deterioration. But it does mean that we have arrived at the present level of crisis without too much help from their population problems.

Even if we limit ourselves to the United States, it is hard to find a direct correspondence between population expansion and rates of environmental deterioration. Using pollution levels as a main indicator, Barry Commoner has found that our environment is becoming contaminated far more quickly than population growth alone can explain. Between 1946 and 1968, the population of the United States increased by 42

---

[24]The major proponent of this view is Paul R. Ehrlich, *The Population Bomb,* rev. ed. (New York: Ballantine Books, Inc., 1971). For a critique of this view and its implications, see James Ridgeway, *The Politics of Ecology* (New York: E. P. Dutton & Co., Inc., 1970), pp. 181–94.

percent, while pollution levels rose from between 200 and 2000 percent (depending on what and how one chooses to measure).[25] Something more than numbers of people is involved here.

All Americans do not pollute equally. As noted in Chapter 1, "Economic Inequality and Poverty," the affluent are more able to consume due to the unequal distribution of wealth and income. Just as rich nations consume and pollute at far higher rates than poorer ones, the affluent minority in this country makes a greater contribution to environmental deterioration than its numbers would indicate.

Obviously, population growth and size have something to do with the demands being made on the ecosystem. But population alone does not explain the problem.

Science and Technology

Many who reject the population argument blame environmental deterioration on modern science and technology. Somehow, it is alleged, modern science and technology have taken on a life of their own. We are now at the mercy of our own cultural ingenuity; the tools that originally were developed to conquer nature have begun to run wild. We have lost control of these tools and are being forced to bow to their imperatives, and environmental deterioration is the result.[26]

The only way to save the environment, according to this view, is to smash the test tubes and machines, close the mines and factories, bury the research journals, and lock the laboratories. We cannot solve the problem with more technology. People must retreat to the "golden years" of the past when small groups of families lived simply, spartanly, and communally in the woods or prairies. Life in those days may have been short and brutish, but at least the entire global ecosystem was not threatened by scientific and technological change. You could breathe the air, drink the water, eat plants and animals, admire the untouched scenery, and enjoy quiet.

As with population expansion, it would be erroneous to say that science and technology have nothing to do with environmental deterioration. On the other hand, neither is it true that these areas of human activity have a life of their own or have created a set of imperatives to which we must bow. Science and technology are tools, and tools can be used in many different ways. How or whether we use them is a matter of *choice*. We can use science and technology to help us live in harmony with the rest of the ecosystem or to hasten its collapse.

[25]Commoner, *The Closing Circle*, pp. 122–37.

[26]This concern is implicit in Heilbroner, *An Inquiry into the Human Prospect*, wherein "industrialization" is seen as a key cause of environmental deterioration. Heilbroner suggests that we may want to use preindustrial societies as a model for our future life-styles.

The uses to which technology is put sometimes damage the environment and harm human beings in sudden and shocking ways. In the late 1970s, for example, some dams burst in different parts of the country, killing scores of people and destroying homes and vegetation. This photograph shows some of the damage that occurred in Georgia in 1977, when a dam overlooking homes and schools burst after heavy rains had weakened it.

Economic Organization

When we look at science and technology as causes of the ecocatastrophe, we must also consider the societal contexts in which such tools are employed. This realization has led some analysts to contrast environmental policies in capitalist and socialist societies, the idea being that the political and economic priorities of a society ultimately dictate the uses to which science and technology are put. According to Barry Weisberg, environmental deterioration

> is rooted in the systemic imbalance between the capitalist organization of society and the life-sustaining capacity of this planet. . . . The trillion dollar economy [of the United States] brings with it a structure of commodities which requires the fantastic production of dangerous chemicals, surplus packaging, solid waste, and effluents which are incompatible with the life-sustaining capacities of the planet itself.[27]

In this view, the ecocatastrophe is a result of a system of economic organization that benefits only a tiny percentage of the world's peoples.

[27]Barry Weisberg, *Beyond Repair* (Boston: Beacon Press, 1971), pp. 1 and 75.

The benefits—wealth, power, and prestige—may prove to be hollow ones for the few that enjoy them.

In capitalist societies such as the United States, economic and political priorities often place profits before people. Environmental abuse is an inevitable by-product of the private pursuit of money. Pollution, land misuse, and resource depletion are "costs" that are being passed on to the population in return for an enlarged Gross National Product. A large GNP means jobs and consumer goods. Eliminate capitalism as a way of organizing and operating America's productive system, say proponents of this view, and you undercut the coming ecological collapse.

It does seem to be true that the activities of business and industry frequently run counter to environmental sanity. Go back and think about who, or whose products, are intimately tied to each of the forms of environmental abuse reviewed earlier in this chapter. Then check Chapter 2, "Concentration of Power," for some ideas about why such abuse is only being monitored, regulated, measured, and studied rather than totally eliminated.

Earlier we cited Barry Commoner's observations that the pollution rates well outstripped population growth. Commoner suggests that the current ecocatastrophe began after World War II. Beginning in 1946, American corporations began to draw upon advances in science and technology to produce new products in new ways, with ecologically devastating results. Why? Commoner strongly believes that the answer lies with short-term profit interests.[28] Since 1946 the GNP has grown enormously, while the ecosystem has been assaulted.

A few examples of developments that have taken place only since World War II will make the point. Plastics are cheaper to produce than many of the materials they have displaced, but while the plastics industry has grown so have the plastic products we cannot get rid of. Synthetic fibers require less labor to produce than wool or cotton and are hence very profitable. They are about as impervious to destruction as plastics. Rearing agricultural animals on feedlots, rather than grazing them in pastures, produces a lot of meat quickly and inexpensively. But the animal wastes pose a monumental disposal problem. Cars built in the post-World War II era have been bigger and heavier, with more powerful engines. They also pollute more and contribute to fuel depletion. They have proven a boon to oil, steel, chromium, plastic, glass, and rubber firms. While fuel supplies have been pressed to keep up with demand, utility companies encourage electric heating, the use of air conditioners and freezers, plenty of lighting, and more. And even while open land is being depleted, land speculators and developers encourage us to "spread out" without regard to the ecological implications. This, of course, means that we must have more roads and highways—a requirement that does not go unnoticed by automobile and oil concerns.

[28]Commoner, *The Closing Circle*, pp. 266–67.

In recounting such post-1946 changes, in which business and industry leaders have been key decision-makers, Commoner concludes:

> Human beings have broken out of the circle of life, driven not by biological need, but by the social organization which they have devised to "conquer" nature: means of gaining wealth that are governed by requirements conflicting with those which govern nature. The end result is the environmental crisis, a crisis of survival. Once more, to survive, we must close the circle.[29]

Capitalism plus science and technology equals environmental deterioration. In other words, the organization and operation of our society, ecologically speaking, harms living things—including people.

Environmental abuse is of concern in noncapitalist societies like the Soviet Union and the People's Republic of China.[30] While the United States is far ahead of any other nation—capitalist or socialist—in its contribution to environmental deterioration, it is not possible to determine the exact reason. Is it because of our corporate capitalist economy? Or is it a result of our advanced levels of consumption and "dirty" production techniques? The socialist societies to which the United States is usually compared tend to be less advanced in terms of industrialization, to utilize lesser amounts of the earth's resources, and to produce fewer consumer goods on a per capita basis.

On the other hand, socialist societies that are not geared toward satisfying the profit interests of a handful of private owners, but instead try to meet the all-around needs of society as a whole, may find it easier to rationalize the costs of environmentally sane operations. In capitalist societies, where business and industry are privately owned, corporate elites do not want to absorb costs that cut into the maximization of profits. They can only pass on some of the costs of pollution control to consumers in the form of higher prices or lower quality goods and to workers in the form of restricted wages. In socialist societies, however, business and industry are typically state-run. The decision to institute environmentally sound economic operations can be made centrally by the government and the costs can be balanced against the well-being of the citizenry.

So it would be much easier to make environmentally sound decisions in socialist societies. But such societies also place strong emphasis on economic growth, and it remains to be seen whether they will avoid capitalism's contribution to the ecocatastrophe. It also remains to be seen whether capitalist nations—the United States in particular—will be able to find a "cheap" way out of their current problems. The prognosis, for this society at least, does not look good.

[29]Ibid., pp. 298–99.

[30]Ibid., pp. 277–81. See also Barry Commoner, *The Poverty of Power* (New York: Alfred A. Knopf, Inc., 1976); and Weisberg, *Beyond Repair*, pp. 146–84. While Weisberg believes that socialism is well-equipped to deal with the environmental crisis, Commoner sees this as an open question.

SEARCHING FOR SOLUTIONS

Why don't we do something about environmental abuse? In this section we will see how our lack of knowledge about the relationship between human beings and the environment has slowed down attempts to correct environmental abuse. We will then look at some of the things we can do in order to protect the environment.

Problems in Combating Environmental Abuse

It is only in the last decade that awareness of ecological matters has existed on a nationwide basis. International interest is even more recent. Some observers believe that national concern began in 1970, with the celebration of the first Earth Day. Since that time, agencies of government and private industry have started to curb environmental abuse—frequently in response to public discontent and aggressive legal actions by citizens' organizations.

The serious implications of everyday environmental abuse are well illustrated by the dangers of fluorocarbons. Fluorocarbons are the gaseous compounds that have commonly been used as propellants in aerosol cans. They enable the cans to give off a fine spray when activated. Fluorocarbons are also used in most air-conditioning and refrigeration units.

During the early 1970s, scientists began to worry about the effect of fluorocarbons. Finally, in 1976, the National Academy of Sciences announced that fluorocarbons do not disappear harmlessly when released into the atmosphere. Instead, they rise far above the surface of the earth. There, it is argued, the gases threaten to deplete the layer of ozone that helps shield the earth from strong solar rays. Scientists believe that one consequence of ozone depletion may be a marked increase in skin cancer fatalities.

The manufacture of fluorocarbons and products employing such gases was an $8 billion industry in the United States. The first response of corporate producers to early warnings by scientists was to launch a public relations campaign. They questioned existing scientific data and called for conclusive research before any moves were made to restrict fluorocarbon production and use.[31] Government officials began weighing both sides in the debate, as the public looked on from the sidelines.

Shortly after the National Academy of Sciences sounded the warnings, we are nearing a resolution of the fluorocarbon debate. Industry is already marketing aerosol sprays that do not use fluorocarbons, and the

[31]For example, Dupont (a leading fluorocarbon producer) ran a proindustry ad in the *New York Times*, June 30, 1975. Depletion of the ozone layer due to such gases is discussed in A. Karim Ahmed, "Unshielding the Sun . . . Human Effects," *Environment*, 17 (April-May 1975): 6–14.

Environmental policy is currently based on the managerial approach, which involves cleaning up polluted rivers and lakes and putting limits on the amounts of pollutants that can be released into the environment. Though efforts to manage the ecosystem have had some success, it is likely that stronger measures will be needed if we are to avoid an ecocatastrophe.

federal government is considering regulation of fluorocarbon production. How many more dangerous problems will we discover? Will we discover them all in time?

Ignorance is a serious problem. We are not even close to a full understanding of the ways in which human activities affect the ecosystem. Until quite recently, scientists were not particularly interested in such practical knowledge.[32] Thus, much environmental damage has been done, and probably will continue to be done, almost inadvertently. It is entirely possible that a process of production or a waste product thought to be harmless today will suddenly be seen as calamitous as its effects become felt in years ahead.

Nor does there seem to be any consensus about the causes of environmental deterioration. Is there a link between abuse of the environment and human nature? Is such abuse an inevitable outcome of population growth? Is it caused by the excesses of capitalism? Or is it a result of lack of foresight in the use of technology, resources, and industrial capabilities? As we have seen, agreement on causes will have a great deal to do with solutions.

Besides our ignorance about the impact of human activities on the global ecosystem and our disagreements about the causes of environmental deterioration, solutions are being held up by other difficulties. Cultural drives, apathy, economic considerations, and political hurdles

[32]See Barry Commoner, *Science and Survival* (New York: The Viking Press, 1966).

seem to work against the total elimination—as opposed to the slow-down—of environmental abuse. The initial sense of crisis of the early 1970s has given way to a process of monitoring and regulating the production and distribution of damage. [33] In other words, now that our efforts to *conquer* our surroundings have failed, we are trying to *manage* the ecosystem. Given the basic ecological principles outlined earlier, this is akin to expecting the tail to wag the dog. We are no longer even asking whether the managerial approach (setting "standards" and "tolerance levels," minimizing "impact," balancing "priorities," etc.) is the wisest course to take, given our past track record.

The financial costs and economic dislocations that may ultimately be required to bring human activities into harmony with the rest of the ecosystem are difficult to estimate. The question of who should be made to bear these costs has yet to be seriously addressed. At present we appear to be looking for the cheapest way out of the ecocatastrophe. Ultimately it must be ended no matter what the costs, if we are to provide for the survival of future generations.

At least one writer doubts that we care about the well-being of future waves of humanity. In the words of economist Robert L. Heilbroner:

> When men can generally acquiesce in, even relish, the destruction of their living contemporaries, when they can regard with indifference or irritation the fate of those who live in slums, rot in prison, or starve in lands that have meaning only insofar as they are vacation resorts, why should they be expected to take the painful actions to prevent the destruction of future generations whose faces they will never live to see? [34]

Changing Institutions and Activities

What are you willing to give up? In return for what? How serious are you about this? Really? The answers to such questions will determine whether people will find a niche in the ecosystem to enjoy after you are gone. From fluorocarbons to billboards, from radiation to plastics, from climatic modification to litter—this particular macro problem is all around us.

Can we end, not just slow down, America's current contribution to ecosystem collapse? We can—but only by fundamentally changing the organization and operation of this society.

Strict controls must be imposed over what is produced in our economy and how. Presently, political and economic policy-makers are much more concerned with increasing the GNP than they are with the environmental impact of the economic activities it represents. We must turn away from a fixation with the dollar value of this society's productive efforts and begin considering the ecological value.

---

[33]This observation is offered in Weisberg, *Beyond Repair*, p. 34.
[34]Heilbroner, *An Inquiry into the Human Prospect*, p. 143.

A start in this direction has already been made by the federal government. In recent years, states and localities have been required to assess the environmental impact of proposed projects and programs prior to receiving federal funding. While this procedure is far from perfect, it has helped promote environmental consciousness in the public sector of the economy.

In the private sector, however, business and industry pour out goods and services that require no environmental assessment or are restricted only after extreme damage has been done. The private sector must be made responsible and accountable for its actions, for example, through the federal chartering of firms. Federal chartering means that firms would be required to obtain a license from the federal government in order to operate. In order to receive this license or charter, the firms would be required to assess and publicly report on the environmental impact of their operations and products. They would also have to agree to be subject to nationwide regulations, tailored to particular types of business and industry, designed to minimize or eliminate negative environmental practices. Any business that failed to abide by the conditions of its charter could either be shut down or placed under public ownership and control—in effect, put under federal receivership—until it met the conditions. Such "infringement" on the freedom of the private sector seems to be unavoidable so long as short-range profit interests continue to override ecological sanity.

Furthermore, we must be willing to alter our own life-styles. Basically, this means directing our consumption patterns into ecologically sane pathways. What is needed is a profound cultural shift wherein the "good life" is no longer defined in terms of the possession of things that are of danger to the environment. Our indiscriminate use of energy and energy-using products could easily be cut down. We could demand increased production of goods made of recyclable materials. A change in life-style also seems to be unavoidable if we have any interest in the world we are leaving future generations. As consumers, we must allow the demands of the ecosystem to begin to manage us as individuals as well as the economic institutions to which we look to meet our basic needs.

SUMMARY

Environmental abuse occurs as humans violate basic principles of ecology. Polluting the air and water, spreading radioactivity into the atmosphere, increasing levels of noise, creating numerous wastes, and consuming irreplaceable resources—all affect the global ecosystem. Since human beings are part of the ecosystem, we too are affected by these activities.

There are a number of major types of environmental abuse. Air pollution is known to have harmful effects on health and property. Pollution of water brings the threat of disease, shortages of clean water, and destruction of plant and aquatic life. Nuclear power poses dangers of radioactive contamination. Solid wastes, many of which are not biologically decomposable, accumulate. Noise and visual pollution are on the increase, the former affecting health and both harming the appeal of our environment. Land is being lost to misuse, often to the detriment of vegetation and wildlife. Finally, irreplaceable resources—e.g., energy-producing fuels and ores crucial to manufacturing—are facing rapid depletion. Conflict over scarce resources—many of which are located primarily in poor Third World countries—promises to emerge in the future.

There are different views on why environmental abuse is taking place. Some feel it is a result of human nature. Blame has also been placed on population growth, as well as on a loss of control over science and technology. Finally, the profit-seeking orientation of capitalism has been blamed. There is little consensus on causes.

Many problems stand in the way of eliminating environmental abuse. Ignorance is a serious problem. Cultural drives, apathy, economic considerations, and political hurdles seem to work against the elimination—as opposed to the slowdown—of environmental abuse. Possible solutions include imposing strict controls over what is produced in our economy and how. We must alter our life-styles by directing our consumption patterns into ecologically sane pathways.

DISCUSSION QUESTIONS

1. Go into a supermarket and record the ingredients from the labels of commonly used bottled, canned, and boxed products. Discuss what you do and do not know about the ingredients and their effects on your health.
2. Take an inventory of all the things you own. How many of these items are made to be disposable or to have a limited useful life? How many are biologically decomposable? How many are cheaper to repair than to dispose of and replace?
3. List the aspects of your everyday activities and life-style that are directly affected by a concern for the ecosystem. List the aspects that are not. Compare your lists with those of others, and discuss the impact you are having on the environment.
4. Is the American Dream of material affluence and luxurious consumption compatible with the basic principles of ecology outlined in this chapter? Why? If we must adapt our life-styles to the demands of the ecosystem, what are the implications for the American Dream?
5. Most people would probably be outraged if someone sprayed them with poisonous air or fed them dangerous chemicals. In effect, this is what industrial polluters and many of their products are doing. Why, then, are people not outraged?
6. You have magically acquired the power to totally eliminate any one type of environmental abuse. Which would you choose and why? What vested interests would your action most adversely affect?

8 Work

Work must be freely available to all. It should be organized cooperatively, with special attention to providing meaning, dignity, and satisfaction.

Most broadly defined, *work* is an "activity that produces something of value for other people."[1] This definition encompasses a broad range of human behavior. As we saw in Chapter 5, "Institutional Sexism," child-care and household tasks are forms of work. Such home labor is socially necessary and economically useful (which is not to say that only women can or ought to do it). So is the informal volunteer work performed in American society. Each year some 32 million people contribute their time and effort to everything from visiting the hospitalized to assisting in political campaigns. While we recognize that the term *work* means more than paid labor, we shall limit our attention in this chapter primarily to work activity for which people receive wages or salaries.

Sociologists have been studying work for a long time. In the nineteenth century, French sociologist Émile Durkheim observed that the division of labor in society made people dependent on one another. Durkheim felt that this interdependence contributed to societal stability and integration, both of which he believed to be necessary for human well-being.[2] Another nineteenth-century thinker, Karl Marx, saw labor as the principal means by which the human species sought to fulfill its potential. Marx believed that the industrializing societies of his day were turning work into a degrading, dehumanizing experience for the majority of workers.[3] As we shall see, Marx's concerns are still relevant.

Contemporary social scientists have suggested a number of ways in which work is central to our everyday lives.[4] Work is the means by which we are expected to pursue the American Dream—the acquisition of material goods and services and financial security. The pay we receive for our labor helps determine our standard of living and our life-style. The jobs we hold are also major determinants of our position in the overall class structure. This is true not only in purely economic terms but also with regard to power and prestige. Thus the nature of our work often tells other people who we are. We may be treated with deference, accepted as an equal, or dismissed as a nonperson depending on our work status.

Social scientists have found that work has a very personal meaning to people. It can serve as an important source of self-esteem. If we are confronted by challenges at work, and if we overcome them, we gain a sense of accomplishment. Work tasks may give us the chance to feel a sense of mastery over our immediate environment and to display particular talents. Our self-esteem may be further enhanced if our work is valued and rated positively by others, both on and off the job. All in all,

---

[1]*Work in America,* Report of a Special Task Force to the Secretary of Health, Education, and Welfare (Washington, D.C.: U.S. Government Printing Office, 1973), p. 2.

[2]Émile Durkheim, *The Division of Labor in Society* (New York: The Free Press, 1965).

[3]T. B. Bottomore and Maximilien Rubel, eds., *Karl Marx: Selected Writings* (New York: McGraw-Hill, Inc., 1964).

[4]See, for example, Lee Braude, *Work and Workers* (New York: Praeger Publishers, Inc., 1975).

work serves as a measure of our social worth and a key source of our personal identity.

Unfortunately, millions of people today are unable to find work or face the prospect of unemployment. Many unemployed men and women, while wanting and needing jobs, have become so discouraged that they have given up looking for them. As we saw in Chapter 1, "Economic Inequality and Poverty," the wages received by the working poor and near-poor are woefully inadequate; and for them, pursuit of the American Dream by means of work is presently impossible. Nor are work status and earnings the only job-related issues that have been troubling millions of Americans. As we shall see, social scientists have detected a serious degree of dissatisfaction among people—especially among the young, women, and other minorities—with regard to the *kind* of work they find themselves doing. Job dissatisfaction appears to exist at all levels of the American occupational system. Before examining some of these topics in more detail, we shall look at the historical trends that have helped shape today's work world.

THE CHANGING WORLD OF WORK

Unemployment, worker dissatisfaction, and other work-related problems are a result of certain historical trends in the world of work. In particular, three trends have, since the Industrial Revolution of the nineteenth century, helped create the work world we know today. The first trend is the shift from an agricultural society first to an industrial and more recently to a service society. Related to this is the second trend, the decline of self-employment among workers. Finally, the past century has also seen a dramatic increase in the bureaucratization of the workplace.

The Post-Industrial Society

Social scientists often divide a society's system of work activity into three sectors: *primary* (agriculture), *secondary* (manufacturing), and *tertiary* (services). Two hundred years ago, most members of the American labor force were engaged in the primary sector. There was little industry, and most of that was in the hands of individual craftsmen and artisans. Then, under the impetus of the Industrial Revolution of the nineteenth century, the proportion of the labor force engaged in agriculture underwent a marked decline. Not only were more people needed to fill the growing numbers of new jobs in manufacturing, but advances in agricultural production meant that fewer workers could provide the American population with food. By the end of the nineteenth century, 50 percent of the labor force was involved in the secondary sector of the economy.

In the present century, particularly since World War II, there has been an explosive expansion of the tertiary or service sector. Technological advances have made it possible for fewer workers to sustain the growth of manufacturing; as a result, the proportion of the labor force engaged in manufacturing has been shrinking. Today over 60 percent of all workers provide services in business, transportation, communications, utilities, education, health, and government. Only about 35 percent are engaged in manufacturing and less than 5 percent in agriculture (see Table 8.1). This latest shift has led one prominent sociologist to call the United States a

Table 8.1. Employed Persons by Occupation, Sex, and Race

Occupation and Race	Total		Males		Females	
	July 1976	July 1977	July 1976	July 1977	July 1976	July 1977
Total						
Total employed (thousands)	89,608	92,372	54,264	55,677	35,344	36,696
Percent	100.0%	100.0%	100.0%	100.0%	100.0%	100.0%
White-collar workers	48.2	48.5	39.4	39.4	61.6	62.2
Professional and technical	14.2	14.3	13.7	13.8	14.9	15.1
Managers and administrators, except farm	10.4	10.5	13.5	13.5	5.5	5.9
Sales workers	6.1	6.2	5.9	5.9	6.4	6.7
Clerical workers	17.5	17.4	6.2	6.2	34.9	34.5
Blue-collar workers	34.2	34.3	46.8	47.2	14.8	14.6
Craft and kindred workers	13.2	13.4	20.6	21.2	1.8	1.6
Operatives, except transport	11.6	11.4	11.7	11.5	11.4	11.2
Transport equipment operatives	3.7	3.7	5.8	5.8	.4	.6
Nonfarm laborers	5.7	5.7	8.6	8.7	1.3	1.2
Service workers	13.9	13.8	8.8	8.8	21.6	21.3
Private household workers	1.2	1.3	.1	.1	3.0	3.1
Other service workers	12.6	12.5	8.7	8.7	18.6	18.3
Farm workers	3.8	3.5	5.0	4.6	1.9	1.9
Farmers and farm managers	1.9	1.7	2.9	2.6	.3	.3
Farm laborers and supervisors	1.9	1.8	2.1	2.0	1.5	1.6
White						
Total employed (thousands)	79,856	82,331	48,931	50,199	30,926	32,132
Percent	100.0%	100.0%	100.0%	100.0%	100.0%	100.0%
White-collar workers	50.0	50.2	41.1	40.9	64.0	64.6
Professional and technical	14.6	14.7	14.3	14.4	15.1	15.3
Managers and administrators, except farm	11.1	11.2	14.4	14.2	5.9	6.3
Sales workers	6.5	6.6	6.3	6.2	7.0	7.3
Clerical workers	17.7	17.6	6.1	6.0	36.1	35.7
Blue-collar workers	33.6	33.8	45.8	46.4	14.3	14.0
Craft and kindred workers	13.7	13.9	21.2	21.8	1.8	1.6
Operatives, except transport	11.0	10.9	11.2	11.1	10.8	10.7
Transport equipment operatives	3.6	3.6	5.5	5.5	.4	.6
Nonfarm laborers	5.3	5.4	7.9	8.0	1.2	1.2

Table 8.1. Employed Persons by Occupation, Sex, and Race (continued)

Occupation and Race	Total		Males		Females	
	July 1976	July 1977	July 1976	July 1977	July 1976	July 1977
Service workers	12.6	12.4	8.0	8.0	19.7	19.4
Private household workers	.9	.9	.1	.1	2.2	2.2
Other service workers	11.7	11.5	8.0	7.9	17.6	17.2
Farm workers	3.9	3.6	5.1	4.7	1.9	1.9
Farmers and farm managers	2.0	1.9	3.0	2.8	.4	.3
Farm laborers and supervisors	1.9	1.8	2.1	1.9	1.5	1.6
Black and other						
Total employed (thousands)	9,752	10,042	5,333	5,478	4,418	4,563
Percent	100.0%	100.0%	100.0%	100.0%	100.0%	100.0%
White-collar workers	33.5	34.6	24.0	25.7	44.9	45.2
Professional and technical	11.0	11.1	8.9	8.7	13.5	13.9
Managers and administrators, except farm	4.1	4.8	5.4	6.6	2.5	2.5
Sales workers	2.7	2.9	2.9	3.1	2.4	2.7
Clerical workers	15.7	15.8	6.8	7.2	26.4	26.2
Blue-collar workers	39.1	38.5	56.0	55.0	18.7	18.7
Craft and kindred workers	8.9	9.4	15.0	16.1	1.5	1.4
Operatives, except transport	15.8	15.1	16.3	14.9	15.2	15.3
Transport equipment operatives	5.0	5.1	9.0	8.9	.3	.6
Nonfarm laborers	9.3	8.9	15.7	15.0	1.6	1.5
Service workers	24.4	24.5	15.8	15.9	34.8	34.8
Private household workers	4.0	4.2	.05	.2	8.8	9.0
Other service workers	20.4	20.3	15.8	15.7	25.9	25.8
Farm workers	3.1	2.4	4.2	3.4	1.7	1.3
Farmers and farm managers	.7	.3	1.2	.5	—	.1
Farm laborers and supervisors	2.4	2.1	2.9	2.8	1.7	1.3

Source: U.S. Department of Labor, Bureau of Labor Statistics, *Employment and Earnings,* 24 (August 1977): 44.

post-industrial society.[5] If present trends continue, our society will become even more service-dominated in the future.

The Decline of Self-Employment

Today, when we think of joining the labor force, we are likely to think in terms of working *for* someone. This was not always the case. At the time of the American Revolution, 80 percent of the labor force was self-employed. (For the purposes of this discussion, we are leaving aside consideration of the sizable slave population.) Most were engaged in family farming. But whatever their role in the division of labor, working people typically owned their own tools and income-producing property.

[5]Daniel Bell, *The Coming of Post-Industrial Society* (New York: Basic Books, Inc., 1973).

Farming was once seen as an occupation in which individuals could be their own bosses and set their own working conditions. Today, however, most of America's food is produced on huge corporate farms, where agricultural machinery and hired workers perform the tasks once done by farmers and their families.

This was the world of "free enterprise" described by Adam Smith in his famous book, *The Wealth of Nations* (1776). It was a world characterized by numerous self-supporting farmers and entrepreneurs serving the needs of local markets in cities, towns, and countryside. Government was for the most part neither an active overseer of the domestic economy nor a source of employment.

By 1880, the self-employed made up only a third of the labor force, and today they represent less than 10 percent of it. In the wake of the Industrial Revolution, industry and then agriculture were progressively taken over by large-scale corporate enterprises. With the expansion of productive capability that stemmed from technological advances, the creation of modern transportation and communication networks, and the emergence of regional and national markets for inexpensively produced goods, independent entrepreneurs (business owners) and family farmers could not compete with heavily capitalized firms. More and more people found that they had to depend on jobs offered by others in order to survive. Today we are a nation of employees, forced to compete with one another for employment opportunities. In the words of one observer, most labor force participants:

> have virtually no access to income from property or control over the production process. [Their] economic welfare is determined by the vicissitudes of the labor market.[6]

Along with the growth of big business and corporate agriculture has come the expansion of public employment. Today, over 15 percent of the labor force is employed by government in service jobs. The federal government employed over 2.7 million people in 1976, while state and local governments had more than 12 million employees on their payrolls. We have come a long way from the days of Adam Smith, when government workers were a rarity.

Bureaucratization of the Workplace

Implicit in the decline of self-employment is a third historical trend, the rise of the formal organization or *bureaucracy* as a setting for work activity. The term *bureaucracy* is not used loosely by sociologists. It refers to places in which the following features are normally present:

1. A clear-cut division of labor, within which each worker is formally assigned specialized tasks and duties;
2. A hierarchy of authority, in which every individual has a supervisor or boss whose work-related directives must be obeyed;
3. Organizational rules and regulations that govern work performance, delineate the rights and responsibilities of each individual, and dictate proper channels of communication;
4. Demands for rationality and efficiency in the performance of work tasks, requiring individuals to set aside their personal feelings when dealing with others;
5. A ladderlike system of material and symbolic rewards based on technical qualifications and the ability to perform specialized work tasks. The rewards are intended to motivate individuals to compete for movement upward in the bureaucracy and to stimulate loyalty to the work organization.[7]

Bureaucratic organization facilitates employers' control over work and workers in the interest of attaining a particular goal. In the corporate world, the goal is generally to maximize profits, while the goal for government is to provide public services dictated by law (for example, tax collection, defense, law enforcement, aid to the disadvantaged). Work

[6]Michael Reich, "The Evolution of the United States Labor Force," in *The Capitalist System,* Richard C. Edwards et al., eds. (Englewood Cliffs, N.J.: Prentice-Hall, Inc., 1972), p. 176.

[7]H. H. Gerth and C. Wright Mills, eds., *From Max Weber* (New York: Oxford University Press, Inc., 1968), Chapter VIII.

policies, the rules and regulations developed to attain the goal, are decreed by those who hold command positions in a bureaucracy. Workers are expected to obey, even if they do not agree with the policies or the organizational goals. Compliance, or doing what they are told, is a virtue expected of those who wish to remain employed.

This is not to say that those who labor in bureaucratic settings are mindless robots whose every action is controlled. Sociologists have long used the term *informal organization* to underscore the nonofficial behaviors engaged in by workers and their peers.[8] Workers may help a bureaucracy operate more efficiently when they bypass red tape and official channels. On the other hand, informal organization may also enable workers to sabotage superiors' planned use of their labor. In either case, the existence of informal organization indicates that bureaucratic control is by no means total.

Beginning with the Industrial Revolution, an ever larger proportion of the American labor force has come to be employed in bureaucratic settings. Today, 20 percent of our industrial work force is employed by a mere sixteen giant corporations. A firm like American Telephone and Telegraph, for example, monitors a system of subsidiary companies employing over a million people. Earlier we noted that the federal government, as a single employer, carries more than 2.7 million people on its payroll.

Not all persons who work do so in bureaucratic settings. But enough do to have caused a federal task force to conclude:

> The trend is toward large corporations and bureaucracies which typically organize work in such a way as to minimize the independence of the workers and maximize control and predictability for the organization.[9]

Work in America most certainly means entering a competitive labor market and seeking to become someone's employee. With increasing frequency, it means taking a job in the growing service sector, though industrial employment still occupies a significant percentage of the labor force. And, finally, work in America increasingly means becoming part of a bureaucracy and submitting to the authority of persons who command higher organizational rank.

UNEMPLOYMENT

Though most persons who wish to participate in the world of work are able to do so, millions of Americans have been unable to market their labor. In the mid-1970s the United States was in the throes of an economic recession more severe than any since World War II. There was a slowdown in production and hiring, and according to the U.S. Depart-

[8]See Peter M. Blau and Marshall W. Meyer, *Bureaucracy in Modern Society,* 3rd ed. (New York: Random House, Inc., 1971), pp. 37–50.
[9]*Work in America,* p. 18.

ment of Labor, the official rate of unemployment reached 9.2 percent in May 1975—the highest rate since the Great Depression of the 1930s. Out of a total labor force of 92,940,000 people, 8,538,000 were said to be involuntarily out of work. Most of the unemployed either had been dismissed from their last job or were new entrants to the labor force who could not find work.[10]

Unemployment in 1975 was a very serious problem. But it is not only during a recession that millions of people are out of work. In our society, a 4.5 percent unemployment rate is considered "full employment." Over time we have come to tacitly accept a permanent pool of jobless people. There have been relatively few years since World War II in which the rate has dipped below the 4.5 percent level, and we have experienced levels well above this throughout the 1970s. What do such statistics mean? Why does unemployment seem to be a permanent feature of American society, even during nonrecessionary years? What impact does joblessness have on people?

Extent of Unemployment

Government statistics on unemployment have been severely criticized for *understating* the extent of joblessness.[11] Much of this criticism is directed at the ways in which the U.S. Department of Labor defines the term *labor force*. The civilian labor force is said to consist of people who are sixteen years of age or older (with the exception of inmates of institutions). To be counted as a member of the labor force, people must either have a full-time or part-time job or have been actively seeking work in the four-week period prior to the Labor Department's monthly unemployment survey. People who do not meet these criteria are not considered members of the labor force and hence are not counted as employed or unemployed.

If the government's definition of *labor force* were not so restricted, say critics, the unemployment rate would be dramatically higher. Many fourteen- and fifteen-year-olds are capable of and interested in holding jobs—at least part-time—but their joblessness is ignored. Many older students would prefer a full-time job to school attendance, but they are not considered in labor force statistics. Housewives, many of whom do not look for work because their pay would not offset extra child-care costs, are also excluded. Then there are the individuals who have become discouraged in the search for employment and have simply given up. They just drop out of existence in terms of official unemployment statistics. Meanwhile, workers who are on strike, on vacation, or ill are

[10]For statistics on unemployment and the labor force, see the *Monthly Labor Review,* published by the U.S. Department of Labor.

[11]Bertram Gross and Stanley Moses, "Measuring the Real Work Force," *Social Policy,* 3 (September/October 1972): 5–10.

counted as part of the employed labor force even if they are not receiving wages.

Thus, a more inclusive definition of the American labor force would probably give us an unemployment rate three to four times greater than that now reported by government. The rate would expand even more if we counted all the part-time workers who need and want full-time jobs. And what about the millions who work full-time and yet live in poverty or near-poverty—does it make sense to call them "employed"?

Government unemployment statistics generally do not depict the changes that take place in the pool of people who are jobless. Over a given period of years, *different* people are constantly becoming employed and unemployed. If we knew how many persons experienced unemployment at any one moment during such a time period, the dimensions of this phenomenon would be more clearly underscored. In the area of poverty, for example, researchers found that between 1968 and 1974 as many as 85 million people (40 percent of the total population) were at one time or another eligible for public welfare.[12] People were constantly moving in and out of eligibility within and between years. Just as such research highlights the unexpectedly large numbers of persons who tread the poverty line, regular inquiries of a similar nature into unemployment would no doubt result in equally dramatic findings.

The statistics with which the federal government depicts unemployment are chosen for their political neutrality, according to the critics.[13] By making the rate of joblessness seem to be lower than it truly is, the government is able to obscure the extent to which satisfactory work opportunities are absent. As unemployment grows, there has even been discussion of moving the "full employment" rate above 4.5 percent in order to discourage discussion of the fact that there are just not enough employment opportunities to go around.

Causes of Unemployment

What factors underlie America's seeming inability to deliver jobs to its people? A quick but erroneous explanation is that millions of people simply do not care to work. There is no evidence that this is the case. On the contrary, surveys indicate that most persons would choose to work even if their financial situations did not require it.[14] Similarly, experimental income-supplement programs for low-income people have not

[12]*The Changing Economic Status of 5000 American Families: Highlights from the Panel Study of Income Dynamics* (Washington, D.C.: U.S. Department of Health, Education, and Welfare, 1974). This study was conducted by the University of Michigan Institute for Social Research.

[13]John C. Leggett and Claudette Cervinka, "Labor Statistics Revisited," *Society,* 9 (November/December 1972): 99–103.

[14]Robert P. Quinn et al., *Survey of Working Conditions, Final Report, November 1970* (Washington, D.C.: U.S. Government Printing Office, 1971), p. 61. This study was conducted by the University of Michigan Survey Research Center.

Among the people who have lost jobs to automation are workers in textile plants. Today many fabrics are produced partly or wholly by machines like these. Some textile manufacturers have even installed computers that run the textile-producing machines.

shown that economic security diminishes the desire to improve one's position in the labor market.[15]

To understand the causes of unemployment we must look beyond the millions of jobless individuals to focus on factors that are largely beyond their control. Just as there are forces creating and perpetuating poverty, so are there forces that the unemployed cannot counter or overcome. Moreover, many of the underlying causes of poverty are the same as those that put and keep people out of work.

Automation and technological change.   One cause of unemployment is the introduction of computers and other "labor-saving" machines into the workplace. Employers install new machinery in order to increase worker productivity and/or cut labor costs. Automation, computerization,

[15]Joseph A. Pechman and P. Michael Timpane, eds., *Work Incentives and Income Guarantees* (Washington, D.C.: The Brookings Institution, 1975).

and other such technological changes often displace workers from existing jobs and also close certain categories of work opportunities for newcomers to the labor force. There are fewer jobs for telephone operators, coal miners, and farm laborers, among others, because of technological displacement. The steel and auto industries have found that substituting machines for people can help hold down labor costs. While automation and technological change do create new job categories—for example, computer programmer and skilled machine technician—it seems likely that more jobs are lost than are created. Furthermore, technologically displaced workers are likely to find it difficult to qualify for and adjust themselves to the new opportunities that open up.

Those hit hardest by technological displacement are unskilled and semiskilled workers, such as clerical employees, laborers, and lower level blue-collar workers. These workers often do not have the educational attainments and training to qualify for jobs requiring more skills. Technical and professional workers and white-collar administrative personnel are more likely to be insulated from technological displacement and are frequently flexible in terms of the work roles they can readily assume.[16]

The precise impact of automation and technological change on unemployment statistics remains a matter of conjecture. But it is clear that, in selected sectors of the economy, people have been put out of work. Observers disagree about the prospects in store for the future.[17] Some downplay the topic of unemployment, suggesting only that changes will be taking place in the nature of work and in the forms of work organization in which people will be employed. Others feel that the growth of new work opportunities will fail to keep up with the natural growth of the labor force and that a steady increase in unemployment will be the result. Still others contend that there will be plenty of work, but that labor force members will have to work fewer hours per week in order to spread job opportunities around. Whatever the future, it is unlikely to be the unemployed who determine its direction. Such decisions are in the hands of public and private employers—those who hold command positions in bureaucratic work settings.

Job export and goods import.   As we noted in earlier chapters, many of the largest American corporations have been opening plants in other countries. Foreign operations have made it possible for such firms to take advantage of cheaper foreign labor and gain better accessibility to foreign markets. According to organized labor, multinational corporations that invest in plants outside this country and/or close down domestic facilities to reopen elsewhere are guilty of exporting jobs.

---

[16]See Ben B. Seligman, *Most Notorious Victory* (New York: The Free Press, 1966).
[17]Ibid. Seligman is critical of the potential impact of automation, as is Donald M. Michael, *Cybernation, the Silent Conquest* (Santa Barbara, Calif.: Center for the Study of Democratic Institutions, 1962). Defenders of automation include Charles E. Silberman, *The Myth of Automation* (New York: Harper & Row, Publishers, Inc., 1966).

Corporate leaders reject this charge, arguing that a substantial percentage of their increased profits flow back into this country. They claim that foreign investments create new jobs in the United States—for example, through the expansion of operations at company headquarters. However, as in the case of automation and technological change, it is not clear that the numbers of jobs being exported are fully offset by the new ones created. Similarly, workers whose jobs disappear due to factory closings may find it difficult to qualify for the new and different work opportunities with which old jobs are replaced.

Corporate relocation has an effect similar to job export. Corporate relocation occurs when employers move their facilities from one place to another within the country. For example, firms that want low-wage, nonunionized workers have at times found it desirable to relocate in the South or even in Puerto Rico, a commonwealth of the United States in which unemployment is usually extraordinarily high. Many workers cannot uproot themselves and their families in order to follow. They must hunt for other jobs, and they are often found among the unemployed. Workers are also left behind when companies move their headquarters and plants out of central city areas—often for tax relief, labor needs, or to gain additional space in which to conduct operations. Left behind are those who cannot afford to relocate or commute far beyond city limits. Over the last fifteen years, the movement of business and industry out of central city areas has contributed to the erosion of the tax bases on which the services of city governments depend. Services mean jobs—from sanitation work to public school teaching. The financial crises of such large cities as New York, in which thousands of public employees have lost their jobs, are linked at least in part to corporate relocation.

Despite the fact that foreign-made goods are often cheaper than their domestically produced equivalents and thus help workers stretch their dollars, their import is another factor bearing on unemployment. The traditional New England footwear industry has undergone a precipitous decline in the face of inexpensive imports from abroad. American automobile manufacturers in Detroit have been hurt by the inroads that small, gas-saving imports have made into the domestic car market. The import of steel from Japan and other nations has forced the closing of at least one American steel plant. Our consumption of foreign-made clothing, tape recorders, cameras, and televisions has a direct impact on the American economy. Solutions are not in sight. One problem is that we want to export some of our own products, and other nations expect us to accept imports in return. Maintaining a balance of trade is a complex process that must go on, but it is accompanied by unemployment for some of the workers involved.

Government spending and taxation.   Since the depression of the 1930s, the federal government has played an ever more active role in determining the overall course of the economy. In two areas—spending and taxation—federal policies directly affect unemployment rates.

Each year the federal treasury is the recipient of billions of dollars that it turns back into the economy. In fiscal year 1976, for example, government revenues were $300 billion. This money came from personal and corporate income taxes, social insurance taxes, excise taxes, and loans from private financial institutions. That year, the government spent $366.5 billion (or $66.5 billion more than its revenues) on the defense establishment, grants to states and localities, payments to individuals, loan debts, and general federal operations.

There are legal limitations on how the federal government may use the money in its treasury. For example, each year billions of dollars must go to social security recipients and federal retirees. However, some flexibility is often permitted within the law, and new legislation is always being passed and old restrictions modified. Given the huge amounts of money involved, spending priorities directly affect the existing structure and growth of work opportunities.

For example, during the 1960s the federal government put billions of dollars into the space program, creating a whole new set of jobs. Aside from industry, funds were allocated to colleges and universities for space-related research and training. Then, in the early 1970s, federal budget makers adopted new spending priorities. There were cutbacks in the space program, and some space projects were eliminated altogether. Thousands of people—from blue-collar workers to highly trained professionals—found themselves out of work. Young people who had obtained advanced degrees in preparation for space-related jobs continue to face a narrowed demand for their services.

A somewhat similar process occurred in the area of public education. In the 1960s the federal government allocated unprecedented sums to encourage the expansion of teacher training programs, to attract young people into the profession, and to permit school systems to enrich their offerings. A shift in federal spending priorities, plus a decline in the school population and escalating costs due to inflation, led to a slowdown in hiring by the early 1970s. In many parts of the country, teachers and other school personnel have been laid off. College graduates who had prepared for teaching positions confront a "teacher surplus," in which the supply of qualified educators outstrips the demand.

Nor is government spending relevant to unemployment only in terms of priorities. At times, as in the mid-1970s, the federal government has tried to restrict annual spending. This strategy, which is considered a way of fighting inflation, also increases unemployment across the country. Federal policy-makers at times tell us that higher unemployment rates are a cost this society must be willing to bear in order to slow down the rising costs of living. The idea is that people will then have more money to spend on consumer goods and services, and ultimately the unemployed (or at least some of them) will be called back to work.

Taxation policy also has an impact on unemployment. Of each dollar flowing into the federal treasury, thirty-eight cents comes from individual income taxes and thirteen cents from corporate income taxes (see Figure 6.1, page 195). When individual income tax rates are lowered, consumers have more money to spend on goods and services. Assuming that they choose to spend this money, sales will increase, creating more jobs in business and industry. When corporate taxes are cut, firms may choose to invest in new equipment, expanded operations, or higher wages for employees—all of which help create jobs. On the other hand, lower personal and/or corporate income taxes also may mean less revenue for the federal treasury and pressure to slow down government spending. The negative effect of the latter on unemployment somehow must be balanced against anticipated job growth in the private sector of the economy—a very tricky balancing act indeed.

Discrimination. We have already seen that institutional discrimination directly affects the employment opportunities open to minorities, including women. Minority unemployment rates are ordinarily quite high (see Figure 8.1). Blacks, for example, are twice as likely as whites to be out of work and are usually jobless for longer periods of time. The unemployment rates for women are normally slightly higher than those for men. Considering the defects of government unemployment statistics, the true rates of joblessness among minorities and women are no doubt considerably understated.

Discrimination on the basis of age is pervasive in the world of work. Young persons between the ages of sixteen and nineteen—especially minority teenagers—have extraordinarily high joblessness rates. Since they are likely to possess few skills and little work experience, it is difficult for them to get a decent start in the labor market. Old age, on the other hand, may mean that education and skills are out of date. Even where this is not the case, employers whose main concern is to cut labor costs often find it desirable to replace older employees with persons who will work for less.

There has been a steady decline in the labor force participation of persons over sixty-five. A good deal of this decline is attributable to the existence of social security and pension plans. In 1900 two thirds of the men aged sixty-five and over were in the labor force; today the figure is around 25 percent and is declining. While some elderly people look forward to retirement from work, others do not. Retirees often face financial problems (one person in five over the age of sixty-five lives in poverty) and/or difficulties adjusting to the loss of a work role and job-related friendships. Forced retirement of workers in their sixties, despite its often negative impact, has been common.

During the 1970s America's "senior citizens" (whose presence is increasingly noticeable because of changes in the age composition of the population) became quite politically active. Their grass-roots organizing has been felt at the national level on such issues as mandatory retirement. In 1978 Congress passed legislation that removed the mandatory

Figure 8.1. Unemployment Rates, by Sex and Race, 1950–76

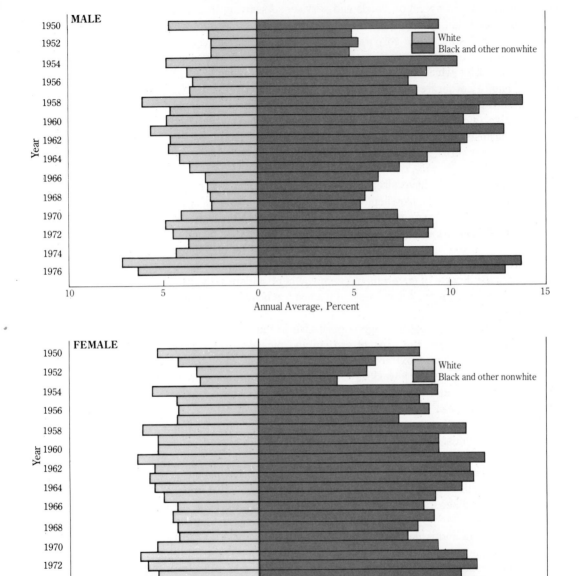

Source: U.S. Department of Commerce, Bureau of the Census, *Social Indicators, 1976* (Washington, D.C.: U.S. Government Printing Office, December 1977), p. 339.

The passage of legislation changing the age of mandatory retirement to seventy in the private sector and removing it from most federal jobs was due, at least in part, to political activism by the elderly. Even with this new legislation, however, older Americans still face discrimination in the world of work.

retirement age from most federal jobs and placed it at seventy years of age for most jobs in the private sector. This action should aid those who otherwise would automatically be pushed out of work in their early or mid-sixties.

The Impact of Unemployment

Individuals who find themselves involuntarily unemployed often discover that their lives and the lives of their families have changed for the worse. For example, Michael Aiken and his associates conducted a study of automobile workers who lost their jobs when their plant was permanently shut down.[18] As their financial resources became depleted, many of the unemployed workers withdrew from contact with friends and relatives because they could not afford to return social favors and obligations. Thus, the unemployed avoided the very persons whose contacts might have been useful in finding new work. Beyond this, the unemployed workers were unhappy over the loss of on-the-job friendships that had helped give meaning to their everyday lives. Not only did they feel a sense of social isolation, but the loss of a work role made them doubt whether they were useful to society. Work was no longer providing personal identity and a sense of social worth. The unemployed had to

[18]Michael Aiken et al., *Economic Failure, Alienation, and Extremism* (Ann Arbor: The University of Michigan Press, 1968).

depend on other family members to bear wage-earning responsibilities, frequently resulting in serious tensions in the home. The economic deprivation stemming from unemployment led many of the persons studied to agree that:

> You sometimes can't help wondering whether life is worth living anymore.

> These days I get a feeling that I'm just not a part of things.

> No one is going to care much about what happens to you when you get right down to it.[19]

The stress, anxiety, tension, and depression Aiken and his associates found among the jobless testify to the central role work plays for people in this society.

Nor are the distresses associated with unemployment found only among blue-collar workers. A recent study of white-collar professionals—including engineers, scientists, and technicians—produced similar findings.[20] The unemployed professionals tended to go through several stages, according to researchers Douglas H. Powell and Paul F. Driscoll. Most of the professionals had been anticipating being laid off as they followed the problems being faced by their employers. So their first feeling was relief when the expected occurred. Given their educational credentials and long employment experience in responsible positions, the professionals were confident about finding new work. They tended to put off looking for a position right away; they wanted to enjoy their newly discovered freedom for a while. Family life, in this initial stage, remained normal.

In the second stage the unemployed professionals began to tire of full-time leisure and to get concerned about not having a job. At this point, they launched highly organized efforts to find work. Economic deprivation had not yet been a problem, as most had savings and other resources to carry them along. Family and friends offered encouragement, and the confidence level of the unemployed was high.

For those whose job-seeking efforts yielded no concrete results, the third stage was characterized by doubt and depression. Their psychological moods interfered with the job search, and relationships with friends and family began to fall apart. The jobless professionals, like their blue-collar counterparts, began to doubt their worth. Confronting feelings of obsolescence, they became alternately frustrated, furious, and filled with despair. Family relations were at their lowest ebb. It was in this stage that suicides were most likely to occur.

In the fourth and final stage, malaise and cynicism set in among the jobless. Job-seeking efforts slowed down to a cursory level, and anxieties decreased as the professionals settled unhappily into their assigned roles.

[19]Ibid., p. 67.

[20]Douglas H. Powell and Paul F. Driscoll, "Middle Class Professionals Face Unemployment," *Society,* 10 (January/February 1973): 18–26.

Family relations improved with the recognition of an extremely difficult situation. In the words of researchers Powell and Driscoll:

> The image of competent and energetic men reduced to listless discouragement highlights the personal tragedy and the loss of valuable resources when there is substantial unemployment. . . . Perhaps more significantly, the situation of these middle-class unemployed further dramatizes the plight of the larger numbers of unemployed non-skilled workers whose fate is to deal with unemployment often during their lifetime.[21]

For workers who fall into the nonskilled category, unemployment simply makes the already difficult challenge of supporting a family that much more difficult. Nonskilled workers feel worthless and doubt themselves even when they are employed. In his classic study, *Tally's Corner,* social anthropologist Elliot Liebow examined the lives of a group of men who lived in a poor neighborhood in Washington, D.C. The men were either unemployed or were construction workers, day laborers, and menial workers in retail and service establishments. Given their position in the occupational structure, all these men had experienced and/or could realistically look forward to bouts with joblessness. Marriages regularly broke down, and some men were reluctant to embark on permanent marital relationships because of their precarious economic situations. According to Liebow: "The way in which the man makes a living and the kind of living he makes have important consequences for how the man sees himself and is seen by others."[22] In their search for some source of pride and self-esteem—since neither work nor home provided these—the men turned to one another, hung around on street corners, and tried to forget their economic, social, and personal sense of failure.

JOB SATISFACTION

If asked, each of us could probably come up with a list of attributes to be found in the ideal job. What kinds of things are most important to working people today? The most comprehensive attempt to answer this question is a University of Michigan study conducted in 1969.[23] As a part of their research project, the investigators conducted lengthy interviews with a carefully selected sample of 1533 employed persons. Those interviewed said that the following things were important in a job: work that is interesting; enough help, equipment, information, and authority to get the job done; an opportunity to develop one's special abilities; the opportunity

---

[21]Ibid., p. 26.

[22]Elliot Liebow, *Tally's Corner* (Boston: Little, Brown & Company, 1967), p. 210.

[23]Quinn et al., *Survey of Working Conditions.* The Michigan researchers repeated this study, with similar findings. See Robert P. Quinn and Linda J. Shepard, *The 1972–73 Quality of Employment Survey* (Ann Arbor: University of Michigan Institute for Social Research, 1974); and Robert P. Quinn et al., "Evaluating Working Conditions in America," *Monthly Labor Review* (November 1973): 32–41.

to see the results of one's work; good pay; and job security. In other words, the content of the job, the resources to do it well, and a chance to realize one's talents were of as much importance as the pay.

If these are the things working people consider important, how satisfied are members of the work force with the jobs they hold? The concept of *job satisfaction* is extremely difficult to measure. Most experts agree that efforts to measure satisfaction and dissatisfaction have been primitive. Thus we must consider any findings as indicative, rather than final and firm.

In some studies workers have simply been asked if their work is satisfying. Over the years, public polling firms such as Gallup have asked this question, and anywhere from 80 to 90 percent of those responding have expressed satisfaction. It is difficult to discern any trends. Critics of such polls assert that this approach does not probe deeply enough into worker attitudes. There is a possibility that most workers answer positively because they have become resigned to their fate. Such criticisms have been lent credence by the University of Michigan's *Survey of Working Conditions*. When the Michigan researchers probed, many of the respondents who claimed to be satisfied admitted to definite complaints about particular aspects of their jobs—for example, their inability to influence supervisors' decisions and to get responses to suggestions on how their work might be better performed.[24]

Another way of measuring job satisfaction has been to ask questions about job choice. In the Michigan study, those interviewed were asked, "If you were free to go into any type of job you wanted, what would your choice be?" In response, 44.4 percent of the workers said that they would prefer some job other than the one they had.[25] The findings of other studies are consistent with the Michigan study, indicating that responses to such a question are closely linked to the *type* of job held by a worker. In one such study, 93 percent of urban university professors and 83 percent of lawyers said they would choose similar jobs again. Among nonprofessional white-collar workers, the proportion was only 43 percent, indicating a sharp difference in job satisfaction within the white-collar category. Among blue-collar workers, the overall percentage of those who would choose similar work again dropped down to a mere 24 percent.[26] When half to three quarters of the persons holding a particular type of job express such opinions, it seems fair to say they are dissatisfied.

In general, the data on job satisfaction indicate that the higher the social status of a job, the more satisfied are those who hold it. The status continuum of occupations and professions tends to be correlated with the

[24]Quinn et al., *Survey of Working Conditions.*
[25]Ibid., p. 61. An additional 6.3 percent of the respondents said they would rather retire or not work at all.
[26]Robert L. Kahn, "The Work Module," in *Work and the Quality of Life,* James O'Toole, ed. (Cambridge, Mass.: The M.I.T. Press, 1974), pp. 203–4.

One way workers express their dissatisfaction with working conditions is to spontaneously walk off the job to conduct a wildcat strike. This photograph shows some striking West Virginia coal miners urging their co-workers to join a wildcat strike to protest cuts in health benefits.

monetary rewards associated with different categories of work. But just as importantly, the ranking of jobs in terms of satisfaction appears to fit with the probable presence or absence of those things workers feel are important about a job. The jobs of nonprofessional white-collar workers and blue-collar workers, unlike those of many professionals, are unlikely to be intrinsically interesting or to allow for the development of talents. Other items that workers see as important—from enough resources to get the job done well to job security—are also likely to be associated with the higher status, better paying professional positions.

Survey findings also suggest that racial minorities and women are extremely dissatisfied with their work situations. This is to be expected, given the overrepresentation of such groups in nonprofessional white-collar and blue-collar jobs and the barriers they face in advancement upward. And, finally, young workers seem to be dissatisfied with much greater frequency than their elders. The Michigan survey, for example, concludes that there is "a significant gap between the expectations or values of young workers and what they actually experience on the job."[27] Since a quarter of the labor force is under thirty years of age, the failure of work to live up to the expectations of youthful workers is by no means a minor problem.

According to a federal task force report, job dissatisfaction reveals

[27]*Work in America*, p. 37.

itself in a number of ways. The productivity of many workers is lower than it should be. In many sectors of the economy, worker absenteeism rates are extremely high, as is annual turnover of employees. Periodically, groups of workers stage wildcat strikes, simply walking off the job on the spur of the moment. Sabotage has grown common, with the production of poor-quality products as one result. The task force detected "a reluctance by workers to commit themselves to their work tasks" and suggested that job dissatisfaction is on the increase in the United States.[28] While no one really knows whether dissatisfaction is increasing, due to the limitations of existing empirical data, it is clear that work today is not meeting the economic, social, and personal needs of a substantial proportion of the labor force.

The Blue-Collar Worker

If we were to distinguish between "brain jobs" and "brawn jobs," blue-collar workers would be found performing most of the latter.[29] Blue-collar jobs, held by some 30 million workers in 1977, encompass a wide variety of skills and skill levels. The unskilled worker is usually employed in a job for which the training requirements are negligible. The required work tasks are so repetitive and routine that they can be learned in a very short time. By contrast, skilled blue-collar work often demands extensive training, ordinarily carried out during a period of apprenticeship. Obviously, the difference between the skill requirements for assembly-line work and cabinet-making is extreme.

In the last fifty years, employment opportunities for the unskilled have steadily diminished. Today only 10 percent of the blue-collar work force is unskilled. Most blue-collar workers hold either skilled or semiskilled jobs, with about 45 percent falling into each of these categories. Such semiskilled jobs as truck driver, machine tender, and short-order cook require relatively commonplace talents but more mental effort than unskilled labor.

Unskilled workers, as we have already noted, are most vulnerable to unemployment and low, often poverty-level, wages. The semiskilled tend to be slightly better off in terms of income, but they still have little job security. The persons who perform semiskilled work are easily interchangeable. Skilled workers are best off economically. However, they

---

[28]Ibid., p. xi. See criticisms of this conclusion and other aspects of *Work in America* in Harold Wool, "What's Wrong with Work in America?" *Monthly Labor Review,* 96 (March 1973): 38–44; and H. Roy Kaplan, "How *Do* Workers View Their Work in America?" *Monthly Labor Review,* 96 (June 1973): 46–48.

[29]The "brain" versus "brawn" distinction is made in Andrew Levison, *The Working-Class Majority* (New York: Coward, McCann & Geoghegan, Inc., 1974). Levison feels that many nonprofessional white-collar and services jobs are essentially of the "brawn" variety. He argues that most members of the labor force—not just blue-collar workers—work primarily with their hands, not their heads.

Public Problem, Private Pain
ON THE ASSEMBLY LINE

While mass production makes it possible for Americans to enjoy a wide variety of consumer goods, it is organized in such a way as to dehumanize those who labor on the assembly line. In this excerpt, Phil Stallings, an auto worker, describes the tedium and boredom of assembly-line work. Stallings, who was twenty-seven years old at the time of this interview, was earning $4.32 an hour as a spot-welder. His job involved putting the first welds on the automobiles that went past him on the conveyer. Stallings has been injured several times on the job, a danger confronting many blue-collar workers.

I stand in one spot, about two- or three-feet area, all night. The only time a person stops is when the line stops. We do about thirty-two jobs per car, per unit. Forty-eight units an hour, eight hours a day. Thirty-two times forty-eight times eight. Figure it out. That's how many times I push that button.

The noise, oh it's tremendous. You open your mouth and you're liable to get a mouthful of sparks. (Shows his arms) That's a burn, these are burns. You don't compete against the noise. You go to yell and at the same time you're straining to maneuver the gun to where you have to weld.

You got some guys that are uptight, and they're not sociable. It's too rough. You pretty much stay to yourself. You get involved with yourself. You dream, you think of things you've done. I drift back continuously to when I was a kid and what me and my brothers did. The things you love most are the things you drift back into.

Lots of time I worked from the time I started to the time of the break and I never realized I had even worked. When you dream, you reduce the chances of friction with the foreman or with the next guy.

It don't stop. It just goes and goes and goes. I bet there's men who have lived and died out there, never seen the end of that line. And they never will—because it's endless. It's like a serpent. It's just all body, no tail. It can do things to you . . . (Laughs.)

Repetition is such that if you were to think about the job itself, you'd slowly go out of your mind. You'd let your problems build up, you'd get to a point where you'd be at the fellow next to you—his throat. Every time the foreman came by and looked at you, you'd have something to say. You just strike out at anything you can. So if you involve yourself by yourself, you overcome this.

I don't like the pressure, the intimidation. How would you like to go up to someone and say, "I would like to go to the bathroom?" If the foreman doesn't like you, he'll make you hold it, just ignore you. Should I leave this job to go to the bathroom I risk being fired. The line moves all the time. . . .

I don't understand how come more guys don't flip. Because you're nothing more than a machine when you hit this type of thing. They give better care to that machine than they will to you. They'll have more respect, give more attention to that machine. And you *know* this. Somehow you get the feeling that the machine is better than you are. (Laughs.)

You really begin to wonder. What price do they put on me? Look at the price they put on the machine. If that machine breaks down, there's somebody out there to fix it right away. If I break down, I'm just pushed over to the other side till another man takes my place. The only thing they have on their mind is to keep that line running.

Studs Terkel, *Working: People Talk About What They Do All Day and How They Feel About What They Do* (New York: Pantheon Books, 1974), pp. 159–61.

are concerned with protecting the rewards that flow from holding a monopoly over a given trade. In times of economic recession, as in the 1970s, even skilled workers confront the issue of job security. The fact that skilled workers are more likely to hold union membership than the other two groups is no guarantee against periodic layoffs.

Despite the differences noted above, virtually all blue-collar workers suffer from low social status. This is reflected in, and no doubt reinforced by, the treatment accorded blue-collar workers in the mass media. Their activities are rarely considered worthy of news reporters' attention, except when there are strikes, layoffs, or serious accidents. With a few ethnic and regional exceptions, blue-collar workers are not commonly the subject of popular music. Television programs typically mock "brawn" workers, portraying them as stupid, closed minded, bigoted, chauvinistic, and politically conservative—erroneous stereotypes rarely applied to white-collar workers. Federal task force interviews with blue-collar workers have

> revealed an almost overwhelming sense of inferiority: the worker cannot talk proudly to his children about his job, and many workers feel they must apologize for their status. Thus the working-class home may be permeated with an atmosphere of failure—even of depressing self-degradation.[30]

Blue-collar work is also physically punitive and often dangerous.[31] Each year almost as many persons die in industrial accidents as were being killed at the height of the Vietnam conflict. According to the U.S. Department of Labor, 5495 people died in industrial accidents in 1975. While the war in Vietnam called forth protest against human carnage, the daily death toll among blue-collar workers generates no such concern. "Brawn" workers are constantly exposed to the possibility of permanent physical impairment and temporary total disability through on-the-job injuries. Occupational diseases—involving everything from respiratory problems to cancer—plague members of the blue-collar sector. We have already noted that blue-collar workers have the highest rates of job dissatisfaction; evidence has begun to accumulate linking this to longevity—the physical and mental stresses at work actually reduce life expectancy.[32]

In recent years, politicians have characterized blue-collar workers as the "silent majority" and the "forgotten Americans." Research indicates a definite relationship between blue-collar status and political alienation. The sense of inferiority, social isolation, and economic insecurity of many blue-collar workers makes them ripe for exploitation by political dem-

---

[30]*Work in America*, p. 29. See also Richard Sennett and Jonathan Cobb, *The Hidden Injuries of Class* (New York: Vintage Books, 1972).

[31]See, for example, Paul Brodeur, *Expendable Americans* (New York: The Viking Press, 1974).

[32]*Work in America*, p. 62.

agogues who know how to channel the frustrations of blue-collar life into the voting booth, while leaving the objective sources of their discontent intact.[33]

The White-Collar Worker

At the turn of the century, the superior wages, social status, and working conditions accorded white-collar workers clearly distinguished them from manual workers. At that time, only 18 percent of the labor force could be counted as white-collar workers. Today the figure is closer to 50 percent. With this growth in the proportion of workers wearing white collars, the sharpness of the distinction between white- and blue-collar work has faded. Particularly affected have been sales and clerical workers. Today there are almost as many nonprofessional white-collar workers as there are professional, technical, and managerial personnel. White-collar nonprofessionals confront some, if not most, of the work-related difficulties under which blue-collar workers tend to suffer.[34]

Like the industrial workplace, large retail establishments and offices are typically highly bureaucratic. In offices, small armies of clerks, typists, secretaries, receptionists, and office assistants perform segmented work tasks under the constant supervision of higher ranking authorities. The same type of bureaucratic environment typically prevails in retail establishments. The social status attached to many nonprofessional jobs is low, and in some cases the wages are less than those accorded semiskilled blue-collar workers. It is for such reasons that job dissatisfaction is high among nonprofessionals, as indicated by the fact that less than half of those surveyed say they would choose similar work again.[35] In the last two decades, nonprofessionals have begun to make up an increasing percentage of the nation's union membership. Faced with low pay and factorylike working conditions, they are turning to the promises of relief and protection unions have long extended to blue-collar workers.

Nor is the world of work consistently rosy even for white-collar professionals, despite their generally high performance on measures of job satisfaction and their relatively high income and status and good working conditions. In libraries, public school systems, hospitals, colleges and universities, and social welfare agencies, as well as in law, architecture,

[33]Aiken et al., *Economic Failure, Alienation, and Extremism.* See also Harold L. Sheppard and Neal Herrick, *Where Have All the Robots Gone?* (New York: The Free Press, 1972).

[34]The changing nature of white-collar work was observed by C. Wright Mills in *White Collar* (New York: Oxford University Press, Inc., 1951). See also Harry Braverman, *Labor and Monopoly Capital* (New York: Monthly Review Press, 1974), pp. 293–373.

[35]Kahn, "The Work Module," pp. 203–4.

and engineering firms, professionals are fighting to maintain their pre-rogatives and autonomy in the face of control by administrative authorities. Pay and the availability of resources have also become major issues. The institutions mentioned above are all client-oriented. Any increase in the number of clients without an attendant increase in professional staff and supportive services is akin to the assembly-line speedup industrial workers are continually battling. Slowly, members of the professional sector are beginning to suffer many of the same work-related problems as lower-level workers. Groups of professionals—for example, teachers—have affiliated with organized labor and engaged in strikes in response.

Another white-collar group facing work difficulties is middle management, bureaucratic authorities who report to the top executives and oversee professional and technical employees as well as lower-level supervisors. Middle managers now represent some 5 percent of the labor force, and the pressures and problems they confront are inevitably felt by those millions who labor below them. A recent study of this group uncovered complaints about salaries, job insecurity, forced early retirement, limits to upward mobility, and heavy responsibilities that are combined with constraints on their authority from above.[36]

Sociologists have typically restricted the term *working class* to refer only to blue-collar workers. In recent years some sociologists have suggested that a "new working class" is in the making.[37] The erosion of white-collar privilege, the bureaucratization of virtually all white-collar work, job-related complaints that sound like those factory workers often voice, movements toward white-collar unionization—all suggest that virtually no part of the labor force is immune to job dissatisfaction.

Job Dissatisfaction and the Consumer Society

Members of the American labor force do more than produce something of value for other people in return for monetary rewards. Workers and their families are also consumers, a fact that must not be divorced from a discussion of the significance of work.

According to Paul Baran and Paul Sweezy, corporate advertisers are constantly "waging, on behalf of the producers and sellers of consumer goods, a relentless war against saving and in favor of consumption."[38] Psychologist Erich Fromm contends that they have been immensely successful:

[36]Emanuel Kay, "Middle Management," in *Work and the Quality of Life,* O'Toole, ed., pp. 106–26.

[37]See Bertram Silverman and Murray Yanowitch, eds., *The Worker in "Post-Industrial" Capitalism* (New York: The Free Press, 1974), Chapter IV.

[38]Paul A. Baran and Paul M. Sweezy, *Monopoly Capital* (New York: Monthly Review Press, 1969), p. 128.

Many Americans look to shopping expeditions as a means of finding the fulfillment missing in their jobs. Since they often cannot afford all the consumer goods they desire, they may buy on credit. With the easy availability of bank loans and revolving-credit plans, consumer credit reached about $200 billion in the mid-1970s.

Modern man, if he dared to be articulate about his concept of heaven, would suggest a vision which would look like the biggest department store in the world. . . . He would wander open-mouthed in this heaven of gadgets and commodities, provided only that there were ever more and newer things to buy, and perhaps that his neighbors were just a little less privileged than he.[39]

Work provides the financial means—at least for most members of the labor force—of entering this visionary heaven here on earth.

[39]Erich Fromm, *The Sane Society* (Greenwich, Conn.: Fawcett Publications, Inc., 1955), p. 123. See also Stuart Ewen, *Captains of Consciousness* (New York: McGraw-Hill, Inc., 1976).

One can speculate that spending money on consumer goods is one way dissatisfied workers can temporarily blot out and separate themselves from the lack of fulfillment provided by their jobs. For most members of the labor force, work is strictly segmented from leisure pursuits. A boring workday can be offset by the hours spent at home tinkering with tools, guns, and cars. In the after-work pursuit of crafts and hobbies, employees who are told what to do all day on the job are transformed into their own bosses. Here they can make up for the lack of opportunities to develop their special abilities, and here they can see the results of their own work. Status denied workers within a bureaucratic setting can be gained by the conspicuous consumption of commodities—from color televisions to camping trailers—that will be noticed and admired by others. Ironically, play, recreation, and leisure have themselves become commodities as corporate advertisers pitch their advertising campaigns to unfulfilled interests and needs.

The wages and salaries of millions of workers are not high enough to enable them to buy all the commodities they are encouraged to crave. Nevertheless, the producers and sellers of consumer products must unload their goods on a regular basis if they are to realize profit goals. Thus, credit has been extended to virtually anyone holding a job. By going into debt—that is, by taking out loans or buying on the installment plan—members of the labor force are able to buy and consume well beyond their immediate means. Producers and sellers prosper. Indeed, easy credit actually means more jobs for workers. But members of the labor force, in order to pay off debts and maintain a credit rating that will allow more debt in the future, must continue to labor. The extension of consumer credit carries with it the subtle effect of forcing workers to the job—even if the job is highly unsatisfying. Workers who would like to quit, to rebel against their bureaucratic superiors, or to take a more satisfying job that pays less must weigh such moves against their debts. Ironically, it would actually harm workers to reject the consumer society, the way the economy is now organized. To reject debt and commodities would not only limit the outlets currently available to the dissatisfied; it would throw millions more people out of work.

CONTROLLING PEOPLE/ CONTROLLING WORK

In the realm of paid labor, people today are forced to function somewhat like objects—subject to economic forces, institutional constraints, and the will of bureaucratic superiors. Becoming employed or unemployed more and more happens *to* people; they have little control over it. Pay, rank, and working conditions are set *for* employees, not by them. Job dissatisfaction is a result of events and conditions that impinge *upon* workers and that cannot easily be altered or escaped.

Work and Other Macro Problems

Many of the macro problems we have considered in earlier chapters simultaneously express themselves in the world of work. With the exception of the very rich, for whom property ownership is the major source of income, the economic well-being of most Americans depends on the marketing of their labor. The income inequalities that prevail in this society and that help determine people's life chances reflect employment policies that are bound to the status quo.

Political decisions at the national level have a direct impact on unemployment, wages, and prices. To the degree political power is concentrated in the hands of a few, decisions in these areas will be made *for* working people rather than by them. The erosion of political democracy is being replicated at the workplace, where people perform dissatisfying labor within the confines of bureaucratic control from above.

Institutional racism and sexism, coupled with inequalities in educational opportunity, arbitrarily disqualify millions who are basically capable of filling positions toward the top of the job hierarchy. Since work is linked to one's sense of self-worth, subordination due to race, sex, or performance in class-biased educational systems creates millions of unhappy, unfulfilled people. They are joined by the aged in their sense of human obsolescence.

The notion of work as an activity that produces something of value for other people is perverted by the dependence of many workers on the "economy of death." While billions of dollars are allocated to upgrade the production of military-related goods, dangerous and disease-producing conditions continue in the underdeveloped, civilian economy. In both the civilian and military sectors, products are developed that pose an immense threat to the surrounding environment and to people.

To alter the world of work, we would want to eliminate unemployment, job dissatisfaction, the stark relationship between work status and life chances, barriers to the full utilization of human talent, and production that leads to the destruction of life, rather than its enhancement. In altering work, we are simultaneously confronted with the challenge of eliminating all the macro problems considered in this book.

Improving the Nature of Work

On the day of the presidential election in November 1976, the official unemployment rate in the United States was almost 8 percent. Both presidential candidates promised to bring this rate down, and each stressed a somewhat different approach.

Gerald Ford saw the answer in new tax reductions, combined with cuts in federal spending (primarily in the area of social services, not defense). This approach presumably would place more dollars in the hands of consumers, whose increased spending would then help stimulate the economy and create more job opportunities. Presumably the new private sector jobs would help out some of the millions of unemployed.

Jimmy Carter took a slightly different approach. Carter called for an immediate increase in federal spending to put at least some of the unemployed back to work right away. This spending, to be paid for by the money saved by eliminating government inefficiency (e.g., in defense outlays), would be coupled with tax reforms favoring middle- and low-income taxpayers. The increased consumption resulting from this mix of strategies would stimulate the economy, thus opening up ever more job opportunities.

While Carter's approach promised more immediate relief for many of the unemployed than did Ford's, neither man chose to confront a number of important issues. Only by resolving these issues will we be able to find solutions to the macro problem of work.

There is a critical need to revise the official definition of *unemployment* so that it reflects more accurately the extent to which our economy fails to provide sufficient work opportunities. Approaches to unemployment that focus only on reducing the officially defined rate ignore the work needs of millions.

There is a need for centralized coordination and control over the introduction of new technologies that displace workers and eliminate jobs. Such coordination and control might be handled through the federal chartering of business firms (see page 246 for a discussion of federal chartering).

There is also a need for control over the degree to which business and industry are permitted to invest money outside this country or to move productive activities elsewhere. The profit benefits of such activities may well be offset by the human and social welfare costs of domestic unemployment. This tradeoff needs to be investigated.

Given the paucity of work opportunities for all who want and need them, federal and state governments should be willing to serve as "employers of last resort." If government is unable to fully stimulate the private sector into providing sufficient work for people to do, it should find ways to organize and allocate its own resources to pick up the slack.

It is time to move beyond the assumption that putting all members of the labor force in a job is sufficient in and of itself. Work conditions themselves are in need of drastic change. There are many possibilities here, including federal incentives for business firms to develop comprehensive programs of worker participation and control. What is needed is increased worker involvement in planning and decision-making, and decreased hierarchy and bureaucratic control from above.

It is also time to begin breaking up concentrated ownership within the private sector, spreading it more widely among the producers of corporate wealth. Federal chartering of business firms, alluded to earlier, might be used to help workers buy the firms to which they contribute their labor. This would be another way of democratizing the workplace.

As we saw in Chapter 2, "Concentration of Power," the interests of elites may run counter to change that is in the general interest. So we should not underestimate the effort it will take to bring about such changes in the world of work. Pressures for change must come from the unemployed and from working men and women who want to leave their children a better world in which to labor.

SUMMARY

Work, an activity that produces something of value for other people, is central to our everyday lives. We are encouraged to pursue the American Dream of material affluence through work. Work helps determine our class position and life-style, and the jobs we do may affect how others treat us. Finally, work is an important source of self-esteem and self-identity.

The world of work has been changing as a result of three historical trends. The United States has moved from an agricultural society to one in which manufacturing and, more recently, the provision of services occupy most workers. Most members of the labor force were self-employed two hundred years ago; few are today. And workers have increasingly become part of large-scale organizations in which they are subject to bureaucratic authority and control.

While our labor force totals over 90 or 100 million people, millions are unemployed. Government unemployment statistics, critics charge, underestimate the true extent of joblessness. Various factors underlie unemployment. These include automation and technological changes that displace workers; the movement of corporate plants abroad or out of urban areas in which the need for jobs is great; government taxation and spending policies that affect consumer and corporate activities; and patterns of discrimination on the basis of race, sex, and age. The impact of unemployment on many of those affected is highly negative—whether we are talking about white-collar professionals or nonskilled, blue-collar workers.

When asked what is important to them in work, people generally mention the content of the job, the resources to do it well, and a chance to realize their talents. These are as important as pay. There are signs that numerous workers are dissatisfied with the jobs they hold—e.g., they would prefer different jobs. Dissatisfaction is greatest among blue-collar workers, followed by white-collar nonprofessionals. White-collar professionals show the least dissatisfaction. The ranking of jobs in terms of satisfaction appears to reflect the presence or absence of those things workers feel are important to them in work. Dissatisfaction is reflected in lowered productivity, high absenteeism and turnover rates, wildcat strikes, and sabotage.

Blue-collar workers perform most of the "brawn jobs," as opposed to the "brain jobs." Wages and job security vary, depending on a worker's skill level. But blue-collar workers in general suffer from low social status. Their work is physically punitive and often dangerous.

White-collar nonprofessionals confront many similar work-related difficulties. They often labor in a setting that is as bureaucratic as the industrial workplace. The social status of many nonprofessional jobs is low, as are wages. White-collar professionals express the most job satisfaction, yet even they face difficulties. In many instances, professionals must fight to maintain their prerogatives and autonomy in the face of control by administrative authorities.

American society emphasizes consumption, and this may be one way that dissatisfied workers can blot out and separate themselves from the lack of fulfillment provided by their jobs. Consumption means that many must go into debt through the use of credit and loans. Such debt carries with it the subtle effect of forcing workers to the job—even if the job is highly unsatisfying.

The world of work is linked to many of the macro problems considered in earlier chapters, and in altering work we are confronted with the challenge of eliminating those problems. Among the steps to be taken to improve the nature of work are revising the official definition of unemployment to make statistics on joblessness more accurate; coordinating and controlling new technologies that displace workers and eliminate jobs; limiting corporate investments overseas that create more domestic unemployment; using federal and state governments as employers of last resort; expanding worker participation in planning and decision-making; and promoting increased worker ownership of the firms to which they contribute their labor.

DISCUSSION QUESTIONS

1. With all the work that needs to be done in this society, how is it that millions of people do not have jobs? Who or what is responsible for their joblessness?
2. Would you rather be self-employed or an employee? Justify your choice. Which are you most likely to be in the future? Why?
3. Think about the work activity for which you most recently received wages or salary. Would you care to perform this work on a permanent basis? Why?

4. If your financial security were guaranteed, would you still want to be a part of the work force? Why?

5. Most of us agree that some positions in the world of work are far less desirable than others. What arguments could be made for and against dramatically increasing the pay and benefits associated with the least desirable jobs?

6. What do you see as the advantages and disadvantages of increased worker participation in planning and decision-making in the organizations where they work? Who or what are the obstacles to such increased participation?

PART II

Micro Problems

I n Part I we examined a number of macro problems, key features of society that do harm to millions of people. Problems also exist at the individual level. We call such individual problems *micro problems*. Micro problems involve behavior that has an adverse impact on other people and/or that is self-harmful. The reasons individuals engage in such behavior are complex and little understood.

The definition and pervasiveness of criminal behavior shifts with changes in the creation and application of law (Chapter 9). Though crimes against people and property seem to be increasing, we do not know how many crimes are actually committed. Many are not reported, and law enforcement agencies are often selective in the exercise of their responsibilities. Given our limited knowledge, and given the fact that there are so many types of criminal behavior, satisfactory explanations of criminal behavior continue to elude us. Meanwhile, the operation of the criminal justice system (police, courts, and correctional institutions) breaks down at a number of crucial points. The system seems to have only a marginal impact on criminal behavior.

The micro problem of mental illness is also difficult to explain and resolve (Chapter 10). Millions of people are mentally troubled. But there is some controversy over whether the behavior of such persons, no matter how bizarre, should be categorized as "illness." Perhaps it is not a disease and thus should not be treated from a medical perspective. Perhaps such behavior is instead a normal, even healthy, way for persons to react to intolerable life situations. As with crime, we do not know how much "mental illness" there is in the United States. And we are not quite sure how to explain the behaviors that come to be labeled as mental illness. Existing forms of treatment—such as drugs and involuntary confinement—may not be addressing the sources of people's troubles.

The most dramatic form of self-harm is suicide (Chapter 11). While it is convenient to assume that persons who commit or attempt suicide are mentally ill, this may not be the case. Instead, such behavior may be considered normal under certain circumstances. In recent years, suicide prevention programs have been initiated, but their full impact is unknown. This is at least partially due to lack of faith in suicide statistics, given the underreporting thought to be involved.

Drug abuse, including the abuse of alcohol, is a form of self-harm in which many Americans are engaged (Chapters 12 and 13). The use of consciousness-altering substances, both legal and illegal, continues to increase. In the case of certain substances—such as over-the-counter and prescription drugs and alcoholic beverages—large-scale business interests contribute to the momentum of use. Why so many people seek to alter their state of consciousness, often risking serious illness or death, remains a matter of debate. Since it is difficult to successfully intervene against behavior that is little understood, efforts to control alcoholism and drug abuse have had limited success.

9 Criminal Behavior

Members of American society should be at peace with themselves and with one another. The vicarious rewards associated with crime and violence should have no attraction.

Periodically, pollsters ask a representative sample of Americans to list and rate the societal problems they consider most serious. No list looks exactly like any other, as new issues are added and older ones receive different ratings. But crime shows up in every poll.

There is a very realistic basis for our concern with crime. National surveys reveal that almost one out of five adults falls victim to crime in any twelve-month period. Most are victims of property offenses rather than crimes of violence. In central city areas, particularly in and around low-income neighborhoods, the rates of victimization are even higher.

For the most part, the phrase *crime problem* primarily means larceny, burglary, robbery, auto theft, assault, rape, and murder to Americans. These crimes touch people very personally. In several, the victims come face to face with the perpetrators. Such experiences are often terrifying, if not dangerous or fatal.

The public is far less concerned about certain other categories of crime, perhaps because these seem rather distant and remote. White-collar crime, which costs billions of dollars more per year than theft, arouses little public ire. Organized crime is more frequently a subject of entertainment programs than a threat to public sensibilities. Political crimes—whether engaged in by dissident groups or government officials—seem incomprehensible to many Americans and are easily ignored. Only the most spectacular incidents or revelations are likely to evoke widespread public concern about these types of crime, and even this is often quite temporary.

Thus, most Americans take a narrow view of the crime problem, focusing only on prospects or memories of personal victimization. This lack of concern about other types of crime is also found in the official crime statistics produced by law enforcement agencies. These statistics regularly indicate increases in the types of criminal behavior Americans fear. When publicized by the news media, official crime statistics reaffirm the legitimacy of public concern. The meaning and reliability of these statistics are rarely questioned, except perhaps by sociologists. Nor do most Americans ordinarily notice that certain categories of crime, such as many white-collar offenses, are absent from official reports.

Because of their concern over the crime problem, Americans support policies and expenditures that claim to be able to restore "law and order." What most do not fully appreciate is that embarrassingly little is known about the *causes* of criminal behavior. In the absence of an adequate understanding of the causes, America's system of criminal justice remains only marginally effective in curbing the crime problem.

In this chapter we will examine crime and criminal behavior in American society today. We will try to answer the question, "What is crime?" and look at sources of crime statistics and their limitations. With these limitations in mind, we will assess the extent and significance of various categories of crime. The chapter then considers physiological, psychological, and sociological explanations for criminal behavior. Finally, we will look at the workings of the criminal justice system.

WHAT IS CRIME?

As we have seen, most Americans define *crime* as behavior that turns individuals into victims, posing a direct threat to their personal safety or property. The behaviors that are defined as criminal in this sense are considered wrong in and of themselves—*mala in se*—such as murder and burglary. No one should have to live in constant fear of harm or loss of personal belongings. No society could continue to function if its members were free to attack one another or take others' property at will. Such acts are condemned in virtually every society. In short, there is universal agreement that certain offensive behaviors are not to be tolerated—they are "wrong" and thus criminal.

But this popular definition of crime as *mala in se* acts does not account for all types of criminal behavior. In order to define crime, we must examine the society's system of law. Legally, the concept of crime encompasses many more acts than the average American has in mind when discussing the crime problem. In the United States, the legal definition of crime is also very precise, referring to acts that are intentional, inexcusable or indefensible, in violation of an existing law, and punishable by government or the state.

The popular and legal definitions of crime do not always coincide. Americans frequently engage in behaviors that are crimes under the law, but that they do not necessarily think of as crimes. For example, workers often remove supplies or tools from their places of employment without realizing that they are committing property offenses. An estimated 25 to 45 million Americans have tried marijuana, but most would not describe themselves as drug offenders. Laws against fornication and adultery are broken daily, but the individuals involved are unlikely to see themselves as sex criminals. Not until agencies of law enforcement attempt to confer criminal status on individuals engaging in such acts are most Americans fully conscious of violating the law. Whether people are aware of or agree with the legal definition of what is crime, it is ultimately the law that makes an activity a crime and allows sanctions to be imposed on violators.

Elements of the Legal Definition

Let us look more closely at the legal definition of crime and the various elements involved in this definition. First, in order to be defined as a crime, an act must have been *intentional*. While the concept of intention is somewhat vague, the law assumes that most people are capable of regulating their behavior and avoiding illegal acts. Hence, those who engage in law-violating behavior must have intended to do so. While intentions are addressed by prosecutors in court, and accused individuals are given the opportunity to defend themselves, the burden of proving an act to be unintentional is placed squarely on the shoulders of the accused.

The legal definition of crime also involves the idea that the act in question is *inexcusable or indefensible.* One of the few excuses is that the individual had no control over the illegal behavior. Thus, individuals are unlikely to be accorded criminal status if they can prove that they were acting under duress—that is, if they were forced by others to violate the law. Likewise, age is considered to be relevant to the issue of control over, and thus responsibility for, criminal behavior. Ordinarily, children under seven years of age are not held responsible for their actions. Special judicial treatment is accorded individuals between seven and sixteen or eighteen years of age, because *juvenile delinquents* are ordinarily considered to be less responsible for their behavior than are adults. Finally, individuals may defend their illegal behavior by claiming insanity. In this case, accused persons must prove that they were mentally incapable of avoiding the act in question or incapable of differentiating between right and wrong at the time the law violation took place.

Juvenile delinquents are considered less responsible for their behavior than adults. As a result, teenage gang members are likely to receive far different treatment from the criminal justice system than their older peers, even when they have engaged in the same illegal behavior.

Ultimately, however, the key element of the legal definition of crime is the *law* itself. The law enables the state to *punish* those whose acts are considered intentional, inexcusable, and in violation of a law by conferring the status of criminal on them. It is not too much of a truism to say that in the absence of law, criminals would not exist. Without law, there is no such thing as crime—at least in the legal sense.

Defining Behavior as Criminal

Why do some acts get defined by law as crime, while others do not? There are conflicting answers to this question. According to some, law is formulated in response to the will of the people. Members of the society, it is said, share common values. Law is the product of a societal consensus about what forms of behavior are to be allowed and what forms are to be condemned and punished. In this view, we live in a democratic, pluralistic society (see Chapter 2), in which equally powerful interest groups compete to direct and express the public will. The state responds by passing laws that serve the self-defined best interests of society's members. The state itself is neutral. It is not under the sway of any dominant group, for there is no such group in American society.

An alternative view holds that law is formulated in response to the interests of the dominant economic and social class. In a society like ours, wealth, status, and political power are unequally distributed. The dominant class—that which is most advantaged in terms of this distribution—is said to be in the best position to influence actions of the state. This class seeks to protect its economic resources and general well-being through the force of law. In this view, the state is not neutral—either in the formulation of law or in practices of law enforcement. Rather, the state acts in the interests of the dominant class.

Sociologist William Chambliss has suggested that the real state of affairs lies somewhere in between these two views.[1] According to Chambliss, there is evidence that some laws are indeed expressions of public opinion and are responses to pressure by interest groups. Examples include laws limiting pollution and statutes protecting minorities against discrimination. Other laws, however, clearly work to the advantage of the economically advantaged. Examples here are tax loopholes and the absence of severe legal penalties for many white-collar crimes. Thus, says Chambliss, there is evidence that members of the dominant class actively use their political power to influence the formulation of law so as to protect themselves.

Chambliss has proposed a third view of why acts are defined as crimes. He calls this view a *conflict theory of legal change*. This theory begins by

---

[1]William J. Chambliss, "The State, the Law, and the Definition of Behavior as Criminal or Delinquent," in *Handbook of Criminology*, Daniel Glaser, ed. (Chicago: Rand McNally & Company, 1974), pp. 7–43.

recognizing that American society is composed of competing classes and interest groups that seek favors from the state. Since these classes differ in their wealth, power, and prestige, conflicts (e.g., over the control of economic resources) will and do take place. These conflicts ultimately cause acts to be defined as crimes:

> It is in the course of working through and living with these inherent conflicts that the law takes its particular content and form. It is out of the conflicts generated by social class divisions that the definition of some acts as criminal or delinquent emerges.[2]

Chambliss notes that the dominant class only wins out in some of these conflicts. Class-based conflicts are often resolved by the state through compromise legislation or legal decisions that seem fair to all.

Meanwhile, according to Chambliss, a variety of interest groups that are not class-based are also competing for favors from the state. Bureaucracies want their interests protected or advanced. "Moral entrepreneurs"—groups with particular moral concerns that they would like to see translated into law—likewise compete for attention. Again there is winning, losing, and compromise as the state responds.

Chambliss suggests that the formulation of law, and thus the creation of the legal definition of crime, is a dynamic, historical process. This process is not totally democratic—in other words, law does not automatically emerge from and serve the interests of all members of society. Nor is the process totally manipulated by a dominant class. It is, however, a political process:

> What gets defined as criminal or delinquent behavior is the result of a political process within which rules are formed which prohibit or require people to behave in certain ways. . . . Nothing is inherently criminal, it is only the response that makes it so. If we are to explain crime, we must first explain the social forces that cause some acts to be defined as criminal while others are not.[3]

Sociologists like Chambliss are just beginning to do research on how laws are formulated, and how this leads to the "creation" of crime. Clearly the answer to the question, "What is crime?" must go beyond a legal definition. The answer must include attention to the sources of any such definition.

CRIME STATISTICS

This chapter will primarily consider crime as it is legally defined. In the United States, our perception of the crime problem is to a large extent based on official reports, such as the *Uniform Crime Reports* issued

[2]Ibid., p. 39.
[3]Ibid.

annually by the Federal Bureau of Investigation (FBI). Data in this report and from other sources as well must be approached with caution.[4]

Official Statistics

The FBI's *Uniform Crime Reports* is a summary of data submitted by thirteen thousand local police departments around the country. These agencies of law enforcement are in a position to gather several types of crime statistics, including the number and kinds of crimes reported to or observed by local police, arrest statistics, and statistics on cases in which conviction took place. In order to assess the amount of crime taking place in the United States, one begins with data on the number of crimes reported to police or otherwise officially detected.

Sociologists have long been aware that the statistics accumulated by police departments and reported by them are of questionable accuracy. Many crimes simply are not brought to the attention of police and thus do not get counted. Murder is almost always reported; but perhaps several times as many rapes occur as are brought to police attention. While most people will report the theft of an automobile, far fewer will report the theft of personal property that is worth relatively little. A woman who is beaten up by a stranger on the street is likely to call the police; one who is assaulted by her husband is far less likely to do so.

In some cases, crimes are not reported to law enforcement agencies because the victims know the perpetrator and want to handle the problem informally. This often occurs for minor offenses. In other cases, people may feel that a crime is not worth reporting because it is unlikely that the police will handle it satisfactorily or solve it. In still other cases, the victims may fear retribution or revenge if they report offenses to the police. Finally, some crimes are simply never detected—or the illegal acts in question are not defined as crimes by those in a position to do the reporting. Whatever the reasons involved, we know that statistics on crime reported to the police grossly underestimate the extent of crime.

Official crime statistics are also subject to distortion by the actions of police themselves. Police departments differ in their vigilance and in the degree to which they are actively concerned with particular categories of crime. Attention to public complaints and police reaction to observed law violations may vary among police departments at different times. Police departments and individual officers have considerable discretion in making arrests. If they choose to avoid arresting individuals, the amount of crime will look smaller than it actually is. Alternatively, police activism may create the appearance of statistical increases in criminal behavior.

A case in point is the way police handle persons possessing illegal drugs. There has been an upward trend in arrests for possession of illegal

[4]See Gwynn Nettler, *Explaining Crime* (New York: McGraw-Hill, Inc., 1974), pp. 43–61.

Table 9.1. Drug Arrest Trends, 1967–76

	1967	1976	Percent Increase
All ages	47,019	295,138	+527.7%
Under eighteen years of age	10,030	71,742	+615.3%
Eighteen years of age and over	36,989	223,396	+504.0%

Source: U.S. Department of Justice, Federal Bureau of Investigation, *Uniform Crime Reports, 1976* (Washington, D.C.: U.S. Government Printing Office, 1977), p. 175. Based on data from 3,035 law enforcement agencies serving a 1976 estimated population of 94,317,000.

drugs in recent years (see Table 9.1). Part of this increase can be attributed to the fact that drug use was not considered an important problem during most of the 1960s, so police rarely made arrests, or else concentrated on certain segments of the population, such as the poor, when looking for drugs. During the late 1960s, however, drug use became both more widespread and a matter of societal concern, and police became more vigilant. Nonetheless, police today continue to ignore many drug offenders—one need only go to a rock concert to see drug laws violated with impunity, often right in front of the police. Such crimes do not find their way into crime statistics.

Furthermore, individual police departments have different procedures for collecting and reporting crime statistics. The Federal Bureau of Investigation has been making notable efforts to encourage standardized procedures across the country, but it has not been totally successful. Moreover, as departments change their procedures to conform with FBI standards, statistics on incidence may change even if the same amount of crime is occurring. There is also evidence that some police departments do not report all the crimes they know of. For example, in the 1960s, the President's Commission on Law Enforcement found that a number of large city police departments kept separate records on crimes that they did not follow up and on those they wanted to keep from the public for political reasons.[5]

There is also the question of just what police are counting. A violation may involve one offender or many; it may also involve more than one law. For example, if two teenagers kill someone in a gang fight, escape by stealing a car after assaulting the driver, and are finally stopped after numerous traffic offenses, who and what is to be counted? When confronted with such dilemmas, police departments are likely to work out their own formulas. They may count crimes by the numbers of victims involved. Or they may count only the most serious crime (in terms of the probable penalty for conviction) committed by each offender. This and other inaccuracies in counting distort official statistics.

If trying to figure out what to make of official statistics is made difficult by such factors, trying to compute crime *rates* is even worse. Crime rates are important for a number of reasons. They make it possible to compare crime in different locales or over periods of time. Sociologists use com-

[5]President's Commission on Law Enforcement and Administration of Justice, *The Challenge of Crime in a Free Society* (New York: Avon Books, 1968), p. 112.

parative crime rates in the search for explanations of crime and criminality. Knowledge of changing rates is also of practical importance to officials interested in evaluating the effectiveness of efforts to prevent or control crime. The public wants to know whether the taxes they pay for law enforcement are being used wisely. People also use crime rates as a barometer of the quality of life in their communities.

Crime rates are calculated in terms of the ratio between the number of crimes officially recorded and the size of the population. For example, the murder rate is expressed in terms of the number of known murders per one hundred thousand people. One would assume that, since most murders become known to police, the murder *rate* is reliable. But there are problems other than the lack of reliability of police statistics. We only count the number of people in the American population every ten years. Even then, the Bureau of the Census misses millions—for example, inner-city residents and members of minority groups are generally undercounted. This means that the population figures so crucial to computing crime rates are only estimates of unknown accuracy. Crime rates can be no more reliable than the statistics that go into them, which means they are not necessarily reliable at all.

Another complication involves the changing composition of America's population. What may appear to be an upsurge in criminality may simply be a reflection of changing population characteristics. For example, young people are responsible for a disproportionate amount of such common crimes as robbery. An increase in the rates for these crimes may simply be a result of an increased proportion of young people. Such changes create problems. Do we know all the factors that must be taken into account in order to compare crime rates among locales or over time? How much weight should be given to those factors we do know about in order to interpret rates and compare them?

At best, official crime statistics provide a very rough picture of the actual amount of crime. Attempts to refine the methods of gathering, reporting, and interpreting such statistics continue, but substantial problems remain. Political considerations in a particular locale will probably always affect police activity and patterns of law enforcement. Individuals will probably never report each and every crime they know about. While the FBI can encourage and demand valid, standardized statistics from local law enforcement agencies, it cannot really do anything about such sources of error—except estimate the biases they introduce in crime data.

Victimization Studies

In an attempt to develop more satisfactory data on the extent of crime, some researchers have gone to the real or potential victims. Beginning in 1972, the Law Enforcement Assistance Administration (LEAA) began funding surveys of victimization in which annual interviews are held with a

Table 9.2.   Crimes Reported by Victims

Type of Crime	Number of Victimizations	Percent Reported to the Police
Crimes of violence	5,599,000	48.8%
Rape	145,000	52.7
Personal robbery	1,111,000	53.3
Assault	4,344,000	47.5
Crimes of theft	16,519,000	26.6
Personal larceny with contact	497,000	36.2
Personal larceny without contact	16,022,000	26.3
Burglary	6,663,000	48.1
Forcible entry	2,277,000	70.1
Unlawful entry	2,827,000	38.8
Attempted forcible entry	1,560,000	33.1
Household larceny	9,301,000	27.0
Completed larceny	8,646,000	27.1
Attempted larceny	654,000	26.5
Motor vehicle theft	1,235,000	69.5
Completed theft	760,000	88.6
Attempted theft	475,000	38.9
Commercial burglary	1,575,000	72.5
Commercial robbery	279,000	86.6

Source: U.S. Department of Justice, Law Enforcement Assistance Administration, *Criminal Victimization in the United States* (Washington, D.C.: U.S. Government Printing Office, November 1977), p. 48.

national sample of people aged twelve and over.[6] In these interviews, individuals are asked whether they had been victims of rape, robbery, assault, or larceny in the past year. Data are also collected on burglary, larceny, and auto theft experienced by households and robbery and burglary affecting commercial establishments.

The LEAA surveys have shown that many crimes are not reported to police and thus never appear in official police statistics. Further, the reporting of crimes to police varies depending on the type of crime (see Table 9.2). The findings of the LEAA national surveys are consistent, in general, with the more limited studies carried out by sociologists in the 1960s.[7]

Victimization surveys can be criticized. One has to assume that the sample of people being interviewed is representative of the population as a whole. One must also assume that those interviewed are providing accurate information—that they are neither consciously distorting nor unintentionally forgetting information. But even with such possible sources of error, victimization studies have opened up a whole new way

[6]See, for example, U.S. Department of Justice, Law Enforcement Assistance Administration, *Criminal Victimization in the United States* (Washington, D.C.: U.S. Government Printing Office, November 1977).

[7]See Albert D. Biderman et al., *Report on a Pilot Study in the District of Columbia on Victimization and Attitudes Toward Law Enforcement* (Washington, D.C.: U.S. Government Printing Office, 1967).

of measuring the extent of crime in the United States. The most serious limitation of the LEAA surveys is their very narrow focus on certain categories of crime to the exclusion of others.

Self-Report Studies

Another way researchers attempt to measure the extent of crime is to ask people to report on their own law-violating behavior. In numerous studies, people have been invited to fill out anonymous questionnaires or submit to confidential interviews.[8] In many cases, researchers have made efforts to validate their interview or questionnaire data against official police records.

The major findings of these self-report studies support common sense. Just about everyone has violated the law at one time or another, committing offenses for which he or she could have been jailed or at least fined. Most of the illegal acts were undetected, at least by law enforcement officials. Most law violators admit to committing only a few minor offenses. A small minority admits to numerous minor offenses and/or some serious crimes.

One of the obvious contributions of self-report studies is that they disprove the belief that only certain types of people (for example, the poor, minorities, and the mentally ill) engage in criminal acts. Such studies also suggest that we cannot generalize about the characteristics of those who commit crimes on the basis of knowledge about persons who are caught.

The findings of self-report studies on the distribution of criminality by age, sex, race, and class are of doubtful validity. For example, some studies suggest that common crimes are disproportionately committed by lower-class people, while others throw doubt on such findings. The two most important limitations are that we do not know if the people who answer questionnaires and submit to interviews are providing accurate information and that we cannot trust the validity of the official police records against which the results of such inquiries are checked. In addition, self-report studies have frequently been undertaken without much concern over the representativeness of the sample of persons studied, so the generalizability of their findings is difficult to judge.

More revealing, perhaps, are the occasional self-reports of individuals who are *not* the subjects of research attention. When, for example, an organized crime figure decides to "sing" during a Congressional investigation, a whole new world of crime and criminal intrigue may be revealed.[9] Such dramatic self-reports underscore the shallowness, if not the questionable accuracy, of official crime statistics.

[8]Nettler, *Explaining Crime*, pp. 73-4.
[9]See, for example, Peter Maas, *The Valachi Papers* (New York: G. P. Putnam's Sons, 1968).

EXTENT AND DISTRIBUTION OF CRIME

Criminal behavior, as legally defined, takes a wide variety of forms. In this section we will examine a number of different forms of serious crime and look at official statistics on their extent. As we have noted, such statistics are known to underestimate the actual amount of crime in the United States. We will also look at victimless crime, illegal activity people engage in voluntarily, in which there is no victim. Since certain types of criminal behavior—white-collar, organized, and political crime—do not show up in official statistics, our coverage of these types of crime will be descriptive rather than statistical.

Traditional Crime

Despite the problems associated with official crime reports, they are still the best existing source of statistics on common or *traditional crime.* In the vernacular of the FBI's *Uniform Crime Reports,* we shall address the extent and significance of *index offenses.* [10] Index offenses are serious law violations which, in the view of the FBI, indicate the gravity of America's crime problem. They are criminal homicide, forcible rape, robbery, aggravated assault, burglary (breaking and entering), larceny (theft), and motor vehicle theft. In 1976 a total of 11,304,800 index offenses were reported to the FBI by local police departments. On the average, this comes out to one offense every three seconds (see Figure 9.1). This was a 91.5 percent increase over the number of such offenses reported to the FBI in 1967. The American population has not grown by 91.5 percent in that time period. Thus, if we leave aside all the limitations of official crime statistics, it must be concluded that there has been a marked increase in the rates of index offenses.

Criminal homicide.   The term *criminal homicide* refers to the willful killing of another person, as determined by police investigation. In 1976, an estimated 18,780 persons were victims of criminal homicide, a 53 percent increase from 1967 (Table 9.3, page 300). Three quarters of the victims were males, most of whom were between twenty and twenty-four years of age. Approximately half were white, meaning that the murder of minorities occurs far more frequently than their percentage representation in the population would lead one to predict. A quarter of all murders occur within the confines of the family, and many others involve people who know one another. Such factors render criminal homicide a difficult offense to prevent. Nonetheless, 79 percent of all known criminal homicides were solved by arrest in 1976—a higher percentage than for

[10]Data in this section are from Federal Bureau of Investigation, U.S. Department of Justice, *Uniform Crime Reports for the United States, 1976* (Washington, D.C.: U.S. Government Printing Office, 1977).

Figure 9.1. Crime Clocks, 1976

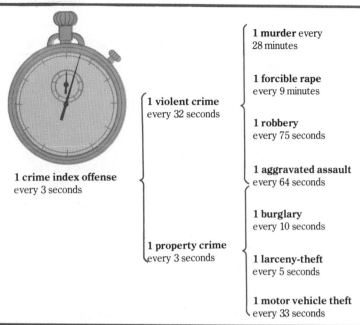

1 crime index offense
every 3 seconds

1 violent crime
every 32 seconds

1 property crime
every 3 seconds

1 murder every
28 minutes

1 forcible rape
every 9 minutes

1 robbery
every 75 seconds

1 aggravated assault
every 64 seconds

1 burglary
every 10 seconds

1 larceny-theft
every 5 seconds

1 motor vehicle theft
every 33 seconds

Source: U.S. Department of Justice, Federal Bureau of Investigation, *Uniform Crime Reports, 1976* (Washington, D.C.: U.S. Government Printing Office, 1977), p. 6.

any other crime. Of those arrested, most were males of the same race as the victim, and 43 percent were under twenty-five years of age. (There has been a notable trend toward criminal homicide among the young in recent years.) Most of those killed died by being shot—in 1976, 63.8 percent of the criminal homicides involved some type of firearms, and in 49 percent of the cases handguns were involved.

Aggravated assault. Serious assaults involve attempts to kill or to inflict severe bodily injury. Police departments reported 490,850 cases of aggravated assault in 1976, up over 90 percent from 1967 (Table 9.3). In most instances, assault takes place either within the family or between neighbors and acquaintances. Unlike criminal homicide, which mainly involves the use of firearms, the weapons employed in aggravated assaults vary greatly. In 1976, 63 percent of the assaults known to the police were solved by arrest. Since the victim, perpetrator, and witnesses are likely to be related to or acquainted with one another, witnesses and victims are often reluctant to testify. According to official statistics, 68 percent of those arrested in 1976 were twenty-one or older.

Forcible rape. Rape is one of the most underreported offenses in the United States. Nonetheless, police departments reported 56,730 cases of forcible rape in 1976, a 105 percent increase from 1967 (Table 9.3).

Table 9.3. Index of Crime, 1967–76

	1967	1970	1973	1976	Rate per 100,000, 1976
Total crime index	**5,903,400**	**8,098,000**	**8,718,100**	**11,304,800**	**5,266.4**
Violent crime	499,930	738,820	875,910	986,580	459.6
Murder	12,240	16,000	19,640	18,780	8.8
Forcible rape	27,620	37,990	51,400	56,730	26.4
Robbery	202,910	349,860	384,220	420,210	195.8
Aggravated assault	257,160	334,970	420,650	490,850	228.7
Property crime	5,403,500	7,359,200	7,842,200	10,318,200	4,806.8
Burglary	1,632,100	2,205,000	2,565,500	3,089,800	1,439.4
Larceny	3,111,600	4,225,800	4,347,900	6,270,800	2,921.3
Motor vehicle theft	659,800	928,400	928,800	957,600	446.1

Source: U.S. Department of Justice, Federal Bureau of Investigation, *Uniform Crime Reports, 1976* (Washington, D.C.: U.S. Government Printing Office, 1977), p. 37.

Like other official crime statistics, those on forcible rape are hard to interpret. The apparent increase could be partially due to greater willingness on the part of women to report rape, which they have been urged to do by advocates of the women's movement and by police officials. The presence and proliferation of rape crisis centers, which provide counseling and legal advice to rape victims, may also stimulate increased reporting. Yet, as we saw in Table 9.2, barely more than half of all forcible rapes are said to have been reported to police in 1976.

Forcible rapes were even less likely to be solved by arrest than aggravated assaults. Only 52 percent resulted in arrests in 1976. Significantly, only 69 percent of the adults arrested on rape charges were prosecuted for the offense, and 49 percent of those prosecuted were either acquitted or had their cases dismissed. These statistics indicate that forcible rape is one of the easiest crimes to get away with, given the low likelihood of ultimate conviction. In 1976, 57 percent of those arrested were under twenty-five years of age; about half were white and half were racial minorities. Contrary to popular stereotypes, virtually all forcible rapes take place within racial groups. Victims frequently are acquainted with the rapist, which helps account for the relatively low rates of arrest and prosecution, since it is sometimes difficult for victims to prove that they were indeed assaulted forcibly and against their will. Sexist attitudes on the part of police and prosecutors often work to give accused rapists the benefit of the doubt.

Robbery. Robbery involves stealing, during which force and violence (or the threat of violence) are employed. Police departments reported 420,210 robberies in 1976, an increase of 106 percent over 1967 (Table 9.3). There was a larger increase in the incidence of robbery than for any other index offense. In 1976, a robbery took place on the average of once every seventy-five seconds (Figure 9.1). Half the robberies known to police were committed on the street, the remainder occurred within households and business establishments. Only 27 percent of robberies were solved by arrest. Victims are unlikely to know the law violators, and it is relatively easy to get away with the crime. If we assume that those who are arrested are representative of robbers, young people are very much involved in this index offense. In 1976, 76 percent of those arrested were under twenty-five years of age; a third were under eighteen. Most of the arrests involved males, and 59 percent of those arrested were black. According to FBI estimates, money and goods valued at $142 million were stolen from robbery victims in 1976.

Burglary. Burglary involves unlawfully breaking into or entering a structure (e.g., a home or business), with the intent of committing theft or some other serious crime. Burglary is a far more common crime than is robbery. In 1976, an estimated 3,089,800 burglaries were reported by

When people worry about the crime of assault, they generally are thinking of the terror of being accosted on the street by strangers. However, most cases of aggravated assault take place within the family and between acquaintances.

police departments, up 80 percent from 1967 (Table 9.3). Sixty-three percent involved residences, and most took place at night. Losses were estimated at $1.4 billion. Despite the volume and costs of burglary, only 17 percent of reported burglaries were solved by arrest in 1976. Of those arrested, 84 percent were under twenty-five years of age, and 51 percent were under eighteen. Sixty-nine percent of those arrested were white, and almost all were male.

Larceny.   In 1976, police departments reported 6,270,800 cases of larceny, making it the most frequent of the index offenses (Table 9.3). This number represented an increase of 100 percent from 1967. Larceny, which does not include motor vehicle theft, involves taking or removing property that belongs to another. In 1976, larceny cost its victims an estimated $1.2 billion. Only 19 percent of all cases of larceny known to the police were solved by arrest. Of those arrested, 43 percent were 'under eighteen years of age. Significantly, almost a third of the arrests involved females—they are arrested far more frequently for larceny than for any other single index crime. In 1976 arrests of whites outnumbered arrests of blacks by more than two to one.

Motor vehicle theft.   In 1976, 1 out of every 139 cars was stolen, and police reported 957,600 cases of motor vehicle theft (Table 9.3). This is up 45 percent from 1967. While most stolen vehicles were eventually recovered and returned to their owners, only 14 percent of such thefts were solved by arrest. The arrest rate for auto theft is lower than that of any other index offense. Most of those arrested were young; 72 percent were under twenty-one, and 53 percent were under eighteen. Most of the arrested were male, and 71 percent were white. As with the other index offenses, one can only assume that those arrested are representative of those who have committed this particular law violation.

Victimless Crime

The seven index offenses are considered by the FBI to be the most serious crimes in America, both in terms of the damage they inflict and their extensiveness. In its *Uniform Crime Reports,* the FBI also presents data on offenses ranging from arson to loitering. Of the 9,608,500 arrests made by local police departments in 1976, well over 70 percent were for crimes other than index offenses (see Table 9.4). A high percentage of these arrests were for alcohol- and drug-related offenses, gambling, sex offenses and prostitution, pornography offenses, and vagrancy.

These crimes, which are entered into voluntarily and do not involve crime victims, are called *victimless crimes.* Victimless crimes are difficult to measure and are a matter of substantial controversy. Though arrest statistics on many victimless crimes are compiled in the FBI's *Uniform*

Table 9.4. Total Estimated Arrests, 1976

Offense	Number of Arrests
Total	**9,608,500**
Murder and nonnegligent manslaughter	17,250
Manslaughter by negligence	3,310
Forcible rape	26,400
Robbery	132,930
Aggravated assault	235,050
Burglary	495,200
Larceny	1,117,300
Motor vehicle theft	134,400
Subtotal for above offenses	**2,161,800**
Other assaults	428,000
Arson	17,700
Forgery and counterfeiting	68,000
Fraud	199,300
Embezzlement	10,000
Stolen property: buying, receiving, possessing	111,600
Vandalism	211,800
Weapons: carrying, possessing, etc.	147,100
Prostitution and commercialized vice	70,200
Sex offenses (except forcible rape and prostitution)	62,600
Narcotic drug laws	609,700
Gambling	79,000
Offenses against family and children	72,400
Driving under the influence	1,029,300
Liquor laws	369,700
Drunkenness	1,297,800
Disorderly conduct	657,500
Vagrancy	39,400
All other offenses (except traffic)	1,619,100
Suspicion (not included in total)	37,600
Curfew and loitering law violations	106,300
Runaways	202,600

Source: U.S. Department of Justice, Federal Bureau of Investigation, *Uniform Crime Reports, 1976* (Washington, D.C.: U.S. Government Printing Office, 1977), p. 173.

Crime Reports, there are no official figures on their extent. Needless to say, arrest statistics grossly understate the extent of such crimes.

Controversy surrounds victimless crimes for two reasons. First, many people believe that the state has no right to impose its version of morality on certain types of behavior. For example, they argue, if people want to enjoy hard-core pornography, possess and use marijuana, purchase sexual enjoyment, or gamble, they should be free to follow their own moral standards without interference by the state. However, others strongly feel that such behaviors should not be permitted under the law.

The second reason victimless crimes are controversial relates to their impact on the criminal justice system. Enough arrests are made for such

The issues related to such victimless crimes as pornography are difficult to resolve. Does the state have the right to deny people the opportunity to buy pornographic books and magazines and see pornographic movies and stage shows? What is the effect on children of being exposed to pornography—or to signs advertising pornographic material? Until such issues are resolved, the criminal justice system will probably continue to be overwhelmed by victimless crime cases.

crimes to clog the system and overwhelm the capacity of the police, courts, and penal institutions. Many experts believe that a new approach to victimless crimes would make the criminal justice system more efficient and less costly. One suggestion is to decrease penalties. In a number of states and localities, for example, possession of a small amount of marijuana is punishable by a summons (similar to a traffic ticket) and a small fine. This frees up the criminal justice system while implicitly recognizing the moral argument for freedom to use this particular drug.

White-Collar Crime

The term *white-collar crime* was made popular in the late 1930s by criminologist Edwin H. Sutherland.[11] Sutherland believed that researchers were not paying enough attention to criminal practices on the part of business executives and other high-status individuals. In his view, expla-

[11]Edwin H. Sutherland, "White-Collar Criminality," *American Sociological Review,* 5 (February 1940): 1–12.

nations for crime had to encompass the full range of law violations—not just the actions of lower-class people that come to the attention of local police. To Sutherland, white-collar crime was "crime committed by a person of respectability and high social status in the course of his occupation."[12]

When Sutherland examined the practices of seventy American corporations over a forty-five-year period, he found that each corporation had a record of one or more law violations. These included false advertising, restraint of trade, unfair labor practices, and financial fraud. Other researchers have since probed various aspects of white-collar criminality, but in a rather piecemeal fashion.[13] Information is often very difficult to obtain. The offices of executives and professionals are not readily accessible to researchers, and the types of behavior in question are carried out in great secrecy. Often the victims do not know they are being victimized. Moreover, in order to prove that white-collar crimes are being committed, researchers may need skills in law, accounting, and economics. Sociologists usually lack this kind of expert knowledge. As a consequence, most of what we know about white-collar crime comes from court cases or occasional government investigations. The information so gained is typically fragmentary and may not be representative in terms of the overall scope of white-collar criminality.

In recent years the narrowness of Sutherland's definition of white-collar crime has come under attack. Scholars have pointed out that individuals other than high-status jobholders also commit acts that are not traditional or common crimes in the course of their occupations. One attempt to expand the definition was proposed by Herbert Edelhertz, a former official of the U.S. Department of Justice. Edelhertz included as white-collar crimes all illegal acts committed by nonphysical means and by concealment and guile, whose purpose is to obtain money or property, to avoid their loss, or to obtain business or personal advantage.[14] This definition focuses on the crime, rather than on the characteristics of the law violator. It not only encompasses financial fraud by corporate executives but also fraud by such lesser mortals as veterans who receive payments enabling them to continue their education under the GI Bill but who do not attend school.

Sociologists still disagree about how to define white-collar crime and what acts the definition should encompass. The law is often quite hazy and ambivalent with regard to criminality. For example, during the 1970s a number of large corporations used secret funds to bribe important officials in other countries into doing business with them. One could consider this a white-collar crime, but in the United States such bribery is not illegal.

[12]Edwin H. Sutherland, *White Collar Crime* (New York: Dryden Press, 1949), p. 9.
[13]Gilbert Geis, "Avocational Crime," in *Handbook of Criminology*, Glaser, ed., pp. 281–82.
[14]Herbert Edelhertz, *Nature, Impact, and Prosecution of White Collar Crime* (Washington, D.C.: U.S. Government Printing Office, 1970), p. 12.

Many law violations never reach criminal courts. For example, false advertising and restraint of trade by corporations are often investigated and adjudicated by governmental review boards or other administrative bodies. When a company is proven to have engaged in false advertising, it may be asked to "cease and desist" its illegal activities. Once it does, the case is closed—there is no "conviction" and no "criminal" insofar as the law is concerned. But has not a white-collar crime been committed?

Difficulties in studying white-collar criminality and the complexities in defining it hamper attempts to estimate its extensiveness. Moreover, like traditional or common crimes, white-collar crimes, however defined, are underreported to an unknown degree. Back in the 1960s, the President's Commission on Law Enforcement estimated that white-collar crime cost far more than robbery, burglary, larceny, and auto theft.[15] The losses stemming from embezzlement, fraud, tax evasion, and forgery are several times greater than those associated with more traditional property crimes. Moreover, some costs associated with white-collar crime are impossible to estimate. For example, what dollar value could be put on a company's failure to abide by civil rights laws, antipollution statutes, or laws regulating product purity?

Because of the ambiguities surrounding white-collar crime, we can only offer illustrations of the directions it frequently takes. During the mid-1970s, for example, Americans were made aware of illegal corporate contributions to political campaigns; failure of a Congressman to divest himself of financial investments that were enhanced by legislation he himself voted on; union leaders' use of pension funds for questionable purposes, including investments from which the leaders personally benefitted; misrepresentation by doctors about services provided patients in order to get more money from government medical programs; and corruption of the judiciary, wherein judges have taken bribes from people involved in criminal cases. This list could be expanded indefinitely, even holding to the definitions of white-collar crime offered by Sutherland and Edelhertz. It should also be noted that the penalties for these white-collar offenses and others are generally far less severe than for traditional property crimes.

Organized Crime

Like white-collar crime, *organized crime* is pervasive in the United States and is more costly to the public than traditional crime.[16] Organized crime is a cooperative endeavor involving thousands of law violators. Its basic focus is on supplying goods and services illicitly to members of the public. Such goods and services include gambling opportunities, loans, drugs,

[15]President's Commission on Law Enforcement, *The Challenge of Crime*, pp. 127–28.
[16]See Donald R. Cressey, *Theft of the Nation* (New York: Harper & Row, Publishers, Inc., 1969).

stolen commodities, and prostitution. Beyond this, organized crime has successfully infiltrated some legitimate businesses and labor unions. In virtually all facets of its activity, the main objective of organized crime is to make money. Some of this money is used to buy power, including protection from politicians and from agencies of law enforcement.[17]

Perhaps the greatest source of income for organized crime is illicit gambling, including numbers games and off-track betting. Since more money is paid in by gamblers than is paid out to winners, high profits are assured. Estimates place annual gambling profits at $6 to $7 *billion*.[18]

Another major source of income is the interest received on loans made to individuals who need funds and cannot get them legally. Organized crime is engaged in loansharking, in which loans have much higher interest rates and shorter repayment periods than is permitted under the law. Borrowers include individuals with gambling debts, narcotics users, and even merchants and business executives who find themselves in financial need. Organized crime encourages borrowers to repay loans and interest on time by the threat or use of force—from murder and beatings to property destruction. No one knows how much money is involved, but it is estimated that annual profits run into the billions of dollars.

The importation and wholesale distribution of illegal drugs—heroin in particular—is another significant source of profit for organized crime. The heroin trade requires international connections and the ability to lay out large sums of money for large-scale importation of the drug. It has been estimated that $359 million changes hands each year in connection with America's heroin usage, at least $20 million of which is pure profit for organized crime.

Although relatively little is known about the matter, law enforcement agencies report that organized crime has invested heavily in legitimate businesses. Organized crime figures gain a thin veneer of public respectability and a visible source of legal income through their involvement in such enterprises. Not all business involvement comes about through direct investment. Firms may be secretly acquired in lieu of full repayment of loans or gambling debts or through extortion. Once in business, organized crime figures may use extralegal tactics in order to ensure high profits. Such tactics range from strong-arming other firms into becoming customers or suppliers to driving competitors out of business. The impact of such business involvement by organized crime remains a matter of speculation. It is often claimed that this involvement has driven up the prices of many goods and services.

It is also claimed that organized crime has infiltrated and gained control over segments of organized labor. Among the results are the limitation of unionization in certain industries and the negotiation of union contracts favorable to business owners—all in return for financial or other favors. Unions collect a great deal of money from their members, and control

[17]President's Commission on Law Enforcement, *The Challenge of Crime*, pp. 446–47.
[18]Ibid., p. 441.

over union funds permits organized crime to divert money into its business investments. When organized crime controls a union, companies must look the other way when merchandise is stolen if they wish to gain union cooperation or avoid labor problems. Stolen goods can then be channeled to firms controlled by organized crime or sold to legitimate businesses at an easy profit.

If law enforcement agencies were vigilant and active in investigating organized crime and intent on enforcing violations of the law, these activities would be more difficult to carry out. So it is to the advantage of organized crime to bribe and threaten politicians and law enforcement officials. No one knows how widespread such corruption is. Its effect is to make interference by agencies of the state unlikely. Thus, even when persons complain about known law violations, little is likely to be done. Moreover, complainants never know whether their "tips" to law enforcement agencies may lead to retributions in return. This helps reduce complaints, and thus the need for corruption.

How extensive and far-reaching is organized crime? No one is certain. In the late 1960s the President's Commission on Law Enforcement surveyed police departments in over seventy major cities. Using the responses of those cities that cooperated along with other sources of information, the Commission concluded that organized crime operates in 80 percent of cities with a population of over a million.

The Commission also reported that there were twenty-four groups across the country that were operating as well-organized "criminal cartels" and whose activities were coordinated by a small group of top-level overseers. These groups were said to have a total of at least five thousand core members, and their activities were assisted by thousands more who were not officially members. Each of the groups was said to be organized in a hierarchical manner, structured like a combination family and business corporation. Policies were made by individual "bosses," and the day-to-day operations were monitored by underlings of different ranks. Those on the very bottom often did not know where orders and directives originated. Group discipline was strictly enforced from within, with systems of internal surveillance used to control members. Membership was restricted, so as to keep out possible informers. The groups were held together by common ethnic ties and by a code of conduct that placed a premium on loyalty and obedience. Collectively, organized crime is popularly referred to as the "Mafia" or "Cosa Nostra," reflecting the belief that most members are of Italian-American origin.

It is important to emphasize that controversy has been growing around the idea that organized crime is only carried out by highly structured, hierarchical Italian-American groups. In the first place, such crime involves people of many ethnic and racial groups, including nonwhites.[19] Second, organized crime appears to vary in the degree to which partici-

[19]Francis A. J. Ianni, *Black Mafia* (New York: Simon & Schuster, Inc., 1974).

Large turnouts at the funerals of organized crime leaders, as in this photograph, public interest in news stories about the lives of syndicate members, and the popularity of movies on this subject all indicate that Americans find organized crime interesting—and not a matter of serious concern. But organized crime is actually extremely costly and has implications for all aspects of our lives.

pants formally structure their activities and relationships.[20] Finally, by focusing on so-called Mafia groups and their activities, certain highly organized and bureaucratic forms of white-collar crime tend to be ignored. For example, systematic criminality within and between business and government could be viewed as "organized crime."[21]

Because of the extent and effects of organized crime, the President's Commission concluded:

In many ways organized crime is the most sinister kind of crime in America. The men who control it have become rich and powerful by encouraging the needy to gamble, by luring the troubled to destroy them-

[20]Albert K. Cohen and James F. Short, Jr., "Crime and Juvenile Delinquency," in *Contemporary Social Problems,* 4th ed. Robert K. Merton and Robert Nisbet, eds. (New York: Harcourt Brace Jovanovich, Inc., 1976), pp. 80–90.

[21]See Dwight C. Smith, *The Mafia Mystique* (New York: Basic Books, Inc., 1975).

selves with drugs, by extorting the profits of honest and hardworking businessmen, by collecting usury from those in financial plight, by maiming or murdering those who oppose them, by bribing those who are sworn to destroy them.[22]

But despite this indictment, federal, state, and local law enforcement agencies allocate relatively few resources to the destruction of organized crime. Leaders of organized crime are rarely prosecuted for violations of the law. Perhaps they are too smart to get caught. Perhaps corruption has effectively safeguarded them from the law. Certainly, they have been able to use legal safeguards of constitutional rights to impede investigations of and prosecution for their activities.

Political Crime

The term *political crime* refers to illicit acts undertaken with the intention of affecting political policies or the political system as a whole.[23] The term is most often used when the powerless challenge the political status quo. Far less frequently is criminal status bestowed by the state on people who misuse the power they possess, such as high government officials. In the latter case, the state is prosecuting its own officials, a difficult business. This is well illustrated by the approach taken by the U.S. Department of Justice to revelations that Central Intelligence Agency operatives had been opening people's mail for twenty years, illegally violating the privacy of tens of thousands of Americans. In 1976 the Justice Department recommended that none of those involved be subjected to criminal prosecution, as they were acting on the basis of directives from government officials at higher levels. Yet, higher-level government officials remain rather hazy about where such directives came from.

Probably the most common situation in which criminal status is conferred on people in connection with political activity occurs when citizens engage in protest and dissent. For example, during the 1960s and 1970s, civil rights and antiwar activists were routinely charged with crimes in connection with acts of peaceful civil disobedience. The federal government even passed special laws designed to restrain the leaders of political change organizations. For example, the so-called Rap Brown Law of the 1960s makes it a federal offense to cross state lines for the purpose of inciting a riot. This law was intended to restrict the mobility of activists and to make them individually responsible for disruptions involving any assembly of people with whom they might have had the remotest contact.

The threat or reality of prosecution can be a potent weapon against those who want to change the political status quo, even those who use

[22]President's Commission on Law Enforcement, *The Challenge of Crime*, p. 485.

[23]See Martin R. Haskell and Lewis Yablonsky, *Criminology* (Chicago: Rand McNally & Company, 1974), pp. 187–236.

The actions of the police during the disturbances at the 1968 Democratic Convention in Chicago were labeled a "police riot" by the Walker Report to the National Commission on the Causes and Prevention of Violence, which investigated the disorder. The confrontation began when the police tried to clear a Chicago park of the thousands of dissidents who had come to Chicago to protest the war in Vietnam. Hundreds of people—including news reporters and bystanders—were injured in the four evenings of violence.

legal channels. There has been reason to believe that government agents have framed dissident individuals during the past ten or so years. In 1972, antiwar activist Father Philip Berrigan and six others were charged with conspiring to kidnap Henry Kissinger (who at the time was President Nixon's foreign affairs adviser) and to bomb government buildings by sneaking into underground heating pipes.[24] The key witness was a paid FBI informer. Though the government was unable to prove these charges in court, Father Berrigan was found guilty of smuggling letters out of the federal prison in which he was confined. The person carrying the letters was the FBI informer.

Not all persons who engage in protest and dissent do so nonviolently. In recent years the United States has experienced political protest that has ranged from mass uprisings in the nation's ghettos to acts of terrorism by "underground" groups. While such activities have gone outside the boundaries of the law, in many instances so has the response of the state.[25] Among the illegal governmental responses of the last decade have been "police riots" involving the indiscriminate use of force and the extensive violation of constitutional rights during criminal investigations.

[24]Jack Nelson and Robert Ostrow, *The FBI and the Berrigans* (New York: Coward, McCann & Geoghegan, Inc., 1972).
[25]See David Wise, *The American Police State* (New York: Random House, Inc., 1976).

When government agencies use extralegal means to contain those engaged in extralegal forms of political expression, it is difficult to tell who the political criminals are.

Political crimes reflect the existence of an unequal distribution of power within the society. They are an important indicator of the degree to which a society is meeting the needs of its members. Despite their significance, neither the public nor the FBI's *Uniform Crime Reports* considers political crimes important enough to categorize as part of America's crime problem.

EXPLANATIONS FOR CRIMINAL BEHAVIOR

As we have seen, many kinds of behavior are considered crimes under the law. Why do people engage in these behaviors? Why do they murder, falsely advertise products, steal, or illicitly repress dissent? No single explanation can account for all crime. The factors involved in any type of criminal behavior are extraordinarily complex, and explanations tend to focus on different aspects of crime and criminality. In this section we will look at some of the explanations that have been put forth.

Physiological Explanations

Efforts to explain criminal behavior as a result of the physiological traits of criminals have a long history. Since the nineteenth century, serious attempts have been made to identify such traits.[26] An Italian physician, Cesare Lombroso, conducted research on soldiers and inmates of Italian military prisons in order to show that the propensity for criminal behavior was inborn and that there were physical differences between criminals and law-abiding citizens. Criminals, in his view, were throwbacks to earlier versions of the human species and were often distinguishable by their primitive head shapes, among other stigmatizing features. Lombroso claimed to have found proof for these ideas. His research was harshly criticized for not recognizing that the Italian soldiers who were most likely to be involved in criminal activity came from a subsector of Italian society in which such activity was culturally acceptable. While members of this subsector—Sicilians—frequently did possess physical features that distinguished them from other Italians, critics observed that these physiological differences could not be accepted as a *cause* of crime since important cultural factors could also be responsible. Lombroso later altered his studies to include such factors.

[26]See Saleem A. Shah and Loren H. Roth, "Biological and Psychophysiological Factors in Criminality," in *Handbook of Criminology*, Glaser, ed., pp. 101–73.

Lombroso's explanation was further discredited by research conducted in the early twentieth century on English convicts.[27] Charles Goring compared a group of convicts with a group of Cambridge University students and found no significant physical differences between the two groups. But Goring's research did reveal a high correlation between imprisonment of fathers and imprisonment of sons and a correlation between fathers' and sons' physical characteristics. Thus, he concluded that criminality was inherited. Critics pointed out that Goring had no way of taking into account the full range of environmental influences that might have accounted for his findings.

Efforts to demonstrate physiological bases for crime continued. In the 1940s, William Sheldon posited a relationship between body build, personality type, and delinquent behavior.[28] Sheldon classified people into three categories. Ectomorphs are thin and fragile, with introverted personalities; endomorphs are soft and fat, with submissive personalities; and mesomorphs are muscular and tough with assertive personalities. Sheldon then examined two hundred American youths who, he claimed, were delinquents. He found that 60 percent of them were mesomorphs. From this he concluded that body build, which has a hereditary basis, was connected with criminality. Sheldon was roundly criticized for weaknesses in his research design and data. Common sense alone tells us that police officers, athletes, and others with muscular builds are not unusually prone to crime. Subsequent studies have not been able to establish the validity of Sheldon's conclusions without confronting similar criticisms.

More recently, research has focused on a possible relationship between genetics and criminality.[29] In recent years, several researchers have claimed that an unusually large proportion of male prison inmates have an extra Y chromosome and that the presence of this extra Y chromosome causes criminal behavior. (Males generally have one X and one Y chromosome; females generally have two X chromosomes.) This theory has been highly controversial—especially since no one knows what proportion of noninmates (or noncriminals) also possess this extra chromosome. Nor does such an explanation help clarify the causes of female criminal behavior.

Only one conclusion can be drawn about physiological explanations: we have no scientifically acceptable evidence that heredity—either in terms of inherited bodily features or genetic characteristics—plays a role in causing criminal behavior. In concentrating on physiological traits, researchers continue to engage in what sociologists call *reductionism.* That is, they are isolating individuals and their behavior from the larger context and are reducing explanations to one very basic variable. There is a sharp

[27]Charles Goring, *The English Convict* (London: H. M. Stationery Office, 1913).
[28]William H. Sheldon, *The Varieties of Delinquent Youth* (New York: Harper & Row, Publishers, Inc., 1949).
[29]See Shah and Roth, "Biological and Psychophysiological Factors in Criminality," pp. 134–39.

parallel between physiological approaches and the explanations for criminal behavior that were popular in the Middle Ages. Then, such behavior was commonly attributed to demons or evil spirits inflicting the souls of the unfortunate. Demon theories also ignore the larger context in which people's behavior takes on meaning and is defined in criminal terms. Physiological explanations are almost ludicrous when one recalls that self-report studies typically find that almost everyone admits to having committed a criminal act. Unless we are ready to claim that almost the entire American population is physiologically marred, such explanations must be rejected out of hand.

Psychological Explanations

Psychological explanations range from those that focus almost entirely on the personality traits of individuals to those that relate personality traits to the immediate social environment. *Psychoanalytic explanations* are based on the work of Sigmund Freud. Most psychoanalytic viewpoints see crime as the outcome of unconscious motivations arising within certain troubled individuals.[30] These motivations, in turn, stem from the workings of components of the personality: the id, ego, and superego. Briefly, the id represents the drive for pleasure and self-gratification; it is present at birth. The ego, which develops later, governs the id's urges, directing the search for pleasure within the limits of surrounding reality. The superego is the guardian of right and wrong; its development marks the emergence of a sense of conscience or guilt over violating the wishes of others in the search for pleasure. In psychoanalytic theory, criminal behavior commonly stems from the failure of the ego and the superego to control the urges of the id. Also, the inadequate development of any of the three personality components may result in emotional problems— from neuroses to psychoses. These problems hamper the ability of individuals to function "normally" and render them prone to crime.

While this explanation may seem compelling, one must remember that the id, ego, and superego are theoretical constructs. Even some professional psychoanalysts do not agree that these components exist. Among those who believe they exist, there are disagreements over their functions and their relationship to behavior. Sociologically-oriented critics would suggest that psychoanalytic explanations for criminal behavior place too much emphasis on individual personality factors and not enough on factors that are external to the individual. Such critics would also point out that known criminals do not in general appear to be any more psychologically troubled than noncriminals.

A second type of psychological explanation involves the belief that

[30]See, for example, Walter Bromberg, *Crime and the Mind* (Philadelphia: J. B. Lippincott Company, 1948).

criminal behavior is *learned.* [31] In this view, people learn to engage in or to avoid such behavior on the basis of *reinforcement*—rewards and punishments. It is assumed that human beings by nature try to seek pleasure and avoid pain. If people are rewarded for criminal behavior, either by other people or by the results of their acts, criminal behavior will have been reinforced as pleasurable. On the other hand, punishment, or the threat of punishment, renders criminal behavior painful and to be avoided.

To an overwhelming degree, this explanation of criminal behavior has been based on experiments with animals, such as pigeons and rats. There is no data on its relevance to actual criminal behavior. One of the major problems lies in the specification and measurement of reinforcers and the meaning of particular reinforcers to different individuals. Moreover, this explanation—like so many others—is always applied after the fact. That is, it is assumed that persons who engage in criminal acts were somehow reinforced into doing so. No one has identified such reinforcers with the precision that would enable predictions of who will commit a crime and under what conditions.

A somewhat related explanation, which relates learning more directly to social factors, has been called *differential association theory.* [32] According to this theory, criminal behavior is learned during the course of communication and interaction with criminals or delinquents. When individuals associate with the criminally-prone, they learn the techniques of crime and the motives, attitudes, and rationalizations for criminal behavior. The neophyte criminal then adopts definitions of the legal codes that favor law violation over law-abiding behavior.

Differential association theory has been criticized on a number of counts. It does not explain who is likely to become associated with criminally-prone people, or why. Nor does it address the question of exceptions—those whose exposure to criminals leads them to reject criminal behavior. Finally, as with so many other explanations, differential association theory tries to cover too wide a variety of law violators. The individual who cheats on income tax, who secretly patronizes a prostitute, or who murders a family member may have *no* history of association with criminally-prone people.

Another explanation that relates psychological characteristics to the social environment is called *containment theory.* [33] Containment theory starts with the premise that not all individuals are equally tempted to engage in criminal behavior and asks why this is the case. The answer is that some people are "contained" or controlled and avoid crime because of outer controls and/or inner controls. Outer controls are social pres-

[31]See Ronald L. Akers, *Deviant Behavior* (Belmont, Calif.: Wadsworth Publishing Co., Inc., 1973).

[32]Edwin H. Sutherland and Donald R. Cressey, *Criminology,* 9th ed. (Philadelphia: J. B. Lippincott Company, 1974), pp. 75–7.

[33]Walter C. Reckless, *The Crime Problem* (New York: Appleton-Century-Crofts, 1961).

sures that condemn criminal acts, such as community standards. Inner controls are a result of socialization. Family, school, church, and peers may encourage self-control in the face of temptations to engage in crime. Indicators of self-control are said to include a positive self-concept, an orientation to realistic and legitimate goals, the ability to tolerate frustration, and favorable attitudes toward law and law enforcement agencies. On the other hand, those who commit crimes are uncontained and lacking in self-control. Containment theory is extremely broad. We know little about the kinds of social pressures or community standards that help "contain" crime; nor do we fully understand the conditions under which individuals are socialized to develop inner controls.

The preceding explanations all have one common feature. They attempt to infer what goes on in the minds of individuals, and these inferences are then taken to be the causes of criminal behavior. Little attention is given to the features of the larger society and how these might relate to the generation of behavior that comes to be proclaimed criminal.

Sociological Explanations

One of the most famous sociological explanations for criminal behavior is *anomie theory,* developed by Robert Merton.[34] Merton observed that our culture places a great deal of emphasis on material success and that materialistic values are thus shared by members of this society. But, Merton points out, success in material terms is not readily achievable by all. Opportunities are denied certain groups more than others—for example, minorities and the poor. There is, in Merton's terms, a dysjunction between cultural success goals and the availability of means to pursue them. This dysjunction creates stress, which takes the form of *anomie,* a sense of disorientation or normlessness. Those affected by anomie may respond in one of several ways. They may simply scale down their success goals and go about their daily lives in a ritualistic manner. They may engage in illegal pursuits, pursuing goals of material success by illegitimate means. They may simply reject such goals entirely, and retreat from any attempt to participate in the mainstream of society. Or they may rebel and attempt to alter the society whose cultural emphases are unacceptable and unattainable.

Merton's theory is highly suggestive, but it remains rather vague in specifying who is likely to experience anomie and how such persons are likely to respond. Moreover, some crimes appear to have little to do with blocked opportunities for material success, and Merton's explanation fails to address these. One example that immediately comes to mind is murder. Both the motivations for murders and the circumstances under

[34]Robert K. Merton, *Social Theory and Social Structure* (Glencoe, Ill.: The Free Press, 1957), pp. 131–60. Anomie theory is also discussed in the Introduction to this text.

Public Problem, Private Pain
A STREET CRIMINAL

John Allen's career of crime began in 1950 with an arrest for theft. He was eight years old at the time. Since then, Allen has been arrested for robbery, assault with a deadly weapon, escape from a federal institution, and homicide. Wounded in the aftermath of a robbery and attempted getaway in a stolen auto, Allen is today a paraplegic. In this excerpt from his autobiography, he talks about some of the personal motivations behind his illicit quest for material gain. Allen's ambitions for economic success and security and his desire to provide for his children suggest that even street criminals are touched by the American Dream.

I always thought of myself as being a hustler. I come from a hustling family. My grandfather told me, when you hustle, what you're really hustling for is so that you won't have to hustle later. If you can hustle and make it, get three or four stores, don't be overcome by your success, and be satisfied to stay at that level. That would be really cool. I ain't never want to be real, real rich, but I want to live instead of just survive.

That's where your goals come in. Your goal while you're doing all your hustling is to get things together enough to do something legal. You might go all the way to the top doing illegal things, like being a really big drug dealer. Or you might go up maybe midway on that ladder and then jump off into legal things. Which way you go depends on the structure you plan and what you're satisfied with. I could strive to be really high on the illegal structure, but at the same time I would be satisfied in the middle.

It seems to me that everyone should be able to do what he or she wants to do as long as they don't hurt anybody in the process. But see, sometimes in my lifestyle, the way I live, people got to be hurt, so you accept that as part of your business, part of your life.

I want to be free inside. Like, many times I went to my mama and said, "Mama, I need some shoes." And Mama said, "I know, but I'm not able to get you shoes because this is rent week. There is nothing." "Hi, Mom, I'm going to graduate from elementary school. Sure be hip to have a suit." "There's nothing I'd like better than buying you a suit. But we've got to pay the grocery bill." So I stole, and I got my shoes and my suit. I looked as good as everybody else. Probably 60 percent of the people in my class stole their suits.

If my children came to me, "Hey, Jack, I need a hundred dollars to buy this outfit I seen," I want to be able to go in my pocket and give it to them without having to say, "I need this money to go toward the rent. I've got to pay this bill or that bill." Then my son comes to me and says, "I want a bicycle," I can say, "Go get a bicycle"; or my daughter saying, "Prom coming up and I need a gown." Some people struggle to get this through legal means or kind of skip the rent and put the kids first. I know my mother did. I know my wife does. She will neglect herself in order that the kids be satisfied. I guess I do that a lot myself. I might have two or three dollars, and if one of them ask me for it, I would give it to them.

I want them to be able, when they leave the prom or the football game, to have a place where they can come and be comfortable and bring their friends and sit around listening to some music. Not lying around the walls, or scared to sit in chairs because they are going to fall apart or on the couch that keeps going to the floor. These are the things that I am talking about.

John Allen, *Assault with a Deadly Weapon: The Autobiography of a Street Criminal,* Dianne Hall Kelly and Philip Heymann, eds. (New York: Pantheon Books, 1977), pp. 232–33.

which they occur vary, and blocked opportunity for material success need not enter into the picture at all.

Other sociological explanations have focused on particular segments of the American population, suggesting that criminal behavior is more closely linked to certain subcultures than to American culture as a whole. Overall, such explanations have limited their attention to crime among low-income groups.

For example, according to sociologist Albert Cohen, lower-class youth possess a distinct subculture within which delinquent behavior has special meaning.[35] Feeling unfairly discriminated against by middle-class society, these youngsters suffer from "status frustration," which they act out in delinquent forms. Low-income boys engage in delinquent behavior precisely because it is abhorrent to middle-class behavioral standards. Much delinquency takes place by youth gangs, which Cohen sees as collectivities within which such behavior receives support and legitimation.

Richard Cloward and Lloyd Ohlin have also concerned themselves with lower-class gang behavior, drawing on Merton's ideas to explain it.[36] In their view, the gap between cultural success goals and opportunities to pursue them cause lower-class youths to form delinquent subcultures. Cloward and Ohlin have identified three types of delinquent subcultures: criminal, wherein property crimes are a main activity; conflict, involving a preoccupation with violence; and retreatist, where drug use predominates. In their judgment, lower-class communities provide support for one or another of these subcultures. If the adults in a community are involved in property crimes, a criminal subculture will emerge to act as a training ground for delinquent youth. In communities in which such adult models are lacking, youngsters are likely to turn to violence for status. Finally, those who are unable to make it in either of the two other types of subcultures tend to band together in retreatist groups and engage in heavy drug use.

Walter Miller has posited the existence of an autonomous lower-class culture within which members are socialized into a unique set of values or "focal concerns."[37] Among these focal concerns are toughness, smartness, trouble, and excitement. The lower-class culture, in Miller's view, automatically brings its adherents into conflict with the law. By contrast, Miller suggests, middle-class subcultural values are more in congruence with behavior required by the legal system.

Such subcultural explanations for crime and criminal behavior have limitations. They address such phenomena only among the nonaffluent. Yet we know—if only from self-report studies—that similar behavior takes place outside the lower class. Moreover, not all sociologists agree

[35]Albert K. Cohen, *Delinquent Boys* (Glencoe, Ill.: The Free Press, 1955).
[36]Richard A. Cloward and Lloyd E. Ohlin, *Delinquency and Opportunity* (New York: The Free Press, 1960).
[37]Walter B. Miller, "Lower Class Culture as a Generating Milieu of Gang Delinquency," *Journal of Social Issues,* 14, No. 3 (1958): 5–19.

on the existence of distinct class subcultures. Among those who do, there is disagreement about whether these subcultural variations *cause* behavior in and of themselves.

Other sociological explanations focus not so much on the groups involved in law violation as on the ways in which people are designated as criminals or delinquents. *Labeling theory* is one such explanation.[38] This theory suggests that criminal behavior exists only if and when certain acts are labeled as criminal. It does not address the origins of the acts in question. But in a way, the labeling process may be considered a "cause" of criminal behavior. For example, when the courts identify certain people as criminals, a whole chain of events may be set into motion. Community members, families, and employers may act as if they expect further criminal behavior. In a kind of self-fulfilling prophecy, the newly labeled may be driven toward the behavior expected by others.

A somewhat related explanation is Richard Quinney's *theory of the social reality of crime.*[39] Like those sociologists who are interested in the labeling process, Quinney has focused on processes of crime definition. In a simple form, his theory is as follows:

1. Crime is a product of law, and law is determined for the most part by legislative action.
2. Legislatures are greatly influenced by the most powerful segments of society.
3. Acts that are in conflict with the interests of the most powerful segments of society are most likely to be addressed under the law.
4. Segments of the society that are not influential in law creation have a high probability of having their behaviors defined as criminal.
5. The behaviors so defined are an outcome of structured opportunities, learning experiences, interpersonal relations, and self-conceptions.
6. Those whose behaviors are defined as crimes come to see themselves as criminals, and to act in response to the expectations that they will fulfill criminal roles.

Thus, Quinney is saying that crime is a social reality that is *constructed*—behavior that is in conflict with the interests of the powerful is declared unlawful. The behavior in question has a variety of underlying causes. In effect, Quinney has not so much come up with a totally new explanation as he has drawn together what he sees as useful parts of other explanations. His theory thus must stand or fall on the strengths of the latter.

[38]Edwin Lemert, *Human Deviance, Social Problems, and Social Control* (Englewood Cliffs, N.J.: Prentice-Hall, Inc., 1967).

[39]Richard Quinney, *The Social Reality of Crime* (Boston: Little, Brown & Company, 1970), pp. 15–25.

THE CRIMINAL JUSTICE SYSTEM

America's system of criminal justice is made up of three interrelated components: the police, the courts, and correctional institutions. [40] As an arm of the state, the main function of this system is to handle those who have violated the law.

Ideally, the criminal justice system operates smoothly and efficiently. The police are supposed to apprehend and arrest those suspected of illegal acts. The accused are to be brought into courts of law, where their guilt or innocence is determined. Those found guilty should be turned over to correctional institutions for supervision and rehabilitation. Needless to say, the system does not work this way. In this section we shall look at some of the reasons it is failing.

The Police

The presence of police helps deter crime in America's communities. Indeed, police spend a good deal of time trying to head off situations in which criminal acts might occur. But an equally important police responsibility is the apprehension and arrest of those suspected of illegal acts. It is at this point that the system first fails to work as it is supposed to.

Of over 11 million serious crimes (index offenses) reported by local police departments to the FBI in 1976, *only 21 percent* were solved by arrests. Of the more than 9 million arrests made in 1976, most were for relatively minor offenses. For example, a third were for law violations related to alcohol. In most large cities, the jails and courts are clogged with persons arrested by police for minor crimes.

There are many reasons that arrest rates for serious crimes are so low. The sheer volume of crimes known to the police is overwhelming, and there are not enough officers to investigate them all. While many serious offenses are reported to police departments, there is often no way for police to identify the law violators. This is particularly the case with regard to property crimes. Thus, the police generally can only apprehend and arrest persons who violate the law right before their eyes and those who are accused by witnesses.

The whole question of arrest is itself a difficult one for police. On the one hand, police have a great deal of discretion in exercising their arrest powers; at the same time, they are restricted by legal rules in their handling of suspects. Legal restrictions are intended to protect the innocent from the violation of their rights. The police must advise suspects that they have the right to remain silent and to obtain the assistance of an attorney. Police are not allowed to use unnecessary force in making arrests, and they must obtain evidence legally. While many police officers

[40]President's Commission on Law Enforcement, *The Challenge of Crime*, pp. 70–81.

violate such restrictions, they do so at the risk that those arrested may be set free if the violations become known.

The arrest activity of police is often hampered by corruption amongst police themselves. In most locales, the police are underpaid. They are expected to do the "dirty work" of society, often at a risk to their own lives. In cities around the country, police have been found accepting bribes and payoffs from law violators, selling confiscated drugs, and even engaging in burglaries. While there is no way to know the extent of such corruption, its existence represents another facet of the breakdown of the criminal justice system. When police themselves become law violators, their credibility as upholders of the law is diminished. Since the police need the cooperation of the public in apprehending and arresting those suspected of law violations, corruption inhibits police work.

The Courts

After individuals have been arrested, they are ordinarily brought before a prosecutor or other official who draws up the charges that will be presented in court. At this stage, problems frequently crop up, effectively undoing the work of the police. Prosecutors may detect or suspect that arrests were made illegally. They may decide that witnesses and/or evidence would not stand up under examination in court. Many prosecutors are faced with a large backlog of cases, and they generally prefer to draw up charges only when they expect those involved to be found guilty. They thus serve as gatekeepers for the courts.

Prosecutors' decisions place many persons arrested by the police back on the streets—often to police dismay. The conflicts that arise between prosecutors and police over the handling of those arrested represent a further source of breakdown in the criminal justice system. Police are likely to lose their enthusiasm when they have to guess at the results that will stem from their efforts.

The courts, especially those in large cities, are faced with far more criminal cases than they can handle. The backlogging of cases has given rise to the routine use of the practice of *plea bargaining*, in which prosecutors offer accused persons the opportunity to plead guilty to a lesser crime. The prosecutor may, for example, offer to reduce a charge of aggravated assault to one of simple assault if the accused will plead guilty. While plea bargaining is intended to lighten the load of the courts and eliminate the need for time-consuming trials, this practice has some serious side effects. Those who are suspected of serious crimes, in the view of police, too often get off lightly. Those who are innocent of violating the law, but who are faced with possible punishment for crimes they did not commit, may be coerced into accepting criminal status and the stigma that goes with it.

Even when accused individuals have their day in court, the criminal justice system often proves to operate inequitably. When there is a backlog of cases, those arrested frequently have to spend a lengthy period in jail before the trial. Affluent persons often can obtain freedom before their trials by raising money for bail. Low-income people have much more difficulty finding bail money, so it is primarily the poor who populate the jails while awaiting trial. Furthermore, in order to convince a judge to grant bail, it helps to have a lawyer who has plenty of time to prepare the case. Again, it is the affluent who are likely to be advantaged in this regard.

The resources available to the accused often affect what happens when cases finally go to court. The nonaffluent usually must rely on attorneys provided them by the courts. These attorneys often handle so many cases that they can give little attention to preparing a defense for any one individual. To expedite matters, they may advise their clients to take advantage of opportunities for plea bargaining. The affluent, on the other hand, can afford legal talent tailored to their interests and needs.

Judges and trial jurors are typically middle-class people, "respectable" members of the community. Though guilt and innocence are supposed to be determined solely on the basis of the evidence presented rather than on personal prejudices, class, race, and other differences do enter into determinations. Accused individuals who are most "like" the jury members are likeliest to receive gentle treatment. Guilty verdicts and punishments, consequently, weigh most heavily on the poor and members of racial minorities. The poor and minorities predominate in jails and prisons across the country, and it is not because they commit the majority of crimes.

Corrections

Persons who plead guilty to crimes or who are found guilty by the courts may be handled in a variety of ways. They may be fined, imprisoned, or allowed to remain free during a supervised period of probation. We shall deal here with imprisonment, which—aside from the death penalty—is the most severe penalty the state can impose on law violators.

Sending people to jail or prison is supposed to serve several different functions. Imprisonment removes law violators from society, thus protecting the public from any further threats they might pose. By taking away freedom, imprisonment serves as a form of punishment and retribution for the offenses committed. The threat of such punishment is intended to serve as a deterrent to anyone tempted to engage in criminal behavior. Finally, imprisonment is intended to place convicted law violators in a controlled environment in order to rehabilitate them.

Prisons are very effective in removing people from society and inflicting punishment. But the threat of imprisonment does not seem to be a major crime deterrent. Given the low likelihood of arrest—even for many serious offenses—criminals have a good chance of avoiding prison. Nor does imprisonment do much to rehabilitate those who experience it. The

Life in prison is characterized by unpleasant housing conditions and boredom as well as by brutality, arbitrary discipline, and inadequate diet and medical care. Hence, it should not be surprising that little rehabilitation of prisoners occurs in American prisons.

vast majority of prisoners either have been there before or can be expected to return in the future. The failure of prisons to turn law violators into law-abiding citizens represents the final stage in the breakdown of the criminal justice system.

The basic problem seems to be the contradictory functions imprisonment is supposed to serve. Isolating law violators and taking away their freedom clearly run counter to goals of rehabilitation. On the other hand, the public does not want criminals to be "coddled." Those who violate the law, it is commonly felt, deserve to pay for it. Criminals deserve punishment, not therapy, or else no one would feel any qualms about engaging in criminal acts. In practice, this view prevails in prisons. Only a small percentage of the resources allocated to correctional institutions goes toward anything that could even loosely be called therapy. Most money is spent to maintain security and to keep inmates under careful control.

In response, the inmates develop their own informal society—a subculture with its own set of rules. Prisons have been called schools for crime, as inmates trade knowledge about their techniques of violating the law. Some inmates use physical force or force of personality to exploit others. Crime is rampant inside prisons. Drug use, homosexual rape, assault, murder, theft, and extortion are common. From the perspective of most inmates, the prison experience is not only brutal, it is purposeless. Few come out in better shape than when they went in. Whatever the reasons inmates had for violating the law, these reasons are not eradicated by locking individuals up.

SUMMARY

Americans rate crime as one of the societal problems they consider most serious. Public concern over the crime problem is essentially focused on personal victimization, such as robbery and assault. Less concern is expressed over white-collar, organized, and political crime, perhaps because these seem rather distant or remote.

Crime is linked to a society's system of law. Whether people are aware of or agree with the legal definition of crime, it is ultimately the law that makes an activity a crime. Under the legal definition, a crime is an act that is intentional, inexcusable, in violation of a law, and punishable by the state.

Why do some acts get defined as crimes, while others do not? Some people believe that law is the product of pluralist democracy and consensus on acts that should be outlawed. Others hold that law is formulated in response to the interests of the dominant economic and social class. Somewhere between these views is the conflict theory of legal change, which sees law creation as the product of conflict between classes and among a variety of interest groups that are not class-based. Sociologists are just beginning to expand research into how laws are formulated and how this leads to the "creation" of crime.

People's perception of the crime problem is to a large extent based on official reports of crime statistics. Such statistics are known to be inaccurate for a number of reasons. Many crimes are not reported to law enforcement agencies. Police may either ignore or be extremely vigilant and aggressive in their handling of certain crimes. The reporting procedures of law enforcement agencies may affect the statistics compiled. Crime rate statistics are also affected by the requirement that they be calculated in conjunction with accurate population statistics—which we do not possess. At best, official crime statistics, such as those presented in the FBI's *Uniform Crime Reports* each year, provide a very rough picture of the actual amount of crime.

Efforts to develop more satisfactory data on the extent of crime have taken different forms. For example, researchers have carried out victimization studies wherein people are asked if they or their businesses have recently been crime victims and whether they reported the crimes to police. Data from such studies indicate that official statistics understate the crime problem to a large extent. Researchers have also conducted self-report studies, in which people are asked about their own law-violating behavior. Data disprove the notion that only certain kinds of people commit crimes and suggest that we cannot generalize about criminal characteristics on the basis of those who get caught.

Criminal behavior takes a wide variety of forms. We have official statistics on common or traditional crime, which includes the serious offenses the FBI calls index offenses: criminal homicide, aggravated assault, forcible rape, robbery, burglary, larceny, and motor vehicle theft. According to official statistics, serious crime has been steadily increasing. But most arrests are for less serious offenses, including victimless crimes. These are crimes entered into voluntarily that do not involve crime victims, like prostitution and gambling. Many people feel that the state should not impose its moral standards on individuals for certain types of behavior. The magnitude of arrests for victimless crimes affects the efficiency of the criminal justice system.

White-collar crime is both widespread and difficult to define. It and organized crime are thought to be far more costly to Americans than traditional property crimes. Political crimes, like white-collar and organized crime, receive little public concern. Political crime reflects the existence of an unequal distribution of power within society.

Why do people engage in criminal behavior? No single explanation can account for all crime. Researchers have put forth explanations based on alleged physiological traits of criminals. They have offered explanations referring to alleged personality traits. And they have offered explanations that suggest that certain features of society cause the generation of behavior that comes to be proclaimed criminal. Embarrassingly little is known about the causes of criminal behavior. In the absence of an adequate understanding of the causes, America's system of criminal justice remains only marginally effective in curbing the crime problem.

The criminal justice system is made up of three interrelated elements: the police, the courts, and correctional institutions. The system does not work smoothly and efficiently, but instead suffers from breakdowns at a number of different points. For example, it catches only a minority of those who break the law; of those it does catch, most will violate the law and probably be caught again.

DISCUSSION QUESTIONS

1. Have you ever been the victim of a crime? Why do you think this particular type of crime occurs in America? Based on your explanation of why the crime occurs, what do you see as the most appropriate and effective solution?
2. Have you ever knowingly violated the law? Who or what led you to do so? What factors would have had to be present to keep you from violating the law? Based on the importance of such factors, what are solutions to this type of crime?
3. Choose a victimless crime. Develop arguments for and against substantially lowering the penalties for this crime. What arguments could be made for and against making this behavior totally legal?
4. Go to your local police station, courthouse, and jail. Talk with as many people as you can and observe the handling and disposition of those accused of violating the law. What changes in this process do you think are needed? Why?
5. In the United States, people are presumed to be innocent of law violation until proven guilty. If the principle were to be reversed (i.e., guilty until proven innocent), what problems would this give rise to? Which principle is most desirable?
6. If you blew up a bridge, set fire to homes and other buildings, and took lives by the score, you would no doubt be accused of crimes. If you did all these things in time of war, you might be called a hero. What does this tell you about the relation of law and crime "creation"?

10 Mental Illness

Members of American society should be at peace with themselves and with one another. The anxieties that provoke mental troubles should be absent.

During the 1972 presidential campaign, the issue of mental illness was brought before the public in dramatic fashion. Democratic candidate George McGovern's running mate, Thomas Eagleton, admitted that he had been hospitalized for nervous exhaustion three times in the 1960s.[1] Eagleton had twice undergone electroshock treatments, which are commonly employed during therapy for mental depression.

Though Eagleton and McGovern insisted that this was all in the past and that the vice-presidential candidate was in excellent health, the news generated great public concern. If the two men were elected, what would happen if Eagleton had to take over presidential duties? Could the presidency—with its power over domestic, foreign, and military affairs—be entrusted to a person with a history of mental illness? Did the choice of such a running mate reflect badly on McGovern's judgment? As public discussion became increasingly intense, Eagleton withdrew from the campaign. McGovern and his new running mate, Sargent Shriver, lost the election to the Nixon-Agnew team, perhaps in part because of the "Eagleton affair."

On one level the Eagleton affair was simply an unfortunate moment in America's complex and often fast-paced political history. But on another level, it was extremely revealing about American attitudes toward mental illness. The Eagleton affair made it clear that Americans harbor deep fears and anxieties about mental problems. There was every reason to believe that Eagleton could meet the demands of high executive office. But there was also sufficient public apprehension about his mental state to deny him the opportunity to prove his capabilities. The vice-presidential candidate, for all practical purposes, was treated as if he were *still* mentally troubled. This suggests that, even if psychiatrists and other mental health practitioners do not feel that an individual is "ill," he or she may be labeled as such by others.

How common is mental illness in American society? Just what is meant by the term *mental illness?* How does labeling fit into the definition of who is ill? What factors are thought to be associated with, or to cause, mental troubles? What happens to people who are confined in mental institutions? We shall address such questions in this chapter.

THE EXTENT OF MENTAL ILLNESS

How mentally troubled are Americans? Numerous attempts have been made to discover, first, the total number of cases existing at any one time and, second, the number of new cases occurring over time. Findings of both types of research have been inconclusive.

[1]See "Crisis Named Eagleton," *Newsweek,* 80 (August 7, 1972): 12–16; and "Eagleton's Own Story of His Health Problems," *U.S. News and World Report,* 73 (August 7, 1972): 16–17.

The Prevalence of Mental Illness

Most of the attempts to measure the *prevalence* of mental illness—that is, the total number of cases existing at a given time—have involved surveying a sample of people and then generalizing from the findings. The best-known empirical inquiry is the Midtown Manhattan study, conducted by sociologist Leo Srole and his associates.[2] These researchers interviewed a sample of adults in New York City, asking questions bearing on their mental state. The data were then turned over to psychiatric experts, who rated each case on a scale ranging from mentally well to incapacitated. The psychiatrists rated only 18.5 percent of those surveyed as mentally healthy. Almost 25 percent were found to be incapacitated or were said to show severe or marked symptoms of mental impairment. According to the psychiatrists, the remainder of those sampled had moderate or mild symptoms of mental illness. If these findings were valid, it would mean that the majority of New York City residents show some symptoms of mental illness!

The findings of similar studies conducted in other communities, from Baltimore to Houston, have varied enormously.[3] Prevalence rates have been found that range from 1 to 60 percent of those surveyed. The most commonly quoted figure is around 10 percent, but many would argue that this figure is conservative.

Why is there no precise information on the prevalence of mental illness? The main reason is the lack of agreement among researchers on the appropriate diagnostic measures. Existing studies use different criteria for identifying the mentally ill, a variety of survey instruments, and various means for classifying cases. This makes comparisons between studies very difficult. Consequently, no one really knows with any precision how prevalent mental illness is among the American people. Our only choice is to accept the rough figure of 10 percent, or over 20 million troubled Americans.

The Incidence of Mental Illness

Efforts to identify the *incidence* of mental illness—the number of new cases occurring over time—have primarily been based on statistics on treatment. For example, one may examine the number of persons receiving aid through outpatient facilities and the number confined in hospitals.

As Table 10.1 indicates, over 6 million persons (many of them children) currently receive treatment in mental health facilities each year. Rela-

---

[2]Leo Srole et al., *Mental Health in the Metropolis* (New York: McGraw-Hill, Inc., 1962).

[3]For an overview of many such studies, see Howard B. Kaplan, *The Sociology of Mental Illness* (New Haven, Conn.: College & University Press, 1972), pp. 49–64.

Table 10.1. Patient Care Episodes in Mental Health Facilities

		Inpatient Services					Outpatient Services	
Year	Total	State & county mental hospitals	Private mental hospitals	General hospital psychiatric service	Veteran's Administration psychiatric inpatient services	Federally assisted community mental health centers	Federally assisted community mental health centers	Other
1955	1,675,352	818,832	123,231	265,934	88,355	—	—	379,000
1965	2,636,525	804,926	125,428	519,328	115,843	—	—	1,071,000
1969	3,572,822	767,115	123,850	535,493	186,913	65,000	291,148	1,603,308
1973	5,248,832	651,857	151,941	475,448	208,416	191,946	982,552	2,586,677
1975	6,409,447	598,993	165,327	565,696	214,264	246,891	1,584,968	3,033,308

Source: George E. Delury, ed., *The World Almanac and Book of Facts, 1978* (New York: Newspaper Enterprise Association, Inc., 1977), p. 960. Data from National Institute of Mental Health.

tively few of them undergo confinement; most are handled as outpatients. The number of people receiving treatment has risen steadily over the last twenty years (see Figure 10.1).[4] This might mean that the incidence of mental illness has been on the increase. But it could also mean that people feel more comfortable about seeking help for mental troubles than they did in the past. Or it could be that more people are defining themselves as ill, having no other way to understand or articulate things that are bothering them. We do know that treatment has become more accessible to Americans. Since the late 1960s, the federal government has provided funds for mental health centers in local communities. This has been done in order to provide alternatives to large, often isolated, residential institutions. However, the trend toward increased use of treatment facilities began before such community centers started to proliferate.[5]

The question of incidence is further muddied when other factors bearing on treatment statistics are considered. Obviously, not all persons who are mentally troubled seek out or are brought to treatment. For example, many of those interviewed by Srole and his associates were considered mentally impaired but were not or had never been under treatment. Furthermore, some troubled individuals who seek aid may not be counted in treatment statistics. This would be the case for those who consult religious leaders or school counselors. Still others—particularly the affluent—rely on private psychiatrists, who generally do not release information about their patients. Thus, these cases do not show up in treatment statistics. For such reasons, it seems likely that estimates of the incidence of mental illness underreport the number of new cases occurring each year.

In the last twenty-five years, there has been a noticeable drop in the

[4]General statistics are available from the National Institute of Mental Health.
[5]See Franklin D. Chu and Sharland Trotter, *The Madness Establishment* (New York: Grossman Publishers, 1974), p. 30.

Table 10.2. Admissions and Confinements, State and County Mental
            Hospitals

Year	Total Admitted	Net Releases	Deaths in Hospital	Residents End of Year	Expense per Patient
1955	178,003	NA	44,384	558,922	$1,116.59
1960	234,791	NA	49,748	535,540	$1,702.41
1970	393,174	394,627	30,804	338,592	$5,435.38
1973	377,020	386,962	19,899	248,562	$9,207.92
1974	374,554	389,094	16,597	215,573	$11,277.23
1975	376,156	391,345	13,401	193,436	$13,634.53

Source: George E. Delury, ed., *The World Almanac and Book of Facts, 1978* (New York: News-paper Enterprise Association, Inc., 1977), p. 960. Data from National Institute of Mental Health.

number of persons confined in mental hospitals at any given time (see Table 10.2). If we limited our attention to the number confined, we might conclude that mental illness—or at least serious mental illness—is on the decrease. However, while this drop has been going on, the actual number of new *admissions* to mental hospitals has been going up each year (Table 10.2). Though more persons are being admitted, the length of confine-ment is decreasing. One reason is that the extensive use of drugs enables people to function outside of confinement. Second, community mental

Figure 10.1. Inpatient and Outpatient Care Episode Rates, Selected Mental Health Facilities

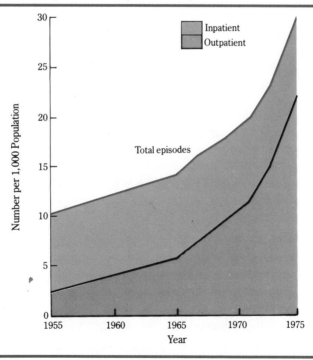

Source: U.S. Department of Commerce, Bureau of the Census, *Social Indicators, 1976* (Washington, D.C.: U.S. Government Printing Office, December 1977), p. 167.

health facilities make it possible for more individuals to be treated as outpatients while continuing to live at home. Third, there has been an ongoing effort to move the aged out of mental institutions and into nursing homes or geriatric hospitals. In the past, elderly persons who could not care for themselves were often left to languish in such institutions. Finally, it costs more to care for the confined. Moving persons out of confinement helps hold down the costs of running tax-supported public hospitals.

One could argue that the incidence of mental illness is increasing. More people are seeking treatment, and the rate of admission to hospitals has been going up. But because of the problem of interpreting available statistics, one must advance such an argument with caution. As with prevalence, the incidence of mental illness remains a topic of debate.

DEFINING MENTAL ILLNESS

Thus far we have used the term *mental illness* rather freely. After all, everyone seems to know what it means. However, there is some disagreement over whether the term means anything at all. We will discuss the problems of definition in this section.

The Medical Model

Only since the nineteenth century have troubled persons been designated as "ill."[6] Prior to that time, they were more likely to be considered "possessed" by spirits, the victims of witchcraft, morally defective, or otherwise afflicted by unknown and unsavory problems. During the nineteenth century, medical practitioners advanced the theory that mental troubles were actually matters of health. They argued that persons exhibiting such troubles should not be harassed and punished or locked up in jails and asylums. Instead, said the doctors, they should be cured and made well.

This approach is usually called the *medical model* or disease model of mental illness. It is based on the belief that just as one's body is subject to injury or disease, so is one's mind. Unusual forms of behavior and/or signs of psychological disturbances are the warning symptoms of the illness. Psychiatrists and other mental health practitioners (e.g., psychotherapists, psychologists, psychiatric social workers) use the symptoms to diagnose the nature of the illness afflicting the troubled individual. Depending on the diagnosis and on the treatment preferences

[6]See, for example, Michel Foucault, *Madness and Civilization* (New York: Random House, Inc., 1965); and George Rosen, *Madness in Society* (Chicago: University of Chicago Press, 1968).

of the practitioner, a method of cure will be prescribed. The cure may involve the intensive probing of a person's thoughts, drug or electroshock therapy, or group meetings attended by similarly ill people. The mentally ill individual is expected to assume the role of patient and to rely on the expertise and advice of the mental health professional.

The evolution of the medical model has been accompanied by the adoption of a system of diagnostic terms. These terms are used to categorize the various types of mental illness that have been discovered by psychiatrists and to help standardize treatment of individuals exhibiting similar symptoms. In the United States, the American Psychiatric Association publishes a guide to this diagnostic system.[7] We will discuss two of the illnesses from this guide—psychosis and neurosis—for illustrative purposes.

Psychosis.   According to mental health practitioners, the *psychoses* are a very severe form of mental illness. Individuals diagnosed as psychotic frequently have their own versions of reality and thus are often unable to perform the roles expected of them in everyday life. Consequently, treatment of the psychoses commonly involves voluntary or involuntary confinement.

Psychotics may suffer from hallucinations, deep changes in mood, or an inability to think, speak, or remember. While psychiatrists have found that some psychoses are *organic*—that is, a result of actual physical damage to the brain or of chemical imbalances in a person's system—they claim that most types of psychosis are *functional*. In other words, in most psychoses there is no known physical reason for the symptoms of illness that are displayed. The mind itself is unwell and in need of cure.

One of the more common psychoses is called *schizophrenia.* This term is used for people who are extremely withdrawn from their surroundings or who act as if they were living in another world. Schizophrenics' thoughts may appear disorganized and bizarre, their emotions inappropriate for the situation, and their behavior unusual. Various types of schizophrenia have been identified and categorized. Persons who exhibit delusions of being persecuted by others are called paranoid schizophrenics. Catatonic schizophrenics act in an excessively excited manner or, alternatively, exist in a mute vegetative state. Childhood schizophrenia, or autism, is marked by withdrawal and repetitive, occasionally self-harming, motor behavior.

In the view of psychiatrists, schizophrenia primarily involves difficulties in thinking. *Affective disorders,* on the other hand, mainly involve changes in mood. In affective disorders, people may become extremely elated or deeply depressed for no apparent reasons. One type of affective disorder, involutional melancholia, is characterized by unrelenting signs of worry. Manic-depressive disorders, by contrast, take the form of sudden

[7]American Psychiatric Association, *Diagnostic and Statistical Manual of Mental Disorders,* 2nd ed. (Washington, D.C.: APA, 1968).

Autistic children are highly withdrawn and generally engage in repetitive behavior. Mental health practitioners have not met with much success in treating autism.

and severe changes in mood. The person may be gleefully boisterous in the manic state and may seriously contemplate self-destruction in the depressed state.

In everyday language, a person designated as psychotic by a psychiatrist is likely to be considered "mad," "nuts," "cuckoo," or "crazy." These terms are not used by those embracing the medical model. To mental health practitioners, such persons are ill and in need of professional healing.

Neurosis. Persons suffering from one or another type of *neurosis,* a second major category of mental disorder or illness, are typically capable of functioning in everyday life. Unlike the psychoses, the neuroses generally do not involve distortions of reality. Moreover, neurotics typically know that there is something wrong with their thinking or behavior.

The principal symptom of neurosis is evidence of anxiety. In mild cases of neurosis, anxiety may be expressed directly. In some severe cases, a person may appear to be in a state of panic. According to psychiatrists, anxiety may also be expressed indirectly, showing up as a variety of other problems—such as blindness, deafness, exhaustion, inexplicable fear of objects or particular situations, and compulsive activity (e.g., hand washing).

In most cases, individuals who are diagnosed as neurotics do not require hospitalization. In fact, mental health practitioners often find it hard to tell if someone is indeed suffering from an anxiety-produced neurosis—i.e., is "ill"—or is merely temporarily responding to pressures that anyone might find distressing.

The utility of the medical model.   The problem mental health practitioners have in determining who is ill and who is well has led some critics to question the whole concept of *mental illness*. How accurate and valid are the judgments made by the most prestigious mental health professionals, the psychiatrists? According to David L. Rosenhan: "There are a great deal of conflicting data on the reliability, utility, and meaning of such terms as 'sanity,' 'insanity,' 'mental illness,' and 'schizophrenia.'"[8] Prevalence surveys and treatment statistics indicate that many people are mentally troubled. But whether their mental states are best viewed and treated as forms of illness is another issue. Could it be that illness is simply a label routinely applied by believers in the medical model?

Rosenhan set up an ingenious experiment in order to pursue this question. He recruited eight people who had no history of mental troubles and were, in the language of the medical model, mentally healthy. At Rosenhan's direction, each of them sought admission to a mental hospital. The staffs of these institutions had no inkling that Rosenhan's associates were "pseudopatients."

Upon arriving at the hospitals, the eight pseudopatients claimed that they had been hearing voices and that they had come to see whether anything was wrong with them. Aside from this deception, they truthfully answered all questions pertaining to their medical backgrounds, lifestyles, and relationships with others. Seven were immediately diagnosed as schizophrenic, and the eighth was judged to be manic-depressive. Their deception was not discovered by psychiatrists. Even though they were healthy, they were diagnosed as ill.

Once they were assigned to psychiatric wards, all eight pseudopatients stopped faking the symptoms that had gained them admittance. They behaved in a friendly and cooperative manner and answered questions about their health by saying they felt fine. But no one—except other patients—doubted that their illnesses were real. After hospitalizations ranging from seven to fifty-two days, the eight pseudopatients were released, their illnesses officially diagnosed as in remission. In other words, they were still considered to be mentally ill, but the symptoms of their illnesses were said to have subsided.

[8]D. L. Rosenhan, "On Being Sane in Insane Places," *Science,* 179 (January 19, 1973): 250.

To further test the ease with which people are termed ill or well, no matter what their true mental state, Rosenhan carried his experiment one step further. He told the staff of one mental hospital—where his pseudopatient trick had become known—that he would seek to admit more such persons to their wards. In effect, he dared the psychiatric staff to uncover his pseudopatients. Following his dare, the staff screened 193 individuals. Of these, 41 were alleged to be Rosenhan's pseudopatients, and many others were considered suspect. Rosenhan had *not* sent anyone to that hospital!

On the basis of his experiment, Rosenhan concluded that "any diagnostic process that lends itself so readily to massive errors of this sort cannot be a very reliable one."[9] His work has helped feed the contemporary controversy over the meaning of mental illness and the utility of the medical model. It lends credence to critics who have urged rejection of the medical model.

Mental Illness as a Myth

The principal critic of the medical model, Thomas Szasz, is himself a psychiatrist. In his writings, Szasz acknowledges the evidence that links brain damage to certain behavior and/or thinking difficulties.[10] Severe cases of syphilis, the excessive use of alcohol, and changes due to aging, for example, can cause people to behave or think in unusual ways. Szasz also acknowledges the effect of chemical imbalances on mental functioning. In such cases, Szasz tells us, it is correct to state that a person is ill. Moreover, such illnesses are most appropriately handled within a medical context.

But Szasz reminds us that most of the illnesses treated by mental health practitioners are functional rather than organic in origin. He contends that these functional disorders are actually individual traits that may deviate from what is considered culturally, socially, ethically, or legally normal. When psychiatrists compare their own standards of what is normal with the traits exhibited by their clients, they are making value judgments about which norms people should follow. They call the people who depart from these norms ill and in need of treatment. Szasz believes that there is a contradiction between judging people as deviant on the one hand and offering them medically-oriented diagnoses and treatments on the other:

> Since medical interventions are designed to remedy only medical problems, it is logically absurd to expect that they will help solve problems whose very existence have been defined and established on nonmedical grounds.[11]

[9]Ibid., p. 252.
[10]See Thomas S. Szasz, *The Myth of Mental Illness* (New York: Delta Books, 1961). His position is most succinctly put forth in "The Myth of Mental Illness," *American Psychologist,* 15 (February 1960): 113–18.
[11]Thomas S. Szasz, *Ideology and Insanity* (New York: Anchor Books, 1970), p. 17.

In our major cities there are women and men who prefer to own no more than they can carry with them and who have no permanent homes, living instead on subways and in the streets. Their social isolation leads people to label them as deviant—and sometimes even as mentally ill. But critics of the medical model remind us that such unusual behavior should not be called sickness and is not necessarily amenable to medically-oriented treatment.

According to Szasz, the symptoms many psychiatrists associate with mental illness are really no more than styles of communication. People designated as ill are simply saying something about themselves, others, and the world around them: "what people now call mental illnesses are, for the most part, *communications* expressing unacceptable ideas, often framed in an unusual idiom."[12] These communications are expressed because people find that life is a difficult struggle. Their relations with other people and their contacts with societal institutions are accompanied by a great deal of personal stress and strain. Often their needs, values, and aspirations are going unmet. They are disturbed by the lack of harmony in American society and by unavoidable conflict with others. In Szasz' terms, people face "problems in living." They are not sick or diseased; they are trying to communicate the difficulties with which they are burdened in everyday life.

By calling individuals with problems in living ill, we are implying that there is something wrong with *them* and that they must change. This is why troubled people are encouraged to become patients and to become dependent on professional care (even against their will). The medical model, in Szasz' view, is an ideology that

[12]Ibid., p. 19.

has succeeded in depriving vast numbers of people—sometimes it seems very nearly everyone—of a vocabulary of their own in which to frame their predicament without paying homage to a psychiatric perspective.[13]

People who face problems in living are encouraged by the medical model to look within themselves for the sources of their difficulties. Only if they accept the fact that they are indeed sick and in need of help can they get better. They must adjust and accommodate their thinking and behavior to that considered normal by psychiatrists.

Those who reject the medical model and the treatments flowing from it still must confront the question of what—if anything—might be done for persons who are mentally troubled. Szasz believes that the latter *can* be helped to deal with problems in living without being told that they are sick. In his view, therapists must establish open, humane relationships with such people. Such relationships should be entered into and maintained purely on a voluntary basis and must not place troubled persons in the subordinate role of patient.

Mental Illness as a Sign of Health

Another well-known critic of the medical model, British psychiatrist R. D. Laing, feels that "humanity is estranged from its authentic possibilities."[14] Laing uses the term *alienation* to characterize the relations that presently exist among family members, generations, sex groups, classes, and races:

> The "normally" alienated person, by reason of the fact that he acts more or less like everyone else, is taken to be sane. Other forms of alienation that are out of step with the prevailing state of alienation are those that are labeled by the "normal" majority as bad or mad.[15]

The abnormally alienated are most likely to be noticed, to seek or be brought to treatment, and to be designated as ill under the medical model.

Laing has suggested that one of the more severe forms of mental illness, schizophrenia, has nothing to do with disease. Instead, according to Laing:

> The experience and behavior that gets labelled schizophrenia is a special strategy that a person invents in order to live in an unliveable situation. In his life situation the person has come to feel he is in an untenable position. He cannot make a move, or make no move, without being beset by contradictory and paradoxical pressures and demands, pushes and pulls, both internally from himself, and externally from those around him.[16]

[13]Ibid., p. 5.
[14]R. D. Laing, *The Politics of Experience* (New York: Ballantine Books, Inc., 1967), p. 12.
[15]Ibid., pp. 27–8.
[16]Ibid., pp. 114–15.

Serious disorders, to Laing, are efforts on the part of an individual to escape from alienating societal arrangements. Laing suggests that these efforts to escape existing realities might actually be considered a sign of health. They are certainly a healthier response than would be living with the problems. "The perfectly adjusted bomber pilot may be a greater threat to species survival than the hospitalized schizophrenic deluded that the Bomb is inside him."[17]

Likening the schizophrenic experience to an LSD "trip" or spiritual journey, Laing feels that psychiatric efforts to cure schizophrenia are more often harmful than helpful. He feels that experienced psychotics should be used to guide those who are in the process of embarking into another level of reality. Needless to say, Laing's ideas—like those of Szasz—are unpopular among those who remain committed to the medical model.

Nonetheless, Laing's observations suggest new ways of approaching those who are troubled. His stress on empathy and understanding, implied by the suggestion of using persons who have "been there" to help others, offers an alternative to telling troubled people that there is something wrong with them.

The Labeling Process

Like Rosenhan and Szasz, Laing emphasizes that mental illness is a label bestowed on people whose thinking and/or behavior is judged unacceptable. The bestowal of such a label is, according to Laing, a *political event,* in which those with medical, legal, and moral authority are in a position to cast an individual into the role of sick person. This labeling process has been spelled out by sociologist Thomas Scheff.

Scheff notes that members of society have handy categories in which to place those who violate commonly accepted rules or norms.[18] Persons who violate the law are "criminals"; those who eat peas with their knives are "ill-mannered." But some forms of behavior are so unusual or unthinkable that they cannot be easily categorized. Such *residual deviance* is likely to be allocated to a catchall category: mentally ill.

Unlike Szasz and Laing, Scheff is not too concerned with pinning down the initial reasons why persons may express unusual thinking and/or behavior. Instead, he simply states that the deviant behaviors called mental illness may arise from diverse sources ranging from the physiological to the socioeconomic.

Scheff contends that the rate of residual deviance is extremely high, and that only a small amount comes to be treated as mental illness. Much

[17]Ibid., p. 120.
[18]Thomas Scheff, *Being Mentally Ill* (Chicago: Aldine Publishing Company, 1966). See also a critique by Walter R. Gove, "Societal Reactions as an Explanation of Mental Illness: An Evaluation," *American Sociological Review,* 35 (October 1970): 873–80.

deviance is either ignored, unrecognized, or rationalized away. Moreover, much of it is transitory. But at least some is labeled mental illness and is treated. The crucial variable, according to Scheff, is *societal reaction.* The label must be imposed by society for mental illness to exist.

When does society impose the label? Scheff posits that we learn stereotypes of what it means to "act crazy" in early childhood. These stereotypes are then reaffirmed, for example, by the mass media and even in everyday conversations. When residual deviance becomes publicly noticed, such stereotypes are mobilized, and the individual is told that he or she is ill.

An individual who has been labeled mentally ill is encouraged to accept this label and to display the traits stereotypically expected of a sick person. Once this occurs, the illness becomes "stabilized": mental disorder becomes a social role. The individual impersonates illness by accepting and acting within the diagnostic labels of the medical model.

Scheff observes that persons may actually be rewarded for playing the illness role. Psychiatrists, for example, are pleased when someone accepts their diagnosis and treatments. Conversely, persons may be punished for attempting to shed the role. Once labeled, so-called mentally ill people—even if pronounced cured—may find it difficult to escape discriminatory treatment (as did Thomas Eagleton, whose experiences were discussed at the start of this chapter). Any additional episodes of

Some types of residual deviance that are today labeled mental illness were given different labels at other times. In colonial New England, for example, when some young Puritan girls in Salem, Massachusetts, began to behave strangely, they were labeled as "bewitched by the Devil." After the girls identified the "witches" who were supposedly responsible, the people of Salem began witch trials that left twenty-two accused "witches" dead.

residual deviance are likely to be interpreted as signs of continued illness. Individuals thus may be caught up in a *career* of being mentally ill, filling this role in response to societal reactions to them.

In sum, there is a controversy over whether most mentally troubled persons are in fact ill. As critics of the medical model contend, such individuals may face problems in living or be alienated from existing societal arrangements. As they respond to their situations with unusual expressions of behavior and/or thinking, they may be labeled as ill and subjected to treatment in a medical context. The critics question the wisdom of such treatment for persons whose troubles are essentially rooted in the social environment in which they find themselves.

FACTORS ASSOCIATED WITH MENTAL ILLNESS

Who are the persons whose behaviors are most likely to set the labeling process into motion? Four factors seem to have a lot to do with being mentally ill. These factors are class, economic disruption, racism, and sexism.

Class

Because of their economic disadvantage, low-income groups face daily problems in living. Thus we should expect many members of such groups to display signs of being mentally troubled. The impact of class on mental functioning has long been recognized. In the 1930s, sociologists Robert E. L. Faris and H. Warren Dunham probed this issue in their research on mental hospitals in Chicago.[19] Faris and Dunham looked at the records of 35,000 persons who had been admitted to the city's private and public mental institutions, checking not only the diagnostic labels that psychiatrists applied to each patient, but also the part of the city each came from. They found that the highest rates of hospitalization were for persons residing in unstable low-income areas. Moreover, the most seriously troubled people—those diagnosed as schizophrenic—tended to come from these same areas.

The study by Faris and Dunham could be criticized for concentrating only on the hospitalized. A more comprehensive inquiry that avoided this pitfall was conducted during the early 1950s in New Haven, Connecticut.[20] This study, which was conducted by August Hollingshead and

---

[19]Robert E. L. Faris and H. Warren Dunham, *Mental Disorders in Urban Areas* (Chicago: University of Chicago Press, 1939).

[20]August B. Hollingshead and Fredrick C. Redlich, *Social Class and Mental Illness* (New York: John Wiley & Sons., Inc., 1958). See also Jerome K. Myers and Lee L. Bean, *A Decade Later: A Follow-up of Social Class and Mental Illness* (New York: John Wiley & Sons, Inc., 1968).

Fredrick Redlich, covered not only the hospitalized but also persons treated in clinics and by private psychiatrists. Hollingshead and Redlich identified the total population of all persons receiving treatment over a five-month period. They divided this group into five classes, based on area of residence, occupation, and amount of education. The classes ranged from Class I (business and professional people) down to Class V (laborers). This division corresponds with differential economic status—Class I being the most affluent and Class V the poor.

The findings of Hollingshead and Redlich's study were consistent with those of the Chicago study. The severely troubled—those designated as psychotic—most frequently came from Class V. Both the incidence and prevalence of serious mental troubles were highest for this group. Those suffering from less serious problems—that is, the neuroses—were most likely to come from Class I. In fact, Hollingshead and Redlich found that the top four classes contributed fewer patients than one would expect, given their numerical representation in the New Haven population.

Beyond this, Hollingshead and Redlich noted that the *type* of treatment patients received varied in accordance with their class membership. People from the lower classes were most likely to be served by public institutions, most of which provided little more than custodial care. Members of the upper classes, particularly Class I, most frequently patronized private psychiatrists; if hospitalization were required, they were likely to enter expensive private institutions. Such differential treatment, it has been suggested, may influence statistics on the high rates of serious disorders among the poor.[21] The prospects for personalized attention and quick release are lower in public, as opposed to private, hospitals. Moreover, the lower classes are more likely to be diagnosed as seriously ill than the affluent, even when they display the same symptoms—an indication of class bias in the application of psychiatric labels.

Both the Chicago and New Haven studies were limited to persons undergoing treatment, which means that they cannot be generalized to any larger population. However, the Midtown Manhattan study, discussed earlier in this chapter, provides some information about the non-treated sector.[22] In this study, the cases were not only classified on the basis of the degree of mental impairment, they were also ranked in terms of the socioeconomic background of the residents. Almost half the persons who came from the lowest economic strata were found to have severe or marked symptoms of impairment, or to be incapacitated. By contrast, little more than 10 percent of those from the highest strata were judged to be so troubled.

Many other studies have been conducted, and their findings are generally consistent: the highest rates of mental illness, particularly of serious

[21]S. M. Miller and Eliot G. Mishler, "Social Class, Mental Illness, and American Psychiatry," *Milbank Memorial Fund Quarterly*, 37 (April 1959): 1–26.
[22]Srole et al., *Mental Health in the Metropolis*.

mental difficulties, seem to be found in the lowest economic strata.[23] The affluent may be afflicted with anxieties, which are relatively minor illnesses within the framework of the medical model. But the poor often respond to problems in living by fleeing from reality. Lacking the finances to pursue private, individualized attention from psychiatrists, poor people who are troubled generally must fall back on the tax-supported institutions reserved for them. There, within a medical context, the poor are told that something is the matter with *them*—not with a society whose organization presents them with problems in living.

Economic Disruption

There is little information about the impact of large-scale societal change on the mental well-being of Americans. One of the few studies was conducted by sociologist M. Harvey Brenner. Brenner hypothesized that "mental hospitalization will increase during economic downturns and decrease during upturns."[24] To test this hypothesis, he examined data on hospitalization and economic conditions in New York State, covering a period of nearly thirteen decades, from before the Civil War to 1971.

Using sophisticated statistical techniques, Brenner succeeded in proving his hypothesis. He discovered that the functional mental illnesses were extremely sensitive to adverse changes in the American economy. Most of the organic illnesses were not sensitive to changes, with the exception of psychoses following excessive alcohol consumption. Evidently, many people try to lose themselves in drink in times of great economic stress. Brenner noted that the people admitted to mental hospitals were typically workers whose occupations were most vulnerable to unemployment or loss of income.

Through his research, Brenner was also able to show that several other factors had nothing to do with changes in hospitalization levels and rates. Among these unrelated factors were the availability of bed space, changing treatment practices, population changes, differences in state treatment facilities, and shifting public and psychiatric definitions of who is ill. By rejecting these alternative explanations, he demonstrated that: "The destiny of the individual is to a great extent subject to large-scale changes in the social and economic structure that are in no way under his control."[25]

In discussing the implications of his findings, Brenner questioned the effectiveness and appropriateness of psychiatric treatment. Since the causes of mental illness lie outside the individual, society—not the pa-

---

[23]Such studies are reviewed in Bruce P. Dohrenwend and Barbara S. Dohrenwend, *Social Status and Psychological Disorder* (New York: John Wiley & Sons, Inc., 1969).

[24]M. Harvey Brenner, *Mental Illness and the Economy* (Cambridge, Mass.: Harvard University Press, 1973), p. 10.

[25]Ibid., p. x.

tient—must be changed in order to reduce mental troubles. Furthermore, he contended:

> Hospitalization is not only a psychiatrically inappropriate response to economic stress; it actually compounds the social impact of economic stress enormously. . . . The patient's economic and social careers can be very seriously damaged.[26]

What Brenner was alluding to here is the fact that individuals who have been hospitalized for mental troubles are frequently stigmatized by the hospitalization. Their "histories" of mental problems make it difficult for them to find economic security, for they are suspected of still being "sick." This, of course, is akin to Thomas Scheff's concept of mental illness careers.

Beyond this, according to Brenner, mental hospitals are vehicles for social control. They function like prisons in that they remove troubled, and possibly troublesome, people from the population and act as safety valves for the society. Since the systemic sources of mental troubles are rarely acknowledged, the very existence of mental hospitals supports the status quo.

Brenner's empirical findings have been underscored by observations during the economic recession of the mid-1970s. Psychiatrists at the National Institute of Mental Health conducted informal telephone surveys of mental health facilities located in areas of high unemployment. The staffs of these facilities reported a sharp rise in treatment for mental troubles, particularly for forty-five- to sixty-year-old men. The psychiatrists observed that millions of people were doubting their ability to keep their economic conditions stable—let alone to achieve future prosperity.[27] Mental troubles, in their view, are a part of the human toll taken by economic adversity.[28]

Racism

As we saw in Chapter 4, racism is a source of harm for millions of Americans. Thus, we would expect to find that minority group members experience mental troubles more frequently than whites. However, studies and data relating to race and mental illness are limited and are confused by the impact of class on minorities. Members of minority groups are overrepresented in the most economically disadvantaged strata, where mental illness is more prevalent. Moreover, most of the

[26]Ibid., pp. 228–29.
[27]*New York Times,* January 27, 1976, p. 6.
[28]Increases in unemployment are associated with increased physical illness as well as with increased mental illness. See M. Harvey Brenner, "Personal Stability and Economic Security," *Social Policy,* 8 (May/June 1977): 2–4.

focus of literature on mental health and racism is on black Americans, not on all minority groups.[29]

Case studies on the impact of racism are of limited utility. One of the best-known studies was conducted in the early 1950s by Abram Kardiner and Lionel Ovesey. In *The Mark of Oppression,* these researchers concluded that black Americans suffer from extremely low self-esteem and from self-hatred.[30] They reached this conclusion on the basis of interviews with twenty-five people who were thought to be psychologically disturbed. Though Kardiner and Ovesey's study had an impact on social science thinking about black problems, it was criticized for stereotyping an entire minority group on the basis of such limited data.

A similar study was published in the late 1960s by two black psychiatrists, William Grier and Price M. Cobbs. In their book *Black Rage,* Grier and Cobbs suggested that blacks who live in a predominantly white society develop "cultural paranoia" in response to racism.[31] Every white is an enemy until proven otherwise. In dealing with their minority status, blacks develop distorted psychological functioning. Behind all this, according to Grier and Cobbs, black Americans are filled with rage. Critics were quick to point out that Grier and Cobbs totally based their claims on contact with black psychiatric patients—people unable to function in American society. The millions of blacks—and all others victimized by racism—who do function were ignored. *Black Rage,* it was noted, failed to shed any light on the mental state of the majority of minority group members. Moreover, as in *The Mark of Oppression,* Grier and Cobb's emphasis on the pathology of black mental functioning clearly failed to address the equally important question of strengths that have enabled such groups to survive racial oppression.[32]

If such case studies fail to shed much light on the mental state of minorities, investigations of prevalence and incidence are at least as difficult to interpret. Social psychologist Thomas Pettigrew has noted that the overrepresentation of minorities in low-income categories makes it difficult to single out racism as an independent source of mental troubles.[33] Minority group members who suffer from serious disorders usu-

[29]See Alexander Thomas and Samuel Siller, *Racism and Psychiatry* (New York: Brunner/Mazel, Inc., 1972), pp. 122–34; and Morton Kramer et al., "Definitions and Distributions of Mental Disorders in a Racist Society," in *Racism and Mental Health,* Charles V. Willie et al., eds. (Pittsburgh: University of Pittsburgh Press, 1973), pp. 353–459.

[30]Abram Kardiner and Lionel Ovesey, *The Mark of Oppression* (Cleveland: World Publishing Co., 1951).

[31]William Grier and Price M. Cobbs, *Black Rage* (New York: Basic Books, Inc., 1968).

[32]See John McCarthy and William Yancey, "Uncle Tom and Mr. Charlie: Metaphysical Pathos in the Study of Racism and Personal Disorganization," *American Journal of Sociology,* 76 (January 1971): 648–72; and Ronald L. Taylor, "Psychosocial Development Among Black Children and Youth," *American Journal of Orthopsychiatry,* 46 (January 1976): 4–19.

[33]Thomas F. Pettigrew, *A Profile of the Negro American* (Princeton, N.J.: D. Van Nostrand Company, 1964), pp. 73–82.

ally cannot afford to patronize private hospitals. Since they are unlikely to have much faith in white-dominated public facilities, they may avoid seeking help until troubles grow severe. These factors may lead to institutionalization of the most deeply disturbed, inflating statistics on, for example, the frequency of psychoses among minorities.

Pettigrew also points out that, in some regions of the country, minority group members are more likely than whites to be involuntarily committed to institutions. Once in large public hospitals, many of which are informally segregated, a lack of quality care and racist practices may result in prolonged stays. Frequent readmissions may follow. All this is to say that estimates of minority mental troubles based on treatment statistics may be biased by factors that do not impinge on whites.[34]

Thus, while statistics for admissions to mental hospitals (Table 10.3) generally indicate that racial minorities have higher rates of admission than whites, it is not easy to interpret this fact. Similarly, the facts that blacks have higher rates of psychosis than whites and that first admission rates for neuroses are highest for whites are also difficult to interpret. It could be that minority group members simply ignore mental disorders that are not incapacitating, so that the most seriously troubled primarily come into contact with treatment agencies.

Furthermore, it is possible that white mental health practitioners may designate minority group members as ill more frequently than they apply this label to whites. Not only is there class bias; there is also ignorance of minority life pressures and ethnic characteristics. Simple things like language barriers may impede understanding the troubles of such groups as Spanish-speaking Americans.

Whatever the facts about the impact of racism on the mental state of minorities and on patterns of treatment, we must remember that the medical model calls for finding fault with the victims. It does not call for fighting the systemic sources of minority mental troubles.

Sexism

Until quite recently little attention was paid to the mental state of American women. Under the impetus of the women's movement, sexism and the problems in living to which it gives rise have become more widely discussed. Nonetheless, as psychologist Phyllis Chesler tells us: "Contemporary psychiatric and psychological theories and practices both reflect and influence our culture's politically naive understanding and emotionally brutal treatment of women."[35]

[34]See Max Seham, *Blacks and American Medical Care* (Minneapolis: University of Minnesota Press, 1973).

[35]Phyllis Chesler, "Patient and Patriarch: Women in the Psychotherapeutic Relationship," in *Woman in Sexist Society,* Vivian Gornick and Barbara K. Moran, eds. (New York: Mentor Books, 1971), pp. 362–63.

Table 10.3. Admissions to State and County Psychiatric Hospitals, by Age, Sex, and Race, Rate per 100,000 Population

Age	Both Sexes			Males			Females		
	Total	White	All other races	Total	White	All other races	Total	White	All other races
All ages	182.2	161.1	321.9	243.7	214.2	444.5	124.7	111.2	212.0
Under 14	17.2	13.8	34.7	22.8	19.0	42.4	11.4	8.3	27.0
14–17	99.1	83.1	186.8	123.1	98.0	262.6	74.3	67.6	110.4
18–24	271.8	234.0	502.6	409.0	343.9	830.3	143.1	129.4	222.8
25–34	332.7	289.2	633.6	457.8	382.4	1026.8	214.1	199.0	311.1
35–44	289.0	244.7	598.6	364.9	304.5	826.1	218.3	187.8	415.3
45–54	277.6	261.4	409.1	359.2	350.3	435.4	201.4	177.8	386.5
55–64	180.7	156.6	406.0	208.4	186.0	422.8	155.9	130.2	391.5
65 and over	91.8	85.3	157.3	136.4	130.9	189.2	60.8	54.0	133.0

Source: U.S. Department of Health, Education, and Welfare, National Institute of Mental Health, *Mental Health Statistical Note,* No. 140 (November 1977): 8.

Chesler notes that men have long dominated the mental health profession. Though women are well represented among psychiatric social workers, men generally hold the more prestigious positions of psychiatrist, psychoanalyst, and psychologist. Thus men have determined how women's mental difficulties will be explained and treated. Women with problems in living who seek help from mental health practitioners are likely to be told that they are at fault, "and this by men who have studiously bypassed the objective fact of female oppression."[36]

Chesler points to studies indicating that women who exhibit—or wish to exhibit—some of the personality traits of mentally healthy men are likely to be thought ill. That is, women who want to be assertive, independent, and aggressive—traits stereotypically associated with the male sex role—may be seen as abnormal. She suggests that there is a masculine ideology in mental health practice, in which the "healthy" woman is one whose personality does not depart from traditional concepts of femininity.[37]

In *Women and Madness,* Chesler draws attention to statistics indicating that, when all modes of treatment are taken into account, women undergo treatment for mental troubles far more frequently than men.[38] Moreover, women have been making up an increasing proportion of those undergoing treatment since the mid-1960s. While there are probably many reasons for this, it seems likely that, as women are growing increasingly aware of and sensitive to their position of subordination, they are searching for ways to cope with the unhappiness they feel. Becoming mentally ill, ironically, may be one of the few ways a woman can find someone who will listen to her troubles.

[36]Ibid., p. 363.
[37]Phyllis Chesler, *Women and Madness* (Garden City, N.Y.: Doubleday & Co., Inc., 1972), pp. 67–9.
[38]Ibid., pp. 306–33. See also Bruce P. Dohrenwend, "Sociocultural and Social-Psychological Factors in the Genesis of Mental Disorders," *Journal of Health and Social Behavior,* 16 (December 1975): 365–92.

What kinds of symptoms do women undergoing treatment most frequently display? Reviewing literature on female patients, Chesler notes they are often "self-deprecatory, depressed, perplexed, suffering from suicidal thoughts, or making suicide attempts."[39] (Fewer women than men actually commit suicide, however.) These are the kinds of symptoms one would expect among a group that suffers from male chauvinism and institutional sexism.

Marriage, long considered to be the proper "place" for women in this society, seems to be a particular source of unhappiness for many. Jesse Bernard, in her review of the many studies that suggest that wives are less satisfied with their marriages than husbands, underscores the dilemma of many married women. While "their happiness is more dependent upon marriage than men's,"[40] women are expected to do the adjusting to their husbands' demands. According to Bernard, the psychological costs of such adjustments are often considerable and "may greatly impair mental health."[41]

TREATING MENTAL ILLNESS

As we have seen, millions of Americans are mentally troubled. Men, women, and children of all races and classes face problems in living caused by the organization of American society. Some of them respond to these problems by behaving in ways that are labeled mental illnesses.

According to the medical model, which dominates the mental health profession, mentally troubled individuals are sick. Private psychiatric care, community mental health centers, and mental hospitals are used to treat the mentally ill and to foster their adjustment to society.

When we include lost productivity due to mental disorders, treatment of mental illness costs more than $20 billion each year. One out of three hospital beds in the United States is reserved for the mentally troubled. More money and resources are used for the treatment of mental illness than for the elimination of the sources of mental anguish. For example, while government programs in the field of mental health have expanded enormously in recent years, this has not been the case with programs to eliminate poverty and discrimination.

In this section we will look at a common treatment given the seriously mentally ill—confinement in large public institutions. We will consider the issue of involuntary confinement and its implications for civil liberties. Finally, we will discuss the possibility of alternatives to confinement.

[39]Chesler, "Patient and Patriarch," p. 371.

[40]Jessie Bernard, "The Paradox of the Happy Marriage," in *Woman in Sexist Society,* Gornick and Moran, eds., p. 149.

[41]Ibid. See also Walter R. Gove, "The Relationship Between Sex Roles, Marital Status, and Mental Illness," *Social Forces,* 51 (September 1972): 34–44.

Mental Hospitals as Total Institutions

As we have seen, not all people who are defined as mentally ill are confined in large public institutions. Who are the people most likely to be confined? According to sociologist Robert Perrucci:

> They are victims of families and communities who can no longer tolerate rule-breaking and problematic behavior. They are victims of poverty, powerlessness, and discrimination and the resulting individual-psychological explanations for their plight as people with a mental illness. They, moreover, are often willing victims insofar as they accept and adopt the roles of madness in order to "solve" the problems of living which they are experiencing. In short, they are not in the hospital because they are mad, but because they have been rejected by society and have no suitable place in it. [42]

In Perrucci's words, mental hospitals function "as a dumping ground for societal rejects." [43]

Large public mental hospitals appear to have a great deal in common with one another. Erving Goffman calls them *total institutions*. [44] Mental institutions are total institutions in that eating, sleeping, work, and play all occur within a schedule set up by hospital administrators and staff. Every patient is required to do certain things at certain times, usually in the company of fellow patients, under a system of rules imposed from above.

The total institution has a great impact on the individual who is confined there. [45] People enter mental hospitals with what Goffman calls a "presenting culture" based on their way of life and the routines they took for granted prior to confinement. They also have a conception of who they are, based on their past participation in social arrangements and interaction with family members, co-workers, and friends and neighbors. According to Goffman, the patients' presenting cultures are ignored in the mental institution; and patients are forced to live in accordance with the demands of institutional authority. In addition, their self-concepts are attacked and altered.

The attack on patients' self-concepts is done through a process of *mortification*. From the moment they enter the institution, patients are cut off from contact with the outside world. They may be photographed, fingerprinted, weighed, measured, undressed, searched, bathed, and disinfected. Personal belongings and clothing may be taken away, and institutional garments provided. The patient may be assigned a number, living arrangements, and a list of regulations. According to Goffman:

> In thus being squared away, the new arrival allows himself to be shaped and coded into an object. . . . This object can be fed into the administrative

[42]Robert Perrucci, *Circle of Madness* (Englewood Cliffs, N.J.: Prentice-Hall, Inc., 1974), p. 30.
[43]Ibid., p. 31.
[44]Erving Goffman, *Asylums* (Garden City, N.Y.: Anchor Books, 1961), p. xiii.
[45]Ibid., pp. 12–74.

Conditions in many large public mental institutions, where less affluent people are generally confined, are often dismal. Inmates are given tranquilizing drugs and often receive little or no therapy. Confinement in such institutions can be extremely harmful.

machinery of the establishment, to be worked on smoothly by routine operations.[46]

The staff carefully observes the individual's willingness to accept being "squared away." Patients who resist may be viewed as troublemakers who deserve punishment. Goffman notes that the staff may actually test new arrivals to see how far they can be pushed. By doing this, the staff gets to demonstrate punishments to the newcomers while simultaneously reminding other patients what happens when someone refuses to defer to staff demands.

Goffman felt that the result of the mortification process is to undermine the patient's sense of autonomy and adult self-determination, placing the individual in a position of childlike dependency on the institutional staff. The staff can then more easily maintain order and routine.

[46]Ibid., p. 16.
[47]Perrucci, *Circle of Madness*, p. 53.
[48]Ibid., p. 64.

Furthermore, the mortification process fits well with the medical model, which sees the inmate as sick. As Perrucci puts it:

> The self that existed prior to hospitalization is defined as having been in some way the cause of the patient's present condition. Thus, the old self must be destroyed, and a new self incorporated through a resocialization process. [47]

Perrucci tells us that the mortification process occurs in a "world of unfreedom." Patients have little control over what happens to them in the institution, so they cannot choose to remain unaffected by it. Perrucci found that patients respond to the pressures in various ways. Some "withdraw" from relations with patients and staff, but comply with institutional routines. Others engage in "accommodation," trying to be perfect patients. Still others respond with "conversion"—imitating the staff's way of relating to other patients. Finally, some "resist":

> Patients operating under this mode are greatly concerned with maintaining their own self-respect and dignity. In this respect, they resist all efforts to place them in the general category of patient. [48]

Hospitalization for more affluent people who have been labeled mentally ill generally takes place in private institutions, which may be characterized by pleasant surroundings and personalized attention. The chances for "cure" and quick release are far better in private than in public institutions.

Public Problem, Private Pain
IN A MENTAL INSTITUTION

In this excerpt from Marge Piercy's novel, the main character, Connie, finds herself involuntarily confined in a mental hospital. She had been hospitalized once before—committed by the courts after a breakdown following her husband's death when she neglected and abused her daughter. This second confinement is a result of Connie's attempt to protect her niece, Dolly, from an assault by Dolly's boyfriend. Connie injured the boyfriend and was herself badly hurt in the struggle. The boyfriend persuaded Dolly to claim that Connie attacked her. Connie's brother believed their story and signed to have Connie legally committed for treatment.

Locked into seclusion, Connie sat on the floor near the leaky radiator with her knees drawn up to her chest, slowly coming out of a huge dose of drugs. Weak through her whole useless watery body, she still felt nauseated, her head ached, her eyes and throat were sandpapery, her tongue felt swollen in her dry mouth, but at least she could think now. Her brain no longer felt crushed to a lump at the back of her skull and the slow cold weight of time had begun to slide forward.

Already her lips were split, her skin chapped from the tranquilizers, her bowels were stone, her hands shook. She no longer coughed, though. The tranks seemed to suppress the chronic cough that brought up bloody phlegm. Arriving had been so hard, so bleak. The first time here, she had been scared of the other patients—violent, crazy, out-of-control animals. She had learned. It was the staff she must watch out for. But the hopelessness of being stuck here again had boiled up in her two mornings before when the patients in her ward had been lined up for their dose of liquid Thorazine, and she had refused. Pills she could flush away, but the liquid there was no avoiding, and it killed her by inches. She had blindly fought till they had sunk a hypo in her and sent her crashing down.

Letting loose like that brought them down hard on her. She was still in seclusion, having been given four times the dose she had fought. Captivity stretched before her, a hall with no doors and no windows, yawning under dim bulbs. Surely she would die here. Her heart would beat more and more slowly and then stop, like a watch running down. At that thought the heart began to race in her chest. She stared at the room, empty except for the mattress and odd stains, names, dates, words scratched somehow into the wall with blood, fingernails, pencil stubs shit: how did she come to be in this desperate place?

Her head leaning on the wall she thought it was going to be worse this time—for last time she had judged herself sick, she had rolled in self-pity and self-hatred like a hot sulfur spring, scalding herself. All those experts lined up against her in a jury dressed in medical white and judicial black— social workers, caseworkers, child guidance counselors, psychiatrists, doctors, nurses, clinical psychologists, probation officers—all those cool knowing faces had caught her and bound her in their nets of jargon hung all with tiny barbed hooks that stuck in her flesh and leaked a slow weakening poison. She was marked with the bleeding stigmata of shame. She had wanted to cooperate, to grow well. Even when she felt so bad she lay in a corner and wept and wept, laid level by guilt, that too was part of being sick: it proved she was sick rather than evil. Say one hundred Our Fathers. Say you understand how sick you've been and you want to learn to cope. You want to stop acting out. Speak up in Tuesday group therapy (but not too much and never about staff or how lousy this place was) and volunteer to clean up after the other, the incontinent patients.

Marge Piercy, *Woman on the Edge of Time* (New York: A Fawcett Crest Book, 1976), pp. 59-60.

Novelist Ken Kesey memorialized the resisters—and speculated on their fate—in *One Flew Over the Cuckoo's Nest.* [49] The novel recounts the experiences of McMurphy, a man who chose confinement in a mental hospital over jail. McMurphy's attempts to humanize his ward by organizing such forbidden activities as gambling and parties run into resistance from a staff member named Big Nurse, who ultimately regains control over McMurphy by forcing him to undergo a frontal lobotomy (a brain operation that can replace aggressiveness with meekness). Kesey's depiction of the struggle between institutional authority and a patient who refused to adapt to it were inspired by his observations in a mental hospital.

There is one more response to confinement. In *Methods of Madness*, psychologist Benjamin Braginsky and his associates found patients who were content to remain confined. [50] They had been in confinement for so long that they could not even bear to think of leaving the institution. Such patients manipulated the staff by affecting symptoms that would bar their release. Through such "impression management," they gained some control over their fate. In Braginsky's view, such behavior was not a result of illness; it was an outcome of the effects of institutionalization itself. [51]

In recent years there have been limited reforms in the administration of large public mental hospitals. And, as we mentioned earlier, the costs of maintaining people in long-term confinement—together with the adoption of drugs that alter the behavior of patients—have decreased the average length of a stay in such institutions. While admission rates have gone up in recent years, so have release rates. Still, the large public mental hospital remains the major focal point for the treatment and mental rearmament of persons who are troubled.

The Politics of Involuntary Confinement

At several points we have alluded to the fact that people may be involuntarily confined to mental institutions. [52] All states have legal procedures that make it possible to hospitalize individuals who refuse to accept the illness label. These procedures often involve having a judge rule that individuals are a danger to themselves and/or others.

The procedures leading to involuntary confinement raise serious civil

---

[49] Ken Kesey, *One Flew Over the Cuckoo's Nest* (New York: Signet, 1962).

[50] Benjamin Braginsky et al., *Methods of Madness* (New York: Holt, Rinehart & Winston, 1969).

[51] To "de-institutionalize" such patients, hospitals have experimented with simulations of nonhospital life in the wards. See Kenneth J. Neubeck, "Capitalism as Therapy?" *Social Policy,* 8 (May/June 1977): 41–5.

[52] This section draws heavily on David Mechanic, *Mental Health and Social Policy* (Englewood Cliffs, N.J.: Prentice-Hall, Inc., 1969), pp. 123–35. See also Thomas S. Szasz, *Law, Liberty, and Psychiatry* (New York: Macmillan, Inc., 1963).

liberties issues. Relatives, social welfare agencies, police, or private citizens may start the process, often when they become aware of individuals who communicate their alienation from the status quo in unusual or disruptive ways or of children or the elderly who do not seem to be able to care for themselves. In other words, the initial judgments about such individuals' mental states are typically made by "accusers" who have no medical or psychiatric training. The judgments are made in terms of value-laden views about what is normal and what is deviant.

In most states, police are empowered to take the "accused" into temporary custody, where he or she may be forced to undergo examination by medical practitioners. Sometimes the examining doctors have no training in psychiatry. Even when they do, as we saw earlier, professional judgments about mental health are not always accurate. Nevertheless, the examining doctor may recommend to the court that hospitalization take place. Since court personnel are not likely to be trained in assessing mental capabilities, they are likely to accept the judgments of medical experts. According to sociologist David Mechanic, "the commitment process has the form of due process of law but is actually vacuous since the decision tends to be predetermined."[53]

Court personnel seem to assume that a person would never have been brought into commitment proceedings unless there was something wrong with him or her. Consequently, many people whose behavior is said to be unacceptable—but who pose no harm to themselves or others—are confined. Even confining those who *may* be dangerous poses civil liberties issues, since there often is no way to predict such behavior. Hospital administrators generally admit that very few of their patients would harm others if released on the spot.

Further, commitment proceedings assume that hospitalization—even involuntary commitment—will help those who are mentally troubled. We have already seen that the impact of confinement in a total institution may actually be harmful. We have also noted that the stigma of hospitalization may plague persons after release. Moreover, since the sources of problems in living do not necessarily reside within the individual, removal from the community may be a questionable solution.

Can't confinement be replaced by some other type of treatment procedure? David Mechanic does not feel that reforms will lead us in this direction:

> Even if we assume adherence to due process in the use of commitment procedures and even if the quality of treatment undergoes impressive improvement, the community will still demand that certain individuals be removed and treated despite no desire on their part for such care. . . . Misfits will always frighten or threaten others, and people will always feel that the interests of the community are best served by placing such deviants in custody. Inevitably what is thought to be in the interests of some is not in the interests of others.[54]

[53]Mechanic, *Mental Health and Social Policy*, p. 127.
[54]Ibid., p. 135.

Mechanic's pessimism may cause us to conclude that the tendency to place "misfits" in confinement is traceable to human nature. In reality, not human nature but *power* plays the central role. The label of deviant or "misfit" is forced on individuals who are mentally ill due to physical causes or who are simply alienated from society. Sociologist Howard Becker has raised and answered the key question:

> Who can, in fact, force others to accept their rules and what are the causes of their success? This is, of course, a question of political and economic power.[55]

Parents may exercise their power to have a troublesome child confined. Children may dispose of their aging parents in the same way. The local ne'er-do-wells whose presence and behavior annoy the "solid citizenry" may be taken away or pressured into voluntary surrender to a mental hospital. In such cases, the ability of the accused to resist confinement may be minimal. Resistance itself, ironically, may be interpreted as further evidence of illness and may be used to justify confinement.

Furthermore, we must not forget that there is much money to be made from the mental health industry. Private psychiatrists often receive fifty dollars an hour for their services. Companies profit from the demand for drugs and equipment utilized by the mental health profession. These people have a vested interest in maintaining today's treatment procedures. Were extensive changes to be made, the status and jobs of many such professionals would be jeopardized.

The Need for Change

So long as the mentally troubled are defined as being at fault for their plight, the features of American society that provoke problems in living are likely to remain unquestioned. It is far easier to pour money and resources into treating the sick minds of individuals than to confront the prospects of altering society so that humanity is no longer estranged from its authentic possibilities.

But we cannot afford to wait for large-scale societal changes while doing nothing to help the millions who are troubled now. The ideas of Szasz and Laing offer some alternatives to confinement. In fact, Laing's idea of having people who have been troubled help others is beginning to be accepted. In many cities, people who face common problems in living can join self-help groups and pool their knowledge and experiences to provide one another with mutual support. Those groups that operate outside the medical model, stress voluntary participation, and offer positive, nonalienating relationships can be expected to make an important contribution.

Moving people out of confinement in public institutions and into the

[55]Howard S. Becker, *Outsiders* (New York: The Free Press, 1963), p. 17.

community must be speeded up. This has been taking place, often simply for budgetary reasons because of the rising costs of inpatient care. But the newly released are too frequently set adrift and left to fend for themselves. Many end up isolated and alone and/or suffering from the stigmatization of their confinement. Trained volunteers might be organized to be special friends and companions to such persons in their home environments. Some of the newly released may like to be placed in the homes of persons who would guide them in their transition to full community participation.

Ultimately, however, the societal factors that seem to give rise to problems in living—from class inequalities to sexism—must be confronted if mental troubles are to be mitigated.

SUMMARY

Millions of Americans are mentally troubled. We do not know the prevalence of mental illness—that is, the total cases existing at a given time—due to problems of definition and measurement. A rough estimate is that 10 percent of the population—over 20 million people—are ill. The number of new cases occurring over time—the incidence of mental illness—appears to be on the increase. But because of the problem of interpreting available data, most of which are based on treatment statistics, one must advance such an argument with caution. Many factors bear on whether or not troubled people seek out and receive treatment.

The dominant approach to the treatment of the mentally troubled is called the medical model. Psychiatrists and other mental health practitioners commonly assume that troubled people are ill and in need of cure. Two major illnesses are known as the psychoses and the neuroses. Psychoses are considered very severe forms of illness wherein individuals have their own versions of reality and are often unable to perform expected roles. The neuroses are considered less severe forms of illness and typically involve expressions of underlying anxieties.

The medical model has come under criticism and is a source of controversy. Questions have been raised as to the accuracy of the judgments made by mental health practitioners in their diagnoses. Critics of the medical model have questioned the very concept of mental illness. It has been contended that the sometimes unusual forms of behavior and/or thinking of the mentally troubled are actually communications stemming from problems in living. So-called mental illness has even been interpreted as a sign of health, a strategy invented by people in order to live in an unlivable situation. Finally, it has been pointed out that the mentally troubled are often subject to labeling. Those whose behavior is deemed deviant may be designated as ill, forced to accept the role of patient, and given treatment within the confines of the medical model.

Various factors seem to be associated with what the medical model labels mental illness. The impact of class on mental functioning has long been recognized, as the highest rates of illness—particularly severe disorders—seem to be found in the lowest income strata. Large-scale economic disruption that adversely affects individuals has been found to be related to increased hospitalization rates. While data are hard to interpret due to the intrusion of class and other factors, minorities seem to suffer from illnesses more frequently than whites. Moreover, women undergo treatment for mental illness far more frequently than do men.

While the treatment of most troubled people is through outpatient facilities, many enter confinement in mental hospitals. Such hospitals have been called total institutions in recognition of authorities' control over almost every aspect of inmates' living conditions and routine. The mental hospital is said to have a great impact on those confined, attacking their self-concepts and encouraging dependency on institutional staff. People who are confined may respond in any number of ways—from withdrawal to resistance. Some, confined so long that they cannot bear the thought of leaving, manipulate the staff by pretending to be ill.

People may be involuntarily confined to mental hospitals. The procedures involved raise serious civil liberties issues, particularly regarding due process. There is a need for change. Mental troubles are typically treated as if the individuals are at fault, despite indications that large-scale societal factors have a bearing on such troubles. Ultimately, such societal factors must be confronted. Meanwhile, self-help groups for the troubled and community support for persons newly released from confinement can be useful.

DISCUSSION QUESTIONS

1. Have you ever wondered whether you were mentally ill? Have you ever been convinced of it? What was the basis for your concern? Did you trace the sources of your feelings to something wrong with you or to the life circumstances confronting you?
2. What are the attitudes of your friends and family toward persons who are thought to be mentally troubled? In your view, are their attitudes realistic and appropriate? Why?
3. On most college campuses, utilization of mental health facilities by students is thought to have been on the increase in the 1970s. Speculate on the possible reasons for this.
4. According to Jesse Bernard, many studies suggest that women are less satisfied with their marriages than men, and the circumstances of marriage may impair women's mental health. In terms of your own experiences and/or observations, is this often the case? Why?
5. Develop a set of criteria that would allow the courts to determine who among the mentally troubled should be involuntarily confined for examination and possible treatment. Compare your criteria with those of others.
6. Prepare a defense for an individual who faces involuntary confinement in a mental hospital because he or she "may" be dangerous to the community, based on your understanding of people's rights under the law.

11 Suicide

Members of American society should be at peace
with themselves and with one another. The
anxieties that provoke suicide should be absent.

By the time you finish reading this chapter, two or three Americans will have killed themselves. According to official statistics, over twenty-five thousand Americans committed suicide in 1976.[1] Perhaps ten times more attempted but failed to do so. Many of those who attempt suicide will try again in the future.

Means of suicide range from the straightforwardly grim to the unexpectedly bizarre. People shoot and slash themselves, ingest poisonous substances, overdose on drugs, asphyxiate themselves with gas, jump from high places, hang themselves, leap in front of trains, electrocute and drown themselves, swallow dangerous objects, tear themselves apart with explosives, pilot speeding vehicles into crashes, and burn themselves. Those who survive suicide attempts are often maimed or disabled.

Most of us think of suicide, in the abstract, as an unnatural and abnormal act, probably related to mental illness. How could a sane person choose death over life? The whole idea is distasteful to contemplate and difficult to condone. As with many other forms of socially unpleasant behavior, people tend to blame the victim for his or her own plight.

In more concrete situations, where the suicidal individual is known, friends and family are likely to react with shock and self-blame. Asking themselves whether there was something they could have done to avert the tragedy, they try to assuage their sense of guilt and rationalize what has happened. Family members attempt to limit public attention to the death, for in this society suicide is considered a shamefully unfortunate affair.

When Americans are confronted with suicide, the first question they ask is "Why?" This same question has preoccupied social scientists for decades; it is a central concern of this chapter. In the following pages we shall focus on the nature and extent of suicide, efforts to explain suicide, and approaches to suicide prevention.

THE NATURE AND EXTENT OF SUICIDE

Before any social phenomenon can be explained, it must be carefully defined. We have already seen the problems involved in defining such phenomena as crime and mental illness. Similar difficulties arise in any discussion of suicide.

The Concept of Suicide

What exactly should someone interested in explaining suicide choose to study? Should suicide research be limited to those who succeed in killing themselves? Or should researchers also study those who attempt to kill

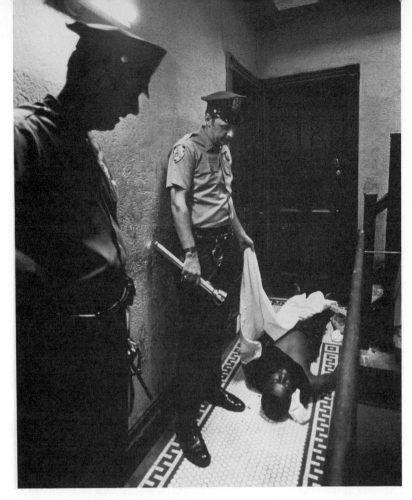

It is extremely difficult to determine intent in many cases of suicide. In fact, it is often hard to determine whether a particular death is actually a suicide. A person who dies from an overdose of drugs, for example, may simply have miscalculated the effects of the amount of drugs taken. Or the person could have consciously—or sub-consciously—wanted to die. The young man in the photograph was probably classified as having died from an acci-dental overdose, since the police have no way of know-ing his intent and degree of consciousness.

themselves, but fail? Furthermore, many persons threaten to kill them-selves and, at least in some cases, follow such threats with suicide at-tempts. Others express, directly or indirectly, suicidal thoughts. Should these forms of behavior be of major concern to someone interested in explaining suicide?

As a result of such questions, social scientists have attempted to categorize various forms of suicidal behavior, believing that there must be some relationship among them.[2] But such categorization creates other questions. One of these is the issue of *intent*. Is it not important to understand the intentions of persons who engage in one or another form of suicidal behavior? For example, researchers believe that some com-pleted suicides are actually accidental deaths caused by errors of judg-ment. This would be the case when a person who takes an overdose of

[1]U.S. Department of Health, Education, and Welfare, Public Health Service, *Monthly Vital Statistics Report,* 25 (December 12, 1977): 27.

[2]See, for example, Edwin S. Shneidman, "Orientations Toward Death," in *The Psychology of Suicide,* Edwin S. Shneidman et al., eds. (New York: Science House, 1970), pp. 3–45.

drugs, expecting to be discovered and saved from death, is not found in time. Shouldn't such deaths be distinguished from suicides in which the intent to die is clear? Or, to take another example, some attempted suicides are staged events. An attempt may be superficial or ambivalent, involving a method of self-harm that is unlikely to cause death. Shouldn't such attempts be distinguished from those that appear serious and potentially lethal?

Intent is closely related to the issue of *consciousness*. Here the question is whether individuals realize that their actions may bring about their demise. Many suicides are both intentional and consciously planned; the person carefully chooses the method, time, and circumstances. In other cases the degree of consciousness is less clear. For example, when individuals kill themselves while under the influence of alcohol or other drugs, we may have no way of knowing whether they are really conscious of the possible outcome of their actions.

To complicate things even more, many people die as a consequence of taking risks with their own personal welfare. For example, medical experts claim that heavy cigarette smokers are slowly killing themselves. While the average person may not categorize heavy smoking as suicidal behavior, social scientists must deal with this phenomenon in terms of its potential lethality for the individuals involved. Is it suicidal behavior? If so, is it intentional? Is it conscious self-harm?

In sum, those interested in explaining suicide continue to face difficulties in categorizing suicidal behavior and in figuring out how to take the issue of intent into account. For the most part, sociologists have focused on completed suicides, frequently using official statistics gathered by agencies of government. In the next section we shall look at some of the limitations of these statistics as well as some of the patterns of suicidal behavior.

Suicide Statistics

As in the areas of unemployment and crime, statistics on suicide are collected by agencies of government. The government calculates the frequency of deaths by suicide, as compared to deaths from other causes. Government data also include information on the age, sex, and race of persons who take their own lives.

In this society, cause of death is ordinarily ascertained by a physician. When there is doubt about the cause of death, a coroner or medical examiner usually conducts an inquiry. In all cases, the death certificate classifies the death as either natural, accidental, homicide, or suicide. Death certificates provide the basis for official statistics.

Social scientists have long been concerned about the reliability of official statistics, suspecting that they underestimate the frequency of suicide.[3] The cause of death listed on death certificates reflects the judgment of the physicians and other medical professionals assigned to ascertain causes of death. Social scientists do not know how these individuals choose to define suicide or whether they agree on a common definition. Moreover, it is suspected that doctors classify some suicides as deaths from other causes to spare the feelings of the victims' families.

Often, it is extremely difficult to be positive that suicide is the cause of death. For example, an individual is found dead from an overdose of drugs. Was this an accident or a suicide? Could it have been a homicide, set up to look like a suicide? A person is found shot to death. It looks accidental, but perhaps the family concealed a suicide note. Or, did the victim purposely manage the circumstances of death to make it look accidental? Could the individual have been murdered? An individual dies in an automobile accident. Did alcohol cause this person to misjudge speed and road conditions? Or did it simply give the person courage to go through with a suicidal act? Perhaps someone tampered with the car.

It is probable that thousands of suicides are attributed to accidental causes each year—whether intentionally or through error. There is no way of knowing how extensive such underreporting is or whether it is systematically skewed in a particular direction. (For example, are the wealthy more prone to hide the fact of suicide, or more likely to gain the cooperation of authorities in doing so, than the poor?) With such cautions in mind, we will briefly examine the statistical picture.[4]

General population. As we mentioned earlier, over twenty-five thousand Americans killed themselves in 1976. This is a rate of 11.7 suicides per 100,000 people. In 1976, suicide was the ninth leading cause of death.[5] As Figure 11.1 indicates, the suicide rate has been relatively constant over the years. (Of course, there is no way of knowing whether the actual suicide rate—as opposed to the official rate—has been quite as constant.) Recently, there have been indications of a slight increase in the suicide rate, especially among young people. There are no reliable statistics regarding the proportion of suicide attempts, but a rough ratio of ten attempts to each completed suicide is thought to exist. This would mean that well over two hundred thousand persons attempt to kill themselves each year.

Age. In general, the probability that persons will commit suicide increases with advancing age (Table 11.1). The relationship between aging

[3]Jack D. Douglas, *The Social Meanings of Suicide* (Princeton, N.J.: Princeton University Press, 1967), pp. 163–231.

[4]For a more detailed discussion, see Sanford Labovitz, "Variation in Suicide Rates," in *Suicide*, Jack P. Gibbs, ed. (New York: Harper & Row Publishers, Inc., 1968), pp. 57–73.

[5]U.S. Department of Health, Education, and Welfare, *Monthly Vital Statistics Report*, p. 6.

Figure 11.1.   Homicide and Suicide Rates, 1965–75

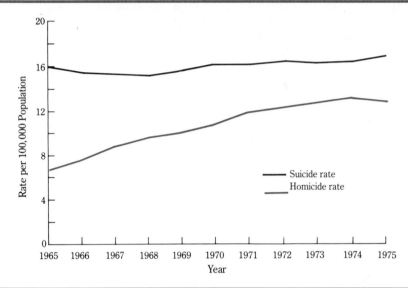

Source: U.S. Department of Commerce, Bureau of the Census, *Statistical Abstract of the United States, 1977* (Washington, D.C.: U.S. Government Printing Office, 1977), p. 167.

and suicide is most marked for men; the suicide rate among males increases steadily for all age groups up through those in their seventies. The pattern for women is slightly different; the suicide rate tends to drop off among women in their sixties, after reaching a peak in the fifties. These statistics obscure the fact that suicide and age correlate differently for minorities. Among blacks, for example, suicide is at its peak among the relatively young—persons aged twenty-five to thirty-four. With regard to attempted suicides, the rate is believed to be higher among the young than among the elderly. Older people are also more likely to use more lethal methods.

Table 11.1.   Suicide Rates by Sex, Race, and Age, 1975

| | Male | | Female | |
Age	White	Nonwhite	White	Nonwhite
All ages	20.1	10.6	7.4	3.3
5–14 years	.8	.1	.2	.2
15–24 years	19.6	14.4	4.9	3.9
25–34 years	24.4	24.6	8.9	6.5
35–44 years	24.5	16.0	12.6	4.9
45–54 years	29.7	12.8	13.8	4.5
55–64 years	32.1	11.5	11.7	4.1
65 years and over	39.4	11.8	8.5	3.0

Source: U.S. Department of Commerce, Bureau of the Census, *Statistical Abstract of the United States, 1977* (Washington, D.C.: U.S. Government Printing Office, 1977), p. 174. Rate per 100,000 population.

Table 11.2. Suicide Methods, by Sex, 1975

Method	Number of Suicides	
	Male	Female
Firearms	12,185	2,688
Poisoning	3,297	3,129
Hanging and strangulation	2,815	846
Other	1,325	778

Source: U.S. Department of Commerce, Bureau of the Census, *Statistical Abstract of the United States, 1977* (Washington, D.C.: U.S. Government Printing Office, 1977), p. 173.

Sex. Men complete suicide far more frequently than do women, at a ratio of roughly 2.5 to 1. On the other hand, suicide attempts are thought to be twice as common among women. For reasons not fully understood, methods of suicide differ between the sexes, just as they do between the old and the young. Men are most likely to choose such violent techniques as shooting and hanging, while women are more prone to use drugs, poisons, and gas (Table 11.2). It is possible that the difference in the methods chosen partially accounts for the different rates of completed suicide by sex.

Race. According to official statistics, the suicide rate among whites is normally twice as high as that among minorities. But there are some important variations. For example, while the suicide rate is lower for blacks than for whites in the southern United States, the opposite is true in the northern states. One investigation of black suicide in New York City found that the suicide rate among young black men exceeded that of whites in the same age group.[6] It has also been noted that the suicide rate is inordinately high among American Indian youth in comparison to white adolescents.

Religion. Overall, suicide is more frequent among Protestants than among either Jews or Roman Catholics. However, it is suspected that there are variations among particular Protestant denominations. It is possible that some Protestant denominations have lower rates than Jews and Roman Catholics.

Marital status. A correlation between suicide rates and marital status has long been noted in official statistics. Single persons are twice as likely as married persons to complete the act of suicide. The widowed and divorced also kill themselves more frequently than the married. These generalizations must be qualified by noting variations. For example, the rate of suicide among young married persons is higher than that among

[6]Herbert Henden, *Black Suicide* (New York: Basic Books, Inc., 1969). See also Carlton Blake, "Suicide Among Black Americans," in *Identifying Suicide Potential,* Dorothy B. Anderson and Lenora J. McLean, eds. (New York: Behavioral Publications, 1971), pp. 25–8.

young people who are single. Among the elderly, suicide is more frequent among those who are married than among those who are widowed.

Place of residence.   In the past decades, official statistics generally showed higher rates for cities than for rural areas. But suicide is not an urban phenomenon. Today, the urban/rural differences are very small. There are also differences in the rates prevailing in particular cities and even in different regions of the country. For example, San Francisco has a higher suicide rate than virtually any other American city. The western states in general tend to have higher suicide rates than other regions.

Occupation.   Even when they are available, official statistics relating suicide rates to occupation are not easy to interpret. Standard occupational categories are not used on death certificates, thus making comparisons between occupations difficult. In some cases, the occupation of the deceased may be unknown. Or those charged with filling out death certificates may simply put down the last known occupation. This could be misleading, for a person could be unemployed or employed in a different job than usual at the time of death. Thus, it is not surprising that the findings of studies attempting to correlate suicide rates with occupation have been contradictory. Nevertheless, there is evidence that suicide is more frequent among the unemployed than among jobholders—at least for men. In addition, certain professions (such as psychiatry) appear to have unusually high rates.

EXPLANATIONS FOR SUICIDE

There are many types of explanations of why people kill themselves. Such explanations can be categorized as physiological, psychological, and sociological. Most of them focus on completed suicides, rather than on other forms of suicidal behavior.

Physiological Explanations

There has been an ongoing controversy about whether the act of suicide is confined to the human species.[7] Those who argue that other species engage in suicide usually point to the lemming—a mouselike rodent native to Sweden and Norway. It is believed that, during their semiannual migrations, lemmings pursue a straight path to their destinations, sometimes falling off cliffs or drowning. Those who dispute the idea that animals commit suicide usually point out that only human beings show

[7]David Lester, *Why People Kill Themselves* (Springfield, Ill.: Charles C Thomas, Publisher, 1972), pp. 18–20.

evidence of intent. We have no wish to enter this debate, but we must point out that it exists.

Researchers have attempted to determine if people who kill themselves differ physiologically from those who show no sign of suicidal behavior.[8] For example, researchers have asked if those who kill themselves are less likely to be physically healthy than nonsuicidal individuals. Some studies have found this to be the case, while others have uncovered no relationship between health and suicidal behavior. This question thus remains open.

Other investigators have tried to determine if there are differences in physical traits, such as weight, between those who commit suicide and those who do not. It has been found that individuals who are disposed toward suicide are often overweight or underweight. However, such individuals could have lost or gained weight on the way toward completing the suicide act.

Hormonal and chemical imbalances have also been investigated. Researchers have theorized that such imbalances are more likely to be present in those who kill themselves than in nonsuicidal persons. The findings of such research have been mixed, and no hard conclusions may be drawn from them.

Finally, research has focused on the possibility that individuals inherit the potential to commit suicide. Though suicide has been unusually frequent in certain families, investigators have no way of determining whether this is a result of environmental experiences or genetic factors. Thus, research in this area remains inconclusive.

These and other efforts to explain suicide in terms of physiological traits all have one thing in common: they focus almost entirely on the constitution of individuals, and they tend to ignore the world in which suicidal individuals live. If most suicides are intentional acts, then explanations must account for the fact that people have minds. Psychologists have tried to provide alternatives to physiological explanations by speculating on the personality traits of those who take their own lives.

Psychological Explanations

The mental makeup of persons who kill themselves is often difficult to ascertain. Frequently, researchers must rely on suicide notes or on people who knew the suicide victim. Occasionally, information on the state of mind of a suicide victim is available from the records of medical and mental health practitioners. The reliability of all such information is open to question, but it has formed the basis for a number of theories on the psychological traits of those who commit suicide.[9]

[8]Ibid., pp. 25–35.
[9]Ibid., pp. 57–71 and 193–218. See also Earl Grollman, *Suicide* (Boston: Beacon Press, 1971), pp. 33–9.

Sleep Good Tonite !!!
I always loved you —
when things went a
little bad you didn't
love me — Very Simple
You gave me every
thing I ever had — So
you take it now
Love (Thank you Don't have)
Karen

For example, some psychologists have suggested that suicide-prone individuals are likely to have suffered from parental deprivation when young. Various forms of deprivation are said to be related to suicide, including the death or absence of parents and parental indifference to childhood needs. Deprivation, it is thought, disrupts the normal psychological development of children and provokes suicidal tendencies.

Others have claimed that suicide indicates—and is a result of—aggression that is directed inward. Children presumably learn to internalize aggressive impulses, rather than express them outwardly, as a result of parental disciplinary practices. In particular, parents who punish their children psychologically rather than physically are thought to foster inwardly directed aggression.

Some theorists believe that all people have both an instinct for self-preservation and an instinct for self-destruction (the so-called death instinct). Suicide is said to represent a breakthrough of the death instinct, a process most likely to occur among individuals who are suffering from mental problems.

It has also been postulated that persons who kill themselves are excessively rigid in their thinking and/or illogical in their reasoning and thought processes. These are considered mental disabilities that interfere with relations with other people and that deny the individual the flexibility needed to deal with everyday life. Suicide is the result.

Suicide has also been portrayed as stemming from a desire to manipulate others—perhaps to invoke love and attention. According to this theory, suicide is a cry for help from persons powerless to proceed in any other way. Alternatively, it has been suggested that suicide is an effort to hurt other people—a means of communicating deep-felt hostility or of exercising revenge.

Finally, mental illness is frequently invoked as a psychological explanation for suicide. In particular, it is thought that depressive psychoses are closely linked with suicidal behavior.

None of these psychological explanations has the backing of firm and convincing evidence. And all of them are limited to the mental state of individuals, ignoring the societal context within which people kill themselves. It is this context that interests sociologists.

Sociological Explanations

Sociological explanations for suicide attempt to remedy the psychologists' omission, but, unfortunately, often at the cost of ignoring the individual. Sociologists are much more concerned with explaining variations in suicide rates, such as those that appear in official statistics.

Durkheim's theory.   The starting point for virtually all sociological explanations for suicide is a theory put forth by French sociologist Émile Durkheim.[10] Writing in 1897, Durkheim tried to demonstrate that the character of a society determined the probability that people would be pushed toward committing suicide. According to Durkheim, suicide could not be explained by physiological traits or psychological variables. Instead, one must look at the social forces impinging on and shaping the lives of the members of any given society. In Durkheim's view, the presence or absence of these forces accounted for variations in suicide rates.

According to Durkheim, suicide is related to the degree to which a society is *integrated*—in other words, the degree to which members of a society share common ideas and goals and sense their ties with one another. Where integration is low, *egoistic* suicides—due to the absence of meaningful social relationships or a sense of belonging—will be frequent. Conversely, where integration is high, individuals will be likely to willingly give up their lives for the group, committing *altruistic* suicides. Such self-sacrifices might take place in times of war or as part of religious rituals.

[10]Émile Durkheim, *Suicide,* trans. John A. Spaulding and George Simpson (New York: The Free Press, 1951).

During World War II, the kamikaze pilots of Japan crashed their airplanes into enemy ships, sacrificing their lives in order to attain military victory. In Durkheim's scheme, the kamikaze attacks would be classified as altruistic suicide.

Durkheim also argued that *social regulation* plays a role in generating suicidal behavior. In a society with a high degree of control over its members' emotions and motivations, *fatalistic* suicide will occur. That is, people kill themselves out of a sense of overmanipulation or of hopelessness about altering their life conditions. Conversely, in a society that provides few guidelines for its members' feelings and inclinations—thereby leaving people unregulated or uncontrolled—*anomic* suicide will take place.

Because Durkheim did not provide measures of integration and social regulation, it has proven difficult to test his arguments. Nonetheless, many sociologists have been influenced by his theory in developing their own explanations. For example, French sociologist Maurice Halbwachs has theorized that suicide is a function of social isolation.[11] According to

[11]Maurice Halbwachs, *Les Causes du Suicide* (Paris: Alcan, 1930). Halbwachs' work is discussed in Douglas, *The Social Meanings of Suicide,* pp. 124–31.

Halbwachs, suicide occurs most frequently among individuals who lack stable and enduring relationships with others. Since such social isolation is presumably more common among city-dwellers than among rural people, said Halbwachs, suicide rates should be higher in cities. Writing in 1930, Halbwachs found that the data on suicide rates available to him supported his hypothesis. Today, however, there is no significant difference between urban and rural suicide rates—at least in the United States—so the social isolation thesis does not appear helpful.

Class and status.   Borrowing some of Durkheim's ideas, Elwin H. Powell has proposed an explanation that relates suicide to the status of different groups in American society.[12] Powell hypothesized that suicide rates would be highest in the lower and upper classes. He reasoned that individuals at the bottom of the class structure would be prone to suicide because they were dissociated from the larger society and had little hope in achieving cultural goals. The upper class, in his view, was so "enveloped" in these goals that many individuals could not find personal reasons for living. Using occupational data from suicide records in Tulsa, Oklahoma, Powell found support for his hypothesis. However, other studies have not found such correlations between occupational status and suicide rates,[13] and Powell's explanation is open to question.

Sociologists Andrew Henry and James Short have also investigated the relationship between status and suicide.[14] These researchers suggested that higher status groups were least likely to be characterized by strong "relational systems" among their members. In other words, their emotional ties were weak. Society, they felt, places few "external constraints"—pressures toward conformity—on the behavior of high-status people. Henry and Short hypothesized that suicide rates would vary directly with social status. Thus, groups to which they assigned high status (men, whites, the affluent, the unmarried) could be expected to have the highest rates of suicide. In general, the statistics they mobilized supported their hypothesis. But there have been criticisms of Henry and Short's work. For example, how does one explain the high suicide rates that seem to prevail among northern blacks in comparison to whites? Such variations in the overall statistics on suicide rates are not easily handled within the framework of Henry and Short's explanation. Also, do unmarried people really have higher status than married people in this society? While this assumption fits with Henry and Short's statistical findings on suicide rates, it does not make much sense.

Role incompatibility.   Other sociologists have hypothesized that suicide rates are related to people's ability to carry out the roles society

[12]Elwin H. Powell, "Occupation, Status, and Suicide," *American Sociological Review,* 23 (April 1958): 131–40.
[13]See, for example, Ronald W. Maris, *Social Forces in Urban Suicide* (Homewood, Ill.: Dorsey Press, 1969).
[14]Andrew F. Henry and James F. Short, Jr., *Suicide and Homicide* (New York: The Free Press, 1954).

assigns them.[15] Jack Gibbs and Walter Martin have pointed out that people must sometimes fill several roles simultaneously—that is, often they have to meet the demands and expectations of a variety of groups. If all these roles are compatible with one another, *status integration* is said to exist, and suicide is unlikely. On the other hand, if the roles are incompatible—if individuals are confronted with conflicting demands and expectations—suicide will be more frequent. In this case, individuals become more suicide-prone because they are unable to satisfy others, and their social relationships with other people weaken. The problem with this explanation is that there is no objective way of measuring the role incompatibility of those who have committed suicide. Instead, we can only assume that role conflict is highest among those who kill themselves. Thus, a crucial aspect of Gibbs and Martin's explanation remains difficult to demonstrate.

Societal reaction.   Another sociological explanation for variations in suicide rates holds that societal reaction to suicide is of key importance.[16] According to this explanation, where members of a society accept or condone acts of suicide, rates will be high; and where suicide is condemned, rates will be low. In other words, the cultural values of a group can either deter or facilitate self-destruction. Proponents of this explanation point to the fact that suicide rates among Roman Catholics, who explicitly condemn suicide, are much lower than suicide rates among Protestants, who do not condemn it as strongly. But the societal reaction theory is not helpful in shedding light on other variations in suicide rates. For example, there is no reason to believe that Americans are more accepting of suicide among men than among women, or among the old as opposed to the young.

The meaning of suicide.   The failure of sociologists to explain variations in suicide rates should be evident. Despite the hints provided by Durkheim and the efforts by many sociologists to reformulate and test his ideas, existing explanations are inadequate. Recognizing this, and concerned by sociologists' willingness to use questionable official statistics to test their hypotheses about suicide, Jack Douglas has proposed an entirely different approach, based on the "meaning" of suicide to persons who take their lives.[17]

In effect, Douglas has called for investigation of the motives or intentions that underlie individual acts of suicide. In calling for sociologists to study the meaning of suicide, he has suggested that research should focus on the goals and objectives that suicidal persons are trying to fulfill

[15]Jack P. Gibbs and Walter T. Martin, *Status Integration and Suicide* (Eugene, Ore.: University of Oregon Press, 1964).

[16]Maurice L. Farber, *Theory of Suicide* (New York: Funk & Wagnalls Book Publishing, 1968).

[17]Douglas, *The Social Meaning of Suicide.* See also Jack D. Douglas, "The Sociological Analysis of Social Meanings of Suicide," in *The Sociology of Suicide,* Anthony Giddens, ed. (London: Frank Cass & Co., 1971), pp. 121–51.

through their behavior. In other words, we should view those who die by suicide as actors, rather than as those who have been acted upon by society.

In Douglas' view, the meaning of suicide can best be ascertained by examining a sample of individual cases. Researchers can document patterns of verbal and nonverbal communication of the suicide victim and of any others involved in the death situation. Douglas attempted to illustrate how this might be done. However, he was forced to rely on published case reports, thereby opening up the question of the reliability of such reports and of those who wrote them. Nevertheless, Douglas is one of the few sociologists who have examined the social determinants of individual suicides, rather than searching for explanations for variations in suicide rates.

Other Explanations

Investigators have studied several other factors that seem to bear on suicide rates.[18] For example, suicide rates tend to vary in accordance with changes in the seasons. In terms of the overall U.S. suicide rate, most suicides are completed in the spring (April or May), whereas the fewest take place in the winter (December). However, when particular geographical regions or cities have been examined, the results have been far less uniform. To date, no one has come up with an explanation for such overall seasonal variations. Nor have researchers found a reliable correlation between suicide and particular days of the week. While the results are somewhat mixed, it does appear that most persons who kill themselves do so during the day rather than at night. Again, there is no explanation for this.

At times researchers have investigated some unusual factors, hoping that they will shed some additional light on suicide rates. For example, research has been conducted to determine the relationship between suicide rates and the appearance of sunspots. No relationship has been found. Less unusual have been efforts to probe the possibility that weather influences suicide rates in some way. A popular idea is that people are most likely to kill themselves on rainy days. But the weather seems to have little to do with suicide.

The Question of Attempted Suicide

As we noted earlier, most of the efforts to explain suicide have been limited to completed suicides, ignoring the question of attempted suicide. Yet an estimated ten times as many persons are thought to make unsuccessful suicide attempts. Between 2 and 5 million Americans are presently living after having made one or more attempts to die.

[18]Lester, *Why People Kill Themselves*, pp. 149–58.

Unfortunately, there are no official statistics on attempted suicides; available information generally comes from hospitals and/or from physicians. These people probably never hear of a significant number of cases. For example, an act of attempted suicide may result in only minor injury. Many such attempts may be intentionally concealed. Finally, it may be difficult to judge whether an attempted suicide has indeed taken place (as opposed, for example, to an accident). Thus our knowledge of attempted suicide remains very limited, as do explanations for it.[19]

Women are more likely to attempt suicide than men, and women who attempt suicide are likely to be younger than men who do so. Women are also more likely to make repeated attempts than are men and to use less lethal methods.[20] Attempts are thought to be most frequent among housewives, in comparison to other groups of women.

Researchers have not been able to explain these differences between the sexes. Some have suggested that women use less lethal methods because they are less aggressive or more concerned with their appearance after death than are men. It has been hypothesized that women often survive suicide attempts because they are the biologically "stronger sex" (which probably means that women generally live longer than men). But none of these observations gets at the question of why so many women attempt suicide in the first place.

One of the few other things we know is that attempted suicide is apparently correlated with age. The average age of persons who attempt suicide is much younger than the average age of those who complete suicide. It is believed that for every completed suicide among adolescents there are a hundred attempted suicides.[21] By contrast, adults have a rate of eight attempts to every completed suicide. Again, there is a difference in lethality of methods, with adolescents tending to use the least lethal of methods. Moreover, it is thought that suicidal behavior among the young is more likely to be impulsive and less likely to be premeditated. As with women, there is no real consensus about why the young attempt suicide so frequently.

The lack of reliable statistical information hampers our knowledge of attempted suicides. Also, there is disagreement over whether completed and attempted suicides involve the same types of people. Do people who attempt suicide and those who complete it make up two distinct groups possessing quite different characteristics? Since most persons who complete suicide have made one or more previous attempts, but relatively few who attempt suicide ultimately kill themselves, researchers have taken a middle position. It is thought that two distinct groups do exist, but that their membership overlaps to some degree. Thus, one can learn

[19]See James Wilkins, "Suicidal Behavior," in *The Sociology of Suicide*, Giddens, ed., pp. 398–418.

[20]Lester, *Why People Kill Themselves*, pp. 36–46.

[21]See Stuart M. Finch and Elva O. Poznanski, *Adolescent Suicide* (Springfield, Ill.: Charles C Thomas, Publisher, 1971).

little about one of these groups by studying the other. But other researchers believe that this position is erroneous, arguing that more information about both attempted and completed suicides is crucial to an understanding of each.[22]

SUICIDE PREVENTION

At the start of this chapter, we noted that most Americans view suicide as an unnatural and abnormal act, possibly linked with mental illness. This view, which draws attention away from the societal context within which people move toward suicide, underlies suicide prevention programs. Such programs view the individual as the problem, not the society. In this section we will look at suicide prevention programs and consider whether people have the right to choose death over life.

Suicide Prevention Centers

Approaches to preventing suicide range from counseling by clergy and mental health practitioners to pleas by police officers called to the scene of suicide attempts. In the last decade, communities around the country have instituted organized efforts to prevent suicide, setting up suicide prevention centers and other crisis projects that try to assist troubled people.

Suicide prevention centers vary greatly in size, resources, and services, and their effectiveness is very difficult to assess. As more centers have opened, many with the help of governmental financing, the number of suicides is thought to have been increasing. It is possible that the presence of such centers—particularly the research involvement of a few—has promoted more careful investigations and record-keeping on causes of deaths. Thus instead of an increase in suicides, we could simply be seeing better detection and recording by medical officials.

Suicide prevention centers seek to keep people from taking their lives by being ready to assist anyone who voluntarily contacts them. Thus, such centers probably come into contact with or learn of only a small percentage of those who attempt and/or complete suicide. Their effectiveness therefore depends largely on how well they handle this minority.

Often, workers at suicide prevention centers have very limited contact with potentially suicidal individuals, perhaps just a telephone conversation with the individual or concerned family members or friends. Workers thus must rely on guidelines to help them determine the seriousness of cases at hand. For example, some centers use the guidelines developed

---

[22]Lester, *Why People Kill Themselves,* pp. 314–16.

by psychologist Edwin S. Shneidman, one of the founders of the well-known Los Angeles Suicide Prevention Center:

1. Persons who are contemplating suicide wish to be stopped or rescued before death. They are mentally torn between wanting to live and wanting to die, and can be pushed toward living.
2. Contemplation of suicide occurs during a period of extreme crisis that may be relatively brief in duration. If the suicidal individual can be gotten through the crisis, the probability of suicide is minimized.
3. Persons who are about to kill themselves are almost always fully conscious of their intentions, although they may not communicate these intentions directly. Few people are unconscious of their intentions.
4. Suicidal behavior usually stems from a sense of isolation and is an act to stop an intolerable existence. Since people define "intolerable" differently, prevention efforts must take into account the perspective of the potential suicide.[23]

Shneidman has pointed out that almost all those who kill themselves drop *prodromal clues* before doing so.[24] That is, they signal their suicidal thoughts to others, often days or weeks before taking steps to die. Such clues may be verbal, involving direct or indirect statements of suicidal intentions. Or they may be behavioral, as when an individual makes a will and sets affairs in order, or actually makes a "practice run" in planning death. Prodromal clues may also be situational—for example, an individual is obviously caught up in conditions involving a great deal of stress-produced anxiety. Finally, the clues may be "prodromatic"—that is, a person appears to be deeply depressed, disoriented, or defiant. Though some persons kill themselves on impulse, Shneidman suggests that even in such cases some kind of warning is given beforehand. The problem is that such clues may go unrecognized or even ignored.

After suicide prevention center workers have used these or other guidelines and have decided that an individual who phones is suicidal, they ordinarily try to talk the person through the crisis period. They may attempt to convince the individual to seek out counseling or therapy. If they know the identity of the individual, they may contact family, friends, or others who can intervene and secure assistance for the suicide-prone person. Therapy typically involves psychiatric treatment and/or drugs. In extreme cases, the suicidal individual may be involuntarily confined in an institution for observation and treatment.

The ultimate goal of suicide prevention centers and other treatment services is to enable persons to function in the prevailing social order. Thus, suicide prevention and therapy do not touch on the question of

---

[23]Edwin S. Shneidman, "Preventing Suicide," in *Suicide,* Gibbs, ed., pp. 255–66. See also Edwin S. Shneidman and Philip Mandelkorn, "How to Prevent Suicide," in *The Psychology of Suicide,* Shneidman, et al., eds., pp. 125–43.
[24]Schneidman, "Preventing Suicide," pp. 255–66.

social changes that might reduce the frequency of self-initiated deaths. Speaking from a sociological perspective, Jack P. Gibbs has stated:

> If any theory on the suicide rate is valid, then conceivably the volume of suicide could be reduced substantially by deliberate social change. However, most theories deal with such basic structural components of society that few policymakers would contemplate making changes, let alone succeed. Further, neither policymakers nor the public is likely to view the "cost" of suicide as sufficiently great to justify undertaking any major remedial action. So in the final analysis, there appears to be only one way to reduce the incidence of suicide, and that is by instituting prevention programs that focus on individual cases. [25]

We cannot share Gibbs' pessimism about the possibility of social changes that will reduce suicide. To write this possibility off, as Gibbs does, is to ensure that such changes will never take place.

Is There a Right to Die?

As mentioned above, the goal of suicide prevention programs is the preservation of individual lives, no matter what the circumstances. Workers in such programs believe that they know what is best for the suicide-prone. The basic precept of suicide prevention is that life is preferable to death and that suicide is a form of deviant behavior that must be fought.

Contrasted to these beliefs is the fact that many members of our society seem to find good reason to kill themselves. (Indeed, even in a utopian society, some persons would probably want to exercise control over their own deaths.) Psychologist David Lester put it this way: "Suicide is a way of living, a way of coping with problems that arise from living, and for many people it is a way of achieving a better life or avoiding a worse life." [26] Though we can all appreciate the pro-life thrust of suicide prevention efforts, it seems valid to consider whether people also have a right to die. A related question is whether there are circumstances under which suicide is rational behavior and efforts to prevent it irrational. Though we cannot provide definitive answers to these questions, we believe them worthy of consideration.

Despite the voluminous literature on suicide, most authors believe that suicide must be prevented—if only to keep from losing people who might otherwise make a contribution to society. One exception is Jacques Choron, who suggests that there is a phenomenon called *rational suicide*. Choron defines rational suicide as suicidal behavior on the part of those who are mentally normal (so far as can be judged), whose reasoning

---

[25]Jack P. Gibbs, "Suicide," in *Contemporary Social Problems*, 3rd ed., Robert K. Merton and Robert Nisbet, eds. (New York: Harcourt Brace Jovanovich, Inc., 1971), pp. 311–12.

[26]Lester, *Why People Kill Themselves*, pp. 325–26.

powers are not impaired, and whose motives can be considered justified. To Choron, justification refers to "approval by contemporaries, in the sense of their agreeing that in similar circumstances they might have done the same thing."[27] With regard to such persons, it could be argued that suicide prevention efforts are misdirected or inappropriate. Perhaps a counselor or therapist should tell them to go ahead, admitting that they are making the best decision.

Choron does not provide many examples of rational suicide, and he admits that we have no way of knowing how many suicides would fit his definition. But the following two cases are illustrative:

A woman learns she is afflicted with a terminal illness for which there is no known cure. The process of dying promises to be long and tremendously uncomfortable. Her physical suffering is likely to have an adverse effect on the emotions of her family and friends. Well before the woman's illness reaches its terminal stage, she takes her life.

A husband and wife, who are extraordinarily active and share a variety of interests in common, sit down and decide to die together twenty years hence. They anticipate a full and enjoyable life for these twenty years, and do not wish to endure old age (wherein they will have to slow down, and possibly cope with illness or death of the other). As planned, they initiate their own deaths when the twenty years is up.

Though cases like these probably would not come to the attention of suicide prevention agencies, that is not the point. The philosophy or ideology of suicide prevention leaves no room for rational suicides of any type. If their intentions were to become known, the woman with the terminal illness and the couple who planned their deaths would be the focus of attempts to preserve their lives.

Suicide prevention workers are sometimes faced with elderly and/or terminally ill persons who indicate intentions to undertake *euthanatic suicide*—in Choron's terms, "easy dying." In such cases, asks Choron: "Should not the multitudes who die painfully and miserably each year be allowed to decide for themselves what is best for them?"[28] In our society, this question is rarely answered affirmatively. The idea that the right to die should be legally protected and that the means for a quick and painless death should be provided to people on request is likely to be greeted with outrage. Meanwhile, many persons do undertake "easy dying" without legal sanction—often unsuccessfully or by violent means:

It would be too much to expect that resistance to the idea of euthanatic suicide will be easily overcome. The most important step in that direction is the realization that considering suicide the wrong cure for the ills of the living does not necessarily exclude the possibility that it may be the right cure for the ills of the dying.[29]

---

[27]Jacques Choron, *Suicide* (New York: Charles Scribner's Sons, 1972), p. 97.
[28]Ibid., pp. 104–5.
[29]Ibid., p. 106.

Public Problem, Private Pain
PLANNING A SUICIDE

When novelist Jessamyn West's sister Carmen was diagnosed as suffering from terminal cancer, she had a decision to make—should she make arrangements to kill herself before the agonizing pain began? Carmen determined on suicide.

Her first idea was to do it alone. But then she changed her mind and decided that she wanted her sister to be with her. Jessamyn West traveled to her sister's home, where she would help Carmen find the means and choose the time of suicide and be at her side when she died.

The following excerpt from Jessamyn West's memoirs underscores the issue of the rationality of suicide. In a similar situation, would you choose self-destruction over the prospect of unwanted agony and lingering death? On what philosophical or moral grounds would you make such a choice? And if someone you loved were dying, would you help that person commit suicide? How would you be able to rationalize assisting in the death of another person?

Many people would agree with Jessamyn West and her sister that, in a case like this, suicide is a rational alternative to waiting for death. But the prospect of a painful death is only one of many problems that lead people to choose suicide. Is suicide in response to, for example, unbearable loneliness or unremitting social and economic pressures any less rational? How do we decide what is rational and what is not when it comes to taking one's life?

All of us know that someday we will die. We do not cry about it. If there were a chance that we would not die, then we might be on the rack; might not be able to stop hoping and wondering and fearing. Carmen had been taken off the rack. There was no more hope for life. There was now an energetic and almost gay period of planning the kind of death she chose: the kind of death and at the time she chose. *She* had not chosen death: fate or genes, or God, which is perhaps the name we give that combination, had made the choice. She at least intended to have some voice in the matter. Why should she spend two or three months in agony? Or so drugged to avoid the agony that she no longer had any existence as a human being? What God would want His children to die in that way? What child of God would so malign his Creator's nature as to believe that such a death was His choice? . . .

Carmen and I became planners, plotters, technicians. We knew what had to be done. We were *pretty* sure how to do it. We intended to be sure. There were those who might try to prevent it. Those we must circumvent. The timing must be right. We would have to decide about that. Death was the goal, but Carmen's kind of death, not nature's savage torture system. Not a slice at a time, the feet in the fire and the testicles squeezed off by the tightening clasp of a drying deerskin pouch; More's death instead, self-elected and not prolonged, was the model.

We were not as joyous as technicians and planners building a ship for launching; or as writers composing a novel whose incidents will reveal (as a life lived cannot) the human condition. We were not prospective mothers carrying babies and eager for their birth. Death was what we plotted. We were not eager for it; but we were eager to make the ordeal of change, which had been decreed, as easy as possible.

Overheard, no one would have guessed from the tone of our voices the nature of our subject: suicide.

Jessamyn West, *The Woman Said Yes: Encounters with Life and Death* (New York: Harcourt Brace Jovanovich, 1976), pp. 114, 120–21.

We have not presented this discussion because we are against suicide prevention or for the right to die. But in the absence of societal changes that might reduce the volume of suicide, much suicide might profitably be viewed as rational. Only when we begin to search for the rational components of self-initiated death—its "meaning" in sociologist Jack Douglas' terms—will more people begin to ask: What is it about the organization and operation of American society that leads so many to suicidal behavior? We must begin to ask this question if, at some future time, thousands of people are to avoid concluding:

> In this life it's not difficult to die.
> To make life is more difficult by far.[30]

SUMMARY

Each year thousands of people take their own lives. Official statistics no doubt underreport the actual number of suicides. Often it is difficult to determine the actual cause of a person's death. Moreover, the fact of suicide may be concealed and death attributed to other causes. There is no way to know how extensive underreporting is.

Official statistics indicate that the suicide rate has been relatively constant over the years, although slight increases have occurred recently (especially among young people). Older adults are more likely to take their lives than the young, men more than women, whites more than minority group members, and Protestants more than Catholics or Jews. Single, widowed, and divorced persons commit suicide at a higher rate than those who are married and living with their mates. City-dwellers take their lives at about the same rate as rural residents. Data on occupations and suicide are mixed, but it is thought the unemployed have higher rates than the employed.

A variety of explanations have been offered for why people kill themselves. Some researchers have sought to find indications that those who commit suicide differ physically from others and have suggested that genetic factors are involved. Others have offered explanations based on the presumed mental states of suicide victims, suggesting that such persons are mentally abnormal. Finally, it has been suggested that both societal forces are involved in pushing people toward suicide and that suicide may have a special social and cultural meaning to its victims.

Attempted suicide is thought to be ten times more frequent than completed suicide. Unfortunately, there are no official statistics on suicide attempts. It is known that women and the young make the most attempts and that they tend to use less lethal methods than men and older adults.

[30]Vladimir Vladimirovich Mayakovsky, "To Sergei Yessenin," in *Mayakovsky*, trans. and ed., Herbert Marshall (New York: Hill & Wang, 1965), p. 350.

There is controversy over whether completed and attempted suicides involve the same types of people.

In the last decade, communities across the country have instituted organized efforts to prevent suicide. Suicide prevention centers have been established, but their effectiveness is very difficult to assess. Such centers probably come into contact with or learn of only a small percentage of those who attempt and/or complete suicide. While efforts to prevent suicides go on, some have suggested that people might have a right to choose death. Are there not circumstances under which suicide is rational behavior and efforts to prevent it irrational?

DISCUSSION QUESTIONS

1. What are the attitudes of people you know toward those who would attempt or complete the act of suicide? To what degree do you share these attitudes?
2. Do you think people should have the right to take their own lives if they wish? If so, should this be an absolute right or are there certain conditions you would attach?
3. If you assist a person in committing a suicidal act, you may be accused of a crime. Can you think of any circumstances under which you would violate the law in this way?
4. Your doctor tells you that by quitting smoking and losing excess weight you may add years to your life. You fail to heed your doctor's advice. Is this the same as committing suicide? Why?
5. According to official statistics, the suicide rate among young people has been increasing in the last decade or so. Speculate on why this is the case.
6. Visit a local suicide or crisis prevention center that often handles calls from persons who are potentially suicidal. On the basis of what the staff is able to tell you about the content of such calls, develop your own explanation for why people kill themselves. (Remember, however, that the center may have contact with only a small percentage of potential suicides.)

12 Alcoholism

Members of American society should be at peace with themselves and with one another. The vicarious rewards associated with alcoholism should have no attraction.

It is a common sight in the low-income, Skid Row districts of American cities. A middle-aged man is sprawled on the sidewalk. His clothing is stained and disheveled, and he looks like he needs a shower and a good meal. He is hugging a bottle wrapped in a brown paper bag. He is drunk—blind drunk. The drugged stupor in which he lies separates him from all surrounding realities. For reasons best known to him, he would rather escape to mental oblivion than stay sober.[1]

An estimated 100 million Americans aged fifteen and older drink alcoholic beverages.[2] Approximately a tenth of them are problem drinkers and alcoholics. Skid Row residents comprise only 3 to 5 percent of the alcoholic population. Nevertheless, until quite recently the Skid Row drunk was the popular symbol of alcoholism. Today this stereotype is breaking down with the accumulation of new knowledge about this society's drinking habits.

Heavy use of alcohol—sometimes to the point of mental oblivion—occurs among both men and women, young and old, at all stations in life. Occasionally, we even learn of important public figures whose lives have come to revolve around drinking. One recent case involved Congressman Wilbur D. Mills, whose heavy drinking was publicly exposed after he and a female companion were found by police to be involved in a drinking binge. Similarly, it has been alleged that Richard M. Nixon became a heavy drinker prior to his resignation from the presidency. Such persons have a much different economic standing and more prestige and political influence than the Skid Row drunk. But they are alike insofar as they pursue the altered states of consciousness that alcohol can provide.

In between the Skid Row resident and the nationally known politician are the rest of the 10 million Americans for whom heavy alcohol use brings both pleasure and problems. Our focus in this chapter will be primarily on this group. We shall begin by describing the general drinking population and considering the distinction between alcohol use and abuse. Then we shall turn to the phenomenon of alcoholism. We will examine definitions of an alcoholic, alternative explanations for alcoholism, the costs of alcoholism and problem drinking, and the various modes of treating alcoholic individuals.

DRINKING IN AMERICA

Alcohol is a drug; pharmaceutically, it is a depressant or tranquilizer. Per capita consumption of this drug (that is, consumption per person) has been increasing steadily since World War II, primarily because an ever higher percentage of Americans have become drinkers. In 1976 per

[1]Life on Skid Row is detailed in Howard M. Bahr, *Skid Row* (New York: Oxford University Press, Inc., 1973).

[2]General statistics are available from the federal government's National Institute on Alcohol Abuse and Alcoholism.

It is hard to imagine American social life without alcoholic beverages. Per capita consumption of alcohol has been increasing steadily in the last thirty years, and it is a rare social event that does not include wine, beer, and distilled liquor.

capita consumption of domestically produced beverages among persons eighteen years of age and older was 31.58 gallons of beer, 2.36 gallons of distilled spirits, and 2.43 gallons of wine.[3] That same year, consumers spent well over $20 billion on such products. In this section we will look at the private and public interests that benefit from the use of alcohol. We will then discuss American drinking practices and patterns of alcohol use and abuse.

Private Profit and Public Income

The term *drug pusher* is usually used to describe persons who loiter around big-city school yards and attempt to lure children into experimentation with heroin. Alcohol is pushed quite openly, though not ordinarily to schoolchildren, by the alcoholic beverage industry. In its role as a drug pusher, this industry actively (and successfully) seeks to cut down on the already-declining percentage of abstainers in the adult population and to increase annual per capita consumption among those who drink. It has been active in efforts to lower the legal drinking age in locations where people must be twenty-one in order to buy alcohol. It is also working to turn the remaining "dry" communities (where the sale of alcoholic beverages is illegal) into "wet" ones.

Though industry advertisements sometimes advise consumers to engage in "responsible drinking," such ads are a recent phenomenon and

[3]*Statistical Abstract of the United States, 1977* (Washington, D.C.: U.S. Government Printing Office, 1977), p. 811.

only emerged after the full dimensions of problem drinking and alcoholism became a matter of public concern. The alcoholic beverage industry still does not publicly acknowledge the fact that it is merchandising a drug. Nor does it advertise the fact that abuse of its product—alcoholism—is the nation's number one health problem.

The industry has a powerful incentive to push alcohol on the public—profit. While some 10 million problem drinkers and alcoholics drug themselves, many to the point of mental deterioration or death, the pushers flourish and seek to increase consumption and production levels.

The alcoholic beverage industry presently employs almost 2 million people, nearly 2 percent of the labor force. Its expenditures on newspaper, magazine, and television advertising—advertising that typically links drinking to youth, sexual pleasure, and relaxation—have risen to over $250 million a year. The industry's total contribution to the American economy was $34.1 billion in 1976.[4]

While the industry counts its profits, government capitalizes on the tax revenues that flow from America's drinking practices. In 1976 federal, state, and local governments took in an estimated total of $9.96 billion in alcohol-related taxes. The federal government alone received $5.43 billion that year.[5] No other tax source—with the exception of personal and corporate income taxes—provides so much income to the federal treasury. Ironically, far more money is taken in from alcohol-related taxes than is spent combating the harm associated with alcohol use. Like the alcoholic beverage industry, government has a vested interest in maintaining consumption of this society's most popular drug.

American Drinking Practices

Over the last fifteen years, sociologists and other social scientists have become increasingly interested in American drinking practices and patterns of alcohol use. As a result of their research, we have gained some knowledge about who the drinkers are. Most of this knowledge is based on surveys of the American population.

A landmark nationwide survey of drinking practices was conducted in 1964–65.[6] This survey studied adults aged twenty-one and over. (More recent investigations often include teenagers.) The researchers found that 68 percent of American adults drank at least once a year, or enough to be classified as "drinkers," while 32 percent claimed to be abstainers. A third of the abstainers had previously used alcohol. Among the drinkers, 52 percent drank once a month or more; the remaining 48 percent

[4]Distilled Spirits Council of the United States, *DISCUS Fact Book, 1976* (Washington, D.C.: DISCUS, 1977), p. 13.
[5]Ibid., p. 29.
[6]Don Cahalan, Ira H. Cisin, and Helen M. Crossley, *American Drinking Practices* (New Brunswick, N.J.: Rutgers Center of Alcohol Studies, 1969).

Table 12.1. Alcohol Consumption

	All Youth (aged 12-17)	All Adults (aged 18 and over)	Young Adults (aged 18-25)	Older Adults (aged 26 and over)
Recency				
Drank alcoholic beverages in past month	31.2%	58.0%	70.0%	54.9%
Drank in past, not in past month	21.4	21.2	14.2	23.0
Within past six months	11.8	8.3	8.0	8.4
Within past year	4.5	2.4	1.8	2.5
More than one year ago	4.2	9.8	4.2	11.2
Not sure, no answer	.9	.7	*	.9
Always a nondrinker	46.5	20.6	15.6	21.9
No answer	.9	*	*	*
Days used in past month				
Current drinkers	**31.2%**	**58.0%**	**70.0%**	**54.9%**
One to four days	24.6	28.7	36.5	26.7
Five to ten days	3.2	11.2	17.3	9.6
Eleven to twenty days	1.8	7.0	9.4	6.3
Twenty-one or more days	1.1	4.5	3.4	4.7
Everyday	.5	6.7	3.4	7.5
Number of drinks on average day				
Current drinkers	**31.2%**	**58.0%**	**70.0%**	**54.9%**
One or two drinks	19.7	37.3	38.6	37.0
Three or four drinks	5.2	12.3	18.1	10.8
Five or more drinks	4.8	7.7	12.4	6.4
Not sure, no answer	1.5	.7	1.0	.7
Number in sample	1272	3322	1500	1822

Source: U.S. Department of Health, Education, and Welfare, *National Survey on Drug Abuse: 1977; Volume 1, Main Findings* (Washington, D.C.: U.S. Government Printing Office, 1978), p. 107. *Less than 0.5%. Some categories do not add to 100% because of rounding.

drank less frequently. Of those surveyed, 12 percent were heavy drinkers.

Since this survey was released, many other studies have been conducted with similar results. For example, the polling firm of Louis Harris and Associates carried out a series of national surveys between 1972 and 1974.[7] The firm surveyed a representative sample of persons eighteen years of age and older. It was found that 42 percent of those surveyed were either abstainers or infrequent drinkers; another 49 percent were light or moderate drinkers; and 9 percent were heavy drinkers. A survey by the federal government in the mid-1970s resulted in similar findings, as Table 12.1 indicates.

Such statistics are, at best, rough indicators of the characteristics of the drinking population. One difficulty is that the definitions of "light," "moderate," and "heavy" drinking differ among surveys. As the definitions change, so do the statistical findings. Furthermore, the findings

[7]Louis Harris and Associates, Inc., Reports prepared for the National Institute on Alcohol Abuse and Alcoholism, 1972–74.

probably understate the percentage of persons who use alcohol heavily, for many alcoholics are unlikely to be completely open about their problem.

Patterns of Alcohol Use

Patterns of alcohol use in the United States are believed to be associated with a number of variables.[8] Sex, age, race and ethnicity, and class-related factors all seem to be related to who drinks and how much one drinks.

Sex.   Drinking has been considered a predominantly male activity. But since World War II, the gap between men and women has been narrowing, and more women than ever are drinking. Today, an estimated 77 percent of all adult men and 60 percent of all adult women drink at least once a year. Men are more likely than women to be moderate or heavy users of alcohol. According to Harris and Associates polls, 16 percent of adult men drink heavily, while only 4 percent of adult women do so.

There has been speculation that women have been closing this gap. In particular, observers have pointed to the increasing numbers of women who are coming into contact with alcoholism treatment agencies as an indication that more women are drinking heavily. However, increased contact with treatment agencies could instead simply mean that individuals who had kept their heavy drinking secret are now seeking help. The fact that well-known women—like former First Lady Betty Ford—have sought aid for problems with alcoholism and drug abuse implies that this may be the case.

Age.   The use of alcohol is not confined to any one age category. But surveys reveal that a higher percentage of young people use alcohol than those over fifty years of age. Older persons are more likely to be abstainers than the young, and it is believed that most persons taper off or stop their drinking altogether with advancing age. Heavy drinking is also correlated with age. Males aged eighteen to twenty and thirty-five to thirty-nine drink most heavily. Among women, the ages are twenty-one to twenty-nine.

In the last few years, attention has been drawn to the drinking practices of school-aged youth. It is believed that drinking, including moderate to heavy alcohol use, has been on the increase among teenagers in the last several years (see Table 12.2). Most of today's junior and senior high-school students have tried alcohol. Among seventh graders, 63 percent of all boys and 54 percent of all girls have used alcohol. The

[8]Much of the data in this section is summarized in U.S. Department of Health, Education and Welfare, *Alcohol and Health: Second Special Report to U.S. Congress* (Washington, D.C.: U.S. Government Printing Office, 1974), pp. 7–18. See also the first special report, published in 1971.

Table 12.2. Current Drinking Among Subgroups of Population

	All Youth (aged 12-17)	All Adults (aged 18 and over)	Young Adults (aged 18-25)	Older Adults (aged 26 and over)
Current drinkers	31.2%	58.0%	70.0%	54.9%
Age				
12–13	13.0	—	—	—
14–15	28.0	—	—	—
16–17	52.0	—	—	—
18–21	—	71.0	71.0	—
22–25	—	70.0	70.0	—
26–34	—	70.0	—	70.0
35 and over	—	50.0	—	50.0
Sex				
Male	37.0	67.0	82.0	63.0
Female	25.0	50.0	59.0	48.0
Race				
White	33.0	59.0	72.0	56.0
Nonwhite	23.0	51.0	59.0	49.0
Region				
Northeast	35.0	71.0	79.0	69.0
North Central	35.0	58.0	73.0	54.0
South	24.0	42.0	57.0	38.0
West	36.0	70.0	76.0	68.0
Population density				
Large metropolitan	36.0	71.0	74.0	70.0
Other metropolitan	30.0	55.0	71.0	50.0
Nonmetropolitan	27.0	47.0	63.0	44.0

Source: U.S. Department of Health, Education, and Welfare, *National Survey on Drug Abuse: 1977; Volume 1, Main Findings* (Washington, D.C.: U.S. Government Printing Office, 1978), p. 109.

percentages shoot up by the twelfth grade to 93 percent for boys and 87 percent for girls. Frequency of drinking and increases in the amounts consumed per occasion also rise steadily by school grade level. A recent survey by the Research Triangle Institute found that nearly 25 percent of all students at the junior and senior high school levels were either moderate or heavy drinkers.[9] Among thirteen year olds, 24.3 percent were moderate drinkers. Only 27 percent of all the students surveyed were abstainers.

Race and ethnicity. Ethnicity has also been found to be correlated with patterns of alcohol use. For some groups, drinking is a part of cultural traditions associated with meals, rituals, or festivities. For other groups, it is not.

Persons whose fathers were born outside the United States are more likely to be drinkers than those with native-born fathers. Among the various American ethnic groups, the Irish, Italians, Poles, and Russians

[9]Pamela Swift, "Bombed Generation," *Parade Magazine,* March 14, 1976, p. 13.

The public has become alarmed over the amount and frequency of teenage drinking in recent years. Studies indicate that a quarter to a third of adolescents currently drink.

have a high proportion of drinkers. Persons of English and Scottish origins, on the other hand, are much more likely to be abstainers.

There does not appear to be much difference between blacks and whites in terms of alcohol use. Slightly more blacks are abstainers. But blacks also have a slightly higher proportion of heavy drinkers in comparison to whites.

Research on racial and ethnic differences in drinking practices is still quite limited. However, it is believed that ethnic groups maintaining cultural norms that limit the use of alcohol have fewer problem drinkers and fewer alcoholics than groups whose attitudes toward drinking are ambivalent or loose. Nevertheless, though group norms may impede or facilitate drinking, alcoholism is found among virtually all ethnic groups.

Class, occupation, and education. As one moves up the class hierarchy, the use of alcohol becomes increasingly common. Members of the lower classes are more likely to be abstainers than are more affluent people. Moreover, it is thought that moderate and heavy drinking also increases as class level rises.

In terms of educational level, the highest percentage of abstainers is found among persons with only an elementary school background. Most college graduates are drinkers, and the proportion of those who are heavy drinkers tends to go up as educational level increases.

The findings regarding class membership and educational level are consistent with those on occupational differences. Business executives and professionals, who stand at the top of the occupational structure, are more likely to be drinkers than almost any other occupational group.

Alcohol Abuse

In most of the investigations of alcohol use, an individual who uses alcohol once or more per year is classified as a "drinker." Knowing how many drinkers there are, along with the correlates of drinking behavior (such as sex and age), gives us a sense of the dimensions of use. But most users of alcohol seem to be able to take it or leave it. Their occasional drinking does not pose serious difficulties for themselves or for others.

Correlates of problem drinking.   At what point can we say that an individual is abusing alcohol to the point where he or she might be called a *problem drinker?* Most experts believe that people who exhibit any one of the following symptoms are problem drinkers:

1. Frequent bouts of intoxication, involving heavy alcohol consumption on each occasion.
2. Binge drinking—periodic episodes of intoxication that last for days at a time.
3. Physical dependence on and loss of control over the use of alcohol.
4. Psychological dependence on drinking in order to relieve depression or escape problems in living.
5. Ruptured relations with family members, friends, and/or neighbors due to drinking behavior.
6. Employment difficulties associated with alcohol use on or off the job.
7. Involvement in accidents and/or contact with law enforcement agencies in connection with alcohol use.
8. Health and/or financial problems due to drinking.[10]

Obviously, the more symptoms that are exhibited, the more serious the consequences are for the individual.

National surveys of adult drinkers conducted in the late 1960s revealed that 31 percent mainfested one or more of these symptoms. The surveys indicated that 43 percent of adult men and 21 percent of adult women were problem drinkers. Such statistics reflect the fact that men are more likely to be moderate or heavy drinkers than women.

For both men and women, *psychological dependence* on drinking in order to relieve depression or escape problems in living was the most common symptom reported. Despite the fact that proportionately more of the poor are abstainers than the affluent, problem symptoms were

---

[10]See Don Cahalan, *Problem Drinkers* (San Francisco: Jossey-Bass, Inc., 1970); and Don Cahalan and Robin Room, *Problem Drinking Among American Men* (New Brunswick, N.J.: Rutgers Center of Alcohol Studies, 1974).

most frequently found among those at the lowest class level. The proportion of drinkers with no problem symptoms was twice as high at the top of the class hierarchy than at the bottom.

Correlates of alcoholism.   If we view problem drinking as a continuum, then *alcoholics* are persons who exhibit numerous symptoms of problem drinking. The line between problem drinking and alcoholism is not clear-cut. Consequently, experts disagree about what characteristics denote alcoholism.

Attempts to define alcoholism have been numerous. The following definitions are typical:

> We define alcoholism as a chronic behavioral disorder which is manifested by undue preoccupation with alcohol to the detriment of physical and mental health, by a loss of control when drinking has begun (although it may not be carried to the point of intoxication) and by a self-destructive attitude in dealing with personal relationships and life situations.[11]

> Alcoholism involves excessive use of the drug to an extent that measurably impairs the person's health, social functioning, or vocational adjustment.[12]

> Alcoholism is a chronic disease, or disorder of behavior, characterized by the repeated drinking of alcoholic beverages to an extent that exceeds customary dietary use or ordinary compliance with the social drinking customs of the community, and which interferes with the drinker's health, interpersonal relations, or economic functioning.[13]

Despite the lack of consensus on how to define alcoholism, it is estimated that at least 5 million Americans are alcoholics. Fully half are employed, and many more are employable. Most live in families. Between 75 and 80 percent of alcoholics are men. The average alcoholic drinks eleven times as much as the average nonalcoholic during the course of a year.[14]

EXPLANATIONS FOR ALCOHOLISM

How does one explain the presence of at least 5 million alcoholics in American society? A number of explanations have been offered, most of which focus on the alcoholic individual.[15] As with the phenomenon of mental illness, the victim is often blamed for his or her own plight.

---

[11]National Institute of Mental Health, *Alcohol and Alcoholism,* rev. ed. (Washington, D.C.: U.S. Government Printing Office, 1972), p. 9.

[12]Joel Fort, *Alcohol: Our Biggest Drug Problem* (New York: McGraw-Hill, Inc., 1973), p. 7.

[13]Mark Keller, "Alcoholism: Nature and Extent of the Problem," *Annals of the American Academy of Political and Social Science,* 315 (January 1958): 1.

[14]U.S. Department of Health, Education, and Welfare, *Facts About Alcohol and Alcoholism* (Washington, D.C.: U.S. Government Printing Office, 1974), pp. 15–16.

[15]These and other explanations are discussed in detail in U.S. Department of

Physiological Explanations

A great deal of research has been conducted to test the hypothesis that alcoholism is linked to the biological makeup of particular individuals. In conjunction with this idea, researchers have also explored the possibility that the chemical properties of alcohol itself or of other ingredients in alcoholic beverages produce alcoholism in certain people.

Some researchers have hypothesized, for example, that alcoholism is a hereditary condition, related to genetic makeup. Other studies have tried to determine whether nutritional deficiencies or hormone imbalances cause alcoholism to develop. It has been suggested that alcoholism is a result of allergic reactions to alcohol and/or to the nonalcoholic components of alcoholic beverages. And researchers have tested the idea that alcoholics cannot metabolize (biologically process and eliminate) alcohol as easily as other people. To date, *none* of these hypotheses has been validated. While the use of alcohol has physiological effects on people—particularly on alcoholics—physiological causes have not been linked to alcoholism per se.

The failure to find support for physiological explanations raises questions about the usefulness of viewing alcoholism as a "disease" in medical terms. As with mental illness (see Chapter 10), the medical model is often applied to alcoholism. The alcoholic may incur health problems in connection with drinking, but so far there is no reason to believe that people drink because they are "sick."

Psychological Explanations

Some psychological explanations attribute alcoholism to particular personality traits that only alcoholics presumably possess. Psychological explanations are also frequently framed in terms of the medical model, on the assumption that the alcoholic's mind is "sick" or "disordered."

One influential theory, which incorporates both physiological and psychological causes, was developed by E. M. Jellinek.[16] In his analysis of questionnaires filled out by a group of alcoholics, Jellinek concluded that alcoholism is a disease that proceeds in cycles. An individual first becomes psychologically dependent on the use of alcohol. As the user begins to lose control over drinking, biological dependency occurs. In other words, according to Jellinek, a personality disorder leads to physical addiction to alcohol. While this explanation certainly sounds logical, no one has been able to demonstrate that alcoholism occurs for such reasons. In particular, there is no evidence that all alcoholics are biologically dependent on or addicted to the drug.

Health, Education, and Welfare, *Alcohol and Health: A Special Report to U.S. Congress* (Washington, D.C.: U.S. Government Printing Office, 1971), pp. 61–70.

[16]See E. M. Jellinek, *The Disease Concept of Alcoholism* (New Haven, Conn.: Hillhouse Press, 1960).

Other explanations have proceeded on the psychological level alone. It has been argued that individuals who received insufficient mothering engage in heavy drinking in order to make up for the oral gratifications they were denied in infancy. Another theory holds that alcoholics are actually latent homosexuals who drink in order to repress feelings they know to be socially unacceptable. Still another explanation suggests that alcoholics are suicide-prone individuals who drink in order to satisfy the urge for self-destruction. In each case, alcoholism is explained in terms of a personality or character disorder traceable to defective parent-child relations. None of these explanations has the support of sufficient evidence.

Another explanation focuses on the idea of an "alcoholic personality." Alcoholics are presumably maladjusted, immature, dependent on others, negative in their views of themselves, suffering from guilt feelings, and incapable of tolerating tension and frustration. However, experts cannot agree on the precise traits characterizing the alcoholic. Nor have researchers been able to develop a list of personality traits that distinguish those who become alcoholics from those who do not.

Finally, it has been suggested that alcoholism is the outcome of a learning process. Certain individuals who are afflicted with deep-seated fears and anxieties learn that drinking can help reduce or eliminate such feelings. It is theorized that alcoholism springs from a basic human instinct to avoid pain and seek pleasure. According to this view, alcohol provides pleasure. However, learning theory does not explain why individuals continue to drink when they begin to suffer from the unpleasant physical, mental, and social effects of alcoholism.

Sociological Explanations

Earlier we mentioned the discovery of a relationship between cultural traditions associated with ethnic group membership and drinking practices. The prevalence of alcoholism is believed to vary among different ethnic populations within the United States, just as it varies among different societies.

Researchers who believe that cultural factors are responsible for alcoholism hypothesize that the alcoholism rate will be low among groups with well-established, well-known, and generally accepted drinking customs. In groups with ambivalence about drinking and the absence of group norms and controls pertaining to the use of alcohol, rates of alcoholism are expected to be high.[17] This hypothesis, which has not been fully tested, addresses overall differences between groups. But it does not address the question of why particular individuals may come to focus their lives on drinking. Even among groups with well-established drinking customs, alcoholism occurs.

[17]See National Institute of Mental Health, *Alcohol and Alcoholism*, pp. 15–6.

Among the questions that existing explanations of alcoholism fail to answer is why some individuals cut themselves off from family and friends to become Skid Row residents and alcoholics.

A second major sociological explanation involves the concept of labeling (see Chapters 9 and 10 for discussions of the labeling perspective). In this view alcoholism is no more than a label attached to persons whose drinking habits are defined as deviant.[18] A number of variables may be involved in determining whether someone will be labeled an alcoholic. These include the quantity, rate, and frequency of drinking; the effects of alcohol consumption on the individual; the reactions of others to the observed effects; the visibility of the drinker to labeling agents (such as police, medical personnel, and employers); the class position of the drinker; and the effectiveness of formal and informal controls over the individual's drinking behavior.

The labeling approach thus implies that there is no identifiable alcoholic individual whose characteristics may be taken as representative of alcoholics in general. Indeed, we have already noted that experts cannot agree on a definition of alcoholism and that it is difficult to draw the line between problem drinking and alcoholism. But the labeling approach sidesteps the question of why an individual adopts the drinking behavior that is at issue. What is it that leads people toward patterns of alcohol use that may, under certain conditions, be labeled alcoholism?

[18]Sidney Cahn, *The Treatment of Alcoholics* (New York: Oxford University Press, Inc., 1970), pp. 36–7.

Alcoholism and Problems in Living

Most experts seem to agree that heavy users of alcohol are engaged in a retreat from reality. According to the Cooperative Commission on the Study of Alcoholism:

> Much American drinking is of an "escapist" nature. That is, alcohol is used as a means of relieving boredom or emptiness, of getting away from authority and restrictions that are considered intolerable, or of overcoming feelings of inadequacy or inferiority.[19]

Thus, the abuse of consciousness-altering drugs—in this case, alcohol—may be viewed as a method by which unhappy people attempt to deal with problems in living.

Unfortunately, the use of alcohol for escape is a false haven. The negative effects often associated with heavy drinking may simply exacerbate the problems in living confronting troubled individuals. With nowhere else to turn, and having no other ways to retreat from unendurable realities, the drug becomes everything, and individuals are destroyed.

In recent years, the idea that alcoholism is a disease has become increasingly popular. For example, the federal government now contends that "alcoholism is a treatable illness."[20] This application of the medical model to alcoholism is in some ways progressive. In the past, alcoholics were likely to be treated as moral degenerates, and it is still common for Skid Row alcoholics to be jailed, rather than sympathetically doctored. Since alcoholism is often accompanied by real health problems, some drinkers need medical help in order to survive.

The problem with conceptualizing alcoholism as a disease is that the medical model implicitly suggests that only the alcoholic needs to be changed. The medical model thereby draws attention away from consideration of societal conditions that may generate problems in living and thus escape through alcohol abuse. It is these conditions that must be changed if the phenomenon of alcoholism is ultimately to be eliminated—or at least reduced.

EFFECTS OF ALCOHOL ABUSE

There are many costs associated with problem drinking and alcoholism, costs that both drinkers and nondrinkers are forced to bear. In this section we will examine the effects of alcoholism on the alcoholic's family

[19]Cooperative Commission on the Study of Alcoholism, *Alcohol Problems* (New York: Oxford University Press, Inc., 1967), p. 130.

[20]National Institute of Mental Health, *Alcohol and Alcoholism*, p. 17.

and health, on highway safety, and on crime and look at some of the monetary costs associated with alcohol abuse.[21]

Personal and Family Relationships

The impact of alcoholism often dramatically affects the alcoholic's relationships with other people, especially family members. Disruptions of family life due to alcohol abuse often end up costing the taxpayer money. Though actual figures are not available, and though many of the costs are nonmonetary, the National Institute on Alcohol Abuse and Alcoholism has observed:

> Unhappy marriages, broken homes, desertion, divorce, impoverished families, and deprived or displaced children are all parts of the toll. The cost to public and private helping agencies for support of families disabled by alcohol problems amounts to many millions of dollars a year.[22]

When we count family members, it has been estimated that 36 million Americans are caught in "alcohol's web."[23] This does not take the impact on friends, neighbors, and acquaintances into account. The personal anguish of many of these millions of people is surely no less tragic than the self-harm alcoholics and problem drinkers impose on themselves.

Personal Health

Problem drinkers and alcoholics pay severe penalties for their drinking. It has been estimated that alcoholics are likely to die ten to twelve years sooner than nonalcoholics. Half die before the age of fifty, which is one reason there are so few elderly alcoholics. The mortality rate (that is, the number of persons per 100,000 who die each year) among alcoholics is more than two and a half times higher than that of the general population.

Alcoholics often die under violent circumstances; serious accidents, homicide, and suicide are not uncommon. This, together with the physical deterioration accompanying alcoholism, helps explain the limits on life expectancy. No one really knows how many deaths are directly attributable to drinking, and all such statistics are estimates. One reason for our limited knowledge is that many physicians do not report alcoholism as the main cause of death out of concern for the feelings of the family of the deceased.

Research on the physiological effects of alcoholism has increased in the

[21]Most data in this section are from U.S. Department of Health, Education, and Welfare, *Alcohol and Health: Second Special Report*, pp. 49–59.

[22]U.S. Department of Health, Education, and Welfare, *Facts About Alcohol and Alcoholism*, p. 16.

[23]National Institute of Mental Health, *Alcohol and Alcoholism*, p. 10.

Public Problem, Private Pain
REVERSION TO DRINKING

Joyce Rebeta-Burditt's novel, The Cracker Factory, *reminds us that alcoholism may be a response to problems in living. The central character in this novel is Cassie Barrett, who is married and the mother of three young children.*

Cassie is a housewife and mother. Her husband Charlie is intent on his career and his leisure-time pursuits with his buddies. Cassie feels closed out of his life and constrained by the traditional female role that Charlie demands she fulfill. She finds Charlie indifferent and insensitive to her feelings of depression and anger. He cannot understand what is "wrong with her." Cassie turns to drinking as a means of getting through the day.

In this excerpt from the novel, Cassie has just returned from the hospital, where she was treated and presumably "cured" of alcoholism. Discovering that her marital situation is the same as it was before her hospitalization, Cassie turns again to alcohol.

One morning I put two poached eggs in front of Charlie, who looked up briefly from his newspaper.

"You've really shaped up, Cassie," he smiled. "A dreadful lady went to the hospital and a very nice Cassie came back. I think you've learned a lesson and honey, I'm proud of you."

He went to work and I started the dishes, trying to feel thrilled at having shaped up for Charlie. *He sounds as though the hospital performed some sort of exorcism,* I mused, scraping egg off the dish with my fingernail. *Evil is banished, goodness restored. Then why don't I feel transformed?*

The dish slipped out of my hand and smashed into the sink, spraying chips over the counter. I looked down at the mess, then at the cluttered kitchen table, and beyond that to the dust on the television set in the den. I pictured the four un-

made beds and the three clothes-strewn bedrooms and the toys in the living room and last night's newspaper on the floor next to Charlie's reclining chair and I yelled at the cat who was licking milk out of a cereal bowl, "What lesson? What goddamn lesson was I supposed to learn?"

I grabbed my coat and the grocery money and was waiting at the liquor store when it opened.

"You find a place where they give it away for free?" the man behind the counter leered. "We haven't seen you for weeks. Where you been?"

"Nowhere," I answered. "I've been nowhere." He gave me my bottle and I walked out thinking that I'd have to start trading at another store where the creeps weren't so free with their remarks.

Once home I pulled the curtains, put on a stack of records and curled up in front of the stereo with a tumbler full of scotch. I sipped and listened and sipped some more, until the barbed wire dissolved and a soft, mellow fog replaced the ache behind my eyes. I must have fallen asleep because the next thing I knew the kids were home and Charlie was due. I knew I'd have to scramble frantically to get to the market and home again, get dinner started and some of the clutter cleared away before he walked in the door. But first, I needed a drink.

And after the drink, I decided, *What the hell. I can open a couple of cans for dinner and if Charlie doesn't like the way the house looks he can clean it up himself.*

I was stirring soup and burning toast when Charlie came in the back door. He looked at the mess, then at me.

"You're drunk," he accused. "You're drinking again."

"Am not," I said, waving the butter knife at him. "I learned my lesson." I gave him my best "nice Cassie" grin.

"Where are the kids?" he demanded.

"In the den watching television. Why?"

"You wouldn't know if the kids were playing in the middle of the street," Charlie snapped, pushing past me.

Charlie called the kids. Greg was the first to arrive.

"I got an A in arithmetic, Daddy," he announced, "the only one in first grade."

"Fine, son," Charlie said absently, stuffing him into his coat.

"Where are you going?" I asked, while Jenny looked from Charlie to me and back again and Steve leaned against the doorway with his arms folded and eyes on the ceiling.

"I'm taking the kids somewhere to dinner, seeing as their mother is too drunk to cook."

"Isn't Mommy coming?" Jenny asked, as Charlie hustled them out the door.

"No," Charlie snapped.

"You can go to hell, too!" I shouted at the closing door. In the kitchen I reached for the bottle I'd hidden behind the oatmeal box and leaned against the sink, drinking and crying, while the soup burned black in the pan.

Later, after the children were asleep, Charlie approached me as I sat staring blankly at television.

"I don't understand, Cass." He shook his head. "Everything was going so well for us."

I took another sip. "For you, Charlie. Everything was going well for you."

Joyce Rebeta-Burditt, *The Cracker Factory* (New York: Macmillan Publishing Co., Inc., 1977), pp. 3–5.

last few years. Heavy drinking is said to be associated with various types of cancer, particularly among persons who also use tobacco. Alcohol use is also thought to increase the probability of coronary heart disease among former drinkers. Alcoholics frequently suffer illness and death from cirrhosis of the liver, a disease in which the liver becomes fatty, scarred, and incapable of functioning normally. In large urban areas, cirrhosis is the fourth most common cause of death among men aged twenty-five to forty-five.

Alcohol affects the brain, often permanently damaging the mental functioning of alcoholics. Drinking may reduce the number of living cells in the brain. Since brain cells do not grow back, alcoholics may suffer from organic psychosis (a mental illness traceable to brain damage), loss of memory, and poor physical and mental coordination. One out of four persons who are admitted to mental hospitals are diagnosed as alcoholics, and 40 percent of all admissions are alcohol-related. Many of the alcoholic inmates are unlikely to recover.

The unborn children of female alcoholics are subject to harm from drinking. Because alcohol tends to be a substitute for a balanced diet, alcoholics are often malnourished. Consequently, the infants of alcoholic women are likely to be less healthy and less well-developed than other babies. Moreover, when a pregnant woman drinks, so, in effect, does her fetus. The newborn children of alcoholic women may die shortly after birth unless they are medically treated for the shock to their systems from suddenly being cut off from alcohol. Furthermore, the impact of alcohol on the woman and her fetus is believed to be a major cause of organically based mental deficiency among the newborn.

Clearly, it is not too much of an exaggeration to say that alcohol kills and maims people. Used heavily, alcohol is a highly dangerous drug. It carries no warnings on its labels, despite its contribution to America's number one health problem.

Highway Deaths

Each year, street and highway accidents take the lives of about as many Americans as died in the ten-year war in Southeast Asia. Of the fifty to sixty thousand deaths due to highway accidents that occur annually, half are estimated to be alcohol-related. Some of those killed, it is suspected, are the victims or the perpetrators of alcohol-related suicides, in which the suicidal individual uses the automobile as the death weapon.

In addition to this annual slaughter, roughly 35 percent of crashes producing serious injuries involve drinking drivers. And approximately a third of the pedestrians who die in traffic accidents each year are heavily under the influence of alcohol. (Presumably, some of these pedestrians may also be committing suicide.)

No other drug has been found to play such a key role in accidental

Deaths and injuries resulting from drunken driving are so serious a problem—especially over certain holiday weekends—that law enforcement agencies across the country have instituted programs to catch drinking drivers before accidents occur. But such law enforcement measures have only limited effectiveness, as is indicated by the fact that the number of alcohol-related traffic deaths continues to increase.

deaths. Despite the occasional warnings by public affairs groups not to mix drinking and driving, the number of deaths continues to rise.

Crime

The use of alcohol is closely tied to certain types of criminal activity and is substantially responsible for the enormous number of arrests made in the United States. Not all alcoholics commit crimes. Not all problem drinkers commit crimes. Of those who do, not all are identified and arrested. Hence, alcohol-related crime statistics—like most other statistics on alcohol—are rough estimates.

Half of all murders and a third of all suicides involve drinking, and twelve thousand people die annually as a result. Physical assaults, child abuse, rape, and other sex crimes are thought to be associated with alcohol use. So are acts of vandalism, arson, and other property crimes.

In 1976 over 9 million arrests were made in this country (see Chapter 9, "Criminal Behavior"). A third of these arrests were for law violations related to alcohol use: public drunkenness, disorderly conduct, vagrancy, and drunken driving. To this we may add many other arrests for crimes against people and property in which alcohol use was involved.

All these arrests do not involve different individuals. Public drunkenness, for example, accounts for about half of all arrests in urban areas.

Most public drunkenness arrests involve persons—e.g., in or near Skid Row districts—who are being repeatedly arrested and released. For such individuals, jail is a "revolving door." In general, a relatively small proportion of the drinking population accounts for the majority of alcohol-related arrests.

Economic Effects

While the alcoholic beverage industry is prospering from the sales of its products and government is benefiting from alcohol-related tax revenues, alcohol abuse is costly to business, government, and, of course, individuals. The federal government, using 1971 figures, has conservatively estimated that the cost of alcohol abuse comes to $25 billion per year.[24]

Reduced job productivity among members of the labor force due to drinking costs the American economy $9.35 billion. Most of this is due to absenteeism, accidents, and inefficiency. This figure covers only male workers and is thus undoubtedly an understatement.

An estimated $8.29 billion goes to pay for medical problems attributable to drinking. This constituted 12 percent of America's total expenditures on health care in 1971. Most of the money goes to cover the costs of hospitalization for alcohol-related health problems.

Fatal traffic accidents involving drinking cost Americans $3.56 billion. Injury accidents cost another $2.38 billion, with property damage adding $500 million more. Of course, no dollar value can be placed on the human suffering that accompanies such carnage.

We have already noted that alcohol-related criminal activity accounts for many arrests. In 1971, the cost of such arrests, subsequent trials, and confinements came to $510 million. Crimes of violence accounted for almost half of this amount.

Finally, alcoholics and their families receive monetary assistance from publicly financed programs—$2.2 billion in income maintenance payments and $135 million in social services in 1971. Not all who were eligible received aid.

Added to the $25 billion accounted for above is the money spent by federal and state governments and private agencies on alcoholism programs. Public and private financing of diagnosis, treatment, rehabilitation, prevention, education, and research totalled a mere $640 million. While the federal government was taking in billions of dollars in alcohol-related tax revenues, it was spending only $127 million on alcoholism programs. Clearly the economic costs attributable to the use of alcohol outweighed the resources being devoted to reduce these costs.

[24]U.S. Department of Health, Education, and Welfare, *Alcohol and Health: Second Special Report*, p. 49.

TYPES OF TREATMENT

Several different kinds of treatment are used in cases of alcoholism. These treatment procedures are directed at altering the physical and/or mental state of the alcoholic. Most of them fall within the context of the medical model, in which the alcoholic is considered ill and in need of being cured. Instead of attacking the societal conditions that may help produce and sustain alcoholism, efforts are made to help the drinker function within the prevailing order.[25]

The "cure rate" for alcoholism is not very high. When we use abstinence for more than three or five years as the criterion for cure, fewer than 20 percent of those treated are cured. If, on the other hand, the criterion is the ability of the alcoholic to maintain control over drinking *most* of the time, the cure rate approaches two thirds of those treated.

The chances for cure depend on the severity of the impact of alcohol on the individual. People who have not been severely affected are much more likely to control their drinking. Persons placed in mental hospitals to be treated for alcoholic psychoses, on the other hand, have only one chance in ten of being cured.

These statistics come from agencies and institutions involved in treatment. It is difficult to know if their claims of successful treatment are real or are instead somewhat inflated. Moreover, millions of alcoholics and problem drinkers never come into contact with treatment facilities. So it is possible that those who are treated are either more—or less—amenable to "cure" than the untreated.

Physiological Treatment

Alcoholics who suddenly stop drinking often suffer from withdrawal symptoms, in which the body, having adjusted to large amounts of alcohol, reacts to the shock of abstinence. Common withdrawal symptoms include trembling, nausea, nervousness, and inability to sleep. Some alcoholics suffer from the DTs, delirium tremens, when they stop drinking. The DTs are often characterized by nightmarish hallucinations, serious convulsions, and feverishness. The individual may be terror-stricken, convinced that snakes or insects are crawling all over his or her body.

The most common method of dealing with withdrawal symptoms is to provide the alcoholic with tranquilizers, a balanced intake of liquids and solids, and bed rest. Once the individual's bodily system has undergone

[25]National Institute of Mental Health, *Alcohol and Alcoholism*, pp. 17–26. See also Don Martindale and Edith Martindale, *The Social Dimensions of Mental Illness, Alcoholism, and Drug Dependence* (Westport, Conn.: Greenwood Press, Inc., 1971), pp. 233–44.

detoxification (i.e., is cleansed of alcohol), further medical treatments may be undertaken to handle physical and mental problems that remain.

Detoxification, or the drying out of an alcoholic, is not the same as eliminating the desire to drink. Thus, further treatment often consists of drugging alcoholics with more tranquilizers in the hope of relieving this desire. The difficulty here is that the tranquilizing drugs may themselves be no more than alcohol substitutes. The alcoholic simply seeks escape from reality through drug treatment.

Attempts have been made to cure alcoholism by using drugs that induce a deep, reflexive aversion to drinking. Deterrent drugs cause headaches, violent nausea, and other physical discomforts whenever alcohol is ingested. The idea is to condition the alcoholic to associate drinking with physical agony and thus to promote abstinence. Deterrent drugs can only be used if the alcoholic is willing to be subjected to such unpleasant treatment. Also, some alcoholics manage to drink themselves beyond the deterrent effects. While deterrent drugs may create an aversion to alcohol, they do not necessarily remove the desire to escape reality.

In general, the physiological approach to treatment does not guarantee abstention from alcohol or the production of "cured" alcoholics. For such reasons, psychologically oriented treatments have also been developed to deal with this "illness."

Psychological Treatment

Psychological treatments for alcoholism are based on the premise that underlying character disorders or weaknesses cause the individual to drink. A variety of approaches are in use. At one extreme, therapists have experimented with LSD, a chemical agent that causes unusual hallucinations and other mental experiences, in the hope that alcoholics will gain insights while under the influence of the drug. The results of such experiments have been minimal.

At the other extreme is psychotherapy, in which alcoholics receive individual counseling and are encouraged to contemplate the deep-seated reasons why they drink. Efforts are made to urge the alcoholic to overcome the psychological problems for which drinking is thought to provide an escape. Psychotherapy is very expensive. And many persons who face problems in living find such attempts to suggest that they are to blame for their own troubles less than helpful.

Group therapy often takes place in hospitals, churches, and mental institutions. About the only organization that claims a high level of success in fostering abstention is Alcoholics Anonymous.[26] In group therapy,

[26]See Barry Leach, "Does Alcoholics Anonymous Really Work?" in *Alcoholism: Progress in Research and Treatment,* Peter G. Bourne and Ruth Fox, eds. (New York: Academic Press, Inc., 1973), pp. 245–84.

Concerned by the increasing visibility of problem drinking, many hospitals and community agencies have set up treatment programs in recent years. Individual, family, and group counseling are popular therapeutic techniques. Though alcoholism treatment programs often help individuals overcome their drinking problems—at least in the short run—such programs generally work with only a small proportion of alcoholics and problem drinkers.

the alcoholic is encouraged to talk honestly with other persons who are trying to or have managed to abstain. The alcoholic thus finds others who have been "saved" from the harmful effects of drinking and enjoys the fellowship of a sympathetic group. Alcoholics Anonymous encourages alcoholics to put themselves in the hands of God and to take encouragement from the experiences and expectations of other AA participants. While several hundred thousand people are presently involved with AA, the religious orientation is not attractive to many other alcoholics. Though it claims great success with those who seek out its services, AA—like alcoholism treatment programs generally—touches only a small percentage of those thought to be alcoholics or problem drinkers.

What Treatment Works Best?

As is evident from our discussion of treatment statistics and practices, no one really knows how to "cure" alcoholism. According to the National Institute on Alcohol Abuse and Alcoholism:

> There is no evidence that any particular type of therapist—physician, clergyman, Alcoholics Anonymous member, psychiatrist, psychologist, or social worker—will have better results than another. The chances of a successful outcome apparently depend more on the combination of right patient and right treatment.[27]

Existing approaches to treatment fail to take into account the possibility that alcoholism may be a response to societal conditions that do harm

[27]U.S. Department of Health, Education, and Welfare, *Facts About Alcohol and Alcoholism*, p. 24.

to people. Unless these conditions are dealt with, it can be very difficult for alcoholics and problem drinkers to confront life in a sober state.

According to Joel Fort and Christopher T. Cory:

> Drug use may be a way for society to keep people with dissatisfactions and frustrations doped up so that they cannot challenge society to eliminate injustice, oppression, political corruption, boring jobs, and unfair economic conditions.[28]

In other words, these experts believe that alcohol facilitates users' escapism, diverting people from struggling against the kinds of problems analyzed in the first part of this book. Presumably, the more people who seek escape from reality and from societal conditions that are intolerable, the more likely it is that such conditions will continue.

SUMMARY

The use of alcohol is an increasingly popular and acceptable activity in American society, even among the very young. Because alcohol is a drug, many heavy drinkers look to it to relieve depression and to escape problems in living that are intolerable when faced in a state of sobriety. One out of ten drinkers uses this drug so heavily that he or she may be labeled a problem drinker or alcoholic.

Experts disagree about what alcoholism is and why it exists, but most, using the medical model, blame the drinker for his or her own plight. Treatment approaches, both physiological and psychological, generally operate within the context of the medical model and attempt to alter the drinking behavior that is in question. Such approaches to alcoholism and problem drinking tend to bypass processes by which people are labeled alcoholics and do not take into consideration the societal conditions that may drive people to drink.

Meanwhile, massive costs are generated as a consequence of such drinking behavior—both for the individual drinker and for American society as a whole. But despite these costs, the alcoholic beverage industry continues to promote and profit from the drug it markets, and the government amasses huge tax revenues from alcohol production and use. Resources devoted to combatting the costs associated with America's drinking practices are negligible in comparison with the profits and tax revenues collected. And alcoholism remains this society's number one health problem and a self-harmful means of escapism from the status quo.

[28]Joel Fort and Christopher T. Cory, *American Drugstore* (Boston: Educational Associates, 1975), p. 61.

DISCUSSION QUESTIONS

1. Are you a user of alcoholic beverages? Why?
2. Does anyone you know appear to meet the criteria for being an alcoholic or problem drinker? How would you explain this person's drinking behavior?
3. What arguments could be made for and against making alcoholic beverages available for purchase by persons of any age?
4. Examine a sample of advertisements for alcoholic beverages. What do these advertisements suggest, directly or indirectly, about the types of people who drink and the benefits of alcohol use?
5. If you normally drink at parties, bars, discos, etc., arrive at one of these settings late in the evening completely sober. How does the behavior of others appear to you when you stand back and view it as an uninvolved observer?
6. Visit a meeting of a local chapter of Alcoholics Anonymous. Summarize the impact of alcoholism on those persons who speak out at the meeting. Compare your impressions with the impressions of your classmates.

13 Drug Abuse

Members of American society should be at peace
with themselves and with one another. The
vicarious rewards associated with drug abuse
should have no attraction.

WHAT IS A DRUG?

ILLEGAL SUBSTANCES

Marijuana

Heroin

Cocaine

LSD

Methedrine

LEGAL SUBSTANCES

Nature and Extent of Abuse of Legal Drugs

Drug Producers, Dispensers, and Users

EXPLANATIONS FOR DRUG USE AND ABUSE

Use of Illegal Drugs

Drug Abuse and Social Conditions

Drugs and Social Control

SUMMARY

T he use and abuse of drugs have become matters of public concern during the last ten or fifteen years. As more people—particularly young adults and adolescents—use drugs for nonmedical purposes, moral, medical, legal, and political issues have emerged. Most of these issues revolve around the so-called problem drugs that are readily available through illicit channels. These include marijuana, heroin, cocaine, LSD and other hallucinogens, and "speed" (methedrine).

Paradoxically, far less controversy and attention surround the increasing consumption of prescription drugs and over-the-counter preparations. Stimulants, barbiturates, and tranquilizers are being used at an unprecedented rate, often for nonmedical reasons. Sociologist Charlotte Muller has characterized the United States as an "overmedicated society" in recognition of the degree to which drugs have become an important adjunct to the daily lives of millions of people.[1]

A discussion of drug use would be incomplete without mention of the use of drugs for social control. In schools, mental institutions, nursing homes, and a variety of other settings, drugs are viewed as an appropriate means of controlling potentially disruptive people. Drugs have also become part of America's military arsenal. They have already been used as a tool in covert intelligence operations, and there are even drugs that can be used as weapons in warfare.

Our emphasis in this chapter will be on self-administered drugs. We will begin with a discussion of the difficulties involved in defining the term *drug.* Then we will examine the nature and extent of abuse of illegal and legal drugs. Finally, we will look at explanations for drug use and abuse, briefly addressing the problem of the administration of drugs for social control.

WHAT IS A DRUG?

The term *drug* is presently subject to a wide variety of meanings and uses, each of which includes or excludes certain substances. From a strictly scientific perspective, a drug is typically defined as "any substance other than food which by its chemical nature affects the structure or function of the living organism."[2] This definition is overwhelmingly broad—under it, even air and water could qualify as drugs. By contrast, medical practitioners ordinarily use the term to mean substances appropriate for use in treating physical and mental illness or disease. In other words, to doctors drugs are medicines. Finally, from a legal point of view, a drug is any substance that is so defined under the law. Thus, law

---

[1]Charlotte Muller, "The Overmedicated Society," *Science,* 176 (May 5, 1972): 488–92.

[2]National Commission on Marihuana and Drug Abuse, *Drug Use in America* (Washington, D.C.: U.S. Government Printing Office, 1973), p. 9.

enforcement personnel may use the term quite differently than scientists and physicians.

Sociologist Erich Goode, an expert on drug use, has asked whether it is possible to arrive at an objective definition that would spell out just what a drug is and is not. In other words, is there any basis on which one could easily distinguish drugs from nondrugs, so that everyone will agree on the meaning of the term? According to Goode, there is not: "There is no formal property which is (1) shared by more or less all drug substances and which is (2) alien to non-drug substances."[3] Instead, any and all substances that are designated as drugs are *socially defined* as such. Society, or some segment of society, labels a substance as a drug, "and the social definition shapes attitudes toward the class of substances so described."[4]

What, then, distinguishes the so-called problem drugs from other drugs and from substances that have not been labeled as drugs? The answer is nothing—nothing, that is, except a different and more negative social definition. This social definition does not necessarily have anything to do with hazards or dangers potentially associated with the use and abuse of a substance. For example, there is one drug that

> has been massively used for decades; its mechanism of action on the brain and other organs is unknown; it accounts for thousands of deaths and illnesses each year, and it produces not only chromosomal breakage, but actual birth defects in lower animals.[5]

This sounds like a description of a problem drug, but actually, the substance is aspirin—which most people probably do not consider a drug at all. Aspirin is associated with far more known health difficulties than, for example, marijuana.

The importance of social definition is indicated by the results of a poll conducted for the National Commission on Marihuana and Drug Abuse. In a national sampling of adults, 95 percent regarded heroin as a drug, and 80 percent labeled marijuana a drug. Only 39 percent regarded alcohol as a drug, and even fewer adults—27 percent—thought that tobacco products deserved this label.[6] While there is no objective and meaningful basis for making such distinctions, the social definitions prevailing in the United States place alcohol and tobacco outside the realm of drug status, and thus not a part of the drug problem.

Social definitions of problem drugs frequently change over time. Within American society, different groups commonly disagree over such definitions. This has been the case with such addictive drugs as morphine and

[3]Erich Goode, *The Drug Phenomenon* (Indianapolis: The Bobbs-Merrill Co., Inc., 1973), p. 6.

[4]Erich Goode, *Drugs in American Society* (New York: Alfred A. Knopf, Inc., 1972), p. 18.

[5]Joel Fort, *The Pleasure Seekers* (Indianapolis: The Bobbs-Merrill Co., Inc. 1969), p. 5.

[6]National Commission on Marihuana and Drug Abuse, *Drug Use in America*, p. 10.

heroin.[7] Morphine first began to be used in the United States in the 1850s. As its pain-relieving qualities became known, its use increased—particularly during and after the Civil War. Physicians enthusiastically endorsed the drug, and medicine companies included morphine in a variety of home remedies. An estimated 2 to 4 percent of the population was addicted by the end of the nineteenth century. While a number of doctors had grown concerned about morphine addiction by that time, neither the press nor the public saw morphine or addiction to it as a problem.

At the beginning of the twentieth century, heroin was introduced into the United States. Physicians found it to be a stronger pain-reliever than morphine, and they believed heroin to be nonaddictive. Use of heroin quickly spread. Like morphine, it could be purchased without a prescription. Before the addictive qualities of heroin became known, the number of drug addicts in the United States further increased. Still, addiction was not viewed in a negative manner by the public.

In the early 1900s, a small group of concerned doctors began pressing for government regulation of addictive drugs. New York passed the first major piece of state legislation in 1904, and other states followed. In 1914 Congress approved the Harrison Narcotic Act. This act regulated the production and distribution of addictive drugs and required users to obtain them by prescription from physicians. Doctors were flooded with prescription-seekers and were soon refusing to supply addicts.

As subsequent drug laws further restricted or eliminated legal sources for addictive drugs, a flourishing black market emerged, in which organized crime came to play an important role. When morphine and heroin became associated with crime and the underworld, public sentiment shifted against the addict and the drugs that were once available in respectable drugstores. Additional changes in the social definition of heroin are currently under way. The federal government has approved experimentation with heroin in the treatment of people who are in terrible pain, such as terminal cancer patients.

Because so many different types of substances can be defined as drugs, it is necessary to limit any discussion of drug use to particular types of drugs. In this chapter, we will focus on *psychoactive substances,* drugs that may affect the minds of those who consume them.

ILLEGAL SUBSTANCES

The so-called problem drugs are illegal substances that are self-administered (knowingly and purposely used). Among the substances most used—and feared—by Americans are marijuana, heroin, cocaine, LSD, and methedrine.

[7]See Troy Duster, *The Legislation of Morality* (New York: The Free Press, 1970), Chapter 1.

Marijuana

Marijuana is the most widely used illegal substance in the United States. The source of marijuana is the *Cannabis sativa* plant, and its potency, in terms of its potential effects on users, stems largely from tetrahydracannabinol, or THC, a chemical ingredient found in a resin exuded from the plant. Because marijuana can have differing amounts of THC, it is difficult to generalize about the effects of the drug on any particular user. Obviously, the smaller the THC content, the milder the effects of the drug.

Effects of marijuana use.   Most marijuana users smoke the leaves, stems, and other parts of the *Cannabis sativa* plant. Some users ingest the drug orally—for example, by mixing it with food. Marijuana often causes

> mild euphoria; stimulation of the central nervous system and increased conviviality. The user experiences a pleasant heightening of the senses and relaxed passivity. In moderate doses the substance can cause short lapses of attention and slightly impaired memory and motor functioning. Heavy users have been known to become socially withdrawn and depersonalized and have experienced distortions of the senses.[8]

Many studies have explored the question of whether marijuana users run the risk of mental or physical damage.[9] Though findings have been contradictory and inconclusive, it appears that adverse effects directly traceable to marijuana use are rare, even among heavy users. Adverse effects may be due to the adulteration of marijuana with other substances, which can occur from the time it is planted to the time it gets to consumers. For example, in 1978 it was discovered that some shipments of Mexican marijuana contained paraquat, a potentially deadly herbicide.

Unlike many other substances, including a large number of legal drugs, marijuana is not a lethal drug. There are no documented cases of deaths directly attributable to unadulterated marijuana, which suggests that lethal overdoses are highly unlikely even among the heaviest users. Nor is marijuana physically addictive. Users do not suffer compulsive cravings, and no matter what the potency of the drug or the frequency of its use, individuals may at any time cease to employ the drug without suffering physical discomfort.

The question of whether marijuana is psychologically addictive—or whether users can become psychologically dependent on marijuana use—has been the subject of much debate. In the absence of firm evidence, particularly on the effects of long-term use, the answer seems to be that it is nonaddictive. Those who use the drug regularly do so because they find it to be pleasurable, just as people enjoy regular exercise or reading. Though a minority of marijuana users employ the drug re-

---

[8]National Commission on Marihuana and Drug Abuse, *Drug Use in America,* p. 158.
   [9]See E. M. Brecher, "Marijuana: The Health Questions," *Consumer Reports,* 40 (March 1975): 143–49.

peatedly, this is no more a sign of addiction than is the fact that men seem "addicted" to wearing pants every day.

Unlike some other drugs, including alcohol, marijuana use does not cause people to engage in serious forms of antisocial behavior, including crime. It is not associated with aggressive or violent activity. The only criminality associated with marijuana is a matter of its illegality—the fact that possession, distribution, and sale of marijuana are against the law.

Extent of marijuana use.   Anywhere from 25 to 45 million Americans are estimated to have used marijuana at least once. The greatest amount of experimentation with this drug has taken place in the last decade (see Table 13.1). During the past ten years, national surveys and polls conducted in schools and local communities have shown a massive increase in marijuana use, particularly among the young, the middle class, and college students. For the most part, those who experiment with or regularly use marijuana are under thirty-five years of age.

According to a 1977 survey commissioned by the U.S. Department of Health, Education, and Welfare, 28.2 percent of all youth and 24.5 percent of adults have used marijuana (see Tables 13.1 and 13.2). All such figures are estimates. Many Americans prefer to conceal their participation in what remains illicit activity, even when anonymity is virtually guaranteed. Conversely, others may think that it is "in" to say that they have used the drug even if they haven't, since marijuana use is so widespread.

The proliferation of marijuana use has resulted in tremendous law enforcement problems. As use has grown, arrests have zoomed, and criminal justice agencies have at times become choked with those caught participating in the victimless crime of marijuana possession (see Chapter 9). Efforts to identify and restrict domestic and foreign sources of marijuana have not been notably successful. A handful of states and communities have taken steps toward the decriminalization of marijuana possession, establishing minimal penalties on a level with a traffic offense. However, it has not been legalized in any community. The prevailing social definition still holds that marijuana is a problem drug, and this view is changing extremely slowly.

Table 13.1. Increases in Marijuana Use

Age	1972	1974	1976	1977	Number, 1977
Ever used					
12–17	14%	22.6%	22.5%	28.2%	7,033,000
18 and older	16%	18.9%	21.3%	24.5%	36,216,000
Used in past year					
12–17	NA	18.6%	17.9%	21.8%	5,436,000
18 and older	NA	10.3%	11.5%	12.8%	18,921,000

Source: U.S. Department of Health, Education, and Welfare, *National Survey of Drug Abuse: 1977; Volume 1, Main Findings* (Washington, D.C.: U.S. Government Printing Office, 1978), pp. 5, 26, and 27. NA = not asked in survey.

Table 13.2. Percent Ever Having Used Selected Drugs

Drug	Ages 12–17	Ages 18–25	Ages 26 and Over
Marijuana and/or hashish	28.2%	60.1%	15.4%
Inhalants (e.g., glue)	9.0	11.2	1.8
Hallucinogens	4.6	19.8	2.6
Cocaine	4.0	19.1	2.6
Heroin	1.1	3.6	0.8
Other opiates	6.1	13.5	2.8
Stimulants	5.2	21.2	4.7
Barbiturates	3.1	18.4	2.8
Tranquilizers	3.8	13.4	2.6
Alcohol	52.6	84.2	77.9
Cigarettes	47.3	67.6	67.0
Total population in age category	24,938,000	30,553,000	117,266,000

Source: U.S. Department of Health, Education, and Welfare, *National Survey of Drug Abuse: 1977; Volume 1, Main Findings* (Washington, D.C.: U.S. Government Printing Office, 1978), pp. 5, 18, 22, and 24. Figures for stimulants, barbiturates, and tranquilizers represent nonmedical use of prescription drugs.

Heroin

Heroin is a derivative of morphine, which itself is derived from opium, a substance found in the *Papaver somniferum* poppy plant. There are several other opiate (opium-derived) drugs. Most heroin used in the United States originates abroad and enters this country from Europe and South America. Once imported, the substance is distributed and sold to users under the auspices of organized crime. Organized crime has not made much of an effort to merchandise marijuana, probably because of its bulk, odor, and relatively low profits. None of these handicaps exists with regard to heroin.

Effects of heroin use.   Much like marijuana, the heroin available to users often varies in potential potency. Before it is sold to individual consumers, heroin is ordinarily "cut" or adulterated with other substances, such as milk sugar, at a number of stages during distribution. The drug is most commonly injected into the bloodstream with a needle and syringe (although it may also be sniffed, smoked, or ingested orally), and the variable potency is a frequent cause of fatal overdoses. Users who unknowingly purchase a unit of heroin that is relatively pure or unadulterated may die immediately upon injecting it because their bodies cannot tolerate the drug's strength. So it is not surprising that the death rate among heroin users is substantially higher than that of nonusers in the same age groups.

The effects of heroin are thought to vary. Nevertheless, most regular users report pleasurable experiences with the drug. Upon injecting it, many users experience a "rush" or wave of sensations somewhat like an intense sexual orgasm. The rush does not last long and is followed by a mild sense of euphoria, the relaxation of tensions, and the disappearance of any physical pains.

Users who take heroin repeatedly develop *tolerance* to it. This means that they must use larger and larger doses in order to achieve pleasurable effects. Tolerance also means that users must take a greater volume of the drug (or stronger dosages) to ward off discomfort similar to that which occurs when heroin use is suddenly discontinued. Increasing the frequency of use and the amounts used exposes individuals to greater risks of overdose.

Heroin and the other opiates are physically addictive. Heroin addicts who stop using the drug suffer from serious withdrawal symptoms, including cramps, nausea, muscle tremors, diarrhea, chills, and extreme nervousness. Withdrawal symptoms typically begin abating after two or three days and are generally gone within a week. But many addicts make the withdrawal symptoms disappear almost instantaneously by taking more heroin—or even other opiates. Regular heroin users are thus literally driven toward continued use of heroin, not necessarily to gain pleasure but to avoid the pain of withdrawal. Besides being physically addicted, regular heroin users may also be psychologically "hooked" in the sense that every waking hour may be spent planning for and ensuring a dependable drug supply.

Most people who use heroin "mainline" it—inject it directly into the bloodstream with a needle and syringe. If they unknowingly inject pure heroin, death may be the result.

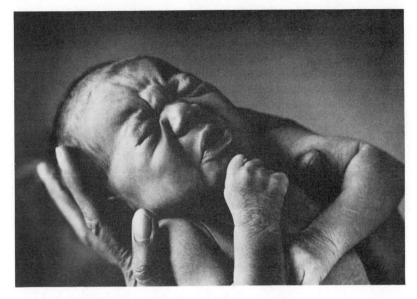

Though heroin in and of itself apparently does not cause physiological damage, it is associated with serious health problems. For example, children born to addicted women are themselves addicted to heroin and undergo withdrawal from the drug upon birth. This four-day-old infant is being treated for withdrawal symptoms.

In recent years a number of long-held myths concerning heroin and its users have begun to be dispelled. For example, the drug apparently does not cause physiological damage (apart from the tragedy of accidental overdose). Though many heroin users are malnourished, this seems to be due to their lack of interest in any pleasures (including eating) other than those associated with the drug itself. Common diseases among heroin users, such as hepatitis and tetanus, are a result of the use of unsanitary paraphernalia—as when several persons share the same needles. Other common illnesses, like pneumonia, are thought to be related to the frenetic life-styles of addicts, who concentrate on the search for a "fix" and lack concern for health and well-being. This is not to say that heroin use is safe. But taken correctly, heroin does not—so far as we know now—damage the human organism. One need only think of the numerous doctors and nurses who have been addicted to one or another opiate drug for years and who continue to function into old age.

Heroin and crime. It has long been believed that heroin causes users to engage in criminal acts. This is not the case. Most heroin addicts—at least those known to law enforcement agencies—had embarked on criminal activity well before becoming hooked. Nevertheless, though heroin itself does not cause crime, the drive to maintain a constant supply of the drug may require breaking the law. Heroin is expensive, primarily because those who market it take advantage of their monopoly position by increasing prices. Users often cannot afford to maintain their drug habits on the wages they could earn on a job. Thus, property crimes such as robbery and burglary may become a way of life. Property crimes committed by heroin users are thought to cost victims hundreds of millions of dollars annually.

Heroin does not, in and of itself, make users aggressive or prone to violence. Involvement in, for example, rapes, murders, and assaults, is far more common among users of alcohol. But addicts who are desperate to get money to feed their habit may resort to violence if the victim of, say, a robbery attempt, fights back.

Extent of heroin use.   There are probably no more than 375,000 heroin users in the entire United States. This number is a rough estimate. We do not know if the number of users has increased in the last few years.

Heroin addicts are likely to be young, male, and residents of large metropolitan areas. A recent survey of men who were twenty to thirty years old during 1974 found that 6 percent had, at some time, used heroin and that 2 percent were current users. By contrast, 55 percent had tried marijuana, and 38 percent admitted to current use. Heroin was found to be the least used drug of nine (including tobacco and alcohol) included in the survey. Only 14 percent of the heroin users said that they had ever undergone treatment for drug use.[10]

Law enforcement efforts have had little impact on the marketing and consumption of heroin. Police have generally concentrated on finding easily identified users and small dealers. They have not been effective in attacking organized crime's control over the heroin market. The people who control the import, distribution, and sale of heroin make so much money that it is well worth it to bribe and corrupt customs inspectors and police. Periodic federal efforts to stem the international traffic in heroin have not yielded significant restrictions in domestic supplies. The poppies that supply opiates are a cash crop in economically underdeveloped societies, and governments in these societies are generally reluctant to outlaw poppies—and thus contribute to their own demise—in the interest of limiting America's heroin usage.

Cocaine

Cocaine is derived from the leaves of the *coca* plant, which is grown in the South American Andes Mountains. (*Coca* plants are also used in the production of Coca-Cola.) Though cocaine is less widely available and more expensive than heroin, it is more commonly used.

Effects of cocaine use.   Cocaine is a stimulant (as are nicotine, caffeine, amphetamines, and methedrine). It is usually taken in the form of a crystal-like white powder that may be sniffed or dissolved in liquid and

[10]John A. O'Donnell et al., *Young Men and Drugs* (Rockville, Md.: National Institute on Drug Abuse, 1976), pp. vii–viii.

injected. Cocaine acts on the central nervous system, producing an immediate rush or surge of extremely pleasurable sensations. This is often followed by feelings of "increased altertness and vigor and suppression of hunger, fatigue, and boredom."[11] The effects of cocaine last only a short period of time.

Continued, long-term use of cocaine may have adverse effects, including loss of mental judgment, impulsive behavior, irritability, aggressiveness, paranoia, and hallucinations. However, cocaine users do not require ever increasing dosages in order to "get high." Nor is cocaine known to be physically addictive, though it is thought to produce psychological dependence. It is possible to ingest an overdose of cocaine, and this often produces loss of consciousness and even death.

Extent of cocaine use.   According to the 1977 survey commissioned by the U.S. Department of Health, Education, and Welfare, 6 percent of adults and 4 percent of youngsters have tried the drug.[12] The National Institute of Drug Abuse survey of men aged twenty to thirty found that this group was more likely to have had experience with cocaine than with heroin. Of the men surveyed, 14 percent had used cocaine at some time in their lives, and 7 percent claimed to be current users. The researchers who conducted this survey believed that cocaine use has been increasing.[13]

Legal attempts to combat the cocaine market and discourage use of the drug have met with little success. Indeed, cocaine appears to be the most popular psychoactive substance among wealthy entertainers. Despite the negative social definition bestowed on this drug by the general public, it is a high status substance among many users—no doubt partly because of its high cost.

LSD

LSD, or lysergic acid diethylamide, is derived synthetically from the ergot fungus (a contaminator of rye). It is often referred to as a *hallucinogen* or psychedelic drug in recognition of its special psychoactive qualities, which include its ability to produce experiences akin to hallucinations. Other hallucinogens are mescaline, peyote, and various synthetic substances.

LSD is normally taken orally in tablet or capsule form. Because it is very potent, extremely small dosages are administered. Like many other drugs that are available only from illegal sources, the quality and purity of

[11]National Commission on Marihuana and Drug Abuse, *Drug Use in America*, p. 163.
[12]U.S. Department of Health, Education, and Welfare, *National Survey of Drug Abuse: 1977; Volume 1, Main Findings* (Washington, D.C.: U.S. Government Printing Office, 1978), p. 76.
[13]O'Donnell et al., *Young Men and Drugs*, pp. vii–viii.

the LSD obtained by users often varies. It is not unusual for hallucinogens to be adulterated with other substances, unbeknownst to users.

Effects of LSD use.   LSD works slowly, and users may have to wait for half an hour before they begin to feel the drug. The resulting "trip," which lasts from six to twelve hours, involves altered consciousness and radical transformations of perceptions, emotions, and thoughts. Interviews with a number of LSD users have indicated that ingestion of the drug often produces:

1. Eidetic imagery. Physical objects are seen to be in motion, often in the form of colorful abstract patterns, when one's eyes are closed.
2. Synthesia. All senses are sharpened and occasionally altered so that music is "seen" and colors are "heard."
3. Perception of a multilevel reality. Objects and ideas may be viewed from a variety of perspectives, often simultaneously.
4. Fluidity. The surrounding environment appears to be in a state of constant flux, with shapes ebbing and flowing.
5. Subjective exaggeration. Unusual and detailed visions may occur wherein objects, events, and moods seem extraordinary and monumental.
6. Emotional liability. Sudden and extreme shifts in emotional states may occur, ranging from ecstasy to despair.
7. Feeling of timelessness. A sense of time, and even the meaning of time, may cease to exist.
8. Irrationalism. The forms of logic through which the world is ordinarily interpreted are replaced by new ways to perceive interrelationships and totalities.
9. Ambivalence. Overwhelming perceptions, thoughts, and emotions may be simultaneously experienced as pleasurable and unsettling.[14]

Effects like these have led some observers to label LSD "psychotomimetic"—a drug that causes users to mimic madness or states of psychosis. The only real parallel between LSD trips and psychosis is the loss of touch with reality that characterizes both.

Despite claims that LSD use can cause physical damage, no physiological harm has been found among LSD users that could be traced directly to the drug. Stories of brain damage and genetic harm have not been substantiated by responsible researchers. Nor is the drug physically or psychologically addictive. In fact, those who use LSD frequently often find it difficult to obtain results such as those outlined above.

Users tend to be able to take LSD or leave it, and most limit their use to a few trials. But there are dangers associated with LSD use. One fairly common experience is the "bad trip," in which users experience intense fear and anxiety and may actually panic. Ordinarily, bad trips are of short

[14]Goode, *Drugs in American Society,* pp. 101–9.

duration, and they often can be handled through the calming influence of individuals who are familiar with such drug effects. In more extreme cases, persons have had to be hospitalized until their minds came back into shape. Less frequently, users may experience "flashbacks"—that is, they begin to "trip" again long after the drug has been taken. Finally, because LSD alters perceptions of reality, users have sometimes exposed themselves to physical dangers, and a few have suffered accidental deaths.

Extent of LSD use. According to the National Commission on Marihuana and Drug Abuse, LSD and other hallucinogens "are generally utilized only for 'spree' circumstantial or recreational use."[15] In 1977 the U.S. Department of Health, Education, and Welfare found that 4.6 percent of youth and 6.1 percent of adults have used hallucinogens.[16] It is thought that the use of LSD has declined somewhat in the last few years, largely because of the dangers associated with use and fears about the purity of available LSD. In the meantime, another hallucinogen—PCP or "angel dust"—has become popular. PCP is a synthetic substance and is thought to be extremely hazardous.

As is the case with marijuana, LSD and other hallucinogens are not associated with serious antisocial behavior or criminal acts. The only criminality involved with LSD use is a matter of the illicit status of the drug. Since LSD is relatively easy to manufacture and to conceal, efforts to dismantle the market within which the drug is distributed and sold have met with little success.

Methedrine

Methedrine, or "speed," is a synthetically derived stimulant that acts on the central nervous system. While methedrine and other stimulants are available legally by means of physicians' prescriptions, an estimated 20 percent of those manufactured are annually diverted into the illicit drug market. Their nonmedical uses are subject to negative social definition.

Speed and such other stimulants as amphetamines are said to "produce in the user a feeling of arousal, acuity, excitation, intensity, focus, energy, competence; contrarily they inhibit fatigue and drowsiness."[17] "Speed freaks" often inject large doses of methedrine for the purpose of experiencing its psychoactive effects. An immediate rush of euphoria is ordinarily followed by a period of dramatic hyperactivity. Users feel compelled to be constantly on the go, often walking and talking incessantly.

[15]National Commission on Marihuana and Drug Abuse, *Drug Use in America,* p. 146.
[16]U.S. Department of Health, Education, and Welfare, *National Survey of Drug Abuse,* p. 68.
[17]Goode, *The Drug Phenomenon,* p. 13.

Public Problem, Private Pain
A BAD TRIP

The following selection is from Peter Stafford's book on the "psychedelic generation," the young people of the 1960s and 1970s who sought to alter their consciousness through the use of drugs. Stafford openly approves of such drug use, which he feels is likely to alter American cultural values, boost creativity, and improve interpersonal relations. Whether mind-altering drugs really do have such an impact—and the degree to which this might be the case—are issues open to debate.

On a personal level, drugs may be a source of pleasure and gratification. But, as this selection indicates, experimentation with drugs also has drawbacks. Problems often occur when the user lacks good judgment or is inexperienced in drug use and when the substance in question is of unknown reliability in terms of its effects.

What follows is a statement by a friend of Stafford's who recounts what happened when he was engaging in experimentation with amphetamines.

The time I took an overdose of about twenty times what I should have, I just dumped the powder in my hand, poured it into applejack and drank it down. I'm not a very scientific guy and didn't realize what I was doing.

Nothing happened for a while but then I began to get obsessed with words. I'd take the letter T, for instance, and find that I could talk in words all of which began with T—even the prepositions. I even seemed to be able to communicate rather admirably in this way, like "Tilly Toiler took Tommy Tutmark, tumbled Tommy twice. . . ." After I had done that for a while I'd begin alternating letters, maybe T and S—such as "Tom

saw Tilly smiling. . . ." I couldn't stop. This went on for hours.

Then occurred one of the scariest things that has ever happened to me. I wrote a letter to a girl I was in love with from twelve o'clock noon to twelve o'clock midnight without stopping—for anything, eating or anything. At midnight I took a little fifteen-minute break and then sat down to revise. I revised the first two pages, but then I got to the third page and my mind started going like a stuck record. I just became extremely critical, so that if I made the wrong loop in a P or something I would throw that sheet away. I revised the first paragraph on the third page from about 12:30 till about 2:30. The room was just strewn with paper, each sheet having maybe two or three words on it. And then I began feeling sick.

Bill, my older brother, came in and said, "Jesus Christ, John, you shouldn't have taken so much." He said something about the stuff being able to burn your brains out. And then I thought, "Oh, God, oh no!"

So I went and I lay down, and my head swelled up until it was about six feet across and my fingertips swelled up till they were huge, heavy things. Just kind of overblown thumbs and fingers. I was sure I was going to die, I was absolutely positive. I got up and wrote a lot of notes to friends—along the lines of "Due to . . ." They were slightly maudlin: "Gee, I'm sorry I did this stupid thing. . . ." I even willed some stuff to people—like, "I don't want anyone but Elsa Helmick to read my diary. . . ."

Peter Stafford, *Psychedelic Baby Reaches Puberty* (New York: Praeger Publishers, 1971), pp. 219–20.

After repeatedly taking the drug and experiencing its effects for several days, users are likely to reach a state of physical and mental exhaustion. When administration of the drug is halted, they are likely to "crash" or pass out and sleep for twenty-four hours. Speed freaks take the drug and crash over and over again, often using other drugs to make sleep possible when the effects of the stimulant become too debilitating.

Experts generally agree that this use of stimulants results in both mental and physical harm. Though overdoses are rare, stimulants may be physically addictive if used over a long period. Heavy users may experience withdrawal symptoms, such as fatigue and depression. Health problems—stemming primarily from the frenetic life-styles of users and the tendency of stimulants to depress appetites—are not uncommon. Users often become physically weakened and susceptible to disease and illness.

Users of stimulants have been known to become mentally disturbed and to be troubled by psychoticlike states. Among the effects noted have been paranoia, loss of memory, inability to concentrate, extreme emotional surges, fixations and hallucinations, and a tendency toward violent behavior. But we are not certain whether such psychological conditions stem directly from the action of the drugs themselves or from the sleepless and hectic life-styles of heavy users—or from a combination of the two.

The illegal use of speed and other stimulants seems to be largely limited to adolescents and young adults. The number of users peaked in the 1960s; use then diminished as some of the adverse consequences became more widely recognized. The popular phrase "speed kills" reflects the feeling that the pleasures associated with the use of such drugs may not outweigh the dangers. Nonetheless, the National Institute on Drug Abuse found that 12 percent of men who were twenty to thirty years old in 1974 were current users of powerful stimulants.[18]

LEGAL SUBSTANCES

As we mentioned at the beginning of the chapter, Americans have expressed less concern over the increasing consumption of prescription and over-the-counter drugs than over illegal substances. Periodically, attention is turned to the abuse of legal drugs—as when Betty Ford, wife of former President Gerald Ford, sought treatment for overmedication and problem drinking in 1978. But in general, public concern fades as quickly as it forms.

[18]O'Donnell et al., *Young Men and Drugs,* p. vii.

Table 13.3. Use of Prescription Drugs, Adults Aged Eighteen and Over

Drug	1972	1974	1976	1977	Number, 1977
Ever used for nonmedical purposes					
Stimulants	5.0%	6.0%	7.9%	8.1%	11,973,000
Barbiturates	4.0%	4.0%	4.4%	6.0%	8,869,000
Tranquilizers	6.0%	3.0%	4.0%	4.8%	7,095,000
Ever used for medical purposes					
Stimulants	13.0%	11.0%	13.4%	12.1%	17,886,000
Barbiturates	20.0%	24.0%	20.9%	19.5%	28,825,000
Tranquilizers	24.0%	30.0%	33.7%	34.8%	51,441,000

Source: U.S. Department of Health, Education, and Welfare, *National Survey of Drug Abuse: 1977, Volume 1, Main Findings* (Washington, D.C.: U.S. Government Printing Office, 1978), pp. 5, 96, and 103.

Nature and Extent of Abuse of Legal Drugs

Among the legal drugs being abused by Americans are stimulants, barbiturates, and tranquilizers (see Table 13.3). Stimulants, as we saw in the discussion of methedrine, act on the central nervous system, producing arousal and intense hyperactivity. Methedrine and amphetamines are legal stimulants. Barbiturates and tranquilizers, on the other hand, are *depressants* that act to relax the central nervous system.

Medical practitioners often prescribe depressants for medical reasons—both physical and mental. Such substances generally have a quieting and calming effect on users, dispelling anxiety and facilitating rest and sleep. In small or moderate doses, barbiturates and tranquilizers relax users; in larger doses, they may produce loss of consciousness. Large doses of some depressants—particularly barbiturates—may cause death. A significant number of accidental deaths and suicides are linked to overdoses of depressant drugs. Moreover, barbiturates and many types of tranquilizers are physically addictive for regular users. Withdrawal symptoms are often extremely severe. In some cases, withdrawal can bring about a coma or even result in death.

There is a small illegal market in legal drugs, and some users obtain the substances from it. But far more users buy the drugs legally—by means of a physician's prescription or even off drugstore shelves. According to Henry L. Lennard and his associates, over 200 million prescriptions for psychoactive drugs, all written by physicians, are filled in pharmacies each year.[19] This astounding figure excludes the use of such drugs by hospitals and other health-related institutions. Lennard and his associates express surprise that such facts have not generated more public concern:

> It is difficult to comprehend that the attention of both the public and most officials has centered upon the use of illegal drugs and that the steady,

[19]Henry L. Lennard et al., *Mystification and Drug Use* (San Francisco: Jossey-Bass, Inc., 1971).

marked increase in the giving and taking of legally prescribed or purchased psychoactive drugs has gone relatively unnoticed.[20]

In the view of Lennard and his associates, certain key segments of American society are directly responsible for the increased use of legal psychoactive drugs. These segments are the pharmaceutical industry and the medical profession. As they pursue their own interests, they are creating an "overmedicated society" whose members are unaware of or confused about the dangers of the drugs to which they are exposed.

Drug Producers, Dispensers, and Users

America's pharmaceutical industry has been undergoing sustained growth since the 1950s. It is presently one of the largest and most profitable sectors of the American corporate economy. In order to remain profitable and to keep growing, drug firms constantly seek out new markets for their products and encourage increased use of existing drugs.

Drug firms aim their advertising at the general public and at medical practitioners. Advertising directed at the public is the major means of pushing over-the-counter psychoactive substances, such as nonprescription sleeping aids like Sominex and Nytol. Prescription drugs are advertised in medical journals for America's two hundred thousand physicians. Drug firms also send traveling sales representatives, who are known as "detail men," to physicians' offices. The detail men press for the adoption of new drugs and sing the praises of older ones, leaving behind free samples and advertising brochures. Furthermore, the pharmaceutical industry sponsors displays and programs at medical conventions, where they try to woo physicians and point out or create the need for psychoactive drugs.

The point of the advertising and sales promotion directed at physicians and the general public is to spread the belief that all problems can and should be viewed in medical terms. If people are anxious, depressed, or lacking in vitality, the solution is medication. Since many Americans find it difficult to understand the sources of their discomfort or discontent, people are eager to try such a simple solution.

Medical practitioners are confronted with endless streams of patients, and they want to handle these patients quickly. After all, the more patients a physician sees each day, the higher the physician's annual income. But doctors also want to handle their patients effectively; they want to help people feel better, and they don't want to admit that they cannot. Over half of all persons who seek out physicians' services, it is estimated, have no easily diagnosable physical ailment. Physicians find that prescribing psychoactive drugs is a handy way of dealing with these cases. Not only is the patient usually satisfied, but the credibility of the

[20]Ibid., p. 9.

College students are one of the main targets of advertisements for over-the-counter drugs that help people stay awake, especially around exam time. Though people may feel that over-the-counter psychoactive substances are solving their problems, such drugs may actually keep them from understanding the causes of their discomfort and discontent.

"healing profession" and the doctor's own sense of mastery over his or her craft are sustained.

One outcome is that patients become mystified or confused about their own problems and potential solutions. They are encouraged to feel that psychoactive drugs are the solution to a lack of sense of well-being. But though the emotional pain may be blocked by drugs, as Lennard and his associates note:

> Drugs do not remedy the unfavorable social and interpersonal arrangements and personal circumstances which generate anxiety or unhappiness. Through the creation of chemical barriers and through the diminishment of gross social deviance, drugs may in fact perpetuate malignant patterns and social arrangements. Were drugs not so readily available, pressure for other solutions and the pursuit of alternative options might be encouraged.[21]

Nonetheless, patients gladly accept drugs, just as the medical profession is pleased to be able to "help" patients with unknown ills. Unfortunately, the prescribed psychoactive substances may not only be inappropriate for whatever is causing patients' distress. There may also be hazardous side effects, including chronic dependence on and physical addiction to certain routinely prescribed drugs.

A subtle side effect of reliance on psychoactive drugs is its effect on the

[21]Ibid., pp. 24–5.

nature of the role of the medical profession. To some extent, doctors downplay their role as healers in favor of the role of drug pusher, promoting the view that drugs are an acceptable and effective way of dealing with problems in living. Their assumption of this role is what helps keep the pharmaceutical industry and the medical profession in a state of affluence:

> It is in the interest of both of these groups to maintain large numbers of persons on drugs. . . . It is, moreover, in the interest of both groups to define more and more problems as medical in order to justify both the medical model and the intervention with drugs. [22]

Figures on the use of legal drugs indicate that these economic interests are being effectively served. For example, one recent national survey found that 20 percent of American women had used prescribed tranquilizers or other depressant drugs in the previous year, while almost 10 percent had used prescribed stimulants. It is thought that use of such drugs by women is increasing. Women are more likely than men to turn to physicians when they are troubled, and men are only half as likely as women to be users of prescribed psychoactive drugs. (Men are, however, heavy users of alcohol.) It is notable that the most frequent reason given by users for turning to their physicians for aid was psychological stress. [23]

Despite the hazards they pose, prescribed and over-the-counter psychoactive substances do not carry negative social definitions in American society. Thus, they are rarely considered part of the drug problem. As a consequence, millions of Americans decry the proliferation of "problem drugs" even while seeking to alter their own states of consciousness.

EXPLANATIONS FOR DRUG USE AND ABUSE

Theories about why people turn to psychoactive substances have generally focused on the use of illegal drugs, implying that the abuse of legal drugs is not a matter of concern or is, at least, an entirely different phenomenon. In this section, we will look at some of the theories that have been put forth to explain the use of illegal substances. [24] We will then present an explanation that covers both legal and illegal drug use. Finally, we will analyze a third type of drug use—the involuntary ingestion of psychoactive substances administered for purposes of social control.

[22]Ibid., p. 38.

[23]Glen D. Mellinger et al., "An Overview of Psychotherapeutic Drug Use in the United States," in *Drug Use,* Eric Josephson and Eleanor E. Carroll, eds. (New York: John Wiley & Sons, Inc., 1974), pp. 333–36.

[24]See Joel Fort and Christopher T. Cory, *American Drugstore* (Boston: Little, Brown & Company, 1975), pp. 10–27.

Use of Illegal Drugs

One explanation of why Americans use illegal drugs focuses on the ready availability of drugs and the interests of those who are in a position to benefit financially from their sale. This so-called peddler or seller theory suggests that drug use is a result of the inability of law enforcement agencies to exercise control over supplies of illegal substances and of the ability of sellers to exert wily promotional and sales tactics on innocent nonusers. According to this perspective, users are manipulated and seduced into illegal drug use. But though availability no doubt has something to do with use, and though some persons may be susceptible to "dope peddlers," this explanation is not very persuasive. Research has shown that most individuals do not embark on the use of illegal drugs as a consequence of contact with sellers.

Another explanation—which has been discredited, at least among sociologists—holds that individuals use illegal drugs because there is something mentally or morally wrong with them. According to this theory, "normal" people are not attracted to such drugs even when they are available. Nor do normal people succumb to the alleged influences exerted by sellers. They simply do not need to alter their minds with psychoactive substances. Thus, say proponents of the theory, those who use illegal drugs must have psychological deficiencies, character disorders, or personal maladjustments. There is no credible evidence to support this theory. Illegal drug use is not reducible to the underlying psychological characteristics of a minority of the population. Research has not discovered psychological characteristics that distinguish users from nonusers. (Of course, the *effects* of some illegal drugs may include undesirable mental reactions.) In sum, an explanation that blames the victim is even more untenable than one that places the blame on the seller.

A more far-reaching explanation for illegal drug use focuses upon the place of drugs in American culture. According to Joel Fort:

> We live in a drug-ridden, drug-saturated society, in which from infancy we have been taught to accept and live the industrial slogan of "Better Living Through Chemistry." We are taught that there is a pill, a drink, or a cigarette for every real or imagined pain, trouble, or problem, and that the more of these substances we use, the better off we will be.[25]

In such a society, according to proponents of this theory, people will use illegal drugs when they have the opportunity to do so.

This explanation has a nice ring to it, but it is overly deterministic. People are not automotons who react to pains, troubles, or problems by taking drugs. Drug use involves a decision—there are, after all, other ways to react to problems. Moreover, this explanation does not address the question of why most Americans continue to shun illegal substances, even while using many that are legal. On the other hand, there is evi-

[25]Fort, *The Pleasure Seekers*, p. 194.

dence that the ready availability and widespread use of legal drugs (including alcohol and tobacco products) makes it more likely that individuals will use illegal substances:

> Users of illegal drugs tend to become recruited out of segments of society that use legal drugs. . . . Abstainers from alcohol, cigarettes, and prescription drugs stand a relatively low likelihood of experimenting with illegal drugs.[26]

This is not to say that the use of legal substances *causes* illegal drug use. Instead, it merely means that there is a correlation between the two. For example, aspirin users are more likely to smoke marijuana than nonaspirin users. But most aspirin users do not do so.

Most recent sociological explanations emphasize that illegal drug use is learned behavior. Specifically, people learn appropriate attitudes and modes of behavior favorable to drug use through social intercourse. For example, there is evidence that parents exert some influence over their children's attitudes toward drug use.[27] The main finding to date is that the children of parents who are themselves users of legal or illegal psychoactive substances are more likely to use illegal drugs than the children of drug abstainers. It is believed that friends and peers play a far more important role than parents. Rarely will parents actually introduce their children into the use of illegal drugs; peer associations and influence perform this function.[28]

The importance of being inducted into the use of illegal drugs was underscored over twenty years ago by sociologist Howard Becker. According to Becker, marijuana users (who, at that time, comprised a comparatively small number of persons) provided assurances to potential users that the drug was safe and worthwhile. In other words, those who already smoked the drug helped convert the neophytes to their view of the drug. Moreover, neophyte users had to be taught exactly how to smoke marijuana, what effects they should expect, and how they should perceive and react to these effects.[29] Obviously, people are most likely to embark into such activity with those they know and trust—their friends and peers.

Sociologists generally agree that becoming a user of illegal drugs involves being a member of and identifying with a group of people who are already users. Participation with others in an illegal and, hence, secret activity may also help cement interpersonal relationships. Group members have something in common with one another, and those who do not use illegal drugs may be viewed as "outsiders." Though Becker's work

[26]Goode, *The Drug Phenomenon,* p. 22.

[27]See Richard H. Blum et al., *Horatio Alger's Children* (San Francisco: Jossey-Bass, Inc., 1972).

[28]See Bruce D. Johnson, *Marihuana Users and Drug Subcultures* (New York: John Wiley & Sons, Inc., 1973).

[29]Howard S. Becker, "Becoming a Marihuana User," *American Journal of Sociology,* 59 (November 1953): 235–42.

deals primarily with marijuana use, more recent investigations suggest that the influence of friends and peers is of importance in explaining the use of illegal drugs in general.[30]

But this explanation does not completely get at the heart of the matter. Though it tells us how people learn to become drug users, it does not explain what users of psychoactive substances—both illegal and legal—are really seeking to accomplish. Only by changing our focus from drug users to society in general can we get at an answer to that question.

Drug Abuse and Social Conditions

In the view of sociologist John Clausen, both the legal and illegal use of psychoactive drugs may be interpreted as

> an aspect or manifestation of a much more general social problem. If substantial numbers of persons find it necessary to use drugs in order to feel comfortable, or if their lives are lacking in meaning and they therefore turn to drugs to provide it, the problem is less in the drugs than in the way of life that has been afforded them.[31]

Clausen's comments suggest that America's recent concern with drug abuse and the drug problem is misplaced in terms of its focus on the illegal substances of the moment and on users. The important questions are rarely brought up in public debate. What is it about American society that makes so many people seek out and accept the effects of psychoactive substances? What is it about this society and "the way of life that has been afforded" its members that renders the pursuit of altered states of consciousness preferable to nondrugged participation in the prevailing order?

As with mental illness, alcoholism, and suicide, widespread drug use may occur because many people are subjected to harmful social conditions. Drug use may be one of a variety of responses troubled people use to cope with problems in living. Psychoactive drugs must be available before they can be used. They must be introduced to nonusers—be it by peers, physicians, or peddlers (a category that includes the pharmaceutical industry). But once such substances are available and introduced, many people grasp onto them as palliatives for ills that may really be societal, not personal.

The tragedy is that drugs are false palliatives, for their use leaves the ultimate sources of peoples' troubles untouched. In the words of Theodore Roszak, drug use "is simply another safety valve. If anything, it allows one to bear up under any grim business-as-usual with a bit less

---

[30]See Johnson, *Marihuana Users and Drug Subcultures.*

[31]John A. Clausen, "Drug Use," in *Contemporary Social Problems,* 4th ed., Robert K. Merton and Robert Nisbet, eds. (New York: Harcourt, Brace, Jovanovich, Inc., 1976), p. 145.

anxiety."[32] Psychoactive substances, Roszak observes, function much like the "soma" described in Aldous Huxley's science fiction novel, *Brave New World,* which helped make otherwise unbearable existences bearable.[33]

Drugs and Social Control

The Brave New World Huxley described was a politically repressive society of social unequals. Drugs were made available to the populace so that rulers could wield their power without the danger of rebellious disruption. The Brave New World was a fictional society, but its use of drugs for social control reflects real-life developments.

The American public has become aware of the use of psychoactive substances for social control through news stories like the one in 1970 that reported that children were being subjected to drug control. In Omaha, Nebraska, for example, 5 to 10 percent of the sixty-two thousand children enrolled in school were ingesting psychoactive substances prescribed by local physicians. These children had been designated by school personnel as hyperactive and disruptive to school routine, and the drugs were intended to make them more manageable.[34] It appears that thousands of children around the country have been learning "Better Living Through Chemistry" during the earliest years of their lives—with parental blessings.

Similar practices are routine in mental hospitals, prisons, and nursing homes. In their report to the Ford Foundation, Patricia M. Wald and Peter Barton Hutt noted the "emerging problem" of the "overprescription of drugs to control the behavior of captive populations" in such settings.[35] For example, Wald and Hutt documented the extensive use of drugs "on elderly patients in nursing homes to keep them from clamoring for the attention of overworked attendants."[36] These researchers predicted that "as the range of behavior-controlling drugs becomes wider, we can anticipate even greater problems in their use in unwarranted situations."[37]

Most studies of drug use in the United States barely mention the ways in which drugs are used for political purposes. The powerless are being subjected to chemical manipulation—students, not teachers; inmates,

[32]Theodore Roszak, *The Making of a Counter Culture* (Garden City, N.Y.: Anchor Books, 1969), pp. 176–77.
[33]Aldous Huxley, *Brave New World* (London: Chatto & Windus, 1970).
[34]Lennard et al., *Mystification and Drug Use,* p. 110.
[35]Patricia M. Wald and Peter Barton Hutt, "The Drug Abuse Survey Project," in *Dealing with Drug Abuse,* Patricia M. Wald et al., eds. (New York: Praeger Publishers, Inc., 1972), p. 11.
[36]Ibid.
[37]Ibid., p. 12.

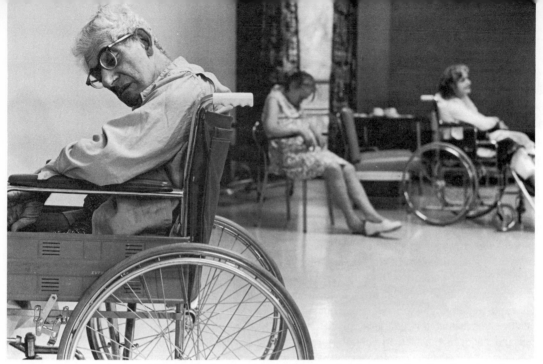

Many nursing homes and other institutions feed drugs to patients in order to keep them from making demands on staff members' time and attention. Practices like this not only infringe upon the rights of individuals but may also have serious medical consequences.

not guards or caretakers; old people, not those who administer the institutions in which the dying eke out their final days. As Howard Becker has observed:

> When the one administering the drug has sufficient control over the user, he can safely ignore the other's interests altogether, and his actions can be designed solely to serve his own interests, personal or (more likely) organizational. [38]

Administrators in charge of schools, hospitals, prisons, and nursing homes find drugs to be a useful tool for the efficient processing of large numbers of people. They are the ones who claim that the best interests of those subject to such chemical pollution are simultaneously being served. The interests of the powerless are being defined from above.

In recent years, drugs have become part of the technology of American military and intelligence forces. The American military has developed the capacity to conduct chemical and biological warfare on an international scale. [39] We know how to use drugs to precipitate death, frightening diseases, and temporary incapacitation among our enemies. During the war in Vietnam, for example, chemical defoliants destroyed vegetation with dangerous consequences to the health of Vietnamese soldiers and

[38]Howard S. Becker, "Consciousness, Power, and Drug Effects," *Society,* 10 (May-June 1973): 31.

[39]See Seymour Hersh, *Chemical and Biological Warfare* (Indianapolis: The Bobbs-Merrill Co., Inc., 1968).

civilians and American military personnel who were directly exposed. Various gases incapacitated persons judged to be members or supporters of enemy forces. Napalm burned many people to death and horribly disfigured others. These substances were never called "drugs," but that was only because of the absence of a social definition. Whatever you wish to call them, their effects on human life and consciousness were a preview of the chemical and biological weapons that might someday turn the world into a grotesque wasteland.

The use of drugs by such American intelligence forces as the Central Intelligence Agency borders on the bizarre. To take but one instructive example, investigations by the news media and Congressional hearings in 1977 revealed that the CIA had set up a secret drug experimentation program in 1953.[40] The purpose of this program, code named MK-Ultra, was to learn how to control the human mind. Presumably this knowledge would be used against foreign enemies. For over twenty years, using $25 million in tax funds, the CIA paid for projects conducted by researchers in eighty-six institutions—including colleges and universities, hospitals, prisons, and pharmaceutical companies.

The CIA-sponsored projects included LSD experiments with federal prison inmates and college students, experimentation with tranquilizers and alcohol on inmates and staff of mental hospitals, and the use of a "knockout" drug on unwitting terminally ill cancer patients. The CIA set up special apartments where researchers could observe the effects of LSD and marijuana on unsuspecting men who had been lured to the apartments from bars. A professional magician was employed to write a manual on the use of sleight of hand and how to secretly slip drugs into drinks. No efforts were made to contact the subjects of experiments later to see whether or how their well-being was affected. The American military is known to have conducted similar experiments on members of the armed forces.

This kind of activity has not been limited to research conducted out of concern with foreign enemies. In 1976 the news media discovered that conspirators involved in the Nixon administration's Watergate scandal had planned to slip a psychoactive drug to Jack Anderson, a columnist critical of President Nixon and his staff. They hoped that Anderson would experience the effects of the drug at a public speaking engagement and make a fool of himself. The plot fell through only because the conspirators failed to get hold of a drug.

There are many more issues regarding drug use in America. Among these issues are the pharmaceutical industry's use of American prisoners and foreign populations as guinea pigs for testing new and occasionally lethal drugs and the sale to other countries of drugs too dangerous to be licensed in the United States. These and other sordid drug-related mat-

---

[40]See "Mind-Bending Disclosures; CIA Testing," *Time*, August 15, 1977, p. 9; and Tad Szulc, "CIA's Electric Kool-Aid Acid Test," *Psychology Today*, 11 (November 1977): 92–4 ff.

ters are part of the drug problem that continues to plague our society.

Clearly, not all the substances we call drugs are harmful. Many drugs, moreover, are known to have extremely beneficial effects. One need only consider the many substances that have helped wipe out serious illness and disease and that have helped prolong people's lives. Drugs are tools that may either be used to enhance human well-being or to harm it. As we begin to learn more about the harmful uses to which drugs are being put—and about the *social* implications of such uses—Americans may begin to react against those forces that have led us to become the "over-medicated society."

SUMMARY

The term *drug* is presently subject to a wide variety of meanings and uses—scientific, medical, and legal. In actuality, there is no single quality that would distinguish substances designated as drugs from nondrugs. Any and all substances that are designated as drugs are socially defined as such. So-called problem drugs (for example, marijuana and heroin) differ from other drug and nondrug substances in that they have a different and more negative social definition. Social definitions frequently change with time, and different groups commonly disagree over such definitions.

Among the most used problem drugs are marijuana, heroin, cocaine, LSD, and methedrine. Marijuana is the most widely used illegal substance in the United States. Less public concern has been expressed over the increasing consumption of legal prescription and over-the-counter psychoactive drugs than over illegal substances. The forces underlying increased consumption include the pharmaceutical industry, which constantly seeks out new markets and encourages increased use of existing drugs, and medical practitioners, who often prescribe psychoactive drugs to patients who have no easily diagnosable physical ailment. Many people have come to believe that drug-taking is an acceptable and effective way of dealing with problems in living. Despite the hazards they pose, prescribed and over-the-counter drugs are rarely considered part of America's drug problem.

There are a number of explanations for why people use psychoactive drugs. Illegal drug use has been said to stem from manipulation of people by drug pushers, moral or mental weaknesses of users, and a cultural environment that extols drug use in general. Each of these explanations is open to criticism. Most recent sociological explanations emphasize that illegal drug use is learned behavior. Peers, and to a lesser extent parents, are important influences and sources of knowledge about drug use. Widespread use of both illegal and legal psychoactive substances may be a response to harmful societal conditions, a false palliative but nonetheless one that helps make an otherwise unbearable existence bearable.

Recently, concern has been expressed over the use of drugs for social control purposes. Drugs have been administered to schoolchildren, inmates of mental hospitals and prisons, and elderly persons in nursing homes. Drugs have been used to make such persons more "manageable." Political use of drugs extends to American military and intelligence forces.

Not all drugs are harmful, and many are known to have extremely beneficial effects. Drugs may be used to heighten human well-being or to thwart it.

DISCUSSION QUESTIONS

1. What arguments could be made for and against legalizing all so-called problem drugs and leaving the choice of use up to individuals?
2. In certain settings, such as mental hospitals, persons may be made to take drugs even if they do not want to. Imagine that you are in such a situation, and present reasons why you should not be made to take drugs involuntarily.
3. During the Prohibition Era, alcoholic beverages were produced, distributed, and consumed widely even though this was illegal. Prohibition laws were repealed largely because they could not be enforced. Speculate on the likelihood and the desirability of similar law changes relating to marijuana.
4. Obtain copies of several medical journals, and read the advertisements for psychoactive drugs. What might be said about the content of these advertisements? Are the sources of the problems to which they are directed necessarily medical?
5. Go to your local drugstore, and conduct an inventory of all over-the-counter products that allegedly will pep you up or calm you down. Record their advertising claims. Develop arguments for and against the passage of a law that would bar such substances from purchase without a prescription.
6. Visit a drug rehabilitation center or other agency that deals with victims of drug abuse. On the basis of discussions with clients, assess the role of drugs in their lives and the reasons they became drug abusers. Compare your findings with those of other class members.

Social Problems: A Critical Approach

Picture Credits

Glossary

A bility groups Groups to which students are assigned in school, usually on the basis of test results, in which they receive differential treatment. (p. 143)

Absolute poverty Material deprivation so severe that survival often becomes an issue. (p. 44)

Academic boot camp A phrase used by Harry L. Gracey to refer to kindergartens in which children are expected to learn the role of student. (p. 94)

Academic track A school curriculum designed to prepare students for additional study beyond high school, rather than to teach them specific job skills. (p. 103)

Addiction Heavy physical and/or psychological dependence on a drug substance. (p. 413)

Aerospace/defense industry A segment of the economy that produces goods and services for use by the armed forces and space program. (pp. 197–99)

Affective disorder Within the medical model, a form of mental illness involving the inappropriate expression of feelings or emotions. (p. 333)

Affective education An educational approach wherein children are encouraged to understand their own and others' feelings and their manner of relating to other people. (p. 116)

Affirmative action Employment and admissions policies that are intended to remedy and offset past discrimination against members of minority groups. (p. 151)

Alcoholic personality So-called personality traits that predispose persons to become alcoholics. (p. 394)

Alcoholism The use of and dependence on alcohol to the point where one's behavior becomes self-harmful and/or harmful to others. (p. 392)

Alienation A sense of estrangement from one or another aspect of the prevailing social order. (pp. 80–81, 338)

Altruistic suicide According to Émile Durkheim, a type of suicide in which persons sacrifice their lives for others. (p. 369)

American Dream A phrase that refers to the American cultural goal of material success and affluence. (p. 250)

Americanization The process of becoming familiar with and adapting to American culture. (pp. 8, 90)

Anomic suicide According to Émile Durkheim, a type of suicide caused by the absence of guidelines for feelings and inclinations. (p. 370)

Anomie A condition in which individuals are without norms to govern their actions. See *anomie theory*. (p. 10)

Anomie theory An explanation for deviant behavior developed by Robert K. Merton, in which deviance is seen as arising from the inability of persons to live by and/or their failure to internalize norms governing the pursuit of material success. See *conformist; innovation; rebellion; retreatism; ritualism.* (pp. 10, 316)

Attempted suicide An unsuccessful effort to kill oneself. (pp. 373–75)

Attribution See *personal attribution; systemic attribution.*

Automation The process of introducing machines to do the work of people or of introducing complex machines to do the work of people and simpler machines. (pp. 259–60)

B iology is destiny The belief that nature has decreed that males and females should play quite different roles in social life. (pp. 160–61)

Black Power The idea that black people should control those community institutions that affect their lives. (p. 150)

Blaming the victim The practice of suggesting that those who face problems in living are themselves at fault. (p. 47)

Blue-collar jobs Jobs primarily calling for manual skills. (p. 270)

Brain drain The large-scale shift of scientific and technical talent from one location or area of activity to another. (p. 208)

Bureaucracy An organizational entity characterized by a clear-cut division of labor, a hierarchy of authority, formal rules and regulations, rationality, and a system of rewards. (p. 255)

C apitalism An economic system in which the means of production (e.g., factories, farms, transportation systems) are largely privately owned. (p. 31)

Class See *social class.*

Competitive individualism A component of American culture that stresses competition for material success and the notion that all individuals can be successful if they really try. (p. 41)

Conflict theory of legal change A theory developed by William Chambliss suggesting that law, which determines what behavior is to be treated as criminal, is the outcome of conflicts between classes and between different interest groups. (pp. 291–92)

Conformist A person who pursues cultural goals of material success through socially acceptable means. See *anomie theory.* (p. 10)

Consciousness raising A process wherein persons sensitive to sexism encourage such sensitivity in others. (p. 180)

Containment theory A psychological explanation for criminal behavior that suggests that crimes occur when people are not subject to social pressures condemning criminal acts and/or when they lack inner controls over their behavior. (pp. 315–16)

Cooling out process   School testing and counseling practices that influence students to lower their academic aspirations. (p. 113)

Corporate capitalism   A capitalist economy that is dominated by very large business enterprises. (p. 202)

Counterinsurgency warfare   The use of specialized tactics in order to thwart the activities of guerrillas and their supporters. (p. 206)

Crime   According to the legal definition, acts that are against the law. According to the popular definition, acts that different people may or may not look upon as illegal. (pp. 289–91)

Crime rates   The ratio between the number of crimes known to have been committed and population size (e.g., murders per 100,000 people). (pp. 294–95)

Criminal justice system   A system composed of the police, courts, and correctional institutions. (p. 320)

Critical approach   An approach to the study of social problems that views the organization and operation of society as problematic. (pp. 12–16)

Culture   A society's way of life, including ideas, practices, and material products that are passed on to subsequent generations. (p. 7)

Culture conflict   A process wherein people must adapt to a new culture while trying to retain all or some of their traditional ways of life. (p. 8)

Decriminalization   A change in the legal definition of an act in which a serious crime is redefined as a lesser offense. (p. 414)

Democracy   A political system based on the consent of the governed, in which important decisions reflect the will of the majority. (p. 60)

Depressant   A drug substance that has a temporary soothing or calming effect. (p. 424)

Detoxification   Medical treatment aimed at eliminating alcohol from the body of an alcoholic. (p. 404)

Deviance   See *deviant behavior.*

Deviant behavior   Behavior that is judged to be counter to prevailing norms. (p. 7)

Dictatorial   A political system in which the power of the state is absolute. (p. 60)

Differential association theory   A psychological explanation for criminal behavior that suggests that criminality is learned during the course of communication and interaction with criminals and delinquents. (p. 315)

Discrimination   Unequal treatment of individuals based on, for example, their racial or sex group membership. (p. 124)

Division of labor   A system of occupational roles within a group or society. (p. 250)

Domino theory   The idea that if one nation moves from capitalism to socialism, other nations will also do so. (p. 207)

Ecocatastrophe   The destruction of the ecosystem. (p. 221)

Ecological zones   Sectors of a community that differ in terms of people's socioeconomic status, life-styles, and patterns of interaction. (p. 8)

Ecology   The interrelationships among living organisms and between such organisms and their nonliving surroundings. (p. 220)

Economic inequality   The unequal distribution of wealth and income. (pp. 30–56)

Economy of death   A phrase used by Richard Barnet to describe an economy in which war-related expenditures and production play an important role. (p. 277)

Ecosystem   A network comprised of living organisms and their nonliving surroundings. (p. 220)

Egoistic suicide   According to Émile Durkheim, a type of suicide caused by the absence of meaningful social relationships or a sense of belonging. (p. 369)

Elites   Persons who hold the most powerful and/or prestigious positions in their chosen fields of endeavor. (p. 69)

Employer of the last resort   A phrase referring to the idea that government should find ways to employ members of the labor force in the absence of work opportunities. (p. 278)

Engineering mentality   A phrase used by Gene Marine to refer to the state of mind of those whose use of land resources is governed by financial and technical considerations, not by interest in the well-being of the ecosystem. (p. 232)

Entrepreneur   A person who undertakes to run an enterprise, such as a business. (p. 136)

Environment   See *physical environment; social environment.*

Environmental abuse   Harm done to the ecosystem as a result of human activities. (p. 221)

Ethnic group   People who see themselves as sharing a common cultural tradition and a sense of identity that places them apart from other societal members. (p. 8)

Euthanatic suicide   A phrase used by Jacques Choron to refer to suicide undertaken to avoid impending agony and death. (p. 378)

Fatalistic suicide   According to Émile Durkheim, a type of suicide caused by a sense of overmanipulation or hopelessness about altering life conditions. (p. 370)

Federal chartering   The idea of having business enterprises get licensed by the federal government before they may operate. (p. 246)

Functional psychosis   Within the medical model, a serious form of mental illness in which there is no known physical reason for the symptoms displayed. (p. 333)

Gatekeeper   As applied to education, the role played by schools in guiding people into another level of the social-class hierarchy or keeping them at the same level. (p. 100)

Gerrymandering   The alteration of voting district boundaries in order to influence the outcome of elections. (p. 139)

Ghettoization   Segregation and isolation of a group of people on the basis of their ethnic or racial group membership. (p. 145)

GNP   See *Gross National Product.*

Governing class perspective   A perspective developed by G. William Domhoff that holds that political power is largely controlled by persons coming from the most socially prestigious and economically privileged backgrounds. (pp. 74–77)

Grass roots   A term referring to self-initiated, organized movements involving the common citizenry. (pp. 82–83)

Greenhouse effect   Pollution-related increases in worldwide temperatures. (p. 223)

Gross National Product   The total value of goods and services produced in a society in a given year. (p. 30)

Hallucinogen   A psychoactive drug that may produce sensations resembling hallucinations. (p. 419)

Hidden curriculum   Ways of thinking and behaving that are encouraged in school apart from what is taught in formal lessons. (p. 92)

Ideology   A set of ideas by means of which people rationalize and justify their particular interests, goals, and practices. (p. 17)

Impression management   Behavior designed to influence other people to hold particular opinions about one. (p. 353)

Incidence   The number of new cases occurring over time. (p. 329)

Index offenses   Serious crimes on which the Federal Bureau of Investigation compiles statistics: criminal homicide, forcible rape, robbery, aggravated assault, burglary, larceny, and motor vehicle theft. (p. 298)

Individualized instruction   An educational practice wherein children work at their own individual pace at different tasks and are monitored for progress. (p. 116)

Industrialization   A process involving changes in the organization of society due to the introduction of machinery to produce goods and commodities on a mass scale. (p. 2)

Inequality   See *economic inequality.*

Informal organization   Spontaneous interpersonal relations and group formations, for example, within a bureaucracy. (p. 256)

Innovation   A mode of behavior wherein people pursue cultural goals of material success in socially unacceptable ways (i.e., through deviant behavior). See *anomie theory.* (p. 10)

Institution   Organizational arrangements created by people to perform certain services or functions within and for society. (p. 126)

Institutional racism   The routine operations of societal institutions as they work to the disadvantage of racial or ethnic minority groups. (pp. 126–27)

Institutional sexism   The routine operations of societal institutions as they work to the disadvantage of females. (p. 160)

Interest group   A body of people sharing common concerns who act to express these concerns and influence policy in the direction of their self-defined interests. (p. 62)

Juvenile delinquency   Law violation by persons who are not legally defined as adults. (p. 290)

Labeling   The process through which individuals are socially categorized and often stigmatized by labels bestowed by others. (pp. 339–41)

Labeling theory   An approach to explaining criminal and other forms of deviant behavior that focuses on the conditions under which individuals are designated as deviant by others and the impact of such labeling on the individuals' behavior. (p. 319)

Labor force   As defined by the federal government, persons sixteen years of age or over (except those in institutions) who are employed full- or part-time or who are actively seeking employment. (p. 257)

Life cycle of social problems   The stages wherein a phenomenon is considered problematic, is brought to the realm of public debate over causes and possible solutions, and is subjected to attempted solution. (pp. 16–22)

Limited warfare   Warfare conducted with conventional (nonnuclear) weaponry. (p. 205)

Macro problems   Key features of society that are problematic because they harm millions of people. (pp. 14–15)

Mala in se   Wrong in and of itself. (p. 289)

Male chauvinism   Attitudes and actions through which individual males display their sense of superiority over females. (p. 159)

Managerial approach to environmental abuse Efforts to measure and regulate harm done to the ecosystem rather than allowing the laws of the ecosystem to regulate human activities. (p. 245)

Marketability   The ability of persons to find demands for their labor in the labor market. (p. 34)

Massification   The outcome of elite domination over mass society. (p. 72)

Massive retaliation   The threat of the use of nuclear weaponry, a threat assumed to act as a deterrent to enemy attack. (p. 205)

Mass society   A large and diverse population which, lacking organization, becomes subject to manipulation by elites. (p. 72)

Medical model An approach to the mentally troubled in which such persons are considered ill and in need of treatment within a medical context. (pp. 332–33)

Mental illness Within the medical model, expressions of thought and behavior that are said to be caused by ailments of the mind. (pp. 332–35)

Micro problems Behaviors on the part of individuals that harm other people and/or are self-harmful. (pp. 15–16)

Middle management Employees whose responsibilities include authority over lower-level supervisory personnel and/or professional staff. (p. 274)

Militarism The propensity to use force or the threat of force in the conduct of relations with other nations and/or in the suppression of perceived internal enemies. (pp. 190–214)

Military-industrial complex According to Richard Barnet, a system made up of the uniformed military, the aerospace/defense industry, national security managers in the civilian government, and Congress. (pp. 190–91)

Minority group A category of people that is subject to subordination and discrimination, e.g., certain racial and ethnic groups and women. (pp. 122–24, 158)

Missions As used by the military, programs of operations against an enemy. (p. 194)

Mobility See *social mobility*.

Moral entrepreneurs Individuals or groups with particular moral concerns that they wish to have reflected in public policy. (p. 292)

Mortification According to Erving Goffman, the process by which peoples' self-concepts are attacked within total institutions; the molding of inmates' ways of thinking and behaving to conform to staff members' expectations. (p. 349)

Multinational firms Business enterprises whose operations extend into other countries, usually to market goods and services or to take advantage of low-cost labor and material resources. (p. 202)

Nationalization Governmental takeover of privately owned properties (e.g., business enterprises). (p. 213)

National security managers A phrase used by Richard Barnet to refer to civilian governmental elites who fashion foreign and military policies. (pp. 199–200)

Near-poor A category of people whose incomes are so low that any slight drop would place them below the poverty line. (p. 46)

Negative Income Tax A proposed tax aimed at the redistribution of income so that a minimum income would be provided to all needy individuals and families. (pp. 54–55)

Net worth tax A proposed tax on the wealth of millionaire families that would allow tax reductions for nonaffluent people who save money. (p. 55)

Neurosis Within the medical model, a form of mental illness in which symptoms reflect underlying anxiety. (pp. 334–35)

New working class White-collar workers whose occupations are conducted under conditions analogous to those of blue-collar workers. (p. 274)

Noise A phrase used by Jules Henry to refer to what children learn in school aside from the formal subject matter taught. (p. 96)

Norm A rule or standard that defines what is socially acceptable behavior. (p. 7)

Normlessness A state in which norms to guide behavior are absent or in which an individual has failed to internalize existing norms. (p. 7)

Nuclear fallout Radioactive debris that travels through the air, e.g., as a consequence of nuclear explosions. (p. 226)

Officer class Career officers in the uniformed military. (p. 193)

Open classroom A school classroom situation that typically allows children freedom to talk and move about and a range of choices of learning tasks. (pp. 115–16)

Open enrollment A policy that allows all persons possessing the minimally required credentials to enroll in an educational program or institution of their choice. (p. 113)

Opportunity structure Avenues within society through which individuals or groups may strive to attain cultural success goals. (p. 10)

Organic psychosis Within the medical model, a form of mental illness caused by brain damage or chemical imbalances. (p. 333)

Organization child Phrase used by Rosabeth Moss Kanter to refer to a child who is most comfortable when those in authority provide supervision, guidance, and roles to be fulfilled. (p. 93)

Overmedicated society A phrase used by Charlotte Muller to refer to the massive use of legal, as well as illegal, psychoactive drugs by societal members. (p. 410)

Ownership class Roughly, the richest 1 percent of the population in terms of wealth and income. (p. 32)

Paramilitary A term referring to semi- or near-military organization and operation. (p. 210)

Peddler theory An explanation for illegal drug use that blames such use on those who peddle or sell drugs. (p. 428)

Peer group A close, intimate group whose members share a common status or set of characteristics. (p. 94)

Pentagon capitalism Seymour Melman's phrase referring to the relationship between the aerospace/defense industry and the Department of Defense wherein the former receives contracts for goods and services under highly favorable conditions. (pp. 197–99)

Per capita   Per person. (p. 384)

Permanent war economy   Seymour Melman's name for an economy in which war-related expenditures and production play an important role, even during periods of peace. (p. 193)

Personal attribution   Attributing the causes of a phenomenon that is deemed problematic to the faults and deficiencies of individuals. (p. 19)

Personal obsolescence   A sense or state of being obsolete—of no use or value. (p. 96)

Personal racism   Individuals' expressions of negative feelings toward persons who are members of racial or ethnic minority groups. (pp. 124–26)

Physical environment   Natural surroundings that are not of human creation. (pp. 220–21)

Physiological explanations   Explanations emphasizing the impact of genetic or biological qualities on human behavior. (pp. 312–14)

Plea bargaining   A practice in which prosecutors offer those accused of crimes the opportunity to plead guilty to a lesser offense. (p. 321)

Pluralist perspective   The view that political power is widely dispersed among competing interest groups, rather than concentrated in the hands of a few groups or individuals. (pp. 60–62)

Political socialization   The process of learning how to view and participate in the political system. (pp. 60, 98–100)

Post-industrial society   A society whose economy is primarily oriented around the provision of services, rather than manufacturing or agriculture. (pp. 251–53)

Poverty   A situation in which people do not possess a means of subsistence capable of providing a secure and adequate standard of living and are, moreover, deprived in comparison to other people in the society. See also *absolute poverty; relative poverty.* (pp. 43–46)

Power   The probability that individuals or groups can implement their desires even though they may be resisted. (p. 20)

Power elite perspective   A perspective developed by C. Wright Mills claiming that political power is concentrated in the hands of those holding top positions in the corporate world, the military, and the executive branch of the federal government. (pp. 69–72)

Prejudice   A negative attitude toward a category of people who allegedly possess undesirable traits. (p. 124)

Presenting culture   According to Erving Goffman, the taken-for-granted ways of life that persons bring with them as they enter a total institution. (p. 349)

Prevalence   The total number of cases existing at a given time. (p. 329)

Primary labor market   That sector of the labor market consisting of the higher-paying, more secure, and most desirable occupations. (p. 131)

Primary sector   That part of the economy devoted to agriculture. (p. 251)

Problem drinking   The use of alcohol to the point where it adversely affects one's ability to function and/or one's relationships with others. Alcoholism may be considered an extreme form of problem drinking. (p. 391)

Problem drug   A drug substance that is socially defined as having harmful or undesirable effects. (p. 411)

Prodromal clues   According to Edwin S. Shneidman, signals or cues provided by potentially suicidal individuals concerning their self-destruction. (p. 376)

Pseudopatient   A person who feigns illness in a treatment setting. (p. 335)

Psychedelic drug   See *hallucinogen.*

Psychoactive drug   A substance that may affect the minds of those who introduce it into their bodily systems. (p. 412)

Psychoanalytic explanations   Explanations for deviant behavior based on Sigmund Freud's theory of the personality, wherein the development of the personality is thought to affect social behavior. (p. 314)

Psychological explanations   Explanations emphasizing the impact of mental processes or personality traits on human behavior. (pp. 314–16)

Psychosis   Within the medical model, a form of serious mental illness characterized by the inability to recognize and function within existing reality. (pp. 333–34)

Psychotomimetic drug   A substance that may cause users to engage in behavior similar to the behavior of so-called psychotics. (p. 420)

Public issue   In the life cycle of social problems, a phenomenon that is judged problematic and becomes a legitimate subject for public debate over its causes and possible solutions. (p. 17)

Public welfare   See *welfare.*

Racism   A set of ideas and practices through which people subordinate others whose racial background is held to be inferior. See *institutional racism; personal racism.* (pp. 124–27)

Radical feminists   A segment of the women's movement that includes two groups: those who define men as an enemy, and those who see capitalism as promoting sexism. (p. 180)

Rates   See *crime rates.*

Rational suicide   Term used by Jacques Choron for suicide by persons who are mentally normal and whose motives may be considered justifiable. (pp. 377–78)

Rebellion   A mode of behavior wherein people attempt to change both the cultural goals of material success and the means by which success is pursued. See *anomie theory.* (p. 10)

Reductionism   The view that social behavior can best be explained in terms of biological or psychological factors. (p. 313)

Reinforcement theory   A psychological explanation for criminal behavior that suggests that people learn to engage in or to avoid such behavior in response to rewards or punishments. (p. 315)

Relative poverty   Material deprivation in comparison to others. (p. 44)

Residual deviance   According to Thomas Scheff, extremely unusual behavior that violates norms and is not easily categorized. (p. 339)

Resocialization   A process in which individuals are encouraged to abandon prior ways of thinking and behaving in favor of the new ways required by new social roles. (p. 351)

Retreatism   A mode of behavior wherein people reject or abandon cultural goals of material success along with the socially acceptable means of pursuing these goals. See *anomie theory*. (p. 10)

Revisionist historians   Historians who reexamine conventional interpretations of history and whose writings tend to emphasize the role of social class and economic forces in creating stability and change. (pp. 89–90)

Ritualism   A mode of behavior wherein people adhere to socially acceptable means of pursuing cultural goals of material success but lower their success aspirations. See *anomie theory*. (p. 10)

Role   A pattern of social behavior that is defined largely by the expectations of other people. (p. 7)

Sanction   A punishment or reward that is intended to thwart or elicit a particular behavior. (p. 126)

Schizophrenia   Within the medical model, a serious type of psychosis in which the mentally ill individual cannot recognize and cope with reality. (p. 333)

Secondary labor market   That sector of the labor market that consists of the lower-paying, least secure, and most undesirable jobs. (p. 131)

Secondary sector   That part of the economy devoted to manufacturing. (p. 251)

Segregation   Voluntary or involuntary separation of people on the basis of, for example, race or sex. (p. 142)

Self-fulfilling prophecy   A process wherein people believe and act as if a situation were real, thereby helping create a reality that coincides with their beliefs. (p. 108)

Self-report studies   Research studies that focus on determining the extent to which people have committed crimes, ordinarily by asking them to admit to any past criminal behavior. (p. 297)

Seller theory   See *peddler theory*.

Sexism   A set of ideas and practices through which males subordinate females on the basis of sex group membership. See *institutional sexism; male chauvinism*. (p. 158)

Social class   A category of people who stand on a similar position in terms of their socioeconomic characteristics and life-styles. (pp. 31–38)

Social control   The process of generating cooperation and conformity with individual or group demands. (pp. 90, 431–33)

Social Darwinism   A body of ideas suggesting that social-class position is linked to biological quality. (p. 5)

Social disorganization approach   An approach to the study of social problems that focuses primarily on the deviant behavior of individuals and assumes that this behavior is largely caused by their immediate social environment. (pp. 6–12)

Social environment   Aspects of society that affect the thoughts and behavior of individuals and groups, including their patterns of interaction. (p. 3)

Socialism   An economic system in which the means of production (e.g., factories, farms, transportation systems) are largely publicly owned. (pp. 181, 204)

Socialization   The process of learning to participate in a society's culture and to fulfill societal roles. (pp. 41, 92–100)

Social mobility   The movement of an individual or group up or down in the social-class hierarchy. (p. 274)

Social pathology approach   An approach to the study of social problems that focuses primarily on the deviant behavior of individuals and assumes that this behavior is largely caused by biological or psychological deficiencies. (pp. 3–6)

Social problem   A social phenomenon that is held to be undesirable or harmful and in need of change. (pp. 2–22)

Social role   See *role*.

Social system   A social group or unit made up of various parts that are interrelated and interdependent. (p. 7)

Societal reaction   Pertaining to labeling theory, the crucial process that must occur in response to norm violation wherein the violator is labeled deviant. (p. 340)

Sociological explanations   Explanations emphasizing the impact of social and cultural factors on human behavior. (pp. 316–19)

Sociology   The scientific study of the organization and operation of society and its components. (pp. 2, 7)

Status integration   A condition wherein the various roles played by a person are compatible—that is, not in conflict with one another. (p. 372)

Stimulant   A drug substance that temporarily speeds up mental or physical functioning. (p. 421)

Structural   Pertaining to the organizational features of a society or group. (pp. 14, 50)

Subculture   A segment of the population that shares certain characteristics—e.g., language, customs, norms—different from the culture as a whole. (p. 318)

Suicide   The act of killing oneself. (pp. 360–62)

Systemic attribution   Attributing the causes of a phenomenon that is deemed problematic to the organization and operation of society or some of its component parts. (p. 19)

T ax loopholes   Legal avenues through which certain individuals are able to minimize their tax liability. (p. 40)

Technological change   Change in knowledge or tools that are used to alter the physical or social environment. (p. 47)

Technological displacement   Job loss due to the introduction of new technology into the workplace. (p. 260)

Tertiary sector   That part of the economy devoted to the provision of services. (p. 251)

Theory of the social reality of crime   An explanation for criminal behavior developed by Richard Quinney that suggests that crime is a product of law. The most powerful segments of society influence lawmakers, and thus the behavior of the least powerful is most likely to be designated criminal. (p. 319)

Third World   The developing nations of the world, as opposed to the highly developed and industrialized capitalist and socialist nations. (p. 204)

Tolerance   The ability to endure or resist the action of a drug substance. (p. 416)

Tooth fairy approach   As applied to political socialization by Jerry Tucker, an approach to learning about political realities that often confuses what is with what should be. (pp. 98–99)

Total institution   According to Erving Goffman, a bureaucratic setting, such as a prison or mental hospital, in which inmates' meals, sleep, work, and leisure are all regulated by administrative authorities and staff. (pp. 349–53)

Totalitarian   A political system in which the state controls the activities of the population and uses this control to perpetuate its own rule. (p. 60)

Tracking   Educational practices that channel students to or away from different school programs or "tracks." Generally used in concert with testing. (p. 103)

Tracks   See *tracking*.

U nemployment compensation   A temporary form of income provided to those who are fired or laid off from their jobs. (p. 48)

Urbanization   A process of societal change involving the progressive movement of people from rural areas and small towns to large urban centers. (pp. 2, 7)

V alue free   A phrase—at times used in conjunction with the term *scientific inquiry*—that refers to the ideal of initiating, conducting, and reporting on research without the intrusion of bias. (p. 7)

Values   Ideas or principles to which people feel strongly bound and which help guide judgments as to what are socially acceptable actions or goals. (pp. 12, 13)

Veto groups   Interest groups strong enough to make an impact on policy decisions and to veto policies that might adversely affect their self-defined interests. (p. 62)

Victimization studies   Research studies that focus on determining the extent to which people have been victims of different crimes, ordinarily by asking them if they have been crime victims. (pp. 295–97)

Victimless crime   Illegal activities in which people engage voluntarily and in which there are no victims. (pp. 302–4)

Vocational track   A school curriculum designed to provide students with specific job skills, rather than to prepare them for additional study beyond high school. (p. 103)

W elfare   A program of financial assistance and services for needy individuals and families. (p. 44)

White-collar jobs   Jobs primarily calling for mental skills rather than manual skills. (pp. 273–74)

White flight   The movement of white residents and white-owned business enterprises out of central city locations, often to suburbs or outlying areas. (p. 134)

Withdrawal symptoms   The physical effects of stopping the use of a drug on which one is dependent. (p. 403)

Women's rights faction   A segment of the women's movement whose goals revolve around ending discrimination against females and encouraging increased participation of women in economic and political life. (p. 180)

Work   An activity that produces something of value for other people. (p. 250)

Worker displacement   See *technological displacement*.

Working class   Commonly refers to that segment of the social-class hierarchy in which most workers hold blue-collar jobs. Also used to refer to all those who neither own nor control a society's means of production and who, to live, must work for those who do. (p. 274)

Name Index

Subject Index